Beyond
the Martyrs

CLASS AND CULTURE
A series edited by
Milton Cantor and Bruce Laurie

Beyond the Martyrs

A Social History of Chicago's Anarchists, 1870–1900

BRUCE C. NELSON

RUTGERS UNIVERSITY PRESS
New Brunswick and London

Library of Congress Cataloging-in-Publication Data

Nelson, Bruce C. (Bruce Christopher), 1951–
    Beyond the martyrs : a social history of Chicago's anarchists,
1870–1900 / Bruce C. Nelson.
        p.   cm. — (Class and culture)
    Bibliography: p.
    Includes index.
    ISBN 0-8135-1344-8   ISBN 0-8135-1345-6 (pbk.)
    1. Anarchism—Illinois—Chicago—History—19th century.
2. Socialism—Illinois—Chicago—History—19th century.   3. Chicago
(Ill.)—Social conditions.   4. Haymarket Square Riot, Chicago, Ill.,
1886.   I. Title.   II. Series.
HX846.C4N45   1988
335'.83'0977311—dc 19   88-6442
                                                                    CIP

British Cataloging-in-Publication information available

Parts of chapters 1 and 8 first appeared in *Chicago History*, 15 (Summer 1986),
and are reprinted by permission. Parts of chapters 2 first appeared in *International
Labor and Working Class History*, 29 (Spring 1986); copyright © 1986 by the Board
of Trustees of the University of Illinois. Parts of chapter 6 first appeared in *The
Haymarket Scrapbook*, edited by Dave Roediger and Franklin Rosemont (Chicago:
Charles H. Kerr, 1986).

Tables 1.3 and 1.4 are reprinted from Edward L. Bubnys, "Nativity and the
Distribution of Wealth," *Explorations in Economic History*, 19 (April 1982), 104 and
105, by permission of the author and Academic Press, Inc.

For Fran and Erik

Contents

Contents

PART THREE

The Haymarket Riot and Afterwards,
1886–1900   *175*

List of Tables

Tables

Acknowledgments

This book began as a dissertation in the Department of History at Northern Illinois University, where I was privileged to study with a group of professors whose scholarship and teaching interlocked. Over a sixteen-year period I had the opportunity to study history with Richard Price, J. Harvey Smith, J. Carroll Moody, Margaret Y. George, Mary O. Furner, and Alfred F. Young. Moreover, I studied with a group of students, especially Leo Bacino, Loomis Mayfield, Richard Soderlund, Joe Wegwert, Clarence Wunderlin, and Paul Street, who were both challenging and supportive. Throughout this project the scholarship of faculty and students in that department sustained and encouraged me; it is a very special place.

I owe much to my dissertation committee: Professors Young, Moody, and Furner; and Dr. John B. Jentz of the Newberry Library. Alfred Young, craftsman and scholar, deserves special thanks: an extraordinary friend and teacher, yet a demanding taskmaster, he convinced me to apply to graduate school in the first place, then guided my program, the dissertation, its revisions, and the pursuit of both publication and employment.

The staffs of Founders Library at Northern Illinois University, the Chicago Historical Society, the Newberry Library, and the state historical societies of Illinois, Wisconsin, and Minnesota were generous with their assistance. Gerd Callesen, Arbejderbevaegelsens Bibliotek og Archiv; Dirk Hoerder, Universität Bremen; Hartmut Keil, Universität München; Josef Polišenský, Charles University; and Vladimir Zahradnicek, Náprstek Muzeum; helped me locate materials in European archives. Rosemary Bowie, friend and nurse, helped with translations from German and Czech sources; Frede Hansen, mechanic and Communist, helped with Danish and Norwegian; John and Frances Mateyko, my in-laws, helped with Polish. I am indebted to all.

An early version of chapter 4 was presented to the Chicago Projekt conference at the Newberry Library in October 1981, and a draft of chapter 5 was presented to the Chicago Area Labor History Group in March 1983. Some of the material in chapters 2 and 8 appeared in *International Labor and Working Class History*, some of chapter 6 in *The Haymarket Scrapbook*, and some of chapters 1 and 7 in *Chicago History*. I am grateful to David Montgomery, David Roediger and Franklin Rosemont, Russell Lewis and Meg Walter for their editorial counsel. Richard Schneirov read parts of the dissertation and generously shared his understanding of Chicago, the Knights, and the labor movement. Steven Rosswurm, David Roediger, Otto Olsen, Paul Street, Milton Cantor, and Bruce Laurie poured over the revised manuscript and helped me clarify its argument and prose. Finally I am grateful to Marlie Wasserman and Marilyn Campbell, of Rutgers University Press, who guided this book through publication.

Since the dissertation was dedicated to my parents, this book is gratefully dedicated to Frances and Erik, who deserve better.

DeKalb, Illinois
February 1988

Beyond
the Martyrs

moved inexorably toward the gallows. While dramatic, the process under investigation was legal, not historical: neither judge, prosecutor, nor jury was interested in the origins or development of the political movement led by the Martyrs, only in the conviction and execution of criminals. At its best, and to steal a phrase from Charles Beard, the history of the Haymarket Affair seems trapped in "juridical interpretation."

We have so many studies of the riot and the trial that it would be impossible to justify another. This book is instead a social history of Chicago's anarchist movement. Who were they? How were they organized? What and how did they think? What brought them to the Haymarket Square? What happened to those who survived the executions? Those questions are simple and basic because they have not been asked by others. The project is justified because it approaches the subject with a new point of view, new evidence, a new periodization, and a new purpose.

First, it considers the rank and file of the city's socialist and anarchist groups, not the martyred leadership. It regards the riot and affair as events within a complex process of industrialization, immigration, alienation, radicalization, and class formation. Second, in posing new questions about the composition, culture, and ideology of those organizations, this study draws on the movement's official organs. The city's working class and its radicals were multilingual, multiethnic, and supported a prodigious number of labor papers. Third, it begins the story of the Haymarket riot more than a decade before 1886 and pursues it for more than a decade after the executions on 11 November 1887. Such a periodization ensures attention to process, change, and context. Finally, this study is concerned less with the trial and justice, and more with the identity, agency, and impact of the unindicted conspirators. Rather than concentrating on the trial, or focusing on representative leaders, I am concerned here with the city's socialist and anarchist movements as a whole. Following Henry David's lead, this book is intended then as "A Study in the American Social-Revolutionary and Labor Movements."

It is intended also as a local study and is written by a provincial. The argument rests upon the twin notions that Chicago's radical labor movement was a community and that it can be approached with the tools of a social historian. Quantitative analysis—of economic growth, population samples, ethnicity, occupation, social mobility, residence, and social affiliation—can be used to analyze and describe a movement of working-class radicals.[3] This study remains one of radicals and radicalism, indeed the most radical socialists in the Gilded Age, and of the most radical city in nineteenth-century America. As such this is a very traditional study, a genre of the Old Labor History. But it is also a social analysis of the relationships between a movement and the community from which it sprang; the answers to the questions posed above will, I hope, lend it a theoretical significance beyond the IWPA and the city of Chicago.

This study is grounded in the words, thoughts, and actions of Chicago's socialists and anarchists. *Der Vorbote, Die Fackel,* and *Die Arbeiter-Zeitung* are rich and accessible sources for such a study; but they have not been extensively used by other scholars. Moreover, many historians have been unwilling to read beyond the editorial pages to the regular reports of movement life and culture. Instead, the four pages of apparently every issue of *The Alarm* have been mined until the historical ore became exhausted. The result of such strip-mining has been a narrow, even nativist, reading of the movement. When I repeatedly criticized a set of books assigned in a reading seminar for consciously ignoring foreign-language sources, one of my classmates irritatedly responded by asking what I expected to find.[4] This book might stand as the answer I could not then provide. Between 1870 and 1900 Chicago's foreign-born constituted at least 40 percent of the city's population; if we measure the ethnicity of households by the birthplace of the father, the percentage rises as high as 75 percent. In short, foreign-language papers illuminate those activities in ethnic neighborhoods, organizations, and institutions that did not interest the commercial, English-language press. To ignore extant and accessible materials in their languages is to perpetuate a Yankee history. This study then is comparative in the sense that it draws on multiple and multilingual accounts.

And it is comparative in the sense that it recognizes that immigrants were also emigrants. American labor historians face some problems on which Europeans can offer little assistance. As provocative and important as E. P. Thompson's *The Making of the English Working Class,* William Sewell's *Work and Revolution in France,* or Wolfgang Renzsch's *Handwerker und Lohnarbeiter in der frühen Arbeiterbewegung* are, European scholars seemingly enjoy the luxury of a kind of homogeneity.[5] Even in southern or rural France, Frenchmen spoke French; in both Munich and Berlin, Germans spoke German. In Chicago, on the other hand, the working class spoke more than twenty different languages. During the 1880s one could live, work, shop, pray, marry, and die without speaking, hearing, or reading a language other than German in Old Town on the North side of the city. The situations in Pilsen on the Southwest side, home to the Czechs, and in Polonia on the Northwest side, were similar. Those linguistic differences conceal equally significant cultural differences, which in turn reinforced political and economic distinctions. Not only must American social historians deal with the problems of language and culture, they must be as sensitive to the experiences of emigration as they are to immigration.[6]

The book's argument is twofold: first that the leadership and active membership of Chicago's anarchist groups were the visible tip of an iceberg of a much larger social and cultural phenomenon. The circulation of the radical press and the numbers of participants in anarchist demonstrations and cultural activities indicate a growing, vital movement. Second, the anarchists' ability to mobilize its sympathetic following grew out of the ethno-cultural traditions and the contemporary experiences of Chicago's Germans, Bohemians, and Scandinavians. The study is focused on the intersection of the movement's active membership and its sympathetic following.

The book is organized in three parts. The first three chapters examine the years from 1870 to 1885 as the foreground to the Haymarket riot. Chapter 1 looks at Chicago's social and industrial setting, chapter 2 at the economic struggle for socialism and the complex relationship between the socialist and labor movements, and chapter 3 at the electoral struggle for socialism. Part II, comprising chapters 4 through 7, is an intensive study of the anarchist movement from 1880 to 1886. This section is organized around a series of basic questions. Who were these socialists and anarchists? How were they organized? How did they agitate? What did they think? Chapter 4 is devoted to a reconstitution and collective biography of the movement's active membership. Chapters 5 and 6 look at their organization and cultural life. Chapter 7 attempts to unravel the movement's ideology by considering it as a cultural system, one expressed by the leadership but shaped and shared by the rank and file. Part III, the last three chapters, is a study of Haymarket's repercussions and aftermath. Chapter 8 recounts the riot within the immediate context of the Eight Hour Movement and the subsequent Haymarket Affair. Chapter 9 returns to the collective biography first presented in Chapter 4 and pursues the movement's rank and file through the affair and on to the end of the century. Chapter 10 serves as both epilogue and conclusion.

Finally, a brief note on my use of the labels "anarchist" and "socialist." As I will argue in Chapter 7, the movement commonly recognized as "anarchist" can be better understood as "socialist." The overwhelming majority of Chicago's "anarchists" came from the Socialistic Labor Party;

despite a sectarian split that became finalized in 1881, the political, social, economic, and cultural similarities between the "socialist" and "anarchist" movements reflect a fundamental continuity. Indeed, the anarchists of the mid-1880s had been avowed socialists in the 1870s. We are stuck then with an inappropriate but widely used label. The reader should be warned that I discovered no alternative: that I have used the label "socialist" to refer to the movement in the period before 1881, that I have had to use both "socialist" and "anarchist" from 1881 to 1886, and that after 1886 the label "socialist" best describes those same people and their movement. I hope this study will contribute to better understanding an historical movement that has been not only misnamed but also misunderstood and neglected.

PART ONE

The Socialist and Labor Movements in Chicago, 1870–1885

. . . Socialism in America is an anomaly, and Chicago is the last place on the continent where it would exist were it not for the dregs of foreign immigration which find lodgement here.

  —Chicago *Daily News*, 14 January 1886

Chapter One

A CONTEXT FOR WORKING-CLASS RADICALISM

Chicago in the 1880s would not be entirely unfamiliar to someone born and raised there in the twentieth century. Its streets are laid on the same grid and the names are similar though the numbering system has changed. Many of the buildings still stand, and some old neighborhoods have been preserved, if only architecturally. The city was smaller and its skyline lower but just as filled with immigrants and just as Democratic. In 1885, the northern boundary was Fullerton Avenue, the southern boundary Thirty-First Street, and Western Avenue appropriately marked the remaining edge. The Montauk Building, the first skyscraper, was not erected until the late eighties and most buildings did not exceed ten floors. In the 1880s, Chicago was the fifth largest German city in the world; in the 1980s, it can claim to be the fifth largest Polish city. And 100 years ago, from 1879 to 1887, the city enjoyed a four-term Democratic mayor who had built the first political machine in its history. The city might be familiar, but it had also changed.

This study is focused on the social history of the most radical working-class organization in the United States during the nineteenth century, a movement composed of immigrant working people and located in Chicago. This chapter is intended as an introduction to that city, to its economy and economic history, to its society and social history, and to the patterns of industrialization and radicalization that form the essential context for understanding that movement. We consider each pattern in turn.

THE ECONOMIC STRUCTURE OF THE CITY, 1870 TO 1900

The Great Conflagration of 1871 seems a convenient point of departure. The fire burned across the city's heart, destroying the commercial district, gutting the finest neighborhoods, and leaving a third of its residents homeless.[1] Yet the city rose, phoenix-like, after the fire. Before it the city's economy had been dominated by commerce, after it by manufacturing. The city's location, at the southwestern shore of the Great Lakes close to the Illinois and Mississippi rivers, proved advantageous and exploitable. The Illinois and Michigan Canal opened in 1848, geographically connecting the Illinois River and Lake Michigan, commercially connecting both north and south, east and west, with Chicago as the hub. Construction of the Chicago-to-Galena railroad started in 1847 and stimulated a boom, first of speculation, later of building. By 1856, Chicago had become the nation's railroad center, boasting ten trunk lines and almost one hundred daily train arrivals. Grain, lumber, and livestock moved east; clothing, shoes, groceries and manufactured products came west.[2] In fact the fire did not date or occasion those changes.

By the time of the Great Fire in 1871, Chicago's economy was already in the process of changing from a merchant-dominated commercial and transportation economy, with a minor craft-based sector, to a modern, corporate, industrial economy producing both capital and consumer goods. In the last four decades of the nineteenth century, fully 45 percent of the city's workers were employed in manufacturing, and by 1880 Chicago had become one of the nation's leading industrial centers. In number of manufacturing establishments it ranked sixth in 1880 and fourth in 1890. In both years Chicago ranked only behind New York City and Philadelphia in number of employees, total wages, capital invested, gross value of products, and value added in manufacturing.[3]

Change within the manufacturing sector was profound. In 1870, the five leading manufacturers included slaughtering, lumber, men's clothing, leather, and flour. Ten years later, slaughtering repeated, but lumber had slipped to sixth and iron and steel and foundry and machine shops had climbed to third and fifth. In 1890, printing and publishing had climbed to fourth, behind meat packing, men's clothing, and foundry and machine shops—ahead of both iron and lumber products. Yet three of the ten leaders in the 1890 census had not been there a decade before. Between 1870 and 1890 manufacturing firm size grew. In 1880, 3,518 firms in the city employed 79,391 workers; the average firm employed 22 workers. In 1890, 9,977 firms employed 210,366 workers, an average of 21 workers per firm. And between 1870 and 1890 each of the ten leading industries increased both their payrolls and capitalization.

Citywide data on firm size, employment, and capital investment obscures wide variations between different industries. In printing, the average firm size grew from 15 employees in 1870 to 20 in 1890; in clothing, the average firm size rose from 63 to 121; in slaughtering from 69 to 336. The most intense capital investment came between 1880 and 1890. The average meat-packing firm increased its capitalization from $120,788 in 1880 to $748,371 in 1890. In foundries and machine shops, capital investment stood at $898 per worker in 1880 and $1,650 in 1890; in furniture, it rose from $543 per worker to $976; in iron and steel, from $1,289 to $5,124 over that same decade. Industrywide data in turn obscures the variations within industries. In baking, one set of firms, both large and concentrated, produced for the national market, while the majority of the city's bakeries were small and competitive, serving only their immediate neighborhoods. In both the metal and furniture trades, production remained "organized in numerous, often medium-sized plants during [both] the Gilded Age and the Progressive Era."[4] (see Table 1.1)

Chicago's industrialization coincided with two periods of depression, the first from 1873 to 1878, the second from 1882 to 1886. Both were part of the international Long Depression from 1873 to 1896. If prices and profit rates fell without affecting the volume of production and trade, growth failed to maintain the levels of the 1870s, and investment continued at falling rates. In Chicago, the effort of rebuilding the burned-out city partially mitigated the first depression, but as money wages fell, real wages rose and promoted recapitalization, the introduction of new machinery, and the expansion of managerial control of the production process.[5] The second depression, which bottomed out in the winter of 1884–85, reinforced the first and was felt more severely. According to the Trade and Labor Assembly's statistician, one-third of the city's carpenters were idle in January 1885, cigarmakers worked only seven hours a day and made about $8 a week, and coopers were averaging $6 to $8. In

11

Table 1.1 CHICAGO'S TEN LEADING MANUFACTURES, 1870, 1880, AND 1890

Product	Value of product (millions)	Number of firms	Hands per firm	Capital per firm (thousands)	Capital per worker	Wage per worker
1870						
Slaughtering	$19.2	31	69	$205	$2,988	$200
Lumber	6.9	37	49	56	1,143	448
Men's clothing	5.7	76	63	25	393	278
Iron & steel	4.7	38	67	93	1,401	592
Leather, tnnd & crd	3.3	27	21	37	1,730	525
Flour mill products	3.1	17	10	38	3,855	747
Distilled liquors	2.8	8	28	72	2,542	766
Malt liquors	2.5	23	17	133	8,037	651
Printing & publishing	2.2	60	15	14	920	584
Tobacco products	2.1	111	9	11	1,281	348
1880						
Slaughtering	$85.3	70	107	$121	$1,131	$454
Men's clothing	19.9	143	72	50	702	396
Iron & steel	10.9	15	207	267	1,289	493
Leather, tnnd & crd	9.3	28	48	86	1,810	653
Foundry & machine shop	9.2	144	35	31	900	486
Lumber	8.9	56	67	40	593	407
Printing & publishing	6.7	151	26	23	872	557
Furniture	6.5	155	32	17	543	439
Distilled liquors	4.4	7	107	167	1,567	440
Tobacco products	3.7	291	7	3	418	394
1890						
Slaughtering	$194.3	52	336	$748	$2,225	$613
Men's clothing	36.3	149	121	99	819	405

Product	Value of product (millions)	Number of firms	Hands per firm	Capital per firm (thousands)	Capital per worker	Wage per worker
Foundry & machine shop	35.2	303	51	85	1,650	607
Printing & publishing	29.1	695	20	22	1,105	713
Iron & Steel	25.0	20	229	1,175	5,124	715
Lumber	20.4	130	72	81	1,119	589
RR cars, steam	14.5	7	840	1,263	1,504	653
Furniture	13.6	157	53	52	976	575
Agric. implements	11.9	6	658	4,745	7,216	500
Malt liquors	10.2	34	60	476	7,899	704

SOURCES: United States, *Ninth Census, 1870,* 3: "Manufactures," 849; *Tenth Census, 1880,* "Manufactures," 391–393; *Eleventh Census, 1890,* "Manufacturing Industries," pt. 2, "Statistics of Cities," 130–145.

Chicago, he said, "39 per cent of the working classes were in enforced idleness." In February, "hundreds" thronged the Relief and Aid Society "looking for bread"; in March 1886, the county poor farm was "literally overrun and infested by tramps from Chicago." "Out of these [two depressions] emerged a complex pattern of political and social movements," Samuel Rezneck has argued, "some of which were even magnified by the sharpened fears flourishing in depression into the vague shape of a Communist scare."[6]

"In America," *Die Chicagoer Arbeiter-Zeitung* noted in 1880, "everything is made by machine, while we made everything by hand."[7] "The most decisive phase of innovation for Chicago's industry," according to Hartmut Keil and John Jentz, "occurred during the very short period from 1879–1883." The ongoing processes of capitalization, the intensification of labor, the expansion of plant size, the introduction of new technologies and productions, deskilling, and the assertion of managerial prerogatives hit unevenly. Some trades were devastated, others only dented, some left seemingly untouched. In meat packing, firm size increased and skilled workers were replaced by "disassembly" line. The baking trade split into small, local neighborhood bakeries, and much larger, nationally marketing cracker factories. In the furniture and metal trades, mechanized, mass-production factories existed alongside artisanal, small, custom shops; in both cigarmaking and the garment industry, small shops of

13

hand workers shared the market with sweatshops employing unskilled women and children.[8]

Such uneven economic development meant very different experiences for Chicago's workers. Some bosses, like Cyrus McCormick, were close and visible, others were distant and unseen. Large factories coexisted with smaller workshops and tenement house work. To be sure the work experiences of skilled and unskilled workers were very different. But there were also differences between male and female workers, indoor and outdoor work, steady and seasonal labor, machine tenders and hand workers, older, dying trades and the new, dynamic ones. Despite a common location and similar long-term patterns, workers did not share identical or homogeneous changes at the point of production.

The wealth produced by Chicago's economic development was unequally shared. Our best source—and unfortunately the categories were abandoned thereafter—for information on the distribution of wealth is the 1870 manuscript census, which recorded both real and personal wealth. Mean total wealth was $6,146 per family in 1870, over ten times the median score of $600. Mean wealth in Chicago was at least 41 percent higher than that for the northern United States: 68 percent of Chicagoans and 65 percent of all Americans owned at least $100 in wealth; fully 85 percent of Chicago's native-born owned property compared to about 71 percent nationally. Of the foreign-born, 64 percent owned some wealth compared to 59 percent nationally.[9] As early as 1870, the distribution of wealth was highly skewed among the city's households. The top decile of families owned 84 percent of all real wealth, 85 percent of all personal wealth, and over 81 percent of total wealth. Real wealth was the most skewed with 40 percent of the city's households owning all; "but personal and total wealth were no less skewed, with 50 percent of the families owning 98 percent of the former and 99 percent of the latter." Fully half of the families in one scholar's sample of the 1870 manuscript census owned barely one percent of the city's total wealth. We have no similar data on the distribution of income, which seems to have improved over time while the distribution of wealth did not.[10]

Those who owned the means of production and distribution reaped the wealth. Philip Armour and John Cudahy made their fortunes in meat packing, Jacob Beidler and Horatio Gardner in lumber, Cyrus McCormick in reapers, R. R. Donnelly in printing, George Pullman in railroad cars, Richard Crane in plumbing fixtures, Erskine Phelps in boot- and shoe-making. Potter Palmer's hotel bore his name, and the fortunes of Marshall Field, Levi Leiter, and John Farwell came from merchandising dry goods. All of these men were Yankees although there were some immigrants within the elite. It was their city; they had built it and then rebuilt it after the disastrous fire.[11]

Those who owned little more than their labor power fared accordingly. The Illinois Bureau of Labor Statistics' *Third Biennial Report*, published in 1884, gathered information on the income and expenses of 354 of Chicago's working-class families. Almost 50 percent were either in debt or on the verge of indebtedness. Food accounted for about 40 percent of their income, rent consumed another 20 percent, clothing about 15 percent, less than 2 percent went to savings, which equalled about one month's rent. In contrast to Potter Palmer's $600,000 English Gothic mansion on Lake Shore Drive, only 7 percent of the Bureau's sample owned their own homes. And in contrast to Mrs. Palmer, "stately, regal, handsome, wearing her diamond tiara and famous rope of pearls, [who] ruled as the queen of America's second largest city," about 26 percent of working-class families supplemented the head-of-household's earnings with those of wives and children.[12]

Thus, the two most striking features of Chicago's industrialization between 1870 and 1900 were its pace and unevenness. Between 1860 and 1870, a rough and tumble frontier town became a major manufacturing center. Chicago was a boomtown, but its development was uneven, interrupted by three depressions, and divergent. And the fact that the wealth produced by that economic development was unequally shared reflected its profound impact.

THE SOCIAL STRUCTURE OF THE CITY, 1870 TO 1900

Chicago's economic development was based upon its incredible population growth: in the last half of the nineteenth century, Chicago must have been one of the fastest growing cities in the country, if not the world. For three decades, from 1860 to 1890, its population doubled every ten years: from 109,260 in 1860, to 298,000 in 1870, to 503,185 in 1880, and to 1,099,850 in 1890. Over those same three decades the city's area grew from 18 to 178 square miles, yet there was no annexation between 1870 and 1880. Thus, the decade that witnessed 69 percent population growth also saw density increase from 8,514 to 14,376 people per square mile.

Nineteenth-century Chicago was an immigrant city. They came in waves: the Irish and Germans in the 1850s, the Scandinavians in the sixties, the Bohemians in the 1870s, the Southern and Eastern Europeans in the late eighties. "In fact," noted the *Northwestern Christian Advocate*, "ours is a foreign city with not more than one-fifth of the population Americans; having more Germans and even more Irish than Anglo-Saxons, and more Bohemians than any city of Bohemia but Prague." With that kind of ethnic diversity, Chicago looks more like Milwaukee, Detroit, Philadelphia, or New York City than it does Troy, Poughkeepsie, Lynn, or Newburyport.[13] (see Table 1.2)

Table 1.2 NATIVITY AND ETHNICITY OF
CHICAGO'S POPULATION, 1870-1900

	Nativity		Ethnicity	Nativity	
Group	1870	1880	1884	1890	1900
Foreign-born	48.4%	40.7%	75.9%	41.0%	34.6%
Native-born	51.6	59.3	24.1	59.0	65.4
German[a]	17.7	15.2	33.6	15.2	10.1
Irish	13.3	8.8	18.3	6.4	4.4
Canadian	4.9	4.3	0.6	2.2	2.1
British Isles[b]	4.9	3.5	4.5	3.6	2.4
Scandinavian[c]	4.6	5.0	7.5	6.5	4.8
Bohemian	2.1	2.4	4.5	2.3	3.1
French	0.4	0.3	1.3	0.2	0.0
Dutch	0.5	0.4	0.5	0.5	1.1
Polish	0.4	1.1	3.7	2.2	3.5
Russian	0.0	0.2	0.2	0.7	1.4
All Other	0.9	1.0	1.2	1.2	1.7
Totals = [d]	100%	100%	100%	100%	100%
N =	298,000	503,185	629,985	1,099,850	1,698,575

SOURCES: Calculated from United States, *Ninth Census, 1870*, 1, "Population," 386–391; *Tenth Census, 1880*, "Population," 538–541; *Eleventh Census, 1890*, "Population," pt. 1, lxvii, 670–673; Abstract of the *Twelfth Census, 1900*, 106–107; the 1884 "School Census of Nationalities by Ward," tabled in Chicago *Tribune*, 18 March 1886, 3.

[a]Germany includes Austria
[b]British Isles includes England, Scotland, and Wales, but *not* Ireland
[c]Scandinavia includes Norway, Sweden and Denmark
[d]Percentages may sum to more or less than 100 due to rounding.

Ethnicity (defined by family origin), not nativity (defined by birth-place), may be more illuminating. The 1884 school census tabulated the city's population by wards and school districts using ethnicity rather than nativity. First and second generation Germans comprised 33 percent of the city—the single largest ethnic group. The native-born of native stock came second with 24 percent, followed by the Irish at 18 percent, and the Scandinavians with 8 percent. The British and Bohemians tied for fifth with 4.5 percent, the Poles comprised 4 percent, the French 1.3 percent, and blacks 1.2 percent. The remaining groups—Italians, Canadians, Dutch, Spanish, and Hungarians—were small and scattered; none accounted for more than one percent of the city's population. By 1890, "only two cities in Germany had more Germans; two cities in Sweden, more Swedes; two cities in Norway, more Norwegians." Measured then by ethnicity, the native-born were not even one-quarter of the population; the "dregs of foreign immigration" and their children comprised 76 percent.[14]

Ethnic differences reverberated throughout the city's occupational structure. The native-born dominated white-collar employment; immigrants dominated the blue-collar work force. In 1870, one-quarter of native-born household heads held high white-collar positions; nearly 40 percent held low white-collar jobs. About 30 percent of the British families held white-collar jobs, only 22 percent of the Germans and barely 14 and 12 percent of the Irish and Scandinavians. By 1900, the structure of native-born occupations had not significantly changed, nor had the overall structure within the city.

The majority of the city's population was engaged in blue-collar occupations where there were wide differences in both the structure and experiences of Chicago's foreign-born population. Skilled workers constituted more than two-thirds of the Scandinavian households in a recent sample of the 1870 census, almost 50 percent of the British, almost 40 percent of the Germans, but only 26 percent of the Irish. Between 1870 and 1900 the occupational distributions within the various economic groups changed dramatically. The percentage of skilled workers declined among all ethnic groups, but most dramatically among the Scandinavians (from 67 to 41 percent). We can measure those changes now with an occupational index, but as early as 1881 Josef Gruenhut, the Trades Assembly's statistician, argued that Chicago manufacturing had become "a European colony": "the American artisan . . . has vanished from the scene," "crowded out" of the skilled trades by immigration.[15] (see Table 1.3)

Table 1.3 DISTRIBUTION OF HEAD-OF-HOUSEHOLD'S
OCCUPATION BY NATIVITY, CHICAGO, 1870 AND 1900

| | White Collar | | Blue Collar | | | Row |
Group	High	Low	Skill	S-skill	U-skill	Totals
1870						
Native-born	25.5%	37.8%	23.4%	10.0%	3.3%	100%
Native-born,						
foreign-stock	7.4	18.5	48.2	14.8	11.1	100
German	3.7	18.9	39.9	12.8	24.7	100
Irish	3.1	11.5	26.6	17.5	41.6	100
British Isles	8.0	25.7	49.6	8.0	8.8	100
Scandinavian	1.7	10.4	67.2	6.9	13.8	100
All other	4.2	15.5	43.7	9.9	26.8	100
City as a whole	8.0	20.4	36.3	12.6	22.7	100
N =						1,143
1900						
Native-born	24.1	32.5	15.7	20.5	7.2	100%
Native-born,						
foreign-stock	5.7	34.1	30.7	21.6	8.0	100
German	5.4	17.9	33.9	22.3	20.5	100
Irish	1.6	19.4	17.7	29.0	32.3	100
British Isles	14.6	17.1	51.2	12.2	4.9	100
Scandinavian	0	4.5	40.9	36.4	18.2	100
Polish	0	21.6	27.0	5.5	45.9	100
Russian	12.5	35.0	37.5	10.0	5.0	100
Bohemian	0	7.5	50.0	7.5	35.0	100
Italian	18.2	45.5	0	0	36.4	100
All other	0	8.3	33.3	16.8	41.6	100
City as a whole	8.2	23.3	30.7	18.8	19.0	100
N =						548

Source: Edward Bubnys, "Chicago, 1870 and 1900: Wealth, Occupation and Education (Ph.D. diss., University of Illinois, 1978), Table 4.3, 72.

In the three decades between 1870 and 1900 the city's occupational structure did not change dramatically, but the size of the skilled contingent declined and that of the semiskilled expanded. The native-born, the Germans, and the Scandinavians experienced a dramatic decline in the proportion of skilled workers, and correspondingly, an increase of both semi- and unskilled labor. The British moved up into white-collar occupations, and the Irish experienced an increase in low white-collar and unskilled blue-collar work, and a decline in the size of the skilled contingent. By 1900, the older, established immigrants had moved up the social ladder and were being replaced by newer immigrants, including Poles, Russians, and Bohemians. At the turn of the century the top rungs were still occupied by the native-born.

There were visible ethnic differences in the distribution of Chicago's wealth. There was no statistical differences between the distributions of native wealth and the city's total wealth. The top 10 percent of the city's native-born, Irish, and British families owned fully 73 percent of each group's wealth. More egalitarian distributions could be found in the German and Scandinavian colonies where the top 10 percent owned 59 percent in the former and 64 percent in the latter. At the bottom of the social ladder the gaps remained just as visible as at the top: only 23 percent of the native-born, but 37 percent of the Germans were propertyless.[16] (see Table 1.4)

In turn, the differences in occupation and wealth were reflected in residential choice. Immigrants tended to concentrate in enclaves, and by the 1870s there were already distinctive neighborhoods: the North side was recognizably German; on the Southwest side the Bohemians claimed Pilsen, the Irish Bridgeport and Canaryville, the native-born elite lived on Pine Street, North Michigan, and South Prairie avenues.[17] The native-born, on the other hand, could be found in each of the city's eighteen wards, distributed quite evenly, showing little concentration. The English-speaking element were almost as evenly dispersed. With the exception of the British, each of the immigrant groups had higher measures of concentration and segregation. One of Chicago's eighteen wards held 65 percent of the city's first- and second-generation Poles, another held 61 percent of the Bohemians, a third 56 percent of the Danes, a fourth 52 percent of the Norwegians. The two largest immigrant groups in the population, the Irish and the Germans, counted for only 22 and 17 percent respectively.[18]

Each immigrant group built its own neighborhood and community. Following recent scholarship, we should understand the first geographi-

Table 1.4 DISTRIBUTION OF TOTAL FAMILY WEALTH IN CHICAGO IN DECILES AND BY NATIVITY, 1870

Decile	All (citywide)	Native-born	German	Irish	English-spkng[a]	Scandinavian[b]
1st	81.4%	79.8%	58.8%	73.0%	73.3%	64.1%
2nd	9.0	11.6	16.5	11.5	15.5	16.4
3rd	4.3	4.9	10.4	7.1	6.4	11.6
4th	2.7	1.9	6.9	4.9	2.7	4.6
5th	1.5	.8	4.4	2.2	1.1	1.8
6th	.6	.5	2.1	.6	.4	.6
7th	.1	.2	.2	.2	.1	.2
8th	.1	.1	.2	.2	.1	.2
9th	.1	.0	.2	.2	.1	.2
10th	.1	.0	.2	.2	.1	.2
Totals =	100%	100%	100%	100%	100%	100%
N =	1,226	258	397	308	120	64
Mean T.W. =	$6,146	$19,257	$2,475	$2,580	$4,346	$2,227
Median T.W. =	$600	$1,050	$800	$300	$300	$300
Mean/Median =	10.2	18.3	3.1	8.6	14.5	7.4
Gini =	.825	.829	.714	.785	.807	.760

SOURCE: Edward Bubnys, "Nativity and the Distribution of Wealth: Chicago 1870," *Explorations in Economic History* 19 (April 1982): Tables 2 and 3, 104–105.

NOTE: "Total Family Wealth" = Real Wealth + Personal Wealth from the entries in the 1870 Federal census schedules.
[a]"English-speaking" = English, Welsh, Scotch, and Canadians.
[b]The size of the Scandinavian subsample precludes rigorous comparison with the others.

cally, the latter much more broadly. These were not ghettoes: for, even in the case of the city's black population, segregation was never complete. Yet the smaller the geographical unit, the higher the measure of concentration. Indeed, both wards and precincts tended to be heterogeneous; the neighborhood was always smaller, and concentration was most striking at the block level.[19]

Despite profound differences, immigrants established remarkably similar institutions, in part because they came form European backgrounds, in part too because they learned from each other. Ethnic neighborhoods centered around churches, parishes, and schools; they grew near industrial areas that employed immigrants and catered to the immigrant trade. Neighborhood institutions provided employment, insurance, benefit, social, and cultural services to both the immediate neighborhood and the larger community. When immigrant groups were small and only recently arrived, they frequently cooperated. Thus the German Immigrant Aid Society's constitution required it to assist all of German origin, "which meant in practice German speaking; it gave aid to people from Bohemia, Moravia, Austria, Hungary, and particularly Switzerland." The earliest ethnic societies in the Scandinavian community were pan-Scandinavian, welcoming Danes, Norwegians, and Swedes alike; similarly the first Czech benevolent society, Slovanska Lípa, was pan-Slavic and attempted to unite Poles and Czechs.[20] Finally, both neighborhood and community played the pivotal role in labor conflicts. Strikes could be won, in some cases only won, when, as Herbert Gutman put it, "elements of the local middle class sided with the workers."[21]

The differences among the city's ethnic communities were more important than their apparent similarities. Among seemingly similar communities there were still strong antagonisms and conflict. The relations between Chicago's different immigrant communities were strained by language differences, competing economic interests, and social and cultural conflict. There was a streak of nativism in the relations between native- and foreign-born, and profound tensions within the foreign-born majority. The German-Republican *Illinois Staats-Zeitung* put it succinctly in 1871: "Between the Germans and the Irish, [and] the Germans and the Americans there is, on the whole, little social intercourse." They spoke different languages, and the language for instruction in the public schools remained controversial well into the twentieth century. Although German was offered until World War I, Bohemian, Polish, Norwegian, and Swedish were not.[22]

Differences in skill and a segmented labor market intensified those conflicts. Older settlers had taken and still held skilled and supervisory positions; new arrivals took semi- and unskilled work. The distribution of occupations reinforced ethnic rivalries. If the native-born and English-speaking dominated the white-collar occupations, then the Germans and Scandinavians dominated the skilled, and the Irish, Bohemians, and Poles the unskilled. On the Southwest side, the Irish in the Fifth Ward and the Bohemians in the Sixth competed for the same unskilled jobs in the lumber district and repeatedly clashed away from the workplace.[23] Within the different trades, wage scales reflected both organizational and ethnic differences. German carpenters and cigarmakers, for example, apparently received lower wages than their native-born coworkers. In the garment trade, there were sharp differences between the wages in the men's and women's divisions, and between native-American seamstresses working in the larger shops and the Russian Jews who took piecework into the tenements.[24]

Perhaps the deepest line of division within the working classes, as David Montgomery has argued, was that of religion. The city's Jewish community was still small, isolated, and invisible; anti-Semitism was not particularly pronounced. The antagonism between Protestant and Catholic was eminently visible, and it echoed within some ethnic communities. The Irish, Polish, and Italians were overwhelmingly Catholic and a growing but decided minority; the English-speaking were just as profoundly Protestant. Chicago was home to the most famous nineteenth-century revivalist, Dwight L. Moody, and there were two major Protestant revivals before Haymarket: the first in 1876, the second concurrent with the Great Upheaval of 1886. We would be wrong to see a simple dichotomy in nineteenth-century Chicago. A third group, of freethinkers and atheists—especially within the German, Czech, and Scandinavian communities—attracted more concern from "Yankee Puritans" than did either Jews or Catholics.[25]

Chicago's ethnic groups behaved very differently in a political arena that was itself fragmented. The electorate was small. Women, those under the age of twenty-one, and those who had not attained citizenship were of course excluded, and in 1886 there were only 81,733 registered voters in a population of 700,000, about 11 percent. Beneath an overlapping set of city, township, and county governments over which the parties competed, a set of factions, or mini-machines, vied within each of the two parties for office and spoils. As a result of both fragmentation and volatile issues, municipal politics remained competitive throughout the period. Although Carter Harrison was reelected four times, neither major party was entrenched: in ten elections between 1876 and 1893 the Democrats won the mayorality six times, the Republicans four.[26]

Even before the 1870s, most Irishmen were Democrats, and most of the Democrats were Irish. The Germans, Norwegians, and Swedes on the other hand were largely Republicans; yet the Danish-Republican *Skandinaven* complained: "The Danes object to being classed as Republicans, because the majority of them are Democrats and Socialists." The English-speaking enjoyed better access to the polls, parties, offices, and the political system as a whole, and the *Tribune* wanted to believe that "the Scandinavians, Bohemians and Poles probably absented themselves from the [voters'] registry through apathy." But as early as 1868, Chicago's *Workingman's Advocate* concluded that both major parties "were the curse of the workingman."[27]

Chicago's working class was fragmented then by differences in skill and occupation, as well as language and culture. Working in different industries, under different conditions, earning different wages, living in different neighborhoods, they worshipped and voted in very different ways. Indeed the hostility and the competition suggest that the singular "working class" could be replaced with the plural "working classes." Despite the common experiences of industrialization and proletarianization, ethnic identifications and conflicts repeatedly undercut a class experience and class solidarity.

THE PATTERNS OF RADICALIZATION

Having taken part in the Civil War, which abolished chattel slavery, the American labor movement, bolstered by a free labor ideology and the vestiges of an artisan republicanism, sought to move "beyond equality." It moved first for a legislated reduction of hours, then for political and financial reforms. It experimented with producers' and consumers' cooperatives as alternatives to competitive industry. In *Beyond Equality* David Montgomery argued that class conflict "was the submerged shoal on which Radical dreams foundered."[28] Skilled workers built local, national, and international unions; but the most characteristic form for unskilled resistance remained that of mass, community-based strikes. The tiny labor movement and the largely unorganized working class were in the process of learning what Eric Hobsbawm has called "the habits of solidarity" and "the rules of the game."[29]

Throughout our period, however, the labor movement confronted the reality of a deeply divided working class. If the city's ethnic groups reacted differently to the process, they shared the combined experiences of industrialization, alienation, and radicalization. The fundamental changes should be located in the social relations of production, in the expansion of wage labor, and in the (self-) conscious presence of a permanent wage-earning, propertyless class. In periods of intense agitation—as in 1867 during the massive strike for the eight-hour day, in 1873 during the unemployment demonstrations, in 1877 during the Great Upheaval, in 1882 during the Knights of Labor's first membership explosion, and in 1886 during the second great Eight Hour Movement—class overwhelmed fragmentation in Chicago. Those events cannot be seen as spasms, triggered by panic and depression. Between 1870 and 1886 Chicago's working class increasingly acted in class ways.

The patterns of alienation and radicalization—the growth of class consciousness—are best reflected in the publishing histories of the city's workingmen's and socialist newspapers. While they lived with chronic insolvency, and frequently died of it, their circulations provide a quantifiable measure of the movement's growth. The press became a central, if vulnerable, institution within the movement. Beyond what the circulations tell us about the membership, and beyond what the editorials tell us about the readership, the very existence of that press illuminates the movement as a whole. Indeed, the publishing histories of individual papers and of the whole socialist press are perhaps the best index of both alienation and radicalization.

Those patterns are visible in each of Chicago's language groups. When an immigrant community reached sufficient size, it generated its own newspapers. The first foreign-language papers—for example, the German *Chicago Volksfreund* (founded 1845), the Norwegian *Frihed's Banneret* (1852), the Czech *Svornost* (1875), and the Polish *Zgoda* (1881)—were commercial ventures that tried to balance conflicting class interests. Under the impact of industrialization, and as the colony's population continued to grow, a "workingman's" paper, such as the German *Der Proletarier* (1854), the English *Workingman's Advocate* (1864), the Czech *Národní noviný* (1870), or the Polish *Nowe Zycie* (1889), subsequently appeared. Some were aborted, others died prematurely, a few survived and competed against the foreign-language commercial press for readership and advertising. At a later point, "socialist" papers appeared—for example, *Der Sozialist* (1876), *The Socialist* (1878), and the Polish *Gazeta Robotnicza* (1894)—in some cases to compete against both sets of predecessors. Circulation remained a function of population: with insufficient readership, advertising, or revenue, a paper died; in some cases three and four papers failed before one survived. The pattern is visible in each of Chicago's larger ethnic communities where an "ethnic" paper came first, followed by a "workingman's" paper, then a "socialist" paper. It suggests the timing of radicalization: the sequence reflects three different kinds of consciousness: ethnic, workingmen's, and class. Finally, both pattern and sequence reveal the leading role played by the city's Germans.

Yet, as David Montgomery has most recently suggested, "class consciousness was more than the unmediated product of daily experience." Chicago's industrialization was mediated by a group who turned to socialism. They were a peculiar group including Forty Eighters like Marcus Thrane, Louis Pio, and Vladimir Klacel; former Radical Republicans, like Harry Rubens and Albert Parsons; members of the First International, like Karl Klings and Conrad Conzett; and several men, like Gustav Lyser and Paul Grottkau, from the Allgemeine Deutsche Arbeiterverein. For these men class consciousness "was also a project, in which 'a militant minority' . . . endeavored to weld their workmates and neighbors into a self-aware and purposeful working class."[30] These men made Chicago an emigré city with something of the milieu of London, Paris, Bern, or Zurich. Chicago's socialists and anarchists played a decisive role in that project by trying to unite across the ethnic, skill, sexual, and craft lines that fragmented the city's working class.

The first evidence of socialism in Chicago dates from 1854 when H. Rosch published a German-language newspaper, *Der Proletarier*. By the end of the Civil War, the city was home to a section of the International Workingmen's Association (IWA), known as the First International, and a socialist movement. In 1874 the IWA fused with the International Social and Political Workingmen's Association to form the Workingmen's Party of Illinois (WPI). Two years later the WPI joined with several other organizations to found the Workingmen's Party of the United States, which in December 1877 changed its name to the Socialistic Labor Party (SLP). By the time of the presidential election in 1880, the SLP in Chicago had split into two factions, and in October 1881, the dissident and radical faction seceded and founded the Revolutionary Socialistic Party (RSP). The Chicago section of the RSP joined the International Working Peoples' Association (IWPA) in 1883 and became the center of the American anarchist movement.

The frequency by which the movement changed its name obscures four essential continuities: of organization, of a corps of agitators unconcerned with labels, of members who followed those leaders, and of ideological evolution. Beneath those changing labels was a process of radicalization that produced a socialist movement. The first groups all called themselves "workingmen's" parties, and it was not until 1878 that the label "socialist" appeared, reflecting an evolution from artisan republicanism to socialism. The changes that mark the process—the decline of artisans, the decay of their institutions, the politicization of the militia, the centralization of municipal government, and the emergence of an avowedly socialist movement—appeared sequentially. If the pace of industrialization in Chicago explains the rate of alienation, the agency of the city's socialists and anarchists explains the pattern of radicalization.

In 1852, Walt Whitman judged New York "the most radical city in America."[31] By 1880 (not 1886) Chicago had assumed that honor. The processes of immigration, industrialization, urbanization, population growth and concentration, individually and in combination, explain the otherwise opaque process of radicalization. In Chicago, one is confronted with one case of radicalization whose clarity is the combined result of its brevity, intensity, and the prominence of its socialists.

Between 1870 and 1900, the city's economy had been transformed from a commercial center to the fourth leading manufacturing center in the United States. Such rapid industrialization was the result of intense capitalization, plant expansion, technological and managerial innovation, deskilling, and combination. Those changes took place within a diversifying economy and reverberated throughout a fragmented social structure. The economic changes hit unevenly among different industries and within the same industries and trades, affecting individuals and groups in different ways. Those changes accumulated, as did surplus value. The *Daily News* was wrong: socialism was not an "anomaly," and Chicago was not "the last place on the continent where it would exist." Despite the differences in skill, trade, gender, and age, each of Chicago's ethnic groups, "the dregs of foreign immigration," as the *Daily News* labelled them, were alienated and radicalized by the processes of industrialization.

Chapter Two

SOCIALISTS, ANARCHISTS, AND THE UNIONS

Historians have readily acknowledged that Chicago's anarchists had close ties to the city's labor movement. Most note, though only in passing, that Albert Parsons was active in the Eight Hour League or that he had served as the president of the Trade and Labor Council in 1880. They have not, however, probed the complexity of that relationship, or how it might have changed over time, or that Parsons was not the only anarchist in the city. On the other hand, in a retrospective series, "Die Geschichte der Arbeiterbewegung Chicago's," published in 1887, *Der Vorbote* claimed that 75 percent of the city's unions were organized by socialists, and that the remaining 25 percent were founded at their instigation.[1] If the traditional wisdom clearly minimizes the role of the socialists, the second claim may only slightly exaggerate it.

By the eve of what Selig Perlman labelled "the Great Upheaval of 1885–1886," three hostile organizations had grown within Chicago's working class. One organization was composed of Irish and Anglo-Americans, and centered in the Noble and Holy Order of the Knights of Labor; the second united both natives and some of the foreign-born in the Trade and Labor Assembly; the third, largely German and Bohemian, had founded the anarchist Central Labor Union. Those three groups had different structures, ideologies, and programs. Despite those differences, however, the memberships of the three organizations overlapped, and their histories intertwined. The task here is to plumb the roots, dimensions, and dynamics of their complex relations. To do that we need to consider the composition of the city's working class and its organized labor movement, as well as the conventional explanation of socialist unionism in the 1870s and 1880s. Then, we turn to the history of two local unions to follow the practice of dual unionism. Finally, we consider the distances between the anarchists and the trade unions, on the one hand, and between the anarchists and the Knights of Labor on the other.

THE COMPOSITION OF CHICAGO's WORK FORCE AND UNIONS

It was an overwhelmingly unorganized working class to be sure. In 1886, Chicago employed about 250,000 wage workers—205,000 men, 45,000 women, and 2,000 children—distributed among 500 different trades and occupations. A report published in the *Workmen's Advocate*, argued that "of these [trades] but 15 are organized on a strictly socialistic basis while 25 others are under the control of the . . . Knights of Labor," "making a total of 40 organized trades out of 500 or 8 per cent." Albert Parsons estimated that 40,000 wage earners were organized, barely 12 percent of the total, and the Illinois Bureau of Labor Statistics confirmed that estimate when it reported some 18,355 members of the Knights of Labor and 23,712 trade union members.[2]

Who were they? Table 2.1 compares the nativity and ethnicity of Chicago's population, Knights, unions. The native-born comprised almost 60 percent of the city's population (measured by nativity), only 13 percent of the trade union members, and almost 34 percent of the Knights' membership. The Irish constituted about 8 percent of the population, and about 14 percent of both the unions and Knights. British immigrants were about equally represented in the two organizations. Chicago's Germans, on the other hand, who comprised 15 percent of the population, contributed 41 percent of union members, but only 21 percent of the Knights. The Scandinavians and the Bohemians followed very different patterns; the former were overrepresented in the unions, the latter in the Knights.

No single variable—not ethnicity, not ideology, not segmentation

Table 2.1 NATIVITY AND ETHNICITY OF CHICAGO'S POPULATION, TRADE UNIONS, AND KNIGHTS OF LABOR, CIRCA 1885

Group	Population		Trade Unions		Knights of Labor	
	Nativity	Ethnicity	Members Nativity	Officers Ethnicity	Members Nativity	Officers Ethnicity
Native-born	59.1%	24.1%	12.6%	18.6%	33.9%	15.5%
Irish	7.6	18.3	13.8	25.2	14.5	39.8
English	2.6	3.2	5.4	41.1	6.8	30.0
Scotch	0.8	1.1	1.0	4.3	0.2	3.5
Welsh	0.1	0.2	0.7	8.1	0.2	3.2
German	15.2	33.6	41.5	1.6	20.7	4.4
Scandinavian	5.8	7.7	17.7	0.8	9.0	1.3
Bohemian	2.3	4.5	1.5		4.6	0.0
Poles	2.3	3.7	1.4		0.2	0.0
Italian	0.3	0.7	2.7		4.9	0.0
All other	4.3	2.9	1.8	0.3	4.9	2.2
Totals =	100%	100%	100%	100%	100%	100%
N =	800,931	623,765	23,712	277	18,355	316

Sources: (Population by nativity) interpolated from *Tenth Census, 1880*, [1] "Population," 538–541 and *Eleventh Census, 1890*, [1] "Population," pt. 2, 650–651; (Population by ethnicity) 1884 "School Census of Nationalities by Ward," tabled in Chicago Tribune, 18 March 1886, 3; (Trade union membership) Illinois Bureau of Labor Statistics, *Fourth Biennial Report, 1886* (Springfield: H. W. Rokker, 1886), 224–225; (Trade union officers) sample compiled from Chicago newspapers and city directories, 1880–1886; (Knights of Labor membership) Illinois Bureau of Labor Statistics, *Fourth Biennial Report, 1886* (Springfield, 1886), 226; (Knights of Labor officers) sample compiled from "District Assembly 24 Minute Book," George Schilling Collection, Illinois State Historical Society, and *Journal of United Labor*, 1880–1883.

—can explain those disparities. By itself, ethnicity can not explain why 80 percent of the city's organized Scottish and Welsh workers affiliated with trade unions while the organized English workers split evenly between the unions and the Knights. Ideology proves just as problematic for German and Bohemian socialists, who were torn between the solidarity of craft organization and the class solidarity of the Knights. And although Irish and Polish workers were largely unskilled, the former split evenly between unions and Knights, while the latter preferred the unions nine to one. Those disparities are so complex as to involve all three variables as well as, following Hartmut Keil, "the underlying structure of the economy, distinct ethnic divisions within the work force and . . . the specific history of labour organisation in the city."[3] In the Gilded Age, that history pitted the native-born against the foreign-born, and the foreign-born against each other; their conflict, and their cooperation, reflect the fragmentation of the city's working class.

Germans were crucial in the reorganization of Chicago's labor movement in the years after the Civil War. German carpenters, carriage and wagonmakers, tailors, and typographers, among others, had organized in the 1850s, and were active in the city's first central trade union body at the end of the decade. When the Civil War shattered their organizations, they were rebuilt during Reconstruction. "Again, German workers were in the forefront of the trade union movement, since they continued to constitute the largest element among Chicago's skilled workers. . . . It was therefore to be expected that they organised along craft lines, exploiting their ethnic common traditions . . . as their most important bases of strength and class solidarity."[4]

The years from 1863 to 1867 marked a period of explosive growth of trade unions in Chicago. Nineteen new unions were formed and "virtually all were multi-ethnic, city-wide unions." These were overwhelmingly skilled workers—bakers, bricklayers, carpenters, coopers, painters, plumbers, stonecutters, and tailors, but they also included sailors, dockhands, and laborers. The city's first Trade Assembly came in 1864, the next year it claimed 8,500 workers in twenty-four unions. Ethno-cultural tensions were already visible. While these unions had multiethnic memberships, their elected leaders remained predominantly English-speaking Anglo-Americans. In ten new unions formed between 1863 and 1867, Richard Schneirov found six Irish, two Germans, one American and one Canadian among the officers. Of all the unions formed in the period, twelve out of fourteen officers (85 percent) were born in English-speaking countries.[5]

Despite the incipient tension, they managed to unite in 1867 for a massive strike for the eight-hour day, but when it failed, the unions disintegrated. By April 1869, the *Workingmen's Advocate* admitted that the Trade Assembly had been "in a dilapidated condition" for months, and it died sometime before October 1870. As the Anglo-American unions collapsed, German skilled workers organized their own unions. In September 1869 they even organized their own citywide trades assembly with its own weekly newspaper, *Der Deutsche Arbeiter*. As the Anglo-Americans turned to English "New Model Unionism," with high dues, extensive benefits, and thriving cooperatives, the Germans converted their orphan branches into viable trade unions. Chicago's German printers formed Typographia No. 9 in 1873; its German furniture workers had set up their union a year earlier, then affiliated with the Furniture Worker's National Union as Local Union No. 1 in 1873. According to Hartmut Keil, the International Workingmen's Association (the First International) "seems to have been a decisive link for trade union organisation between the '60s and 70s." Both union movements collapsed in the depression of 1873 to 1879 as unionization became impossible.[6]

Socialist influence in Chicago's unions was always public. It was most visible when the members marched through the city's streets in processions arranged by the Socialistic Labor Party. Who marched with the socialists? The *Inter Ocean* listed the units in a procession arranged by the Socialist Labor Party in June 1878:

Division No. 1

Furniture Workers' Union, comprising the upholsters, finishers, woodcarvers, gilders, frame-workers, and wood-turners' unions.
Carpenter's Union
Box-makers' Union
Schleswig-Holstein Verein
decorated wagon

Division No. 2

Iron Moulders' Union
Socialistic masons
Bakers' Benevolent Society
Machinists' and Blacksmiths' Union
Socialistic Shoemakers
Socialistic Tailors' Union

Typographical Union No. 9
Masons' Benevolent Society
Handwirksbuscher (tramps)
decorated wagon

Division No. 3

Great Western Light Guard Band
Bohemian Workingmen's Benevolent Society
Workingmen's Benevolent Societies Nos. 1, 2, and 3
Scandinavian Singing Society
Vorwaerts Singing Society
Free singers [Freier Sangerbund]
Allmania Mannerchoir [sic]
Rothmanner singers and more wagons
Scandinavian section of the Socialistic Labor Party
English
Bohemian
French
German.

It was an impressive demonstration: the *Inter Ocean* reported "not less than 7,000 men in the line."[7] Yet few of the units in the parade were very large: the Sozialistische Schumacher Verein did not exceed 50 members; the Tailors' Union had perhaps 100; the mason's barely 40; and Typographia No. 9 about 50.

The first unit in that parade, the Furniture Workers' Union—properly Die Möbel-Arbeiter Union No. 1 von Chicago—was one of the largest. Tracing their roots back at least as far as an 1852 strike, and prominent in the 1867 general strike, Chicago's German cabinetmakers had played a leading role for a national union, in the Eight Hour Movement of the late 1870s, and founded a cooperative factory in 1879. Die Möbel-Arbeiter Union became a mainstay to the socialist movement, yet with no more than 200 members in 1879, out of almost 3,000 in the trade, the union was small but growing.[8] Die Möbel-Arbeiter Union was not the only socialist union. The German Typographical Union No. 9 enjoyed a closed shop from the radical press. The German and Bohemian bakers' unions, and the German butchers' union, which emerged out of benevolent societies, were each organized by socialists, as was Die Metall-Arbeiter Union, which would play a central role in the McCormick strike in

1885–1886. Each of these socialist unions grew up alongside, and competed with non-socialist unions. And we are ill-equipped to understand either their rivalry or their histories.

THE "MARXIST VERSUS LASSALLEAN" DICHOTOMY

The traditional wisdom has perceived a split between political socialists, "the Lassalleans," and economic socialists, "the Marxists." In Chicago during the seventies and eighties, that dichotomy obscures more than it illuminates.[9] To be sure, the Workingmen's Party of Illinois was Lassallean when it argued that political action was the only way out for the working class, and denounced trade unions "since they never led to any lasting betterment for the workingmen." The issue was far from settled: after the WPI failed to elect a single candidate, Klings lost the editorship, and Conrad Conzett, a member of the First International, a Marxist, took over. Under his direction, *Der Vorbote* reopened the question of strategy. With the depression in its second year, Conzett attacked the unions even as they disappeared, arguing that they "fully observed the rod of economic depression," but hoping "the movement in general will profit from these hard lessons" if only it could be forced "to broaden its program toward attacking the wage system itself."[10]

After the Tilden-Hayes election in 1876, the *Labor Standard*, an organ of the Workingmen's Party of the United States, "offered sound advice to the members of our party and [to] those who ought to be members. It is to drop political action altogether . . . and in the meantime to organize the [WPUS] and Trades Unions and to agitate in them labor questions only. There is absolutely no other way to a *future* victorious political action."[11] Overemphasis on the word "party" can only confuse us now: this was not a purely or strictly Lassallean party.

Chicago's SLP relied on trade union support, yet only a handful of the city's trade unions were organized "on a socialistic basis." Peter McGuire almost defined the criteria for such an evaluation: "Our party proposes to start them ahead by opposing their fossilized policy of resistance to capital, and by making them aggressive in their form of organization. That is to advocate their organization or reorganization upon a socialistic basis." He explained, "I do not attack Trades Unionism, but I do attack the existing form of trade union organization." That spring Paul Grottkau wrote his first article for *Der Vorbote*, boldly calling for the economic organization of the working class and arguing that political freedom in the face of economic dependence and servitude did not make sense.

"Political action of the workers without a strong organization and without real means of power in this country is the equivalent of fighting windmills." Grottkau's reputation and enthusiasm proved contagious as the SLP charged into unionization, calling mass meetings, scheduling speakers, arranging parades, and organizing.[12]

By June 1878, *Der Vorbote* could list over twenty trade unions in the city that had endorsed the SLP. Under Grottkau's leadership the SLP cooperated with the larger labor movement.

> The trade-union organization always appears to us as the natural and fundamental organisation of the working-class, and, being convinced that it should be entitled to all the support we can possibly give it, for its own sake, we cannot utter too strongly our feeling of protest, when here and there the over-zealous but unintelligent followers of the political labor movement desire to use the trade unions as mere auxiliaries for the Social-Democracy and demand that they should become socialistic in the sense in which the word applies to our political party.

Grottkau criticized the politicos, though he argued the issue had become obsolete: "If it were obliged to choose between trade union and political agitation, its choice would invariably fall on the former. We have no such alternative before us; therefore, we can be active in both spheres. We must always place economic action above political."[13]

Grottkau and Parsons were editors and ideologues, but they were not the only unionists or organizers within the movement. To understand the relationship between Chicago's socialists and the city's labor movement, we have to read beyond the editorial pages, first to the movement that supported these editors, then to the unions themselves. Oskar Neebe had organized among the brewery workers, Samuel Fielden among the teamsters, and Louis Lingg among the carpenters. The relationship between the socialists and the labor movement need not be defined solely by the Haymarket Martyrs. Of 542 members of the SLP identified in a sample reconstitution, 57 can be positively identified as trade union officers, fully 1 in 10. Moreover, 146 of 723 identified members of the IWPA in a second sample can be identified as union officers, 1 in 5. Most never achieved notoriety. John Dusey and Jacob Winnen were successive presidents of the Stairbuilders' Union; Ernst Legner served as the president of Die Möbel-Arbeiter Union; Josef Pondelicek became the first president of the Bohemian painters' union; Mathias Schmiedinger headed the Bäcker Unterstützungsverein and later the

Baker's Union; and August Winiger was the president of the German Typographia No. 9. A list of IWPA members elected vice-presidents of their unions would include: Wilhelm Kempke of the CigarMakers Union No. 15; M. Klepac of Union No. 54, the Bohemian carpenters and joiners; Wilhelm Medow and Julius Stegeman, both of Typographia No. 9; and Henry Schiefelbein of Die Lumberyard Arbeiter Union.[14]

Those lists belie the simple dichotomy of Marxists and Lassalleans. In Chicago, economic agitation preceded, then accompanied, and after 1880 even replaced political organization. Where electoral activity proved intermittent, and success elusive, unionism and socialist agitation within the trade unions were a continuous thread from the 1860s through to Haymarket.

THE PRACTICE OF DUAL UNIONISM

Throughout this period, Chicago's socialists and anarchists practiced a peculiarly nineteenth-century form of dual unionism by erecting and maintaining organizations that rivalled local, national, and international unions.[15] The Sozialistische Schumacher Verein, for example, competed with the Anglo-American Knights of St. Crispin, the German and Bohemian International Carpenters and Joiners with the Brotherhood of Carpenters and Joiners, Die Metall-Arbeiter Union with the Blacksmiths and Machinists Union, German *bäckers* and Bohemian *pekařs* with English-speaking bakers.[16] At its simplest, a polyglot work force posed real problems for would-be organizers. "As W. T. Henderson, a Chicago carpenter, stated, 'We have German, French, Bohemian, Scandinavian, and English-speaking members. Now how can all these different tongues ventilate before one body? It would take you a week to go through a meeting.'"[17] The most common solution involved ethnic branches; just as frequently those branches that became socialist broke with their erstwhile comrades. The political distinctions between socialist and non- or (more often) anti-socialist unions were, in turn, reinforced by ethnic and cultural divisions.

The histories of the carpenters and cigarmakers' unions may illuminate the relationship between the socialist or anarchist and labor movements in late nineteenth-century Chicago. The carpenters, who remained skilled, comprised about 12 percent of the IWPA's members, the second largest occupational group; the cigarmakers, beset by mechanization and semiskilled, accounted for 10 percent of the SLP's members, the largest occupational group within a sample of its membership. Combined, the two trades account for about 16 percent of the two organizations, about one in six. In both trades there is a pattern of secession and subsequent reunification of socialist and antisocialist locals.[18]

Socialists, Anarchists, and the Carpenters' Unions
Chicago burned in 1871 and had to be rebuilt in the rest of the decade: carpenters, and building-trade workers in general, were in demand. Immigrants were crucial in the formation of Chicago's carpenters' unions. German Forty Eighters were actively involved in the earliest attempts to organize carpenters, and in 1855 they formed the Schreiner-Verein. These were radicals, if not socialists, and already in the 1860s, "the strength of the German unionists was reinforced by their working-class neighborhood associations and ethnic cultural institutions." A multiethnic union appeared eight years later as did a competitor in 1872. Both disintegrated following failed strikes in 1867 and 1873, with only the German and Scandinavian branches surviving.[19]

Between 1877 and 1884, Chicago's carpenters build an impressive local organization with a complex of twelve branches, identified by ethnicity; a citywide executive board, with local officers; and an extensive program of benefits and insurance. However impressive, that structure was flawed: "the leadership was overwhelmingly Anglo-Irish while the local membership was more heavily German, Bohemian, Scandinavian, and French. Even more important, many [of the] active unionists in Chicago were Germans and Bohemians, whose socialism and ethnic cultures divided them from the Brotherhood's leaders."[20]

The socialists were ensconced in branches 7 and 12, two of the five German-speaking branches, a few more in branch 5, which was Bohemian. Although expressed in different languages, the dissension within Local 21 was not so much ethnic as political. The first defections surprisingly came from a group of Anglo-Americans who fled the brotherhood for the Knights of Labor in September 1882. It surfaced again almost a year later when Carl Steckelberg, the corresponding secretary of branch 7 and a member of the IWPA's Gruppe Sudwestseite, supported the Progressive Cigarmakers against their international union. The German and Bohemian carpenters were "nothing but oppressed dues payers," locked out of both leadership and policy-making positions, and upset when the Anglo-American "labor reformers" endorsed temperance as a solution to the labor question. The two groups interpreted cooperation differently: the Anglo-Americans saw their building association as an effective program for evolutionary change; the German and Bohemian socialists, on the other hand, advocated an independent labor party and later revolutionary action for what they called "the cooperative state."[21]

A long, disastrous strike in spring 1884 occasioned, but did not cause, the destruction of Local 21's edifice. In September, McGuire denounced "Anarchists in Trades Unions," describing two "classes of Anarchists": the "political anarchist who makes capital for political parties"; and the "Social Anarchists" who "talk of petroleum, revolution and dynamite." Some of the latter had "gained entrance into the trade unions and constructive labor movement. . . . In Chicago, Carpenters Union No. 21 has had examples of this kind, but now these disturbers are powerless. . . . They can't be reasoned with, nor are they subject to discipline." McGuire advised, "Kick them out wherever they are!"[22]

The "disturbers" had already been rendered powerless in July when the local's executive board decided to consolidate into two branches— "one German and the other American"—bound by an executive committee composed of delegates from each. The new officers were not new; and there were no socialists among them. In any case, consolidation destroyed the socialist position just as it ignored the Scandinavians and Bohemians. In October 1884, the new corresponding secretary predicted "our union will do well. But we must get rid of all the crazy Johann Most shouters, for they only want to use our union for their propaganda or else destroy it." The Bohemians withdrew, asking for a charter as a second local; the Germans followed with the same request. Both were ordered to pay off Local 21's debt as a precondition. Instead the dissidents ("known here as Anarchists" according to the loyalist secretary) severed their ties with the brotherhood and with the city's Trade and Labor Assembly and affiliated with the new Central Labor Union (CLU).[23]

In July 1885, Local 21 advised *The Carpenter* of "an armed organization of a dozen carpenters of the Anarchist stripe. These fellows were either too poor or too stingy to pay their dues [to Union 21]. Now they are buying $12 guns and playing soldiers." There were not many members of the "Armed Organization of the International Carpenters and Joiners' Union No. 1" or in the Independent Carpenters and Joiners' Union, the CLU's new affiliates; nor were there many left in Local 21. While its correspondent reported "a creditable showing" in the Labor Day parade that September, only fifty (the smallest of the units) marched with Local 21 and the Trade and Labor Assembly; 1,200 carpenters had marched to the CLU's picnic a day earlier.[24]

By the fall of 1885, there were three separate, parallel, and hostile groups among Chicago's carpenters. The first, led by the Irish, organized within the Knights; the second of Anglo-Americans, in the growing brotherhood and the Trades Assembly; the third of German and Bohemian socialists, in the revolutionary Central Labor Union. Despite sustained and aggressive organizing by two of those groups—the Knights and the CLU—the majority of the city's carpenters remained outside all three.

Socialists, Anarchists, and the Cigarmakers' Unions

The dynamics of dual unionism, of socialist competition with non- or anti-socialist unions, are just as visible in the history of Chicago's cigarmakers' unions. There had long been a protective union in the city with ties to the national organization and in 1867 Local 11 had even won a closed shop from one of the largest employers. It disappeared in the long depression: "between 1874 and 1877 there is no record of activity from the cigarmakers' union in Chicago." When it reappeared with a reissued charter in January 1877, it "was a different organization than its predecessors in several respects."[25]

As early as the eleventh convention of the Cigarmakers' International Union (CMIU) in 1877, socialists had proposed that the CMIU declare itself "in harmony with the platform of the Workingmen's Party of the United States." The motion was of course tabled, and Adolph Strasser later revealed that comments of socialist delegates had been stricken from convention records.[26] Outmaneuvered nationally, the socialists retained a strong base in the Chicago local. Its new president, Polish-born, German-speaking Sam Goldwater, and many of its officers were socialists; several had already stood as candidates for the WPUS and the SLP. The revitalized union dismissed talk about harmony within the trade. In May 1877 it published a warning to employers threatening to list those who used the truck system.[27]

Such militancy grated on those who cherished craft harmony, and in March 1879 they withdrew from Union No. 11 and received a second charter as Local 14. Each of the rivals grew; yet combined, they accounted for barely 7 percent of the city's 1,600 cigarmakers. About 1,000 struck against a wage cut in October 1879. At a mass meeting of both factions, speakers from Local 11 condemned the International as "a fraud, and a leech sucking the life-blood of the cigarmakers throughout the country." In its place they urged a unified local powerful enough to go it alone. The strike collapsed; in its wake Local 11, "which was evidently neither more nor less than a socialistic club," according to Strasser, lost its charter. [28]

In May 1880 the local reinitiated several members of the "suspended union" as the socialists trickled back into the fold. Within a year the union's meetings were again arranged and addressed by socialists, SLP'ers like Fred Korth, Joseph Hack, Wilhelm Betting, Jacob Selig, and Wilhelm Kempke were again the recognized leaders and elected officers. One of their most consistent opponents later conceded that within three months of the socialists' return the union's membership has risen from a mere 60 to more than 300. [29]

In July 1882, Local 14 resolved to "sustain the authorized Union 144" (in New York City, Gompers's local), denouncing "any party or clique that tries to create dissatisfaction in our ranks" and prefiguring subsequent developments in Chicago. Like Gompers's opponents in New York, the socialists remained unwelcome, distrusted, and uncomfortable in No. 14. That fall they arranged a mass meeting to organize a separate "Progressive Union"; when 500 men responded, Cigarmakers' Progressive Union No. 15 established itself in October 1883. The socialists, not the conservatives, had seceded this time. The citywide Trades Assembly immediately denounced the new union as "a piece of socialistic agitation which could only bring harm to the workingmen." Led by Korth and Selig, the Progressives rejected the union bureaucracy, cract insularity, and apolitical stance of both Local 14 and its International, arguing instead for a principled "progressive" stand. One principle was immediately acted upon: the formation of a union for the semiskilled cigar packers. [30]

Secession could not have come at a less propitious time as the manufacturers' association exploited the competition with a lockout. Despite joint meetings and declarations of harmony, the Progressives found themselves striking against the International. They undercut the union scale and Local 14 denounced Progressive president Jacob Selig as "the champion scab of Chicago" when the smaller local imported workers from New York's Progressive Union. When the strike finally ended, the International retained its bargaining position. In June 1884, the Progressive Union "had the horrible gall" to apply for membership in the Trades Assembly. Opposed by Local 14's delegates, they lost by a unanimous vote of all twenty-three member unions. When the Progressives struck again, unsuccessfully, Local 14 claimed "a great victory," quoting one large manufacturer who conceded, "You fellows will break anybody's back." [31]

Beaten twice in five months the Progressives neither folded nor disappeared. They sponsored the initial call for the new Central Labor Union, and were active in its processions, demonstrations, and agitation. By late September 1884 they had reached some kind of truce with Local 14 and with the International: *Progress* headlined "Common Sense in Chicago," reported "a protocoll [sic] of cooperation," and announced the two locals would "fraternize." Both continued to grow, though they rarely met together. Indeed, Local 15's corresponding secretary complained that "our 'friends' of the Int[ernational] Union cannot make up their minds yet that a Progressive Union is in town to stay." By the time that Local 15's delegate arrived at the second convention in May, the national CMPU was prepared to reunite with the older International. Both locals overwhelmingly supported amalgamation, although Local 15 continued to be reticent; eventually Progressive Union No. 15 rejoined the International as Local 15.[32]

As the Eight Hour Movement caught fire late in 1885, unionists remained a minority of the city's cigarmakers. Like the carpenters, the cigarmakers had built separate, parallel, and mutually hostile organizations in the Trades Assembly, the Knights, and the Central Labor Union. If the hostility between the Knights and the International union did not surface until after Haymarket, that between the International and Progressive unions remained barely disguised.

THE CENTRAL LABOR UNION

In the summer of 1884, Chicago's anarchists escalated the practice of dual unionism to a citywide level by founding a Central Labor Union in opposition to the Trades and Labor Assembly. It was, in fact, the second such challenge. Just before the fall elections in 1879, Darwin Streeter, then president of the Trade and Labor Council, and the leaders of the city's Eight Hour League endorsed a Democrat for county treasurer. The socialists countered by labeling Streeter "a veritable Judas among the workingmen"; in turn, his allies charged that Morgan, Goldwater, and Schilling had also been bribed. At the council's next meeting, the socialists defeated a motion to censure the *Arbeiter-Zeitung* by a margin of twenty-four votes to ten. One of the losers, Cornelius McAulliffe, a printer, Greenbacker, and Knight, then denounced the socialists, charging that "the Council had been run as the fag-end of the Socialist Labor Party, and he wanted no more of it." By the end of January 1880, there were two trade and labor councils.[33]

While some Chicagoans saw only a personal fight between Streeter and Morgan, there was more at stake, and the conflict exposed the underlying tensions in the movement. First, the margin of the censure vote, and the fact that the council's majority stayed with Morgan and the socialists testifies to their strength in the city's labor movement. During the split the socialists retained the support of the silver gilders', iron moulders', Amalgamated Engineers', tanners', curriers', stairbuilders', carpenters', wood carvers', German tailors', furniture workers' and the socialist shoemakers's unions. When the anti-socialist faction seceded to form the Trade and Labor Assembly, it included the typographers, painters, Knights of St. Crispin, sailors, and butchers. Second, the Knights of Labor's delegates played an important role. Until they split they had consistently voted with the secessionist bloc. Since the Knights remained clandestine, Morgan successfully maneuvered to expel them for not being unionists and for belonging to a secret society. Finally, and however short-lived, the secession identified the fundamental political issues. The SLP expected the council's loyalty, and considered the endorsement of a Democrat as betrayal. The unionists, on the other hand, sought a more flexible policy, one which could pose workingmen's demands to the traditional parties.[34] The rivalry lasted almost four months. According to the *Times*,

[the] great question [is] whether the regular Trade and Labor Council presented as good an opportunity to the leaders of the Council to put money in their pockets by selling their supposed influence with the workingmen to office seekers while remaining an independent organization, or [if they] could arrange matters so as to obtain control of the regular Trade and Labor Council and return to it.

At the beginning of May the two factions reunited, under the secessionists' name, as the Trade and Labor Assembly with Albert Parsons as a compromise chairman. In the name of solidarity the socialists surrendered the most important offices and remained content with finances and statistics; for their part the unions got an apolitical assembly.[35]

Four years later, when the Trades Assembly rejected their application, the Progressive Cigarmakers called for the formation of a new body, "a Central Labor Union after the pattern of the CLU in New York." As early as October 1883, during one of its confrontations with the CMIU, *Progress* had published a letter from Chicago reporting that "the Brassworkers Union, the Union of the Furniture Workers, and all the socialistic labor organizations of Chicago, who all defend the rights of labor to the full fruit of what it produces, have promised us their sympathies and support."[36] With only eight charter members—CMPU No. 15, the Deutsche Zimmerleute und Bauschreiner Union, Die Möbel-Arbeiter Union, the Metall-Arbeiter Unions of Chicago and North America, Typographia No. 9, the Custom Tailors' Union, and the Fresco Painters' Union—the CLU did not enjoy an auspicious beginning. Within two months they were joined by the Cigarpackers Union and the Fleischergesellen Unterstützung Verein, bringing the total to ten. Despite their hostility, both the SLP and the IWPA came together to launch the CLU: from the former, T. J. Morgan, Samuel Goldwater, and Julius Vahlteich; from the latter, Albert Parsons, Paul Grottkau, and Josef Pecka.[37]

Modelled after the IWPA, the CLU became a federation of local unions; its officers rotated, with a new chairperson for each meeting and a secretary elected for short periods. Gompers would never have tolerated the lack of discipline or order in such a participatory democracy. Because it took the Pittsburgh Manifesto as its own and reported its meetings in the anarchist press, the CLU should be regarded as an "anarchist" or "socialist" body. Although we can not be sure of the affiliations of individual members, virtually all of its officers and delegates came from either the IWPA or the SLP.

The CLU and the Trades Assembly were antagonists and rivals. Their antagonism dated from the mid-seventies and their rivalry lasted, like the CLU itself, beyond the turn of the century. The Europeans' secession left the assembly an Anglo-American body whose meetings were conducted in English. Of 277 officers between 1880 and 1886, fully 53 percent had Anglo-American surnames, another 25 percent were Irish, no more than 21 percent were European. (See Table 2.1) Theirs was an organization of, by, and for skilled workers who held the assembly as their own; the unskilled were conspicuously missing. The assembly seemed "an aristocracy of labor which mind their own business and blackguard the Socialists." *The Alarm* and *Die Arbeiter-Zeitung* denounced the assembly as a "bogus labor organization," composed of "businessmen, not union men," whose members were "lickspittles," "dough faces," "shallow pates," and "flunkeys". In January 1885, the assembly narrowly passed a set of resolutions denouncing anarchist rhetoric and agitation. According to *The Alarm*, "many of the delegates," opposed the resolutions, "and some of them avowed their sympathy for and belief in the principles of Socialism." The IWPA and the CLU then challenged the conservatives to a debate: if they could harmonize labor and capital, "the Socialists promise[d] . . . to discontinue their agitation." Not a single officer from the assembly showed up.[38]

Embittered by its experience with the socialists at the end of the 1870s, the assembly prohibited political discussions, although its members were free to campaign at election time. Its officers were tied into (not by) the regular political parties, and expected to be courted at election time. Carter Harrison proved a congenial mayor who could be entreated by trade union delegations. And if Harrison hired some of the assembly's leaders for city positions, if he listened to them, if he repeatedly re-strained the city's police force, and proposed reform legislation for them, such was, in Richard Schneirov's words, "the price he paid for the refusal of unionists to engage in independent labor politics" under a socialist banner. Unionists in turn came to expect patronage and viewed the city's health department "as a legitimate source of sinecures for their leaders." Between 1882 and 1886, the assembly worked out what Selig Perlman described as a program of "political collective bargaining." Indeed, as Schneirov has argued, "the configuration of municipal politics was as much the result of an accommodation [by] Harrison to labor's political strength as the opposite." The CLU was continually shocked by the assembly. In November 1885, the assembly chose "a member of a Chi-cago militia regiment" as its delegate to the Federation of Trades in Washington. An initial uproar evaporated when he promised to resign when his enlistment was up, only five years in the future. Where the CLU was outraged by the conflict of interest, the delegate believed it "far more honorable to be a member of the militia than it is to go around with a gang of Socialists and Anarchists who want to destroy other people's property."[39]

Thus, we should contrast the CLU and the Trades Assembly on three levels: composition, strategy, and politics. Where the assembly's mem-bers were Anglo-American and skilled, the CLU was composed of European immigrants, skilled, semiskilled, and unskilled. The cigar-makers, for example, had established a cigarpackers' local, and from its beginning Die Möbel-Arbeiter Union had organized skilled, semiskilled, and unskilled in its local. The fundamental contrasts were political. The anarchists in the CLU declared themselves revolutionaries; the unionists, evolutionaries. To the anarchists, the assembly's members had "no higher aims"; they were content with ameliorative reforms. While the anarchists taught "class hatred," the trade unionists refused "to declare war on capital." Clearly, the central issue was property ownership: to the conservatives the anarchists meant "to destroy other people's property";

for the CLU and the anarchists the system of private property had to be destroyed, "by all means, i.e., by energetic, relentless, revolutionary and international action." Jacob Selig, who spoke for the Progressive Cigar-makers and for the CLU, best expressed the contrasts and the conflict:

> The Trade and Labor Assembly[,] composed of the English-speaking unions, is controlled by the office-seeking element in the trade and labor organizations, men who have no higher aims than the abolition of prison labor, the enforcement of the eight hour day, prohibition of children under 14, fair days-wages for a fair-days work[,] and political office from the Republican or Democratic party, [they] don't care which.

The Metall-Arbeiter Union echoed that last clause when it withdrew from the assembly in 1884 and affiliated with the new CLU: "We are tired to be [sic] the tail with which the Republican and Democratic party [sic] wag."[40]

SOCIALISTS, ANARCHISTS, AND THE KNIGHTS OF LABOR

Rivalled on one side then by the Trade and Labor Assembly, the anarchists simultaneously competed with the Noble and Holy Order of the Knights of Labor. Chicago's first Local Assembly, LA 400, had nineteen charter members in 1877 and the order grew sporadically during the next decade. Even after it dropped the cloak of secrecy, in January 1882, the order's growth remained slow, uneven, and out of step with national growth for the next four years. Then, in the Great Upheaval of 1885–1886, the order exploded; from 551 members in July 1885, District Assembly (DA) 24 claimed 14,019 twelve months later. Chicago's second district assembly, DA 57, experienced the same pattern. Founded in July 1882, it grew slowly, then leapt from 1,355 members in 1885 to 7,734 in 1886. With 27,000 members at the time of the Haymarket riot, the Knights more than equalled the Trades Assembly and dwarfed the CLU.[41]

The Knights and the trade unions differed in composition, purpose, and methods. The trade unions organized skilled workers; the Knights organized workers, regardless of skill. Where the unions were based on the monopoly of craft skills, the Knights initially promoted mixed assemblies which subsumed craft with class. Thus trade unionism embraced, even institutionalized, craft identifications; the Knights proclaimed that "An Injury to One is of Concern to All." If the unions challenged capital,

44

but not the capitalist system, the Knights challenged the capitalist order, but not capital. Finally, the trade unions depended on high dues, an extensive benefit system, and the strike; the Knights offered a decentralized system, few benefits, and preferred mediation and the boycott.

Before 1881, Chicago's Knights and unionists remained distant, if not estranged. When the anti-socialists seceded from the Trades Council in 1879, the Knights had sided with them, but a rupture came in 1880. As Philip Van Patten wrote to Terence Powderly, "Why must our [assemblies] in that city persist in running the Trades Assembly in the way they do? The regular unions denounce our Order as a know-nothing political league and it is working great injury." Van Patten, then secretary to both the SLP and the Knights' general executive board, pleaded with the Grand Master Workman, "Advise our bro[ther]s to work in and through the *regular* unions and thus get control of the regular Trades Assembly." Powderly then intervened, and by May the Knights officially withdrew from the assembly.[42]

After 1881, when secretary and politics ceased to be divisive, unionists and Knights worked together. They held joint parades, picnics, and demonstrations. And they organized together. Myles McPadden wrote Powderly in February 1882 to announce: "I have spoken before 21 different local unions," including the tinners, painters, clerks, moulders, printers, and the Amalgamated Society of Machinists, Blacksmiths and Engineers. He closed by predicting we will "have over 10,000 men in Chicago in two months." That hope proved unfounded, but for a time the order grew quickly. "In fact we have a revival as the *Evening Journal* puts it. Three local unions of the Iron Moulders joined in a body." That spurt can be traced to two changes within the Knights. The first was an unprecedented accommodation to European immigrants, and the Germans came into the order in such numbers that there was talk of a second German District Assembly. The second development was as significant. Until 1882 the order in Chicago had been based on mixed assemblies. In fall 1881 Richard Griffiths, the District Master Workman, asked Powderly's sanction for a Local Assembly (LA) of brass finishers. When he approved, McPadden brought in the moulders and Chicago's Knights organized not mixed but trade assemblies.[43]

The spurt stopped as quickly as it had begun for DA 24's roll book of delegates contains cryptic remarks like "lapsed," "severed," "lapsed and turned over effects" next to many of those new locals. The District Assembly, whose motto advised "Cavendo tutus" [Safety through Caution], was unprepared for such explosive growth. New, aggressive, and Irish organizers like McPadden, William Halley, and Joseph O'Kelley ran too far ahead of the older Knights. According to Halley, those in DA 24, like Powderly, seemed "to dread rapid organization," the "making haste slowly process did not keep out bad men or politicians in Chicago, to the ruin of nearly all the old assemblies."[44] The Irish then withdrew from DA 24, feeling out the Trades Assembly first, then pursued a charter for a second DA.[45]

There was little hostility between Chicago's Knights and unionists, even less between the Trades Assembly and the District Assembly. In 1881, the Knights endorsed *The Progressive Age*, which was then owned by the city's unions, as its official local organ. A year later, in October 1882, DA 24 argued: "It will be conceded by all that the Order is a trades union to all intents and purposes, and in its early days in this city it was fostered, maintained and kept alive solely and entirely by trade unionists." Even when the Knights forsook mixed assemblies and concentrated on trade assemblies, the order continued to cooperate with the unions and their assembly, and some LAs sent delegates to both the DA and the Trades Assembly. In 1886 the state Bureau of Labor Statistics found that 17 percent of the state's trade unionists were simultaneously members of the Knights.[46]

The earliest historian of the Knights, Norman Ware, was adamant that "the only direct connection between the Chicago anarchists and the Knights of Labor lay in the fact that Parsons was a member of the Order." Ware admitted that Parsons "had joined Local Assembly No. 400, . . . in 1877, and . . . [later] transferred . . . to Local Assembly No. 1307 of which he was a member until his execution." In fact, Albert Parsons was the first Knight in Chicago, having been initiated on 4 July 1876 while in Indianapolis. Moreover "Old 400" was the first Knight assembly in the city, and at least four of its original nineteen members were intimate with the socialist movement: Andrew Adair, George Schilling, Van Patten, and Parsons.[47]

Dual membership continued: at least forty-eight identified members of the SLP were also members of the Knights, as were at least thirty-seven identified members of the IWPA. Within District Assembly 24 the socialists tended to represent craft assemblies by a ratio of two-to-one: C. P. Wakeman, LA 1754 (bricklayers); Julius Krueger, LA 1790 (shoemakers); Charles Wheeler and Alfred Gould, LA 1802 (machinists); Carol Fleischhammer, LA 1821 (German tanners); August Spies and Oskar Neebe, LA 1995 (German printers); and Jacob Selig, LA 3045 (cigar makers). Reflecting their class rather than craft consciousness, the anarchist-Knights tended to represent mixed assemblies by a ratio of three-to-one: thus Albert Parsons served as one of LA 400's delegates, as did O. A. Bishop from LA 828; Tim O'Meara, LA 852; Albert Berndt, LA 1617; Lizzie Swank and Julia Bishop, LA 1789 (the women's assembly); and Wenzel Thorek, LA 2220 (Bohemian). Both socialists and anarchists were initially trusted by the Knights, then feared and excluded. As late as 1882, socialists were still prominent in DA 24, three years later the anarchists were no longer as visible.[48]

The two organizations, the two movements, were never mutually exclusive. In Chicago, as in Detroit and elsewhere, some Knights were socialists, and some socialists were Knights. Between the 1877 Great Upheaval and the 1880 presidential election, one can speak, as Richard Schneirov has, of a "socialist hegemony over the local labor movement" in Chicago. Socialists became prominent in both the unions and the Trades Assembly; they offered both a political forum and a critique of contemporary political economy, and they had successfully elected candidates to state and municipal offices. While the Noble Order remained secret, even furtive; the socialists enjoyed visibility, even prominence. Yet, as Schneirov points out, "it is important to distinguish between the organizational hegemony of the Socialist[ic] Labor Party and an ideological hegemony of socialism."[49]

The relationship between Chicago's anarchists and Knights remained ambiguous. From his jail cell August Spies remembered that he "was also a member of the Knights of Labor once—about three years ago—but the assembly to which I belonged dissolved, and I never since have renewed my membership, principally, because I never liked secrecy or ceremonies in any organization. But I have frequently lectured in meetings of "Knights," when invited. Oskar Neebe recalled:

> Often the remark has been made 'we were working against the interests of the Knights of Labor,' but that was not so, we were not against them, only against the ways these organizations were made up and kept. Did not hundreds of our speakers speak to the workingmen to organize themselves, no matter in what form as unions or Knights of Labor, that in organization lay their strength.

Albert Parsons, Chicago's first Knight, addressed an open letter to the Grand Master Workman in August 1886: "The foundation principle of socialism, or anarchy, is the same as the Knights of Labor, viz., 'the abolition of the wages system' and the substitution in its stead of an industrial system of universal cooperation."[50] That Parsons wrote from jail, facing

47

conviction, does not explain his comparison as delusion. Both he and Powderly had been members of the SLP, both were Knights, and Parsons maintained that "the platform of the Knights of Labor contains nothing else by socialistic demands, the realization of the whole of them would amount to Socialism." Beyond their seeming ideological affinity, the Knights and the CLU shared much of the same commitment. Both grew out of existing organizations of skilled workers; but where the unions remained trapped in craft identifications, both the Knights and the CLU aimed at the larger working class. Both tried to organize the unorganized; both sought to be inclusive, rather than exclusive. Both were egalitarian.[51]

The crucial differences were again ethno-cultural. The Knight's base, its membership, and their elected officers were decidedly Anglo-American. In 1886, based on the material published by the Illinois Bureau of Labor Statistics, fully 34 percent of Chicago's Knights were native-born; another 22 percent came from Ireland and the British Isles. In sum, at least 56 percent of the order's membership were English-speaking. Yet those figures were skewed by the order's phenomenal growth during the Great Upheaval and the Knights' composition should instead be measured in the period before the Upheaval. From 1882 to 1886 some 342 people served as delegates and officers of Chicago's two District Assemblies. Of a subtotal of 316 whose ethnicity can be determined, 52 percent had Anglo-American surnames, another 40 percent were Irish; no more than 8 percent had German, Scandinavian, Czech, Jewish, French, or Dutch surnames.[52] (see Table 2.1)

The Noble Order never actively excluded European immigrants or those who could not speak English. Yet from 1877 to 1885–1886, Chicago's Knights remained an Anglo-American organization. That pattern became visible as early as 1882 when Germans had rushed into the order in such unprecedented numbers that a separate German district assembly in the city was discussed. Both rush and discussion fizzled. The Knights made few concessions to foreigners, even less effort to meet and organize them. The *Adelphon Kruptos* and the constitution had been translated into German, for example, as early as 1880, but remained unpublished and uncirculated until January 1882, when the order went public. Moreover, while DA 24 had recommended a German-speaking organizer as early as November 1880, it was not until June 1882 that they actively pursued the Germans. And it took another five months before William Halley wrote to Terence Powderly about "a new Bohemian A[ssembly], the first of its kind."[53]

In the spring of 1883 Chicago got a charter for a second district assembly, No. 57. Though it drew on the city's southern and more industrial parts (Pilsen, Bridgeport, and the suburban towns of Lake, Cummings, and Pullman), its officers remained overwhelmingly Irish. Indeed, twenty-seven of its first twenty-nine officers had Irish surnames; the other two were German and Czech. DA 57's leaders, like the Grand Master Workman, enjoyed close ties to the Irish community, the Clan-na-Gael, the Land League, and the Catholic Church. DA 57 rejected DA 24's caution and preferred the boycott and strike to arbitration. The two DA's rarely cooperated and on some issues actually fought one another.[54]

Socialism, not political action, divided anarchists and Knights. The Grand Master Workman had himself joined the Socialistic Labor Party in the summer of 1880 and remained on cordial terms with a few of its officers for some time.[55] His timing was important. Powderly, a Greenbacker, joined the SLP only after it merged with the national Greenback Party for the presidential campaign that year. From his office in Scranton the Grand Master Workman explained in 1882 that as long as socialists were "temperately discussing social questions as we meet them[,] I find no fault with *socialism*. But when violence, robbery, etc. is contemplated, I object. There is an attempt being made to make our Order a scapegoat for Socialism of this kind.[56]

Chicago's Knights were less cordial. Powderly's chief correspondent in the city, Richard Griffiths, a Welshman and Grand Old Man of the Order, felt threatened by socialist and anarchist agitation. In 1882 he denounced William Halley to Powderly, saying that Halley "is not a Socialist, he is too soft for that." Griffiths later tattled when Halley shared the platform with the cursed socialists during a memorial service for John McAuliffe. In 1885 Griffiths and Parsons were invited to a Fourth of July celebration. Griffiths accepted reluctantly, telling Powderly his appearance might "lead some to think that I am neck and crop a Socialist and dynamiter." Concern about fraternization was not a personal idiosyncrasy, for Powderly's other Chicago correspondents consistently sought to distance themselves from the radicals. When J. H. Randall, for example, wrote the Grand Master Workman, he pointedly announced, "I am not a member of the Red Flag school."[57]

Although some of Chicago's Knights hated the socialists and anarchists, Powderly initially feared only that they would tarnish the order's reputation. In April 1886 he threatened one alleged anarchist, demanding:

Are you an organizer for the International Society? [A]re you instrumental in raising an emergency fund among the Assemblies? Do you make the statement in the Assemblies that the K. of L. is but a stepping stone to Socialism and Anarchy? Did you ever make the statement that I was an Anarchist, a Socialist or an advocate of the use of dynamite? Did you prevent the formation of a D.A. by stating that it was a political machine?

A month later, only two days after the Haymarket riot, Powderly recalled the man's commission saying "the Order . . . was not intended to be used as a school for the spread of anarchist ideas . . . and I will not tolerate it in the future."[58]

On the eve of the Great Upheaval, Chicago's labor movement embraced only a minority of the city's working class. Despite the combined efforts of trade unionists, the Knights of Labor, and the Central Labor Union, less than 12 percent of the city's wage earners had been organized. With few exceptions women remained outside as did Poles, Italians, Jews, and blacks. While both the Knights and the CLU had made great strides, semi- and unskilled workers were without organization. "Continuous formal organization," as Beatrice and Sidney Webb once phrased it, came in the wake of the Great Upheaval, and it was unevenly enjoyed.

Such failure must be traced to the conflicts and competition within the city's labor movement and working class. That movement had organized around three poles or camps. Anglo-American skilled workers had created and maintained the Trades and Labor Assembly; led by an aroused leadership, many Irish-American reformers sat in the Knights of Labor. The remaining European immigrants, led by socialists and anarchists, had broken with the assembly and, rejecting the Noble and Holy Order, formed their own Central Labor Union. Those three organizations reflected fragmentation of ethnicity, ideology, segmentation, and the history of Chicago's labor movement.[59]

And yet those three camps interlocked and interacted, for their memberships overlapped. Socialists in the seventies and anarchists in the eighties participated in each of the other's organizations. If the trade unions represented the skilled, both the Knights and the Central Labor Union organized the semi- and unskilled. And if the Knights and the unions openly cooperated, the CLU competed with both. In the eighties, anarchist dual unionism, especially among the carpenters and the cigarmakers, pursued a course far to the left of both Knights and unions.

Indeed, one is tempted to argue that the very divisions within the labor movement facilitated the organization of Chicago's working class.

Before we can pursue that competition and those divisions into the Eight Hour Movement and the Great Upheaval, we need to examine labor's struggle for political power, the rise and fall of the city's socialist labor party.

Chapter Three

SOCIALISTS, ANARCHISTS, AND THE POLLS

In April 1879, Ernst Schmidt, a German-born Forty Eighter, physician, and former abolitionist, ran as the Socialistic Labor Party's (SLP) first mayoral candidate in Chicago. He polled almost 12,000 votes, some 20 percent of the total. A party composed of working-class immigrants, the socialists seemingly exploded into the political arena. The party was ecstatic, the commercial press shocked. As Protestant ministers sermonized over "communism," the bourgeois press rushed to discover the origins of socialism; both sermons and articles reeked of nativism. If most could not see past the Paris Commune, the *Tribune* knew that "the origins of this socio-political association [began] with the revolution of 1848" and that "the entire edifice of our present state of society . . . [and] the distribution of wealth" was at stake.[1]

The story of the Socialistic Labor Party's electoral efforts is almost familiar, but deserves reevaluation for several reasons. That story has usually been told as one aspect in the national history of the party, and, as such, nuance, circumstance, and agency have been lost.[2] We need to know something of the movement's composition, program, and agitation

52

in the 1870s in order to understand what those same radicals were doing or trying to do in the 1880s. Indeed, electoral socialism was the antecedent for revolutionary socialism.

ORIGINS AND INITIAL EFFORTS, 1873–1879

By 1860 there was an active section of the International Workingmen's Association (IWA, the First International) in the city. It published a weekly newspaper, *Die Deutsche Arbeiter*, a name that reveals the dominant ethnic group. Many Germans were active, but it was not wholly German. At the IWA's celebration of the first anniversary of the Paris Commune in 1872, there were six speakers: three Germans, one Swede, one Norwegian, and one Englishman. The IWA was not small, the *Tribune* reported 400 members at the end of 1873, and by then the organization was actually in decline.[3]

The IWA achieved notoriety in December 1873 when it organized mass demonstrations of the unemployed during the first winter of the long depression. The editors of Chicago's English-language press were flabbergasted by the thought of workingmen demanding public relief, but the editor of the German-language *Illinois Staats-Zeitung* understood the portent of those mass demonstrations: "Chicago now has, like Berlin, its Bebels, its Liebknechts, Mendes and Tolkes. Here too is war declared on the disgraceful 'moneylenders,' the contemptible 'capitalists,' and the 'property owning class' and a division of property is demanded in the name of the 'right to live.'" The IWA was joined by new speakers and its crowds were soon addressed in French, Polish, and in English with an Irish accent. In a city racked by nativism, the phenomenon was disturbing. On Christmas Day, 1873, the *Tribune's* editor saw something unusual: "The fraternization of immigrants of different nativities in America is not often observed. . . . If ever they unite, it is not love for one another that brings them together, but opposition to some common enemy, to the attainment of something which all want, but which divided, they are powerless to obtain."[4]

Although First Internationalists were prominent, the movement that emerged from the unemployment and relief demonstrations of December 1873 was not a socialist movement. Rather the IWA offered speakers, discussion, and argument to workingmen who could appreciate their contribution. The IWA temporarily dissolved itself into the Workingmen's Party of Illinois (WPI) and by February 1874, that party had created ten German clubs, one Bohemian, one Polish, one Scandinavian, and one

53

Irish club, and established its first official organ, *Der Vorbote*, a German-language weekly. Three months later there were reportedly thirteen German sections, two Bohemian sections, one Polish, and one now described as Danish.[5]

Theirs was a typically nineteenth-century workingmen's movement composed overwhelmingly of artisans with a sprinkling of socialists. If one, signing itself "Proletaire," wrote to the Republican *Tribune* and attacked the characteristic features of "the capitalistic system," the IWA's general council still fretted about bourgeois and petty bourgeois elements within the party. In March 1874, the WPI offered a slate of candidates for Northtown offices. None was successful, although they polled almost 1,000 votes. The IWA was seemingly reborn in the aftermath of that election and in June "a hundred men and about four women" met to form an English section. A week later, "because there were plenty of women who liked to join," they changed its name to the International Working Peoples' Association." Intriguingly, "two colored gentlemen" were now active.[6]

Perhaps because they celebrated the memory of the Paris Commune, more likely because it identified them with the worst image of alien labor movements, the IWA and the WPI became "the commune" or "the communists." Both disappeared from the commercial press, only to reappear for a disastrous showing in the fall elections. Despite the activities of a voter registration committee and of increasingly capable speakers, the party polled all of 785 votes and failed to elect a single candidate in the county elections that fall. Louis Nelke and Joseph Gruenhut were subsequently expelled from the party for accepting $260 from the Republicans, $10 each had been offered to three other members, and "a large amount" to *Der Vorbote*'s editor, but all had refused.[7]

Following the Commune celebration in March 1875, the *Tribune* denounced the hypocrisy of "The Chicago Communists": "The men can get no work; the female[s] are threatened with every description of trouble, yet they have enough money to rent a hall, buy beer and wine, decorate, employ a band and arrange tableau[x]." The workingmen's party looked moribund, choosing not to run candidates that spring, yet remained so fearsome that the *Tribune* called for a National Guard garrison in the city. More expulsions, again for collaborating with the Republicans, followed the fall elections.[8]

Two developments took longer to bear fruit. The first was the emergence of a socialist press. *Der Vorbote* had been established in 1874 and grew to a circulation of 3,300 within two years. Encouraged by its success, the Germans launched the *Illinois Volks-Zeitung* as a tri-weekly in June 1876, without discontinuing their weekly. As Marcus Thrane, an exiled Norwegian Forty Eighter, became increasingly active, first in the IWA and then in the WPI, he devoted more space in his monthly *Dagslyset* to socialism and the socialist movement. As significant was the emergence of a national movement embodied in the Workingmen's Party of the United States (WPUS), which emerged from a unity congress in the summer of 1876.[9]

Held in Philadelphia, this congress forged the WPUS out of the old IWA, Cincinnati's Social Political Workingmen's Society, the Social Democratic Workingmen's Party of North America and the WPI. While "the Socialistic Labor Party of North America" was suggested for the party's name, one of *Der Vorbote*'s correspondents expected that the word 'socialist' would frighten English-speaking workers and noted, "we will be called communists regardless of what name we adopt."[10] Chicago's delegate, Swiss-born Conrad Conzett, "pledged his honor that there were 593 members" in his party; nationally the WPUS claimed almost 3,000 adherents. Conzett was an important delegate, voting with Friedrich Sorge and Joseph Weydemeyer against a clause permitting a local-election movement. He and Gustav Lyser (who would come to Chicago and edit *Vorbote* a year later) prepared the party's constitution, and he offered to sell his paper to the party for a promissory note.[11]

In March 1877 *Der Vorbote*, the party's official Chicago organ, announced: "Wir haben heir 700 bis 750 Parteimitglieder." Buoyed by its continued growth, the party decided, against national advice, to enter the spring municipal elections. With a campaign fund of $97, it ran just three aldermanic candidates. In the Sixth Ward a Czech, Prokup Hudek, a captain in the Bohemian Sharpshooters, polled almost 20 percent of the vote; in the Fourteenth Ward Swiss-born Frank Stauber, a hardware-store owner, polled 7 percent; and in the Fifteenth Albert Parsons, a native-born printer, polled almost 16 percent. The party grew to six sections: four German, one Scandinavian, and one English, and at the end of the month *Der Vorbote* began advertising German and Skandinavian Frauensektions.[12]

When the Great Railroad Strike of 1877 swept into Chicago, the *Tribune* had only to headline "It is Here" as workers fought the combined forces of the police, the militia, and federal troops. The same week, the unorganized wholly outnumbered the party and generated their own leaders, as the WPUS tried to organize and moderate those crowds, urging "every honest workingman to help us to preserve order." As Marianne Debouzy noted:

> In reading the press one does not know what they fear more: the unorganized working class, despisingly considered as mob, or the organized workers controlled by communists. They are equally concerned about the absence of leaders and the presence of agitators. They blame the mob both for its boldness and for its cowardice. And the position of the dominant class swings between two contradictory extremes: fear of the mob, fear that the insurrection might arouse the scum of the underworld, and fear of organization, of the Commune.[13]

The Great Upheaval loomed over the county elections in that fall. In addition to the Republicans and Democrats, the field included a curious sprouting of workingmen's parties. The WPUS struck first with a mass meeting of "about 1,000," offering multilingual speakers and a platform. The *Tribune* lambasted the "longhaired idiots and knaves," dismissing their platform as nonsense that flew in the face of social mobility and the American dream. The next month a convention "of the anti-socialistic element" met in Maskell Hall and took the name the Workingmen's Industrial Party (WMIP). If the credentials and executive committees reflected the party's ethnic composition, then it was 80 percent Irish. A month and half before the election, a Greenback committee, overwhelmingly native-born or Anglo-American, and led by Andrew Cameron, editor of *The Workingman's Advocate*, met with the WMIP, but each "attempted to swallow" the other. Despite some initial disgust, they quickly merged; and the tactic of "swallowing" or "capturing" party meetings continued.[14] The Workingmen's Industrial Party evaporated just before the election when General Lieb "and his hirelings" captured a second convention for the Democrats. Outraged, some of the former members allied with the Greenbackers to form a local Greenback-Labor ticket.

Four days before the election the *Times* predicted the socialistic ticket "chiefly draws its strength from the Bohemians and the lower strata of the Scandinavian element; . . . outside of these people it finds but few supporters. Its votes will be equally drawn from the Republicans and Democratic parties and will in nowise affect the general result." More optimistically, the party's candidate for city treasurer, Frank Stauber, predicted about 7,000 votes based on *Vorbote*'s 3,500 subscribers.[15] Paced by Stauber, Parsons, two Irishmen, John McAuliffe (an engineer), Tim O'Meara (a foreman at the Rock Island carshops), Sam Goldwater (a Polish cigarmaker), and Lauritz Thorsmark (a Danish cabinetmaker), the WPUS captured 12 percent of the votes, but none of the offices. Confirming Stauber's estimate, the WPUS polled 6,592 votes, while the Greenback-Labor ticket drew only 1,673; confirming the *Times* analysis, about one-third of the WPUS's total vote came from the Bohemian parts of the Fifth and Sixth wards, the heart of the riot district the previous July.[16]

The socialists, not the Knights of Labor, and certainly not the "labor reformers," assumed the legacy of the 1877 Upheaval. The socialists enjoyed four advantages over their rivals. First, while they shared the Knights' commitment to organizing the unskilled and winning political reforms, the socialists already constituted a party. Second, the SLP's platform favored transforming trade unions into revolutionary bodies, but they viewed their party as a supplement to the unions, not an alternative as the Knights did. Third, because they were as yet untainted by corruption or scandal, the socialists could claim the mantle of reform. Finally, the socialists offered a party and platform that were public and visible: "labor reform" had become amorphous and the Knights remained secret.[17]

Both legacy and mantle fit awkwardly at first. The party had spent only $425 on the election, and it was "decidedly pleased with the vote." With only forty-three cents in their treasury, the socialists were still optimistic about the spring elections: they established a central committee, were "perfecting a ward organizations," and talked of electing "at least 5 aldermen." Their rivals were in disarray. The Greenback-Labor party had been soundly beaten, the WMIP—identified again by the *Tribune* as "anti-Communistic"—discredited. At the end of the year the Knights challenged the socialists for control of the city's Trades Assembly. The result was a draw, or rather a withdrawal, and for a time Chicago's labor movement enjoyed both an assembly and a rival trade council.[18]

Chicago's section of the WPUS sent a delegation to the 1877 national convention that founded the Socialistic Labor Party of North America (SLP in English, SAP in German). That convention changed the party's name, not its agitation. At the end of January, a new local platform emerged, consistent with the national one. The first four planks demanded the eight-hour day, the abolition of both prison labor and conspiracy laws, and the repeal of vagrancy acts. New legislation was to be ratified by the citizenry. Planks six through nine promised to prohibit child labor, abrogate existing city streetcar contracts, establish municipal ownership of streetcars and gas works, and prohibit the contract system on city projects. The tenth and last was the financial plank of the Greenback Party.[19]

United on that platform and hoping to demonstrate the organization's "energy and vitality," the party contested all of the offices. Before the election the Democratic *Times* reported that the socialists believed they controlled eight wards, yet in a ward-by-ward analysis the paper could find little corroboration. The SLP polled 6,809 votes out of 49,644 cast, almost 14 percent of the total. Again the socialists did well in the Fifth, Sixth, and Fourteenth wards, polling 21, 21, and 41 percent of the vote. They also did well in the Fifteenth and Sixteenth wards with 30 and 37 percent. Convinced they had done even better, 150 party members protested fraud in the Fifteenth Ward, charging Albert Parsons had been counted out. That election produced the SLP's first victory, a seat in the City Council, and prompted the Republican *Inter Ocean* to observe: "The Fourteenth Ward sends a Socialist, [Frank] Stauber, who is a man of some intelligence, and who will doubtless do what he can to further the interests of the party which elected him. In the Council he will be powerless."[20]

The "communists" had been ridiculed, then despised; as "socialists" the same people became feared. The *Tribune,* ever the voice of reform, described "The Dangers of Communism": now that a single socialist had been elected, the paper feared "plunder and misgovernment," in a word, "Tweedism." Four days after the election, the *Tribune* reported rumors of fusion between the hated Democrats and the cursed socialists. According to the *Inter Ocean,* "the recent performances of the Commune" had alarmed the forces of order. "A number of our citizens called yesterday at military headquarters to ascertain how far the city could depend on the army in case of trouble with the Communists." One solution, first voiced by the *Tribune* and now endorsed by the *Inter Ocean* was "to have a regiment quartered here to ballast, as it were, the militia," and a letter to the *Tribune* from "veteran cavalryman" urged a mounted unit "prepared to quell any outbreak that might occur."[21]

The occasion for another of Chicago's red scares had been a parade by the Lehr- und Wehr-Verein, a working-class militia affiliated with the SLP. When the Bohemian Sharpshooters were seen drilling on vacant lots wild rumors of an uprising spread throughout the city. Interviews with Parsons, who "stated the aims and means of his party," with Joseph

Wondreyka and Prokup Hudek, who "ridicule[d] the idea of any uprising by their people," and with another "prominent member . . . identified with the Commune movement" all branded "the senseless verbiage" about an uprising as "absurd." In an editorial on these "Perilous Days," the *Inter Ocean* worried: "There is distrust, dissatisfaction, discontent about us everywhere. Communism proper has little to do with it, but a common feeling of disgust, discouragement, and uncertainty feeds the flame that makes the communistic kettle boil, and increases the temptation hourly."[22]

Measured by the expansion of the socialist press, the party continued to grow, even to mature. German readers still enjoyed two papers: the *Illinois Volks-Zeitung*, a two-year-old triweekly, and the venerable *Vorbote*, now four years old. In October 1877, after the Great Upheaval, the WPUS considered "the publication of a daily and weekly paper entirely in the interests of workingmen to be owned and controlled by a cooperative association consisting of reliable trade union members and friends of the cause of labor." A press committee and mass meetings publicized the effort, but nothing came of it for almost a year.[23] The movement needed Scandinavian and English-language organs. It got the former when Marcus Thrane closed *Dagslyset* and returned to Chicago. With a currently arrived partner, the exiled Danish socialist Louis Pio, he began *Den Nye Tid* as a weekly in the spring of 1878. Within months it claimed 600 readers in the city; within a year 1,000. An English paper took longer. The National Executive Committee (NEC) did not think the party could support two English organs, but when the Cincinnati *National Socialist* ran into debt, the Chicago section was allowed to buy its subscription list, hire its editor, and move the paper. When *The Socialist*'s first issue appeared in September 1878, Albert Parsons became Frank Hirth's assistant editor.[24]

The party continued to broaden its base. By the fall of 1878, Chicago boasted a German section with four branches, as well as Bohemian, French, Scandinavian, and English branches. Women had appeared at party meetings; that summer the party began actively to enroll them as members. When a mass meeting founded the Working Women's Union in July, the president announced "that she expected capitalists would call it a communistic meeting, but it was not." "Communistic or not," the *Inter Ocean* noted, "a number of the leading socialists were present and cheered the speaker to the echo." Party meetings and social functions were regularly reported in the bourgeois press. In August, 5,000 people gathered to celebrate the electoral success of the Sozialistische Partei

Deutschland (SPD) in Germany, later that month the SLP arranged an anti-Chinese rally to support striking shoemakers. About 1,000 socialists paraded through the city's streets to a picnic in Ogden's Grove in September where "not less than 3,000" feasted. And in December the SLP admitted ten new members, including "two swarthy sons of Africa," "the first colored gentlemen that have cast their lot with the party."[25]

After the fall elections in 1878, the *Inter Ocean* wrote of "Tickled Socialists." "Their vote reached to surprisingly proportions, and caused the community to open its eye[s] to the fact that the party was more formidable than anyone was willing to admit a month before." *The Socialist* headlined "A Great Triumph for Socialism" when four candidates were successful: one state senator, Pennsylvania-born Sylvester Artley (a picture-frame maker); and three state representatives, Leo Meilbeck (a Moravian cabinetmaker), and two Germans, Charles Ehrhardt (a cloth cutter) and Christian Meier (a brushmaker). The party's representatives were instructed to introduce bills for women's suffrage, bureaus of labor statistics and factor inspection, the reform of prison contract labor, and to support another party member for U.S. senator.[26]

The prospects scared Chicago's old-line politicians. As early as September, the Democrats fully expected the SLP to forego its own candidates and support theirs. After the election some of the politicos talked briefly on redistricting the city, disfranchising socialist voters by gerrymandering. That talk fizzled when redistricting seemed to threaten some of the redistrictors. Equally calculating members of the Fourteenth Ward's Republican Club questioned "whether it would not be a good plan to combine with the Democrats so that . . . a Communist Alderman would not be sent to the Council" in the spring. Initially tabled, the question was later revived. Aware of all those machinations, *The Socialist* asked only for "a fair election and a fair count."[27]

The picture was not without clouds. *The Socialist* faced financial disaster weekly. In January, for example, its receipts covered only half its expenses and twice during 1879 its press committee called the business manager to account. The first time they exonerated him; the second time he resigned before being fired. There had been rumors of internal dissension before, but these were more serious. T. J. Morgan spoke directly to the problem in his organizer's report: "The efforts of certain cliques" had resulted in "discordant and disgraceful meetings." Morgan suggested either quieting or ejecting the "disturbers," or else "anarchy would prevail in the party."[28]

The problem was party discipline. According to the National Board of

Supervision in New York, *Der Vorbote* had repeatedly compromised "the interests of the whole party" and the editors of both *Vorbote* and *The Socialist* used the columns of their papers to "ventilate personal quarrels." The board urged the editors to refuse "personal items which have nothing to do with principle," then contemplated its own organ, and finally appealed to the local sections to exercise more control. Those same problems surfaced in Chicago. In January, complaints against State Senator Artley appeared in the bourgeois press. Two months later, Albert Parsons was unceremoniously kicked off the *The Socialist*'s press committee. In March, Morgan specified the charges against Artley: he "kept apart from his party comrades in the Legislature," had voted with the Republicans for speaker of the house while the rest of the SLP's delegation abstained, and had entered the Republican caucus, and then introduced legislation independent of his comrades and party. In short, Artley "seems to have deserted the party, and remains in Springfield as an independent legislator."[29]

AMBIGUOUS SUCCESS: THE MUNICIPAL ELECTIONS OF 1879

The party postponed its investigation of those charges as it turned to the municipal elections in April 1879. The Greenbackers had preempted the Democrats by nominating Carter Harrison and abruptly adjourning, hoping to anticipate fusion. The Republicans had already nominated Abner Wright as their candidate when 300 delegates gathered for the SLP's convention. They hammered out a local platform and nominated Ernst Schmidt for mayor before filling the slate with eighteen aldermanic candidates.[30]

The socialists waged an experienced and vigorous campaign, electing ward and precinct captains, selecting election judges, and then calling nightly agitation meetings. The high point of the campaign came when 40,000 people jammed into the Exposition Building to celebrate the anniversary of the Paris Commune as "The Dawn of Liberty" and to meet the party's slate. Two days before the election the *Inter Ocean* tried to analyze "The Communistic Vote":

We thus prove, with a nicety approaching a mathematical proposition, that communistic recruits are from the Democracy. The liberty-loving German, Irishman, Frenchman or Swede naturally affiliates with the Republican party, while the ignorant of all nations affiliate with Democracy and surely the wild follies of communism can only find followers among the ignorant and debased. . . . If the communists maintain or increase their vote . . . a Republican victory next Tuesday is assured.

The editor of the German-Republican *Staats-Zeitung* knew better; for a month before the election he tried to warn his party against overconfi-dence. Anton Hesing feared that the temperance issue would split the Republicans. Throughout March he fought to tone down the "fanatical drys"; failing that he turned on Abner Wright's opponents, warning that Harrison would lead to Irish control and corruption. Finally, he condemned a vote for Schmidt as effectively supporting the dreaded Harrison. Temperance became paramount and Schmidt was the only candidate to unequivocally oppose it. It was no surprise that the German Saloonkeepers Association endorsed him; but the *Staats-Zeitung* also reported that hundreds of German businessmen had gone public with their support.[31]

Dr. Schmidt garnered almost 12,000 votes, fully 20 percent of the total. He drew them from every ward, although the party's strength continued to be concentrated in the German Northwest and Bohemian Southwest sides: wards 14 through 16 contributed 36 percent of the party's total; wards 5 through 7 accounted for another 36 percent. In the Sixth and Sixteenth wards, Schmidt decisively beat the regular party candidates, polling 47 percent in the former, 51 percent in the latter. Although Schmidt lost, the party won three more seats in the City Council. In the Sixth Ward, John Altpeter, a German jeweller, won with 47 percent of the vote; in the Fourteenth (which had already elected Frank Stauber to a two-year term), Reinhold Lorenz, a German saloon keeper and member of the Lehr- und Wehr-Verein, won with 40 percent; and in the Six-teenth, Chris Meier, the former state representative, won with 58 per-cent. The party was ecstatic, but the *Times* offered the most perceptive of the postelection editorials:

The vote received by Dr. Schmidt . . . can in no sense be accepted as clearly indicating the strength of the socialist-communistic organization in Chicago. Dr. Schmidt is deservedly popular among the Germans of the city, who were largely dissatisfied with both the regular party candidates, and besides, he only represents the socialistic-communist doctrines in an exceedingly mild and innocuous form. The distinctive political theories of the communist organiza-tion were not brought forward prominently in the canvas; there was really no discussion of them, and the result must have been very different had they been. His vote indicates his personal strength and dissatisfaction with both of the other nominees and NOT the voting power of the communist element.[32]

Who voted for the SLP? Ernst Schmidt ran best on the Southwest side, wards 5, 6, and 7; and on the Northwest side, wards 14, 15 and 16; polling more than 72 percent of his vote in just those six wards. In contrast he ran a distant third across the center of the city: wards 1, 2, 8, 9, 11 and 12, which produced barely 12 percent of the SLP's total. The Northwest side was a German colony, the residence of about 36 percent of the SLP's membership; the Southwest side was of more mixed ethnicity, home to about 36 percent of the party's membership. In contrast, the center six wards were overwhelmingly native-born and English-speaking, home to barely 13 percent of the SLP's membership. That data clearly suggests a relationship between ethnicity and the socialist vote.[33]

Ecological regression across the city's eighteen wards, with ethnicity as the independent variables and the SLP vote as the dependent variable, can be used to define that relationship. The correlation coefficients are presented in Table 3.1, which deserves, indeed requires, some explication. It shows a high correlation between a ward's socialist vote and its ethnic composition. The correlation between native-born voters and the SLP ($r = -.86$) is strong and negative; that is, the higher the percentage of native-born voters in a ward, the lower the SLP vote. We can disaggregate the nativities of the foreign-born, first by language; the correlations are stronger, but still in the same direction.[34] The last set of correlations are the most revealing, and are confirmed by other evidence. German wards strongly correlated with the SLP vote ($r = +.93$), Bohemians and Polish only moderately ($r = +.42$ and $+.41$); predictably the Irish voter strongly correlated with the Democracy ($r = +.84$), and the Scandinavians split between the SLP and Democrats ($r = +.20$). Chicago's leading German papers, the bourgeois *Staats-Zeitung* and the workingman's *Vorbote*, had predicted a strong German turnout for Schmidt. The leading Czech paper, *Svornost*, knew the contest in the Bohemian community would be between the Democrats and the SLP; five days before the election it boldly endorsed the SLP, describing its candidates as "honorable and educated men." Finally, while the SLP had made dramatic overtures to the Irish, the *Times* reported little progress.[35]

SLP National Secretary Philip Van Patten glowingly described "the electoral successes of Chicago." Yet three questions must still be posed. First, was Dr. Schmidt, "one of the most popular and best-loved men in

Table 3.1 CORRELATIONS OF THE SOCIALIST LABOR PARTY
VOTE AND THE NATIVITY OF REGISTERED VOTERS, MAYORAL
ELECTION OF 1879

[Ward-level data, Pearson's r, r^2]

Birthplace	r	r^2
Native-born	− .845	.713
Foreign-born	+ .845	.713
English-speaking [a]	− .924	.853
Non-English-speaking [b]	+ .924	.853
Germany	+ .931	.867
Ireland	+ .147	.022
Bohemia	+ .423	.179
Poland	+ .411	.169
Holland	+ .238	.056
Scandinavia	+ .203	.041
Canada	− .549	.302
British Isles [c]	− .725	.527
All other	+ .537	.288

SOURCES: (election returns) Chicago *Tribune*, 2 April 1879, 1–2; (nativity of registered voters) [1884] by ward, *Tribune*, 7 April 1886, 3.

[a] "English-speaking" = Native-born, Canada, England, Scotland, Welsh, and Irish.
[b] "Non-English-speaking" = all others.
[c] "British Isles" = England, Scotland, and Wales, but not Ireland.

Chicago . . . an old associate of Karl Marx," a party member?[36] Second, was a vote for Schmidt a vote for the SLP? Finally, was 20 percent a success?

Schmidt later recalled the campaign:

Because of [Carter] Harrison's understanding and sympathy for the workers' plight, I consented in 1879 to become a candidate on the Socialist[ic] Labor party's ticket. . . . With me, a rank outsider, running for mayor . . ., Chicago faced a three-way mayoralty battle. The Republican candidate . . . had the support of 450 businessmen and the press, especially *The Tribune*, which was backing Wright's anti-labor policy and labeling Harrison and me 'advocates of communism.' . . . Democrat Harrison was not conceded a chance against Wright because of the latter's Republican backers from Prairie Avenue. . . . But we of the SLP hoped to get enough votes away from Wright to enable Harrison to win, and this we did.

Schmidt had not been prominent in the IWA, the WPI, the WPUS or the SLP *before* the 1879 election. Six months after it, an embittered Benjamin Sibley charged that Schmidt was put up by the party without being a member and Schmidt seemingly confirmed the charge. Sibley contended that the whole campaign had been managed by Morgan and Schmidt as "a put-up job for Harrison"; again, Schmidt's own words lend credence to the charge.[37]

Analysis of the two previous mayoral elections confirms Schmidt's account of the SLP's electoral strategy. German-Republican wards abruptly split between the Republicans and the SLP; Harrison and the Democracy squeaked through the gap. They were grateful, according to Schmidt: "After the election Harrison asked me to name a few friends of mine for appointment to positions in the municipal government, which I declined to do." Harrison's gratitude and patronage extended into the leadership of the SLP. Gabrienne Davoust lost a spot on the party slate the next fall because he asked Harrison for a job. Others did not have to ask: William Barr, a Greenbacker-cum-socialist, became a city milk inspector; Maurice Bowler got a sewer inspectorship; and Joseph Gruenhut got an appointment first in the Health Department, later as the city's factory and tenement inspector.[38]

If Schmidt was not really a party member, were his votes socialist? Probably not. The platform had been "exceedingly mild and innocuous," there had been "no discussion" of "the distinctive political theories of the communists". In March 1879, 20,000 to 40,000 people filled the Exposition Building to kick off the party's campaign; yet *Der Vorbote* reported only 870 good-standing members. We still need to account for almost 11,000 other voters. According to P. J. McLogan, leader of English-speaking Typographical Union No. 16, most trade unionists who voted for Chicago's SLP between 1877 and 1879 viewed the party as a vehicle for protest. The socialists, recounted McLogan, "were reinforced . . . by the trade unionists, who considered themselves oppressed and went in at that time and voted the socialistic ticket. I know a great many . . . who voted the socialistic party's ticket; I know I did it myself by way of protest." They found Harrison more congenial than the SLP and, after 1879, they flocked to the Democracy. Seven months after the mayoral election, the SLP's vote was down by 66 percent.[39]

Finally, 20 percent of the mayoral vote was a peculiar kind of success. On the one hand, it generated the delusion, shared by bourgeois and socialist alike, that the SLP held the balance of power in municipal politics. On the other, the *Tribune* or the *Inter Ocean* would later laud the socialist aldermen as men of integrity and conscience largely because they had been impotent in the City Council. In 1878, Frank Stauber had marched into the council's chambers to represent the Fourteenth Ward. The *Illinois Staats-Zeitung* reported the decisions on his first five bills: an appropriation for public bathing houses lost nine to twenty with four abstentions; a second, to pay aldermen $3.00 per session, lost four to twenty-five; one to open public reading rooms was tabled; another to supply kerosene lamps where gas lines had not been laid was ruled out of order, as was an appropriation for a contingency fund for epidemics. A year later, four socialist alderman faced an insurgent council that rejected the mayor's committee appointments. The socialists were relegated to minor committees (wharfing privileges, harbors and bridges, and farmers' markets), then separated so as not to form even an irrelevant voting bloc.[40] Twenty percent of state power proved an insufficient base for municipal socialism.

THE DECLINE OF THE SLP AND THE RISE OF THE IWPA, 1880–1886

Both Jacob Winnen and George Schilling judged the 1879 mayoral election to have been the "zenith" of the SLP's political power. It had been greeted with headlines proclaiming the "Great Success of the Socialists!" Only seven months later, the *Tribune* could find solace in "The Abatement of Socialism." The SLP failed as a political party, but merely dating that failure is inadequate: we need to understand the decline of the SLP.[41]

The election euphoria had quickly evaporated. In April, the party's Central Committee criticized State Senator Artley's independence. In July, Grottkau offered to resign his editorship "in the interest of the party and in defense as to my spotless past." In August, the English section censured the *Arbeiter-Zeitung* for its ongoing criticism of Sam Goldwater, a party member and then president of the Trade and Labor Council. In October the *Tribune* savored the infighting during the party's county convention and one member's objection to another's candidacy because he had asked Mayor Harrison for a job.[42]

During the convention Benjamin Sibley, a leading member and perennial candidate, dramatically resigned by "sending in his red card" and publicly explained his defection. He charged that T. J. Morgan had forged a letter from the Harrison campaign promising to "well consider" socialists for mayoral appointments. When Morgan admitted the letter, the party had hushed it up. He objected to Schmidt's candidacy because he had not been a party member for the required two years. Finally, Sibley charged that Schmidt and Morgan's actions were but "one grand scheme put up in the interest of Carter H. Harrison." Beyond the charges, Sibley pointed to the prestige of the Germans and the debility of American socialists. The *Tribune* and the *Staats-Zeitung*, which had opposed both Harrison and the SLP, continued to delight in "socialist fraud," "corruption," and additional resignations. As the insults increased, the internal fight turned vicious and personal. In September 1879, *The Socialist* expired and the English branch was without a paper. Paul Grottkau, editor of the *Arbeiter-Zeitung*, was denounced as a "dictator" and compared to Bismarck; in return Van Patten, secretary of the party's NEC, was accused of "frequenting disreputable houses."[43]

The first attempt to heal the split came in January 1880, at the biannual elections of new officers when the party constitution was simply amended. The hitherto independent ethnic branches were now to recognize the authority and discipline of the Central Committee; in addition there was a new prohibition on party business independent of the main section. To some extent the conflict was fought over the ethnic lines within the party. The German and Scandinavian branches, "the radicals," led by Grottkau, were arrayed against the English and French branches, "the conservatives," led by Morgan. The amendments barely resolved the split: "The different [branches] met in different rooms and were in session all afternoon . . . [eventually they] ratified the new platform and resolutions."[44]

Ostensibly united, the party turned to the 1880 municipal elections as the two factions nominated separate slates and then came together to thrash out the official one. Although the SLP had run a full slate of eighteen candidates in 1879, it mustered only sixteen in 1880. Charges of vote fraud appeared even before the polls opened. On the day after the election, the *Tribune* reported that one of seven districts in the Sixth Ward had failed to file its returns and in the Seventh Ward one of seven districts "will not be counted until today . . . but will not change the result." The SLP's vote fell in every ward save one. In the Third Ward it received only two of 1,322 votes; in the Eleventh, only eleven; in the Twelfth, only twelve. And the *Tribune* was premature, the full returns from the Sixth Ward changed the results significantly. At 1:00 A.M. the socialist was leading a three-way contest, but the final tally had him with losing to an independent by twenty-nine votes.[45]

The situation was even closer in the Fourteenth Ward. On election night, the *Tribune* reported that the Socialistic candidate had 50.6 percent of the vote. George Schilling tells the story best:

> The results were declared at the precinct in the presence of three Election Judges, two Clerks, party challengers, and a police officer. Two of the judges . . . took the ballot-box and tally-sheet home, and on learning that the election had resulted in the defeat of their candidate . . . they stuffed the box and changed the result. . . .
>
> This change gave McGrath a majority and he was seated by the Council. A long litigation ensued, costing the workingmen about $2,000 and keeping Mr. Stauber out of his seat for nearly a year. . . . Walsh and Gibbs, the two election judges who had stuffed the ballot-box and forged the tally sheet, were tried for the offense and acquitted, Judge Gardner declaring that, while they had violated the law, there had been no evidence showing that had been their intent.[46]

Election fraud proved bitter and intensified the fight within the local party that resumed in July 1880 when the Germans convened the main section without notifying the incumbent officers. Since the English branch was "almost entirely uninformed," it was easily packed by Germans who elected a new central committee. The conservatives retained only one of the seven offices, and "the resolution formerly passed to expell [sic] Grottkau, Peterson and Bartels [the leading insurgents] was voted down."[47] As early as February 1880, Schilling had analyzed the alignment of forces. In a letter to Van Patten he described a three-way fight, between radicals and conservatives, with himself in the middle. He labelled the Grottkau faction "the anarchists"; the first use of that label by anyone *inside* the movement. The split was tactical or ideological and cut across ethnic lines. The Grottkau faction claimed perhaps a majority of the Germans; "some of the English, among them A. R. Parsons," according to Schilling; and a majority of the Scandinavians. Morgan's base lay in a clear majority of the English-speaking section, probably all of the small French section, and a minority of the Germans. The Bohemians

English abbreviation, IAA in German). Chicago sent a delegation of six to the congress: one English-speaking, three German, one Scandinavian, and one Czech.[62] By the end of 1883, the radicals had organized thirteen IWPA groups in Chicago. In December they invited SLP sections to withdraw from the party and affiliate with the Black International.[63]

The few who remained in the party had to be struck by the IWPA's vitality. Despite a five-year-old tactical and ideological dispute, despite its own inactivity, the SLP proposed yet another harmony meeting and the possibility of reconciliation. "By the time the meeting adjourned, the breach between the two factions was wider and the animosity deeper." When Wilhelm Kempke returned from the SLP's 1883 Convention he reported "a decided falling off in the number of English-speaking Socialists. Some of the Germans present denounced them as traitors and utterly unreliable. Others took the ground that the English members were doing effective work outside the party and that someday the English[-speaking] wage workers . . . [would] make the fur fly." Neither the IWPA nor the SLP participated in the 1884 elections. While the anarchists raved on about revolution, when the socialists infrequently met they continued to extoll "the best interests of labor."[64]

The two branches had little in common beyond their origins and history. Both celebrated the anniversary of the Paris Commune, but the anarchists commemorated the death of Marx while the socialists preferred their Lassalle fests. In May 1884, the Chicago section invited Alexander Jonas of the party's NEC in New York to address the SLP and the IWPA at two separate meetings. In the course of the second Jonas asked whether the members of the IWPA "were anarchists in the classical meaning of the word." From the audience, August Spies replied "that he supposed they were, [but] that there was no difference between the [IWP] Association and the [Socialistic] Labor party."[65]

There were differences. Chicago's SLP had now become almost wholly German: the French section had evaporated, the English section was all but extinct, and the Bohemian and Scandinavian sections had joined the IWPA en masse. While there were few converts, some new blood arrived from Germany. Wilhelm Langner, a shoemaker, was expelled under the Sozialistgesetz in 1880, and Julius Vahlteich, Lassalle's secretary and an SPD delegate in the Reichstag, arrived in 1883. The next year Paul Grottkau was publicly humiliated in a debate with Johann Most and replaced as editor by August Spies. He rejoined the SLP, but left the city.[66] New recruits were outnumbered, however, by those who joined the IWPA or dropped out altogether.

In January 1884, the Chicago section needed only 200 dues stamps to cover its membership; in April, the party's minutes recorded a membership of 120: 14 in the English branch, 22, 28 and 56 in the three German ones. There was no fresh blood and "the old officers were reelected" repeatedly in the English branch. According to John Blake, its organizer, its "agitation had been left to take care of itself." Blake "declined to act as organizer any longer," explaining "he had undergone a change of heart, and no longer believed in political action," but was reelected nonetheless. In July the *Herald* headlined "Socialism on the Wane in Chicago":

> Enthusiasm has been lacking in their organization for some time, and it was a sorry lot of reports that were made at the semi-annual meeting yesterday. The German contingents have been doing something, and have sent $50 to the old country to be used in electing Socialists in the Reichstag, but the English section has done absolutely nothing. Attempts have been made to vaccinate the Scandinavians, but they would have none of it.[67]

After the aldermanic elections in the spring of 1882—when it contested only five wards—the SLP ceased to be a political party. Carter Harrison sought his second reelection in 1883, his third term as mayor, but "a resolution to pledge the SLP to Harrison was voted under the table or in the stove with some indignation." The main section operated under the delusion that it "held the balance of power between the two great parties, and could change the complexion of the city's politics at any time." Before the 1884 presidential election, Morgan explained the English branch's position: a "Democratic administration can not help us anymore than a Republican administration did. We, as socialists, must agitate and wait." They did more of the latter. The Germans recognized that the party was without organization or candidates, and one told the *Times*, "We will vote the Democratic ticket straight." Indeed, a letter in *Der Sozialist* admitted that the section had been voting Democratic for six years.[68]

Nor could the SLP function on a social level. Picnics declined and the party lacked enough marchers to have a respectable parade. There was "a very small attendance" at its last picnic in May 1884, even the speeches were cancelled. "'If we have the speeches it will take away the business of the bar for a time,' explained a member, 'and if we sell enough beer it will pay expenses.' This conclusion appeared satisfactory to everybody," according to the *Tribune*. After January 1885, the SLP was comatose: its festivals and meetings went unreported locally; the organization and its agitation had become inert; and the section announced its meetings in *Der Sozialist*, published weekly in New York City. Throughout 1885 that paper advertised the meetings of four branches in Chicago, all German. But only 106 members voted on an important party issue in May, and the next month the central committee mentioned that one branch had to be reorganized. By January 1886 there were only three advertised branches, and the section needed only $3 worth of dues-stamps to cover its membership.[69]

Then, in the enthusiasm of the Great Upheaval, especially in the early months of 1886, the SLP and the IWPA reached some kind of detente. When the party's financial secretary died in January, both the SLP and the IWPA passed subscription lists to aid his survivors. Far more important, the Eight Hour Movement drew the two factions together. The socialists began by debating their own position on the issue, for, like the anarchists, they were initially hostile, then ambivalent, finally enthusiastic. And the SLP's members found themselves much more welcome inside the anarchist Central Labor Union than they were in either the Knights of Labor or the Trades Assembly. Socialists spoke often at the mass meetings called by the CLU or the IWPA, where they shared anarchist platforms and audiences.[70] In the last months before the Haymarket riot, even the English branch revived when "a few members of the old Socialistic Association met . . . for the purpose of re-organization" and Morgan returned from his suburban exile assuming he would again lead the party. Sometime between March 1885 and March 1886, the English branch had apparently been dropped by the party: in April 1886 "twenty-five to thirty well known socialists had reorganized, but were not yet ready to affiliate with the national SLP."[71]

The Workingmen's Party of Illinois put up the first socialist slate in 1874 and polled almost 1,000 votes, but failed to win a single office. The movement chose not to run for the next three years. Only after the 1877 Great Upheaval did Chicago's socialists become a force in municipal politics. The SLP relied on foreign-born and working-class voters, drawing its strongest support from Germans and Bohemians, to a lesser extent from Scandinavians and the Irish; the party never attracted the native-born or Anglo-Americans.

Socialists ran in every aldermanic election from 1877 to 1882, when they abruptly withdrew from electoral politics. Parliamentary socialism peaked in 1879 when the SLP ran a full slate of candidates; led by Ernst Schmidt, who polled 11,818 votes for mayor, the party elected three aldermen. That was "the zenith" of political power: the next year the party did not file a full slate, and in 1881 and 1882 the Morgan faction retreated to its strongholds, then failed even there. The SLP elected one state senator, three state representatives, and five aldermen, who did not enjoy brilliant legislative records. Beyond establishing a state Bureau of Labor Statistics and a municipal factory and tenement inspectorship, they failed to deliver any of their program. At the state capital they were outvoted by rural representatives and the two-party system; within the City Council they proved powerless, consigned to minor committees, their bills tabled or ruled out of order. At both levels the socialists ran into the entrenched defenders of bourgeois property relations.

The SLP had decisively defeated the rival Workingmen's Industrial Party and the Greenbackers to assume the legacy of 1877. It was their misfortune to compete with Carter Henry Harrison as he led the Democracy into a broad-based coalition that would hold the mayoralty from 1879 to 1887. After defeating Abner Wright, Harrison held off Republican challenges in 1881, 1883, and 1885. In addition to offering jobs to the socialists, and cooperating with the emerging ward bosses, Harrison built the city's first political machine. Indeed, the Republicans did not recapture the city until after the Haymarket Affair, when the working-class coalition, which had supported the Democracy, ran its own candidate. Facing defeat, Carter Harrison chose not to run.

PART TWO

The Movement as a Whole

The socialist element are sowing seed daily which they, no doubt, hope will bear fruit directly. Their agents are now canvassing for recruits, button holing people on the street corners, and volubly advancing their 'cause.' Such agents carry printed prospectusses of their platform, which retail for 10 cents, and copies of a Cincinnati organ, for which a nickle [sic] is modestly demanded. Whether the proceeds go toward the establishment of a skirmishing fund is unknown.

 —Chicago *Inter Ocean*, 10 June 1878

[The anarchists] had already an armed group; they had meeting places in all sections of the city; they had missionaries out among the workingmen; they printed thousands of pamphlets; they had a daily newspaper and they never missed an opportunity of pushing themselves to the front, or of demonstrating their strength at workingmen's meetings, or in political gatherings.

 —John Flinn, *The History of the Chicago Police Force, From the Founding of the Community to the Present Time* (1887)

Chapter Four

THE FOREST, NOT THE TREES

Assuming that its readers "labored under the belief that there were but few communists" in the city, in March 1879 the *Tribune* tried to explain how the socialists had been able to fill the huge Exposition Building on the Lakefront with a crowd estimated between 20,000 and 40,000 strong:

> Skim the purlieus of the Fifth Ward, drain the Bohemian socialist slums of the Sixth and Seventh Wards, scour the Scandinavian dives of the Tenth and Fourteenth Wards, cull the choicest thieves from Halsted, Desplaines, Pacific avenue and Clark Street, pick out from Fourth Avenue, Jackson Street, Clark Street, State Street and the other noted haunts the worst specimens of female depravity, scatter in all the red-headed, cross-eyed and frowsy servant girls in the three divisions of the city and bunch all these together and you have a pretty good idea of the crowd that made up last night's gathering.

That crowd came to celebrate the eighth anniversary of the Paris Commune; it was multiethnic and polyglot, included whole families; and it drew its participants from "a Socialistic community." Any of those features might have provoked that reporter's reaction, but what most scared him and what he hoped to convey to his readers was "The Extraordinary Turnout of 'The Reds.'"[1]

Who were these people? The historians of Chicago's social-revolutionary movement have been unable to get below the surface of that "mob." They have presumed that the eight Haymarket Martyrs were representative of the anarchist movement and that their biographies were an appropriate microcosm. If neither "the mob" nor "martyrdom" are particularly sophisticated lines for historical analysis, scholarly research on the movement seems to start and finish with *The Autobiographies of the Haymarket Martyrs*.[2] A collective biography of the rank and file, of the movement behind those leaders, should improve our understanding by specifying their composition and characteristics. A collective biography can supply empirical answers to a set of simple questions. How old were Chicago's social-revolutionaries? How long had they been in the city? What were their ethnic backgrounds? What were their occupational experiences? Where did they live? Were they single or married? How big were their families? What were their labor and associational affiliations? What distinguished the city's radicals from their cohorts? With such information we might approach Chicago's socialists and anarchists on human terms, rather than as judicial and historical victims. Empirical studies of the rank and file can shift our understanding of radicalism away from biographical studies of prominent leaders and back to the movement itself.[3]

THE PROCESS OF RECONSTITUTION

How many socialists, how many anarchists, did Chicago have? In July 1876, the socialist party had about 600 members, in March 1877 about 750; at its height, in March 1879, the SLP had about 870 members and drew almost 12,000 votes. In August 1884, Samuel Fielden claimed that Chicago's IWPA had "one thousand members, . . . more when the Bohemian groups were included." Eight months later, in April 1885, Albert Parsons boasted that the association had "over 2,000 active members [and] a sympathetic following of 10,000 more." By the time of the riot, another thirteen months later, the movement's sustained growth had made Parsons's estimate—one traditionally regarded as exaggerated—obsolete. Writing nine years after the affair, William Holmes of the American Group remembered 3,000 members of the IWPA at the organization's zenith.[4]

One hundred years after Haymarket it is still possible to reconstitute both organizations. Two membership lists have survived. The first, comprising some 106 names, was compiled by the financial secretary of the SLP's German section for the years 1880–1884 and recorded name, occupation, address, and dues received. The second, reportedly compiled by the financial secretary of the IWPA's Gruppe Nordseite late in 1885, contains 232 names, was captured by the police after the riot, and published as an appendix to Michael Schaack's sensational exposé of the anarchist conspiracy. Although the first list is authentic, the second needs to be verified.[5]

That can be done by combining Chicago's socialist and anarchist press for the names of members. *Die Chicagoer Volkszeitung, The Socialist, Die Arbeiter-Zeitung,* and *The Alarm* published regular reports of the city's socialist and anarchist meetings as well as the reports of the Allgemeine Comite, which coordinated their activities. From those reports we can learn who presided at meetings, who lectured, who served on which committees, and who served as delegates to the Allgemeine Comite. Similar lists can be combed from the city's bourgeois newspapers. Finally, the single best source for the composition of the anarchist movement is Michael Schaack's *Anarchy and Anarchists.* In 1886 Lieutenant (later Captain) Schaack directed the police investigation of the Haymarket conspiracies. He compiled the interrogations and "confessions" of some seventy-odd anarchists, including information on the ages, nationalities, occupations, addresses, marital status, and family sizes of his suspects.[6]

The German section's membership list, supplemented by the names combed from socialist newspapers and the commercial press, identify 542 members of Chicago's SLP. Gruppe Nordseite's membership list, supplemented by the anarchist papers, the commercial press, and Captain Schaack's interrogations, identify 723 members of Chicago's IWPA. Since the Socialistic Labor Party claimed a membership of about 900 in 1879, and the International Working Peoples' Association about 2,800 in 1886, these two sets of names constitute samples of approximately 60 and 25 percent respectively. These samples are recognizably skewed. Reconstitution from German and English-language sources underrepresents Bohemian and Scandinavian radicals, and—because ethnicity appears related to occupation and mobility—that underrepresentation reverberates throughout the sample.[7]

Those names can be traced into the annual city directories from 1870 to 1886 and then into the manuscript schedules for the 1880 census to learn something of the people they identify. Although record linkage is tedious and inconvenient, it is the core of this research.[8]

WHO WERE THESE SOCIALISTS AND ANARCHISTS?

Age

How old were Chicago's socialists and anarchists? Were they teenaged radicals, or adults? The socialist sample had a mean age of 41.7 years in 1886; Chicago's anarchists had a mean age of 37.5 years in that year. For 201 socialists whose age could be determined, out of 542 identified members of the SLP, the median (middle) age was 39, and the mode (most frequent score) was 38. For 255 anarchists, the median and mode were both 36. Socialists ranged in age from twenty-three-year-old Friedrich Luebbers to seventy-one-year-old William Barr; anarchists ranged in age from fifteen-year-old John Theilen, the son of an anarchist couple, to seventy-six-year-old Dr. James Taylor. (see Table 4.1)

The range reflects the movement's diversity. About 10 percent of these

Table 4.1 AGES OF CHICAGO'S SLP, IWPA, AND POPULATION

Age	SLP	IWPA	Chicago
Less than 5			12.8%
5-9			10.6
10-14			8.9
15-19		0.8%	9.1
20-24	2.0%	7.5	11.4
25-29	8.1	16.1	11.5
30-34	14.1	18.0	9.6
35-44	43.4	33.3	12.5
45-54	19.2	16.9	7.6
More than 55	13.1	7.5	5.7
Age unknown			0.3
Totals =	100%	100%	100%
N =	201	255	1,099,850
Mean (years) =	41.7	37.5	~25.8
Median (years) =	39	36	~21

SOURCES: (SLP) 1880 manuscript census schedules; (IWPA) 1880 manuscript census schedules; Michael Schaack, *Anarchy and Anarchists* (Chicago: F. J. Schulte, 1889); (Chicago) calculated from United States, *Eleventh Census 1890*, "Population," pt. II, 117.

socialists were under thirty years of age, 40 percent were in their thirties, almost 30 percent in their forties, and 20 percent over fifty. Of the anarchists, about a quarter of the sample were under thirty, almost 40 percent were in their thirties, another quarter in their forties, and about 10 percent over fifty. If we convert those ages to year of birth, we can learn something about their experiences. About 20 percent of the socialists and 38 percent of the anarchists were born before 1836: that is, they were old enough to have experienced the revolutions of 1848 before emigration. Yet 80 percent of the socialists and 62 percent of the anarchists were born after 1836. If 1848 belonged to their parents, these two samples had lived through the Franco-Prussian War and the Paris Commune. All of the socialists and three-quarters of the anarchists were alive during the American Civil War.

Those distributions were not unusual. If we exclude those under twenty and those whose age was not recorded, then the distribution of ages within both the SLP and the IWPA looks remarkably like that of Chicago's population in 1890. A study comparing union and nonunion members in various states in the mid-to-late 1880s, discovered that both groups averaged under forty years of age.[9] With mean, median, and mode clustering together in the late thirties, the "average" SLP member, like the "average" anarchist, was not a teenager, but an adult. In short, age does not distinguish our two samples in any significant way from their cohorts in the city's population or from those in the American labor movement.

Length of Residence

How long had these socialists and anarchists been residents of Chicago? Were they new arrivals or older settlers? Did they bring their peculiar brand of socialism with them from Europe, or was it the product of indigenous conditions? Both the city directories and the 1880 census schedules provide the material to answer those questions. The first and last citations in a directory can be used as one measure of the date of arrival and of the length of residence. Whenever a name showed up in the 1879, 1880, or 1881 directories it was pursued into the census, which recorded the age of the oldest child born in Illinois and can be used as a supplementary measure of residence.

Julius Vahlteich arrived in 1883, four years after the SLP's zenith, Julius Hoppock, a typesetter at the *Arbeiter-Zeitung*, arrived in December 1885, only five months before Haymarket; yet Dr. Taylor, or the IWPA's American group, had been in Chicago for forty-four years, that is since

Table 4.2 LENGTH OF RESIDENCE OF CHICAGO'S
SLP AND IWPA

Years in Chicago	SLP	IWPA
Less than 1	1.6%	4.5%
1	2.1	6.8
2	2.7	8.4
3	2.1	2.0
4	4.3	6.6
5-10	62.8	51.1
11-15	13.8	6.1
16-20	3.7	12.6
20-25	4.7	0.9
More than 25	2.1	1.1
Totals =	100%	100%
N =	188	57
Mean (years) =	6.5	8.2
Median =	8.0	7.0

SOURCES: Chicago city directories, 1870, 1875–1886; manuscript census schedules for Chicago, 1870 and 1880.

1842. Mean length of residence for the socialist sample can be calculated at 6.5 years; mean length of residence for the anarchists at 8.2 years. The base years are however different: 1880 for the socialists, 1886 for the anarchists; simple subtraction can produce the year of arrival. The "average" socialist had been a Chicago resident since 1873; the "average" anarchist since 1879. On the other hand, 92 percent of the socialists, but only 15 percent of the anarchists had experienced the Great Upheaval of 1877 and were still active in the radical movement at the time of the 1886 riot. (see Table 4.2)

This kind of distribution again suggests the movement's diversity. While some had only recently arrived in Chicago, two out of three social-ists and one out of six anarchists had been here for ten years; 44 percent of the socialists and 15 percent of the anarchists had experienced the

Great Chicago Fire of 1871. This diversity in turn implies something more complex than the simple dichotomy between imported and indigenous radicalism by suggesting the interaction of recent immigrants and older settlers; other evidence confirms that interaction. Recognition and reputation linked the struggles back home, across the Atlantic, with new and different ones in America and Chicago.

The pattern is perhaps clearest among the Scandinavian radicals. Acclaimed as "the founder of the Norwegian labor movement," Marcus Møller Thrane had fled to Chicago in 1863, after seven and a half years in prison, and remained active in workingmen's clubs and socialist politics until he left the city in 1884.[10] Thrane's partner in *Den Nye Tid*, the organ of the SLP's Scandinavian section, was Louis Pio, "the founder of the socialist movement in Denmark" and a member of the First International, who had been exiled in 1877. Before coming to Chicago Pio and his secretary, William "Sorte" Hansen, had experimented with rural, utopian socialism in Kansas.[11] Thrane and Pio were prominent in the WPUS and SLP, Hansen in the IWPA.

The most prominent of Chicago's Czech Socialists was Lev Palda, a member of the First International, who edited *Národní noviný*, a weekly, "as a social Democratic publication." Bohemian-born Martin Baumrucker emigrated to Chicago in 1867 and opened a tailor shop. According to his obituary, his "only ambition was to improve the situation of Bohemian workers" and he represented Chicago's Czechs at the founding convention of the WPUS. Born in Moravia, Lev Mielbeck became the first Czech elected to the Illinois General Assembly as an SLP candidate in 1878.[12] As the SLP declined, a second wave of Czech immigrants, including Jakub Mikolanda, Norbert Zoula, and Josef Pecka, emigrated in 1882, 1883, and 1884 respectively, after imprisonment; each fled the Austrian anti-socialist laws and quickly rose to important positions in Chicago's Czech radical community. As *Budoucnost*'s editorial collective, they linked American socialism with Bohemian nationalism and free thought.[13]

The same pattern was also visible among the German radicals. Conrad Conzett had been a member of the First International in Switzerland; Gustav Lyser was expelled from the Social Democratic Workingmen's Party by the Eisenach Congress in 1873; Paul Grottkau had edited a bricklayer's journal and an SPD organ in Berlin before he immigrated to Chicago in 1876. Until August Spies took over the Socialist Publishing Society in 1884, each of its editors had made his reputation before emigration, Spies was the first to rise with an American reputation.[14]

Nativity and Ethnicity

In April 1886, the *Tribune* described the Central Labor Union's Eight Hour procession and suggested that "the majority of the marchers were Communistic Germans, Bohemians and Poles." John Flinn, the official historian of the Chicago Police Force, observed in 1887 that "Sclavonic [sic] names predominate among the anarchists." And the *Times* straightforwardly reported that one anarchist crowd was composed of "a lot of Poles, Bohemians, Germans, Hungarians, Laplanders, Siberians, Frenchmen and here and there an Irishmen [sic]."[15]

The material presented in Table 4.3 confutes those casual observations. Information on place of birth could only be located for about 40 percent of the two samples and, as a result, I have relied on an ethnic identification of the member's surname. Reported to be 83 percent accurate (it undercounts the native-born), this method permits an identification in 501 of the socialist sample of 542, about 92 percent, and 630 of the 723 anarchists, about 87 percent.[16] The figures in Table 4.3 should be corrected for two reasons. First, it has proved impossible to locate *Den Nye Tid* or to get access to the movements' Czech-language newspapers: without them the sample overrepresents those names combed from German-language papers. Second, an ethnic identification of a surname undercounts the native-born, especially in an immigrant city. There is no way to correct the size of the native-born contingent; but access to the Czech and Scandinavian newspapers should increase their numbers while decreasing the Germans.[17]

Table 4.3 compares the ethnic compositions of the SLP and IWPA with that of Chicago's population. With about 45 percent of the SLP and IWPA's membership, the Germans were probably overrepresented in these calculations. That anomaly may be solely due to the skewness of the sample, but as the *Arbeiter-Zeitung* proudly noted, Chicago was the fifth largest German city in the world. Both Bohemians and Scandinavians were similarly overrepresented in the SLP and IWPA; on the other hand, the native-born, Irish, and Polish were underrepresented. In 1879 Benjamin Sibley estimated that 25 to 30 percent of the SLP's votes were Irish, but only 10 percent of its membership. After the riot Leo Meilbeck lamented that there had never been more than 100 Irish socialists in the city. While evidence suggests irreligion was the divisive issue, only the absence of the Irish and Polish is important here.[18]

The SLP had been dominated by immigrants, but the IWPA's Thanksgiving Day demonstration in 1884 marked, for August Spies, "the birth of a new phase in the social struggle. Hitherto the revolutionary movement

Table 4.3 ETHNIC COMPOSITIONS OF CHICAGO'S SLP, IWPA, AND POPULATION, CIRCA 1885

| | SLP | | IWPA | | City |
Group	Observed	Corrected	Observed	Corrected	Population
German	57.0%	45.0%	66.3%	45.0%	33.6%
British Isles	9.9	10.0	4.9	4.0	4.5
Bohemian	7.6	7.0	11.3	15.0	4.5
Scandinavian	6.8	10.0	3.2	10.0	7.7
Native-born	5.8	10.0	6.5	15.0	24.1
Irish	4.0	10.0	1.4	5.0	18.3
French	3.8	3.0	0.2	0.3	1.3
Polish	2.2	3.0	1.6	3.0	3.8
Dutch	1.6	0.5	0.9	0.5	0.4
Swiss	0.6	1.0	2.1	1.0	0.1
Belgian	0.2	0.2	0.1		0.1
Luxembourg	0.2	0.2	0.2	0.1	
Canadian	0.2	.1	0.6	0.7	0.6
Russian			0.6	0.5	0.2
All other					0.9
Totals =	100%	100%	100%	100%	100%
N =	501	1,000	568	2,800	623,765

Sources: (Observed and Corrected SLP, Observed and Corrected IWPA) samples described in text; (Population by Ethnicity) calculated from the 1884 "School Census of Nationalities by Ward," tabled in Chicago *Tribune*, 18 March 1886, 3.

has been restricted to the better situated and more intellectual German, Bohemian and Danish workingmen. . . . Yesterday, the typically American working class carried the red flag through the streets and thereby proclaimed its solidarity with the international proletariat." Neither organization was, as Friedrich Engels complained in 1887, "made up almost exclusively by German immigrants."[19] With the size of the German contingent corrected, the ethnic compositions of these two organizations closely resembled the city's population and its labor movement.

Occupation

Were Chicago's socialists and anarchists artisans and skilled workers undergoing proletarianization, or were they already unskilled workers? What were the occupational structures of the two organizations, how "working class" were they, and how did their occupational structures compare with that of the city? Finally, how much occupational mobility had these socialists and anarchists experienced in the period before the Haymarket riot? The occupations of 364 socialists (69 percent of the sample) and 572 anarchists (79 percent) could be identified. Chicago's socialists came from fifty-four different occupations, the anarchists from fifty-one. (See Table 4.4)

Not surprisingly, most were skilled and both organizations reflected the diversity of the city's work force. Cigarmakers comprised the single largest occupation within the SLP, laborers within the IWPA.[20] Manufacturing trades (furniture, clothing, printing, cigarmaking, shoemaking, tanning, baking, and so forth) accounted for some 40 percent of the total. In a city devastated by fire in 1871, and which doubled its population every decade between 1860 and 1900, it is not surprising that the building trades (carpenters, painters, masons, bricklayers, stonecutters, and plasterers) comprised the second largest group of occupations, some 13 percent of the SLP's membership, 20 percent of the IWPA's. The remaining occupations were widely scattered.

Table 4.5 presents the occupational structures of the two organizations. About 74 percent of the socialists and 82 percent of the anarchists were blue collar; about 26 and 18 percent white collar. The categories here were not rigid: the latter included bookkeepers and clerks, saloon- and shopkeepers, editors and reporters, foremen and superintendents, musicians, teachers, doctors, salesmen, and so on. The borderline between skilled and low white collar was particularly fluid: of the twenty-one saloonkeepers within the IWPA, for example, fifteen had been skilled workers. Of the thirteen anarchist shopkeepers, eight had been skilled workers and George Engel, a painter, opened a toy shop so he could devote more time to reading and the movement.[21] Table 4.5 also compares the occupational structures of the two samples to that of Chicago. White-collar professionals comprised 3 percent of the SLP, only one percent of the IWPA, and 8 percent of the city's population. Skilled workers comprised 40 percent of the SLP, 43 percent of the IWPA, but only one-third of the city. At the bottom, the unskilled accounted for 8 percent of the SLP, 15 percent of the IWPA, but 21 percent of the city. Compared to the SLP, the IWPA drew less from the top of the social ladder and more from

Table 4.4 OCCUPATIONS OF CHICAGO'S
SLP (CIRCA 1880) AND IWPA (CIRCA 1886)

Level [a]	Occupation	SLP	IWPA
S	Cigarmakers	9.9%	4.2%
S	Carpenters	7.7	11.7
UN	Laborers	7.7	14.2
SS	Seamstress/Tailors	6.9	8.0
SS	Cabinetmakers	6.6	6.1
LW	Saloonkeepers	4.9	3.7
LW	Shopkeepers	4.9	2.3
SS	Shoemakers	4.4	3.5
S	Machinists	4.1	3.0
S	Painters	3.6	3.7
S	Printers/Lithographers	3.3	7.3
LW	Bookkeepers/Clerks	3.3	5.2
LW	Editors/Reporters	3.0	1.9
LW	Foremen/Superintendents	2.2	1.2
S	Masons/Bricklayer/Stone	1.9	2.6
SS	Bakers	1.6	.9
SS	Teamsters/Drivers	1.6	2.4
S	Butchers	1.4	1.7
SS	Housekeepers	1.4	.7
S	Jewelers/Silversmiths	1.4	.5
LW	Agent	1.1	.5
LW	Barkers	1.1	.3
SS	Broom/Brushmakers	1.1	.5
HW	Doctors/Physicians	1.1	.5
S	Metalworkers	1.1	1.4
LW	City Inspector	.8	
S	Coopers	.8	.3
SS	Cutlers	.8	
S	Harnessmakers	.8	
HW	Architects	.5	
SS	Bartender/Cook	.5	
S	Clothcutters	.5	
LW	Conductor	.5	
HW	Lawyers	.5	
UN	Polisher	.5	
SS	P.O. Carriers	.5	.3
HW	Real Estate	.5	

Table 4.4 (continued)

Level [a]	Occupation	SLP	IWPA
LW	Teachers	.5	.9
S	Barbers	.3	.3
S	Bellowsmaker	.3	
S	Brewers	.3	.3
S	Blacksmiths	.3	1.6
S	Bookbinders	.3	.7
S	Draftsman	.3	.2
S	Furrier	.3	
SS	Janitor	.3	
LW	Lumber Inspector	.3	
S	Plater	.3	
S	Plumber	.3	
*	Retired	.3	.3
LW	Surveyor/Civil Engineer	.3	.2
S	Tanners/Curriers	.3	1.4
S	Upholsterer	.3	.2
S	Wagonmakers	.3	.3
S	Musicians		.9
SS	Fringe/Awning/Tasselmakers		.5
S	Plasterers/Calciminers		.5
UN	Watchmen		.5
SS	Gardners		.3
LW	Pinkertons		.3
LW	Contractors		.2
SS	Carpetweaver		.2
*	Clairvoyant		.2
SS	Midwife		.2
LW	Notary Public		.2
S	Telegrapher		.2
S	Telephone operator		.2
Totals =		100%	100%
N =		364	572

SOURCES: (SLP) Chicago city directories: 1870, 1875–1880; (IWPA) Chicago city directories: 1870, 1875–1886; Michael Schaack, *Anarchy and Anarchists* (Chicago: F. J. Schulte, 1889).

NOTES: (a) HW = High White Collar, LW = Low White Collar, S = Skilled Blue Collar, SS = Semi-skilled Blue Collar, UN = Unskilled Blue Collar, * = Unknown. These categories are used again in Tables 4.5 and 4.6, below.

Table 4.5 OCCUPATIONAL STRUCTURES OF CHICAGO'S
SLP, IWPA, AND POPULATION

Level	SLP 1880	IWPA 1886	Chicago 1885
High white collar	3%	1%	8%
Low white collar	23	17	22
Skilled blue collar	40	43	33
Semiskilled blue collar	26	24	16
Unskilled blue collar	8	15	21
Totals =	100%	100%	100%
N =	363	569	
Occupational index =	− 0.14	− 0.36	− 0.20

SOURCES: (SLP) Table 4.4, above; (IWPA) Table 4.4, above; (Chicago) interpolated from Edward Bubnys, "Chicago, 1870 and 1900: Wealth, Occupation and Education" (Ph.D. diss., University of Illinois, 1978), 72.

the bottom. Although their occupational indices do not significantly differ, the distributions within the three samples were not identical.[22]

Table 4.6 presents material on the occupational mobility of IWPA members between their first appearance in Chicago and 1886. Two-thirds of the sample started and finished at the same level; 22 percent enjoyed some success and climbed up the ladder, 12 percent slid down. Only one anarchist managed to climb into the high white-collar ranks, the remaining four had started there. About 70 percent of those finishing at the low-white-collar level had started there; 77 percent of the skilled workers had started there; 30 percent of the semiskilled and 40 percent of the unskilled did not taste mobility.

Most of Chicago's socialists and anarchists had served their apprenticeships before emigration, most owned their own tools, most followed a single trade, most worked in small shops, not factories. These were not artisan radicals, but workers from both the skilled trades and those that had become sweated. And again, this is neither unusual nor unexpected.

Table 4.6 OCCUPATIONAL MOBILITY OF CHICAGO'S
IWPA MEMBERS TO 1886

(in numbers)

Earlier Occupation	Last Occupation					
	Unskilled	Semiskilled	Skilled	Low White	High White	(rt)
High white	0	0	0	0	**4**	(4)
Low white	5	3	11	**45**	1	(65)
Skilled	18	6	**188**	32	0	(244)
Semi-skilled	7	**8**	8	3	0	(26)
Unskilled	**35**	4	36	13	0	(88)
(ct)	(65)	(21)	(243)	(93)	(5)	
N = 427						

SOURCES: Chicago city directories, 1870, 1875–1886.

NOTE: Boldface entries (e.g. **188**) indicate those whose occupational levels did not change (N = 280, 66 percent of the total); those above the diagonal were "social sliders" (N = 50, 12 percent); and those below the diagonal were "social climbers" (N = 97, 22 percent of the total).

Address

The *Tribune* had implied in 1879 that the city's socialists were concentrated in "the Bohemian socialist slums of the Sixth and Seventh wards," in the "Scandinavian dives of the Tenth and Fourteenth wards," and on "Halsted, Desplaines, Pacific avenue, . . . Clark Street, Fourth avenue, Jackson Street, . . . [and] State Street." Milwaukee, Clybourn, and Sedgwick streets on the city's Northwest side (Fourteenth Ward) were the heart of the immigrant German colony. According to an 1886 police report, "there are more Anarchists in the upper end of the Sixth Ward than in any other part of the city. The most violent of the dynamiters live on Seventeenth, Eighteenth, Oakley and Van Horn streets," on the Southwest side (Sixth Ward), in the heart of Bohemian Pilsen.[23]

In fact, while socialists and anarchists could be found in all but one of the city's eighteen wards, they clustered closer than neighborhood or street. On the Southwest side, the police "investigated the houses at nos. 64, 66, 68, and 70 on the same street, all occupied by Anarchists" in a house-by-house search after the riot. Louis Lingg, the convicted bomb maker, boarded with William Seliger and his wife; Balthasar Rau and Mikhail Malkoff roomed together in a boardinghouse. The Spies family, with seven identified members of the IWPA, and the Schnaubelt family, with another five, shared the same houses; and Otto Lehman's wife told Captain Schaack that her family lived in a two-story boardinghouse with eight other families, bragging that "all of them were anarchists." If Chicago's socialists and anarchists huddled together, these two samples are no more concentrated than some of the ethnic groups within the city's population.[24] That concentration produced, and then reinforced, a sense of community.

Gender

Contemporaries were horrified at the presence of women within the movement. Captain Schaack was shocked by "The 'Red' Sisterhood": "crazy women," "these creatures in petticoats," "the most hideous-looking females that could possibly be found," especially one who "looked as though she might have carried the red flag in Paris during the reign of the Commune." The *Times* was only slightly more restrained: "Scattered through the procession were not a few of the she-communists, attended by a contingent of sucking, communists who were imbibing some of the resources of civilization." Women regularly appeared in both socialist and anarchist demonstrations: in tableaux, on wagons, in plays, and carrying banners at the head of processions. The workingmen's parties supported a "deutsche Frauensektion" and a "skandinavische Frauensektion" as early as 1877; and a Bohemian women's section of the SLP appeared in February 1882. We know something of their activities, little about them.[25]

They were not many. Of 542 identified members of Chicago's SLP, only five were women, not even one percent of the sample; of 723 anarchists only thirty-eight were women, barely 6 percent of that sample. The WPI, the WPUS, and the SLP had each endorsed women's suffrage, but, as political parties, none had much use for the disfranchised. At a meeting of the Allgemeine Comite in October 1883, "the speaker emphasized especially the necessity of drawing more women, than has been done in the past, into the socialist movement." The Pittsburgh Congress's *Plan of Organization* for the IWPA, on the other hand, explicitly called for the participation of "both men and women." The very choice of that name, the International Working People's Association, rather than the Workingmen's Association, may well have been aimed at recruiting them. They figured more prominently in the IWPA's American Groups than in the other sections. Lizzie Holmes was the assistant editor of *The Alarm* from its first issue; Lucy Parsons contributed articles to it and frequently shared the rostrum with her husband. When Sam Fielden testified to about 175 members of the American Groups, he included "about 15 to 20 ladies among them." Sarah Ames and Ann Timmons chaired meetings of the group; Frau A. Sauper served twice as Gruppe Sudwestseite 1's delegate to the Central Committee.[26]

Unlisted in the city directories, most of these women remain obscure. They seem to have been younger (mean age = 33.9 years) than the rest of the movement, but Louis Lingg's girlfriend, Elise Friedel, was only twenty-two while Sarah Ames was sixty-four in 1886. More of the women were native-born than in the movement at large and had been city residents longer. Their most frequent occupations were seamstress and housekeeper, but they included a midwife, a printer, and a clairvoyant; yet in twenty-six of the thirty-eight cases (68 percent), information on occupation was unavailable. Of the total, two were widows, five were single, nine of undetermined marital status; the remaining twenty-two were married to other members of the IWPA.

At least seven of the anarchist women were members of the Knights of Labor, including Sarah Ames, who served as Local Assembly 1789's Master Workman; both Lizzie Swank and Julia Bishop served as delegates to District Assembly 24. Others had been active in the Working Women's Union in the late seventies. Lizzie Swank later married William Holmes but continued to be *The Alarm*'s assistant editor; both she and Lucy Parsons were frequent public speakers. The other women worked in the movement's theater groups and in anarchist Sunday schools. These "she-communists" did more than sew revolutionary banners and serve beer.[27]

Marital Status and Family Size

The number of women whose husbands were also active suggests an investigation of marital status within the movement. The figures here are suggestive, rather than precise: six years elapsed between the 1880 census and the 1886 riot. Of the SLP sample, 87 percent were married, 13 percent single, and one percent widowed; for the anarchist sample the figures were 78, 18, and 4 percent respectively. Because 56 percent of Illinois trade union members were married, single males may well be underrepresented in both samples, and the number of marriages over-counted.[28]

In 1883 the *Arbeiter-Zeitung* announced the "socialistic christenings" of three children named Karl Marx Kaiser, Ferdinand Kiesling, and Martha Sophia Dannenberg. Those christenings and a Union League Club member's suspicion that the Bohemian anarchists "were so organized as to embrace entire families, even down to thirteen-year-old girls," suggest that we examine the families of SLP and IWPA members.[29] What kinds of families did Chicago's socialists and anarchists live in? Were they different from others in the city?

Information on family size and composition is as imprecise as that on marital status for the same reasons. Family size could be determined for 148 of the 184 marriages within the SLP sample (about 80 percent), and for 166 of the 221 marriages within the IWPA (about 75 percent). Socialist families contained, on average, 2 adults and 2.6 children; family size ranged from 23 childless couples to 3 families with 8 children each. Anarchist families were slightly smaller with a mean of 2.3 children. For the city as a whole, mean family size has been reported at 5.06 in 1870 and at 4.44 in 1900: simple interpolation produces a mean family size of 4.75 members in 1885.[30] If anarchist families were slightly smaller than socialist ones, these two samples do not differ significantly from other Chicago families except in their politics.

From the census we can learn that the widow Wilhelmine Lange was August Neukopf's sister-in-law; along with his wife, all three were members of the IWPA's Gruppe Nordseite. From Captain Schaack we know that the husband, wife, son, and stepson in John Theilen's family were members of that same group; and from newspaper accounts of their arrests we know that Rudolph Schnaubelt was Michael Schwab's brother-in-law. We know of at least thirty couples in which both husband and wife were active in the IWPA; of five father-son pairs; of eleven sets of brothers, totaling twenty-six more members; and at least ten children who were christened by the movement. Like the SLP then, the IWPA included not just two but even three generations of radicals; in Chicago, socialism and anarchism were family affairs.

Affiliations

The processes of reconstitution and prosopography also churn up material on the movement's social life. While the manuscript census schedules help to reconstruct the familial networks within the IWPA's membership, city directories and newspaper reports allow us, to some extent at least, to reconstruct the associational network that enmeshed the SLP and IWPA. However, incomplete, those fragments reveal something about both intra- and extra-movement activities.[31]

Among the socialists, we can identify ninety-four members who served as candidates for the WPI, the WPUS, or the SLP between 1874 and 1882. At least forty-three people served on the board of the Socialist Publishing Society, which published *Der Vorbote, Die Chicagoer Arbeiter-Zeitung* and *Die Fackel,* and another three from the *Illinoiser Volks-Zeitung*'s publishing company. A total of sixty-one members of the movement's paramilitary organizations can be identified: twenty-three in the Lehr- und Wehr-Verein, twenty-one of the Bohemian Sharpshooters, fifteen from the Jaeger-Verein, but only two of the Irish Fifth Ward Labor Guards. Six of the socialists were identified with the movement's theatrical societies, eleven more with its various singing societies.

Only twelve of the anarchist sample had ever been political candidates. Among the anarchists, we can identify fifty-four people who served on the boards of the Socialist Publishing Society, The Alarm Publishing Company, The New Age Company, which published *Den Nye Tid,* and the editorial collectives that issued *Die Anarchist, Budoucnost,* and *Lampcka.* Although they were outlawed and driven underground in 1879, a total of ninety-six members of the movement's paramilitary organizations can be identified: sixty-six in the Lehr- und Wehr-Verein, twenty-three of the Bohemian Sharpshooters, only seven from the Jaeger-Verein. At least eighteen of the anarchists participated in the movement's theatrical socie-ties, ten more in its Gesangvereine. (see Table 4.7)

Chicago's socialists and anarchists were not isolated in their commu-nity: the evidence is even thinner here but clearly suggests the scope of their social affiliations. We know of three different kinds. At least 130 socialists and 159 anarchists belonged to fraternal lodges and benevolent societies, including the Deutsche Ordnung Hermann Sohne, the Odd Fellows, the Order of the Harugari, and the Knights of the Golden Rule. Both the SLP and the IWPA were permeated with irreligion and their members were prominent in freethinking organizations: three socialists and eight anarchists were active in the Liberal League, which is usually associated with Robert Ingersoll; another two of the SLP and four of the IWPA were members of the Skandinavisk Fritaenkere Forening, a largely Norwegian equivalent; three more with the Bohemian freethinkers society. Both organizations enjoyed links to the artisan-republican Ar-beiterverein and the Skandinavisk Arbeiderforening; both socialists and anarchists also had close ties with a set of immigrant workingmen's

Table 4.7 SOCIAL AFFILIATIONS OF CHICAGO'S
SLP AND IWPA MEMBERS

(in numbers)

Affiliation	SLP	IWPA
Intra-Movement		
WPI/WPUS/SLP candidates	94	12
Socialist publishing		
societies	46	54
Theatrical societies	7	18
Gesangvereine	11	17
Lehr- und Wehr-Verein	23	66
Bohemian Sharpshooters	22	23
Jaeger-verein	15	7
Fifth Ward Labor Guards	2	0
Extra-Movement		
Fraternal Lodges and		
Benevolent Societies	130	159
Turnvereine	4	19
Bohemian Sokols	3	3
Cooperatives	3	0
Irish Land League	3	3
Liberal League	3	8
Skandinavisk Fritaenkere		
Forening	2	5
Arbeiterverein	3	0
Skandinavisk Workingmen's		
Association	7	2
Totals =	378	396

SOURCES: Chicago city directories, 1870, 1875–1886; *Chicago Directory of Lodges and Benevolent Societies for the Year 1883* (Chicago: C.F. Lichtner, 1883); *The Alarm*; *Chicagoer Arbeiter-Zeitung*; *Chicagoer Volkszeitung*; *Dagslyset*; *Die Fackel*; Chicago *Herald*; *Illinois Staats-Zeitung*; Chicago *Inter Ocean*; *Svornost*; Chicago *Times*; Chicago *Tribune*; *Der Vorbote*; Michael Schaack, *Anarchy and Anarchists* (Chicago: F. J. Schulte, 1889).

gymnastic societies, including the German Turnverein, the Scandinavian Turnerbrotherhood, and the Bohemian sokols.[32]

Both organizations were intimate with the city's labor movement and contemporary sources reveal something of their trade union activities. (see Table 4.8) The evidence here is fragmentary, confined in most cases to those who served as officers, rather than members, but at least forty-eight socialists and thirty-seven anarchists can be identified as members of the Knights of Labor. Chicago's radicals more closely identified with the trade unions: 58 of the socialist sample of 542 and 153 of the 723 anarchists were active in the city's trade unions; indeed, 49 socialists and 114 anarchists served their unions as elected officers. The largest number of socialists could be found in the cigar makers' and the citywide Trade and Labor Council. Within Chicago's IWPA we can identify thirty-five members of the various carpenters' unions, another thirty-four members of the German Typographical Union No. 9, and twenty-eight members of the various cigar makers' unions; those three unions account for almost two-thirds of the known union affiliations of IWPA members. The remaining third of the affiliations are scattered.

THE MARTYRS AND THE RANK AND FILE

Who were Chicago's socialists and anarchists? Previous scholarship has focused on the martyred, the articulate, and the English-speaking for answers; it has mistaken eight trees and ignored the forest. This chapter has assembled some of the biographical information available on 542 members of the SLP and 723 members of the IWPA. By looking at the age, residential, ethnic, occupational, gender, marital, and family characteristics of the two movements we can move beyond the leadership. With a collective biography we can approach both the socialists and anarchists as historical actors.

We know quite a lot about them and can use modal frequencies to generalize about the average socialist and the average anarchist. He was male, thirty-six years old in 1886, and had already been in Chicago for seven years. He was German and a skilled worker, most likely in a manufacturing trade. He lived on the city's North side and among his comrades. He was married, with at least two children, and his wife was active within the movement. He was a union member, may well have served as an officer, and probably belonged to a fraternal or benevolent society.

But to write of the "average" socialist or anarchist is to obscure the

Table 4.8 LABOR AFFILIATIONS OF CHICAGO'S
SLP AND IWPA MEMBERS

(in numbers)

Affiliation	SLP	IWPA
Knights of Labor		
members	48	37
Trade Unions		
Cigarmakers	12	28
Trade and Labor Council	10	5
Mobel-Arbeiter [Furniture Workers]	7	12
Eight Hour League	5	1
Machinists	4	0
Typographical #16	4	3
Iron Molders	2	0
Soz. Schuhmacher [Shoemakers]	2	0
Typographical #9	2	34
Working Women's	2	3
Clothcutters	1	0
Bakers	1	2
Fleischer-Gesellen [Butchers]	1	1
Pictureframemakers	1	0
Stairbuilders	1	2
Knights of St. Crispin	1	0
Woodcarvers	1	0
Masschneider [Custom Tailors]	1	0
Carpenters		35
Metall-Arbeiter [Metalworkers]		9
Lumberyard Workers		4
Hodcarriers		3
Terra Cotta Workers		3
Brewers and Maltsters		3
Teamsters		1
Bohemian Painters		1

Table 4.8 (continued)

Affiliation	SLP	IWPA
Bookbinders		1
Saddlers		1
Maurer [Bricklayers and Masons]		1
Gerber Verein [Tanners]		1
Totals =	106	191

SOURCES: *The Alarm*; *The Carpenter*; *Chicagoer Arbeiter-Zeitung*; *Chicagoer Volkszeitung*; *Cigarmakers' Official Journal*; Chicago *Herald*; *Illinois Staats-Zeitung*; Chicago *Inter Ocean*; *Journal of United Labor*; Chicago *Knights of Labor*; *Progress*; *Progressive Age*; *The Socialist*; *Svornost*; Chicago *Times*; Chicago *Tribune*; *Der Vorbote*; and Michael Schaack, *Anarchy and Anarchists* (Chicago: F. J. Schulte, 1889).

movement's diversity. Within the IWPA's ranks, for example, the mean age of 37.5 years seems to conceal fifteen-year-old John Thielen and seventy-six-year-old James Taylor. The mean length of residence dismisses the fact that Julius Hoppock had only arrived in the city five months before Haymarket just as it ignores the forty-four-year residence of Dr. Taylor. Such obscurity is the price of statistical generalization; the reward is the ability to compare. Measured by age, ethnicity, occupation, and family size, these samples of the SLP and IWPA's membership compare well with the population of Chicago. In fact, the rank-and-file socialists and anarchists look very much like late nineteenth-century Chicagoans.

The memberships of the SLP and IWPA were not identical. Between 1879 and 1882, sectarianism escalated, as we have seen, from insults ("a frequenter of disreputable houses," "a little Bismarck") to fistfights and competing socialist slates. In 1878, there was one socialist organization in Chicago, the SLP. It had elected one state senator, three state representatives, and its first alderman. The party reached its "zenith" the next year, then "ceased to be a political factor." In 1881, there were two socialist slates for the city elections: the SLP and the new Revolutionary Socialist Party. After 1882, Chicago's socialists and anarchists withdrew from electoral action. The SLP became moribund, if not comatose, as the IWPA renounced parliamentary socialism and embraced social revolution and the Paris Commune. By 1886 and the Great Upheaval, Chicago's SLP had dwindled to about 100 members, as the IWPA grew to about 2,800.

The explanation of this split is not to be found within some of our variables: not in age, or marital status, or family size. The explanation might be in found in length of residence, in occupation, and in ethnicity. Those who had been active in the WPI, the WPUS, and the SLP had been in America and Chicago longer; anarchism appealed, in George Schilling's words, to those "of the more recent importations . . . in whose breasts the flames of revenge are most easily kindled."[33] In 1880, about one-quarter of the SLP was English-speaking, six years later only about one-fifth of the IWPA spoke English: those from Britain, Ireland, and Canada had left the SLP and did not join the IWPA. The changes in occupational distribution were at least as important. In 1880, the SLP had drawn about 26 percent of its membership from white-collar ranks; in 1886, only 18 percent of the IWPA's membership held white-collar occupations. Simultaneously, the proletarian components within the two organizations changed. The IWPA drew 43 percent of its membership from the ranks of skilled workers and 15 percent from the unskilled; the SLP had drawn 40 percent and 6 percent respectively. Chicago's anarchists were newer arrivals, less white collar, and more unskilled than its socialists. Those three changes mark the differences between the two organizations.

Chicago's SLP and IWPA were international, working-class, and heterosexual. Both organizations were international, for their membership hailed from eighteen different nations; the two organizations mixed first- and second-generation immigrants with some of the native-born; and their members spoke at least nine languages. Both organizations were proletarian: although skilled workers predominated, the single largest occupational group within the IWPA were laborers; less than 20 percent of their membership held low-white-collar jobs. And both organizations mixed men, women, and children in its organization and agitation. If the Socialistic Labor Party's name suggested its politics and social composition, the International Working People's Association's name accurately described the rank-and-file membership.

Chapter Five

THE MOVEMENT'S
INTERNAL ORGANIZATION

Having identified Chicago's socialists and anarchists, we turn now to a discussion of their organization and agitation. There is no irony in the juxtaposition of the terms "anarchist" and "organization" if the latter is used as both noun (the final product of activity) and verb (the act or process of organizing). Chicago's social-revolutionaries generated their own institutions and this chapter focuses on both act and process. A study of the movement's structure may explain its attraction to both the active membership and sympathetic following; it may also suggest the sources of cohesion and continuity, the traditions, that the movement tapped.

Two crucial institutions can be readily identified, two centers around which those movements organized: club life and newspapers. The publishing histories of Chicago's socialist and anarchist press stretch back from Haymarket to Hermann Rosch's *Der Proletarier* in 1854, then forward to *Der Vorbote*, which survived for fully fifty years before dying in 1924. Similarly club life stretched back to the sections of the First International even before the Civil War, through the ward organizations of the workingmen's parties of the 1870s, to the groups of the Socialistic Labor Party and the International Working Peoples' Association at the time of the riot and beyond. Club life served as a lyceum, library, schoolhouse, benefit society, and social center. Socialist newspapers served as the movement's public face, presenting the movement to the city's working people. Both institutions sought to provide continuity as the movement grew and developed. Club life and the press recruited new members as they strengthened existing bonds of solidarity.

SOCIALIST AND ANARCHIST CLUB LIFE

By May 1886, the IWPA had organized at least twenty-six groups in the Chicago area. Five of those groups supported armed sections that were accorded additional representation on its citywide Central Committee. The groups reported their weekly meetings in the anarchist press and those reports reveal the organization, size, and recruitment of the movement's active membership. Between 1883 and 1886 the groups grew in number. Six had survived from the days of the SLP; in the six months before January 1884, five new groups organized. By its first issue, in October 1884, *The Alarm* could list a total of sixteen with their meeting times and places. From the directories of Chicago's IWPA groups, and from their reports to the Central Committee, we know of at least twenty-six active groups in the city at the time of the Haymarket riot.[1]

Between 1883 and 1886 the groups grew in size. The radical press frequently mentioned that "three," "four," "five," or "several new members joined the club." But on May Day 1886 word reached Chicago that a membership list had been confiscated by New York's police "and all comrades compromised have been arrested." To avoid that mistake *Die Arbeiter Zeitung* advised, "Away with all rolls of membership and minute books where such are kept." Fearing infiltration and "because some of our members were [already] black-listed and persecuted," some groups issued membership cards inscribed only with numbers; after February 1885, the Lehr- und Wehr-Verein engraved its rifles with numbers, not names. The Seliger-Lingg lists captured by the police will probably remain the exception.[2]

Despite the destruction of those membership lists, we have some data on the size and growth of three of Chicago's IWPA groups. *The Alarm* published a short history of the English-speaking group in May 1885 as part of the minutes of the Central Committee. The American group, it reported, organized with only five people in November 1883; a year later it had grown to 45 members, by April 1885 to 95, in November 1885 to 150. During the Haymarket Trial, Samuel Fielden, one of the original five, testified that in early 1886 it "had about 175 members," with "probably 15 to 20 ladies among them." Then in March 1886, barely two months before the riot, *The Alarm* ran this open letter on its front page: "Comrades: By the courteous assistance of the first American group here, we were enabled to start another group, with a membership of eleven, to be known as American Group No. 2 of Chicago." The circumstances surrounding the formation of that second American group remain unclear. It may have split away from the original one; more likely it was composed of wholly new recruits. Even if those circumstances are not clear, the fact is that the English-speaking section of the IWPA in Chicago was growing.[3]

A Bohemian-speaking branch had been prominent within Chicago's SLP, but most of its members switched their loyalties to the IWPA after the Pittsburgh Congress in 1883. In January 1884, its delegates were reporting to the Central Committee from two separate and growing groups. In November 1885, six months before Haymarket, they announced the establishment of "another group" and reported four already existing ones "mit einer Mitgliederzahl von etwas über 200." In three years then the Bohemian section grew from one to five groups; by the time of the riot in 1886 we can account for at least 209 Czech and Moravian members.[4]

Similarly complete information is available for only one other group: the North side German-speaking group whose membership lists were captured by the police. Reports in *Die Arbeiter-Zeitung* announced a membership of 103 in June 1883; the group had grown to 130 in April 1884; that August "Die Gruppe hat 150 gutstehende Mitglieder." William Seliger testified during the trial that there were 206 members when he became the group's financial secretary late in 1885. And when they were confiscated by the police after the riot, Seliger's lists included the names of 232 and 21 women in Gruppe Nordseite.[5] (see Table 5.1)

The clubs grew by a process of mitosis, of cellular division, or as George Engel put it, "I belonged to the Northwestside Group, the mother group of other groups in the same part of the city." When Michael Schwab arrived in the fall of 1881 he found "thousands of socialists in the city" but "inner dissensions had at that time nearly destroyed all socialistic organizations." Schwab then joined Gruppe Nordseite which "commenced a lively agitation."

A movement started whose aim it was to build up an entirely new organization . . . to form clubs like the Northside Club all over the city. It was hard work to do that, but it was done. I was one of the organizers and I attended many and many a meeting where only six to twelve persons were present, and always the same old faces! But we knew we were right. . . . Slowly we gained a foothold and then we adopted constitutions. . . . [By] the fall of 1883 [sic, 1884] we had established about 20 clubs in the city . . . most of them prospering."

A cadre set out from the established clubs, carrying the message with an almost missionary zeal, into new neighborhoods, found halls, and agitated to form new clubs. The movement's best speakers scheduled the first meetings, then the group elected its own officers, sent its delegates to the city Central Committee and "conduct[ed] its work [in] its own way."[6]

The workingmen's parties of the early 1870s had adopted their ward clubs from the established parties, socialists and anarchists subsequently developed a very different mode. The organizational structures of the SLP and IWPA were similar, although the IWPA permitted more autonomy. *The Alarm* described it this way:

How To Organize

Nine persons can organize a group of the [IWPA]. A group is organized in this manner, viz.: The persons who desire to form a group assemble and select one of their number to act as chairman. They then select one of their number to act as recording and corresponding secretary and another person to act as treasurer. For convenience these functionaries act continuously at the pleasure of the group. The chair is selected at each meeting. The work of propaganda, viz., the obtaining of additional members, the spread of economic information, the organization and arming of the working people, both men and women, is the work of the group in its respective locality. . . . Each group is autonomous (independent) and conducts its work its own way. The funds collected are controlled by the group [collecting] it. All groups adhere to the programme laid down in the Manifesto of the Pittsburgh Congress.[7]

In practice the number of officers varied from the three suggested by *The Alarm* to a more common six: a chairman; recording, corresponding, and financial secretaries; a treasurer; and a librarian. In addition, each group elected a delegation to the Allgemeine Comite proportionate to the size of its membership. The most elaborate configurations were found in the oldest German groups, the least in the American groups. Each group

Table 5.1 REPORTED MEMBERSHIPS OF CHICAGO'S IWPA GROUPS, 1883–1886

Group/Gruppe	Date Est.	Membership by Year				Members Identified
		1883	1884	1885	1886	
American #1	Nov 83	5	45	95	175	57
American #2	Feb 86				11	
Bohemian #1	Original					}
Bohemian #2	Jan 84					}
Bohemian #3	Aug 84 ?				} 200	} 71
Bohemian #4	Apr 85 ?					}
Bohemian #5	Sep 85				9	}
Bridgeport	Jan 84		51			19
Bruderlichkeit	Dec 83	27	45			20
Einigkeit	Feb 84		15			11
Freiheit	Jul 83		32			13
Jefferson #1	Dec 83	14		30		11
Jefferson #2	? 85					
Karl Marx	Jan 86				13	9
Lake #1	May 83		33	31		16
Lake #2	Aug 85			20		1

Group	Date					
Lakeview	Dec 83	17				4
Nordseite	Original	75	150	206	253	257
Nordwestseite	Original	39	66	101		54
Pullman	Dec 84		40	75		2
Revolutionary Cigarmakers	? 85					17
Südseite	Original	72			200	20
Südwestseite #1	Original	33	36			34
Südwestseite #2	Jul 83	16	38			10
Südwestseite #3	Jan 84	35				18
Vorwaerts	May 83		52	59		22
Totals =		333	603	617	861	666
# groups reporting =		10	12	8	10	
Mean group membership = (a) =		33.3	50.3	77.1	95.1	
# active groups = (b) =		13	18	24	26	
Total membership = [a * b] =		433	905	1,851	2,473	

SOURCES: *Die Chicago Arbeiter-Zeitung*, 1883–1886; *The Alarm*, 1884–1886; *Der Vorbote*, 1883–1886; Chicago *Inter Ocean*, 1883–1886; Chicago *Tribune*, 1883–1886.

however rotated its officers every six months; and each meeting opened with the election of a new chairman. Although some prominent members served many times, none were repeatedly reelected. Such an organization blurred the distinction between officers and members, between the leadership and the rank and file, by deliberately emphasizing mass participation.

During the 1870s the workingmen's parties had been largely *ad hoc* organizations. "Our forums," recalled Tommy Morgan, "were street corners, vacant lots, a room over a saloon, and in the trade unions and our resources, the nickels and dimes from the workers' pay." In 1877 Charles Zepf advertised his Wein und Bier Saloon at 54 W. Lake Street as the "Hauptquartier der Sozialisten"; by the 1880s the movement became more established as IWPA groups met weekly in neighborhood saloons. The police had magnificent intelligence on those meetingplaces, and by 1886, could list "10 small halls, 17 saloons (3 of which had small halls connected to them), and 12 other saloons which had rear rooms where the 'reds' sat to talk." Bohemian Hall, also known as Smrz's and Liberty Hall, at 63 Emma Street, was the meeting place for the LWV's Second Company and Gruppe Karl Marx; and Thalia Hall, at 703 N. Milwaukee Avenue, was home to Gruppe Nordseite; Koster's Hall, 2833 S. Wentworth, served Gruppe Südwestseite.[8]

The "notorious Florus' Hall," at 71–73 W. Lake Street, near the city's center, was the largest of the Red halls: four stories high, with a restaurant and cooperative saloon on the first floor, meeting rooms and an assembly hall on the second and third, and rented rooms above. The American Group met there, as did Gruppe Freiheit, the Möbel-Arbeiter Union No. 1, the Metal Workers Union No. 1, and the Central Labor Union. Most of the halls were smaller, behind, above, or below a barroom. Schaack's book presents drawings of some of them. One of the interior of Moritz Neff's Hall shows it draped, presumably with red crepe, above a number of neatly arranged tables, with a bust of Ferdinand Lassalle before a small raised lectern. These halls held up to a hundred or so; they entertained mixed crowds from the neighborhood; and the German ones welcomed families, including women.[9]

> According to Police Captain Michael Schaack the saloonkeepers always looked to it, the first thing in the morning, that plenty of anarchist literature and a dozen or so copies of the *Arbeiter-Zeitung* were duly on the tables of their places, and in some saloons beer-bloated bums, who could manage to read fairly [well], were engaged to read aloud such articles as were particularly calculated to stir up the passions of the benighted patrons.

He knew that the saloonkeepers "shouted louder than anyone else for Anarchy," that "they made substantial contributions to the movement," that they rented their halls "no questions asked," and that they "never found anything worth reporting" to the police. Schaack was convinced that the saloonkeepers were parasites; yet their relationship to the anarchist movement was more complex. The owner of Greif's Hall, for example, a former butcher, served on the *Vorbote* Presse Komite, had been the president of the Fleischer Unterstützungsverein, and an SLP member and candidate in the 1870s. Thomas Greif was one of eighteen saloonkeepers within our sample of SLP members, the second largest occupational group; another twenty-one were among the IWPA sample, comprising its sixth largest occupational group; of the total of thirty-nine, at least seventeen had been skilled workers before buying their saloons.[10]

Club life mingled the movement's diverse membership. Women were welcome, at least in the German saloons, and occupied prominent positions in the American Group. IWPA groups were based in the immigrant enclaves. As neighborhood clubs, their locations had important ramifications for club life.[11] Unlike unions, whose memberships were occupationally homogeneous, socialist clubs, like some Knights' assemblies, mixed different trades at each meeting. Thus carpenters met with tailors, metalworkers with lumber shovers; while each club's membership reflected the neighboring crafts and industry, no group was dominated by any one trade. Club life transcended other divisions, too, by mixing skilled, unskilled, and petty proprietors together. And it mixed old and young, apprentices and journeymen, recent immigrants and older settlers. On the other hand anarchist club life both preserved and undercut language differences.[12] Some should be identified as "German" or "Bohemian," yet Gruppe Nordseite included German, Bohemian, Swiss, Polish, and Russian members; and the American Group mixed native-born, Canadian, English, Irish, Scotch, Welsh, a few Germans and Scandinavians. Few other nineteenth-century organizations—except, of course, the two omnipresent political parties—could claim to be as diverse.

The clubs' activities are as interesting as their ambiance. The IWPA's groups met weekly, alternating agitation meetings with business ones. In October 1885, *The Alarm* described a recent and "well attended" meeting of the American Group: "Every phase of the labor question in its bearings upon social life are freely discussed. The first speaker usually entertains the meeting with a 30 minute speech followed by 10 minute criticisms from different persons in the audience until 10 o'clock P.M. Free discussion, everybody invited." Two weeks later *The Alarm* further explained: "The discussions are generally conducted in this wise: The topic for each meeting is assigned at the previous one and one or more persons [are] appointed to prepare either orally or in writing short addresses, after which the subject matter is open to discussion by the audience."[13]

Within the movement, club life was more than a meeting place, lyceum, library, schoolhouse, benefit society, and recreational center. It served as the movement's core, the basis for organization, recruitment, and agitation. As *The Alarm* indicated, the central feature of those meetings was a speech presented by a member chosen in advance, both he and his topic being announced in the movement's press. Little remains of those lectures save the titles and occasional three or four sentence summaries. O. A. Bishop lectured on "Christ Considered as a Socialist," J. P. Dusey on "The Irish Land League and the Social Struggle in America," Mikhail Malkoff spoke about "The Revolutionary Movement in Russia," Comrade Fehling on both "The Tactics of the IWPA" and "The Development of Socialism."

Back in May 1879, a letter to the editor of *The Socialist* had complained that "Socialists, competent to explain our doctrines, are few in numbers, for they are mostly comparatively uneducated men. Not that they are incompetent for want of natural ability, but because few of them have been Socialists long enough to gain the knowledge that is only to be acquired by patient study." A solution to the problem had already been proposed. Joseph Labadie wrote from Detroit: "the mode adopted by [the Typographical Union] consists in having certain members appointed by the President to either read a paper treating upon the subject or deliver short discourses on some labor subject." Labadie judged the idea "a good one" and recommended that it "should be adopted by all labor organizations."[14]

The next month the SLP's English section resolved to set up a "school of public debate—a lyceum", and the Revolutionary Socialist Party (RSP) explicitly recommended "lectures [and] labor lyceums" so that workingmen might educate themselves. Where the Knights advised their local assemblies to devote ten minutes of each meeting to the study of political economy, the IWPA was more committed to the education of its members. The first steps came late in 1879 when the socialists opened a library. Each of the groups elected its own librarian, and the Allgemeine Comite reserved a seat at its meetings for the association's librarian. The

Arbeiter-Zeitung's offices held the central library; presumably each group had a smaller collection.[15]

In April 1884, the Allgemeine Comite's librarian reported a collection valued at $300 and was authorized to make another $50 purchase. We know little about those holdings. Marx, Engels, Lassalle, Bebel, to be sure. Judging by the lists of "Socialistic Reading Matter" published in *The Alarm* and *Die Arbeiter-Zeitung*, the library also held works by Hyndman, Bakunin, Kropotkin, Reclus, Lafargue, and Lawrence Gronlund. Alongside Johann Most's *Revolutionare Kriegswissenschaft* (The science of revolutionary warfare), there probably were other scientific manuals and journals. Surely there were novels, including works by Sue, Sand, Turgenev, and Zola (*Germinal* had been serialized in *Die Arbeiter Zeitung*). The libraries also subscribed to a variety of European and American socialist and labor papers. They apparently resembled both English and European workers' libraries.[16]

We may assume the anarchists turned to their libraries to prepare their lectures. Michael Schwab read from Marx's *Die Burgerkrieg im Frankenreich* at one meeting; at another he commented on Bebel's *Die Frau unter dem Sozialismus*. The Hocking Valley strike in 1884 occasioned lectures on "Coal Mining in Pennsylvania," "Mine Murders: Right and Justice," and on the strike itself. A number addressed religion: "Relief from Serfdom Through Religion," "Is There a God?" "The Demoralizing Influence of Catholicism," and "The Religion of the Exploiters." Theodore Fricke, business manager at the *Arbeiter-Zeitung*, who had lived in Mexico, lectured on that country and its population; Russian-born M. D. Malkoff on "die Revolutionare bewegung in Russland." Albert Parsons spoke on "The Recent Riots in Cincinnati" after a visit. It should not be surprising to find lectures on "The Crisis of the Workers," "The Development of Socialism," "The Distribution of Wealth," "The Development of Agricultural and Industrial Conditions in America," or "Der Klassenkampf in Amerika" within a movement of social-revolutionaries. Political economy was not the only subject. Genossen Fleiser, a butcher, once spoke on "The Adulteration of Food"; H.E.O. Heinemann, a reporter for the *Arbeiter-Zeitung*, lectured on "Nourishment and the Human Body"; and after Fricke presented his Mexican travelogue, August Spies reported on China. The Martyrs lectured regularly, touring the city's groups presenting lectures with the same titles. But they were not the only speakers. In a sample of ninety-four lectures presented between 1883 and 1885, only eighteen (19 percent) were presented by those subsequently convicted in the Haymarket Trial; 81 percent were delivered by IWPA members who did not figure in the grand jury indictment.[17]

Lectures and lecturing educated the movement's active membership. From the lectures they learned of modern socialism, political economy, philosophy, American and European history, and current events; by lecturing, the members learned oratory and rhetoric, organization and argument. Club life taught the anarchists how to schedule and conduct meetings, to deal with people and groups, to account for funds and members. The structure of club life in turn reinforced those lessons. By rotating their elected offices, the anarchists trained a growing cadre that could call and direct meetings, speak in public, account for funds, and correspond with old comrades and new recruits. However simple, those skills were crucial to both organizing and unionization. Club life then served as a schoolhouse for the movement's membership.[18]

And for their children. In 1881 T. J. Morgan charged that public school teachers were "transcending their duties in instructing children in political matters and in villifying socialists." O. A. Bishop "said that his progeny had come to be spotted in school as 'children of that socialist, Bishop,' and that they were held up to ridicule." Thus in May 1879, at the height of SLP activity, both *The Socialist* and *Die Arbeiter-Zeitung* proudly announced the opening of "The First Socialistic School," with about 100 pupils. We know little about the school's history, teachers, or curriculum. It could not have survived very long, for the movement lacked the financial resources to operate a school, and in 1882 Gruppe Nordseite set up its own "Sonntagschule."[19]

Socialist Sunday schools enjoyed more longevity. Captain Schaack thought them "the most conspicuous feature of the propaganda of the Internationale [sic] in Chicago to-day" when he described them in 1889. By then there were four schools, all on the city's North side, with about 560 children enrolled, and "the number of pupils is increasing from day to day." Schaack remains our only source:

> The schools are of Socialistic and Anarchistic origin. Nothing is taught relating to dynamite or bombs. The German language is used in all the schools, and all the ordinary branches of education are embraced in the curriculum, but underneath and above all is the spirit of contempt for law and religion. The children are instructed that religion is nothing but a humbug; that there exists no God and no devil, no heaven and no hell; and that Christianity is only a preventive system adopted by the capitalists to rule the working people and keep them under. After this they are to be taught the spirit of revolution. In all, the main point is agitation for Socialism and Anarchy.[20]

Dr. Kleinholdt, "one of the chief teachers" according to Schaack, described a curriculum that included "reading, writing, natural history, geography, literature, general history and morality—so much of ethics as young minds are capable of receiving." He protested that the schools did not teach either socialism or anarchism; but admitted "We desire the children to grow up into Socialists, that they be worthy successors of their parents."[21]

Finally, club life served as a social center. The anarchists staged "entertainments" and festivals year-round; with picnics and excursions in the summer; dances and masquerade balls in the fall, winter, and spring. Some of the groups set up singing societies that performed popular songs, musicals, even operettas. One mounted a theatre group, which started by staging "tableaux vivants," and later presented historical dramas, including some original pieces; still another formed a brass band that marched in the movement's parades. The IWPA's groups held frequent benefits for the anarchist press and for their own members' families in times of illness, unemployment, or death. They contributed to creating a rich social and cultural life for the movement.[22]

THE ROOTS OF CLUB LIFE AND
THE ASSOCIATIONAL NETWORK

That kind of club life was not unique to the SLP, the IWPA, or Chicago. Its roots ran both deeper and wider. As John Jentz has recently argued, the same "culture of entertainment," found in Neff's Hall during the 1880s, had been "promoted by the Anglo-American mechanics' institutes during the [early] nineteenth century." The mechanic's institutes were intimately bound up with artisan culture. Founded in 1842, the one in Chicago was the project of master craftsmen, but membership was never limited to the mechanical classes: editors, publishers, and merchants were also admitted. By 1850, the institute housed a library of some 5,000 volumes and boasted of a full-time librarian. Beyond a reading room and books, the institute offered lecture courses, night-school classes with paid instructors, genteel entertainment, and a moral atmosphere for its members. That membership was active in the reform movements of the mid-nineteenth century, especially in temperance and abolitionism.[23]

The historian of the Chicago Mechanics' Institute has argued for the centrality of three beliefs expressed by the institute. The first held to the dignity of labor, a belief that powered the membership's abolitionism. A second cherished competence, with frugality, perseverance, and morality as the keys to success. Education, both moral and mechanical, became the third article of faith. Equal opportunity, a labor theory of value, the pursuit of a competence, the assertion of dignity: the institute was a bastion and forum for artisan republicanism. It is not surprising that its members fought against the slaveholders, or that they returned from the Civil War as heroes and claimed success in business.[24]

The institute's building burned in the Great Fire in 1871, but neither its antebellum form nor its membership had survived the Civil War. From its beginnings the institute had two governing boards. Mechanics had served prominently as its elected officers, but a board of directors made policy decisions. Indeed, "between 1843 and 1860 the elective offices were gradually dominated by an elite, with common tradesmen almost totally excluded." As early as 1843, its second year, the board included a merchant jeweler and, after 1860, Cyrus McCormick.[25] By the end of the Civil War, the Chicago Mechanics' Institute had become a social club for successful masters, inventors, and entrepreneurs. Unable to adapt to the changes in the economy or in the social relations of industrial production, the institute was at the same time unwilling to adapt to the city's changing population and made no attempt to attract immigrants.

Rejected, they drew upon their own traditions and set up their own artisan clubs, the Arbeiter-Verein, during the financial crisis of 1857–58. By the early 1860s, there were three branches of the Arbeiter-Verein in the city. In 1861, the central organization had 250 members, $500 in the bank, a good library, a piano for its new singing club, and a debating society. Two years later, the membership had passed 1,000 and the library had grown to 740 volumes.[26] The Arbeiter-Verein became the German-immigrant equivalent of the Mechanics' Institute. Like the institute, the verein "united artisans, proprietors, and lower level professionals"; similarly "the acceptance of members of higher status—like lawyers and editors—prompted discussions in the Association's debating society." Like the institute, the verein was a republican institution grounded in the local artisan movement and culture. Both marched in public demonstrations; both were active in the abolitionist movement. Beyond its use of German, the Arbeiter-Verein differed from the institute in at least two important respects. First, it served beer before, during, and after its lectures, meetings, and social events. It actively opposed the temperance movement and served as a meeting point for that opposition. Second, while there was an important educational purpose to the verein, that purpose was never as explicit as it was in the institute. While both organizations offered classes, those in the verein emphasized English as a second language.[27]

And like the Mechanics' Institute, the Arbeiter-Verein could not survive what David Montgomery once termed "the shoals of class conflict" in the years after the Civil War. Capitalist industrialization dissolved the artisan community of masters and journeymen; the process of proletarianization, though uneven, rent the social relations of production. As early as 1861, the issue of middle-class control surfaced in debates within the verein, just as they had within the institute. Growing conflict between the working-class membership and the middle-class reformers who directed both organizations split them apart.[28] As the Arbeiter Verein declined, its proletarian members seceded to form their own organization, the Socialer Arbeiter-Verein, which affiliated with the First International. By 1872 that organization became the International Social and Political Workingmen's Association and organized not just Germans, but also Bohemians, Poles, Norwegians, French, Danes, and less successfully, the native-born. Thus, even before the long depression of the 1870s, class consciousness grew in the fertile soil provided by ethnic organizations.[29]

Socialist and anarchist club life then grew out of the traditions of both the Mechanics' Institute and the Arbeiter-Verein. In the seventies and early eighties club life meshed, sometimes neatly, with an existing network of immigrant or ethnic societies. Anarchist groups met in ethnic saloons in ethnic neighborhoods, but they scheduled their larger events, festivals and mass meetings, in the German and Bohemian turnhalles where many of the anarchists were members and a few served as officers. The movement cooperated with a wide range of immigrant societies, including gymnastic societies (the German Turnverein, the Bohemian sokols, and the Skandinavisk Turnerborderna); friendly societies; fraternal and benevolent groups, and singing societies in which socialists and anarchists were frequently members and officers.[30]

THE SOCIALIST AND ANARCHIST PRESS

Socialist club life antedated the socialist press to which it devoted so much energy. German immigrants, members of the International, issued *Der Proletarier* in 1854, *Stimme des Volkes* in 1860, and *Der Deutsche Arbeiter* in 1869. When Lev Palda issued *Národní noviný* in 1870–1871, it became the first Czech-language socialist paper in Chicago and the United States.

In turn, a socialist press predated the organized socialist movement. In April 1880, *Der Vorbote* asserted "Die Geschichte der Arbeiterbewegung in den Vereinigten Staaten ist zugleich [at the same time] die Geschichte der Arbeiterpresse."[31] The insight is important, and although expressed in German, we need not stop with the German press, nor with German editors. By 1886, there were seven or eight anarchist newspapers issued in Chicago, five of them official organs of the IWPA, published in three languages: German, English, and Czech. Their publishing histories became crucial to the movement's development; their circulation histories reveal the growth of a sympathetic following.

The oldest of the papers were published in German by the Socialist Publishing Society (SPS), which issued stock only to its subscribers. *Der Vorbote* (The harbinger), the oldest, was founded in 1874 as a weekly, and the society grew out of the Verein Vorboten. The owner and publisher of *Der Sozialist*, a WPI organ, offered to sell his paper to the WPUS at its Union Congress in 1876; it is not clear that the WPUS ever paid off the debt, but the SPS assumed ownership and subsequently transferred it to the SLP, still later to the IWPA.[32] In June 1877, the SPS felt confident enough to issue a second paper, *Die Chicagoer Volks-Zeitung* (Peoples' newspaper), as a triweekly. It expanded coverage of local news, leaving *Der Vorbote* as the main paper with a weekly summary. As early as October 1877, the movement discussed a daily paper, and in May 1878 *Die Fackel* (The torch) which was subtitled an "independent organ of instruction, entertainment and amusement," appeared as a Sunday weekly. One year later, in May 1879, as the SLP continued to grow in members and the SPS in confidence, *Die Volks-Zeitung* became the daily *Die Arbeiter-Zeitung* (Workers' newspaper).[33] By the time of Haymarket, the SPS issued three papers: a daily and two weeklies.

Based on his study of German workers, labor leaders, and the labor movement in Chicago, Hartmut Keil concluded that "listing the editors of *Vorbote, Chicagoer Arbeiter-Zeitung,* and *Fackel* is almost equivalent to enumerating Chicago's outstanding German labor leaders of the period." Between 1874 and 1886 the SPS enjoyed the services of at least seven editors who were hired and fired by the society: Karl Klings, Conrad Conzett, Paul Grottkau, Gustav Lyser, Wilhelm Rosenberg, August Spies, and Michael Schwab. All were immigrants, all but Swiss-born Conzett were German, all but Grottkau came from working-class families, all but Klings and Spies had been journalists.[34]

The German monopoly over Chicago's socialist press continued through the Great Upheaval of 1877. That fall, Louis Pio issued a pamphlet calling for a national organization of Scandinavian workers in America and announcing a new paper, *Den Nye Tid* (The new age). Pio, founder of the socialist movement in Denmark, was soon joined by a coeditor, another exiled Scandinavian Forty Eighter, Marcus Møller Thrane, father of the Norwegian labor movement. Even in exile, Pio and Thrane were perhaps the two most famous Scandinavian socialists of the nineteenth century. And yet the comrades ousted Pio in May 1878, when they discovered that he was simultaneously editing a Methodist paper. A freethinker, Thrane proved more acceptable, and the paper "adopted a strongly anti-clerical and atheistic stance." In fall 1880, he too got ousted by a group of insurgents led by Peter Petersen, Olaf Ray, and Norman Hafstad during the split over fusion with the Greenback Party. In October 1881, the Revolutionary Socialist Party named *Den Nye Tid* an official organ; two years later it became one of the IWPA's organs. Combining socialism and rationalism, it survived through April 1884, perhaps even longer.[35]

An English organ, *The Socialist,* took another six months. It might have appeared earlier but the SLP's national executive committee had concluded that the party could not support two English organs. When the Cincinnati *National Socialist* went under, the Chicago section bought its subscription list, paid off its debts, hired Frank Hirth, a German-born cigarmaker, and moved the paper. Renamed *The Socialist*, it had as its announced goal to organize workers "into one grand political labor party for the purpose of securing labor's rights." Hirth got fired about a month before the paper died in August 1879 and Albert Parsons briefly assumed the editorship. With its death came the defection of the Irish from the SLP; in its wake Chicago's English-speaking socialists were without a paper for fully five years.[36]

The four remaining papers all appeared after the Grottkau-Morgan factional dispute, after the Turner Hall Congress, and were anarchist papers. The Czech-language *Budoucnost* (The future) appeared first, in June 1883, initially as an eight-page biweekly, then as a weekly, issued from a small printing shop in a basement in the heart of Bohemian Pilsen. The only contemporary account described it as "a very small sheet . . . having only a limited number of subscribers," and contended that its articles were largely "translations from the German daily, the *Arbeiter-Zeitung.*" Its editorial collective was composed of very recent immigrants, all of whom worked outside the paper. Josef Pondelicek was a painter (and president of the first Bohemian painters' union); Jacob Mikolanda, a carpenter and officer in the carpenters' union; and Norbert Zoula a silversmith; only Josef Pecka had any experience as a journalist.[37]

Five years after *The Socialist* collapsed, Chicago's English-speaking socialists finally got another paper when the first issue of *The Alarm: A Socialist Weekly* appeared in October 1884. Editorial responsibilities were apparently shared by Albert and Lucy Parsons, assisted by Lizzie May Swank, who had been a dressmaker active in the Working Women's Union. *The Alarm* appeared as a weekly for three months, then found "our expenses being too heavy [and] the prospects . . . gloomy", and reluctantly became a fortnightly. Like its predecessor, *The Alarm* was never solvent: benefit picnics, dances, and evening entertainments had to be scheduled frequently to keep it afloat. Although it was "owned and controlled" by the IWPA, Parsons claimed that he had exercised very little control:

> This paper belonged to the organization. It was theirs. They sent in their articles—Tom, Dick, and Harry; everybody wanted to have something to say, and I had no right to shut off anybody's complaint. *The Alarm* was a labor paper, and it was specifically published for the purpose of allowing every human being who wore the chains of monopoly to clank those chains in the columns of the *Alarm*. It was a free press organ. It was a free speech newspaper.[38]

Chicago's last two anarchist papers had much shorter histories. We know very little about the first, *Lampcka* (The lantern), a Czech weekly published from August 1885 through April 1886. The same day the police suppressed *Budoucnost*, they raided and subsequently closed the tiny basement office of *Lampcka*. After describing it as "a Bohemian Anarchistic paper," the *New York Times* and the *Chicago Tribune* reported "the proprietor and editor . . . bears the name of Hradecny" and that he had fled the city the night of the riot. Anton Hradecny later returned to Chicago, but he never revived the paper.[39]

In December 1885, Gruppe Nordwestseite complained to the Allgemeine Comite that the *Arbeiter-Zeitung* was "nicht radikal genug" [not radical enough]. Led by Adolph Fischer, a compositor at the *Arbeiter-Zeitung*, and George Engel, a painter turned shopkeeper (both executed on 11 November 1887) the group began its own four-page organ, *Der Anarchist*, in January 1886. It was a monthly, and only four or five issues appeared before its staff was arrested and the paper suppressed in the wake of the riot. Its subtitle proclaimed it as the "Organ der Autonomen Gruppen der I.A.A.," and it reportedly followed Johann Most's violent editorial line, but in its short life was never recognized as an official organ of the IWPA. *Der Anarchist* may provide an explanation for two competing Bohemian anarchist papers: if *Lampcka* was an anarchist paper, it was probably more radical than *Budoucnost*.[40]

What did an anarchist paper look like? Through 1900 the SPS's papers were printed with traditional fraktur type, few commercial advertisements, and infrequent illustrations. The daily *Arbeiter-Zeitung* had four pages; *Der Vorbote*, the Saturday political weekly, eight; and *Die Fackel*, the cultural Sunday issue, twelve. The first page offered national and international "telegraphic despatches," the second carried editorials, the third page serialized a novel, and under the headline "Stadt Chicago" the last page held local news. Every issue published directories, announcements, and reports of the labor and social-revolutionary movements. The daily concentrated on the local movement, *Der Vorbote* offered a weekly review but aimed beyond the city limits, and after 1881 *Die Fackel* offered a "Kleine Frauen-Zeitung" to women. These papers specialized by language: while the *Arbeiter-Zeitung* occasionally reported meetings of the American Group, *The Alarm* never reported the meetings of any of the other ethnic groups within the movement. *Den Nye Tid* claimed to be "the only Danish-Norwegian workers' newspaper and organ for the Scandinavian socialists in the United States"; judging only from its first issue *Budoucnost* concentrated on Bohemian activities. Parsons and Swank devoted much of their paper to readers' letters, the Germans featured European news, especially from the homeland, and particularly on the SPD. The German papers and *Budoucnost* reported on fraternal societies, including the Turn Verein and the sokols; the Germans published streetcar schedules and market prices; and announced births, marriages, and deaths. If the English and Scandinavian papers addressed far-flung radicals, the German and Czech ones served concentrated and local communities.[41]

What did an anarchist paper sound like? All of Chicago's anarchist papers would have subscribed to *Den Nye Tid*'s credo:

> Its purpose is to safeguard and promote the interests of the worker and to spread socialist teaching among our countrymen. It will work to gather all workers in one association to establish a social order which will grant the worker his rights. It will oppose corruption, rottenness, exploitation and capitalist domination. It will fight against monopoly and the predatory nature

of the system and will aim at liberating work from the yoke of capitalism. It will contain editorials on social, political and economic matters. It will bring news about the workers and workers' movement in all continents. . . . It will not be written in a haughty or pompous language, but in a style understood by the common man.

The Alarm's articles "ranged from the impudent, to the imprudent, to the totally outrageous" as Parsons and Swank filled its pages with lively social commentary; with reports on strikes, union meetings, and demonstrations; editorial opinion and educational articles on revolutionary theory; extensive correspondence from its readers; and reprints from other socialist journals. *The Alarm, Die Arbeiter-Zeitung,* and *Budoucnost* revelled in baiting the bourgeois press; an infrequent cartoon showed a dog, variously labeled "Daheim" or "Staats-Ztg" baying at a moon labeled "Arb. Ztg." and its editors invited at least three libel suits. Perhaps *Die Fackel* best expressed the movement's "feverishly combative character." The Sunday edition took its slogan "Giving the serious and the funny its due, and despising nothing but the base." Its "Skitzen aus dem Leben der Grosstadt," a regular column, reported fads and fashions, popular theater, rumors, and street conversation. In the remarkable hands of Gustav Lyser, *Die Fackel* revelled in "the spirit of rebellion 'against everything,' against bourgeois culture and morality, conservative trade unionism, and above all, against the state." Lyser, and those who succeeded him, could be irreverent, satirical, witty, and sarcastic; and *Die Fackel*'s masthead featured the torch of liberty and its own name in the flames of revolution.[42]

Each paper was issued by a publishing society: the German papers by the SPS, *The Socialist* by The Chicago Socialist Press Association, *Den Nye Tid* by The New Age Company, *The Alarm* by The Alarm Publishing Association. Their political purpose was explicit: according to the WPUS's Union Congress, "The press shall represent the interests of labor, awaken and arouse the class-feeling amongst the workingmen, promote their organization as well as the trade-union movement and spread economical [sic] knowledge among them." All were cooperative ventures, which meant that only subscribers could buy stock (and few expected any dividends), that the staffs had to respond to the readership, and that editors were responsible to a board of directors.[43]

We know the most about the Socialist Publishing Society, which was the oldest and most copied. Its directors included editors, reporters, compositors, and carriers; there was no distinction between management and labor. The society defined its mission as exceeding that of a labor paper. According to its statutes, its purpose was to "cultivate and develop its members' understanding of morality, history, political economy, statistics, philosophy and other sciences, through debates, readings, lectures, pamphlets, newspapers, journals, and other publications." At the end of 1883 *Der Vorbote* reported that 15,729 books and pamphlets had been distributed by the Chicago groups. *The Alarm* published a more comprehensive report about two years later. During the preceding ten months, 387,537 books, pamphlets and circulars had been distributed by the organization.

> The number of books and brochures sold was 6,527. (They were mostly valuable books, viz.: Marx, Lassalle, Bebel, Hyndman, Bakunine, Reeclus [sic], Gronlund, etc.) From the brochures of Comrade John Most there were circulated 5,000; Address to Tramps, by Mrs. Parsons, 10,000; 'How to Put Down the Commune,' 5,000; Communistic Manifesto, 25,000; Pittsburgh Proclamation, in English, German, French and Bohemian, 200,000; gratis copies of THE ALARM were circulated 96,000.

Despite such impressive production, the press rarely enjoyed solvency. In 1876, Conrad Conzett listed *Der Vorbote*'s weekly expenses at $106.75, "an average weekly income of $108.00" and a profit of $1.25. Three years later, when *The Socialist* died, it had an income of $45 and expenses of $87 per week. Despite 3,600 subscribers and a circulation of 4,500 respectively, each week threatened to be a socialist paper's last.[44]

The SPS did not buy its own printing press until after the riot. Instead, its compositors set the type, then delivered the galleys to a job printer for the press run. The SPS's rented offices occupied the whole building at 107 Fifth Avenue (now 41 N. Wells), a three-story building with a restaurant on the first floor, editorial and composing departments for the three German papers and *The Alarm* on the second, meeting rooms and the IWPA's central library on the third. In contrast, both the Scandinavians and Bohemians owned their presses, although hardly comparable offices. *Lampcka* and *Budoucnost* was issued from tiny basements on the city's westside, *Den Nye Tid* came out of a "hole"—"an unimpressive wooden building on Milwaukee Avenue." According to one of its printers, "Daylight came from windows in the roof and at night there was an oil lamp. . . . All the book printing was done on a monster job press that was operated by foot power. We had great trouble getting anyone to feed and tread that press."[45]

When the police raided the society's offices the morning after the riot, they arrested twenty-two of the staff: reporters, compositors, even the printers' devil. All were members of the German printers' union, Typographia No. 9. Of eighty-two people who sat on the SPS's board of directors between 1873 and 1886 at least ten were members of Typographia No. 9, about 12 percent of the total.[46] Both statistics point to an important relationship between that union and the radical press. Conrad Conzett, *Vorbote*'s editor, served as president of the union local in the 1870s; Herman Pudewa, the arrested composing-room foreman, served as the local's secretary or vice-president from 1883 to 1886, as well as being an SPS director and an active member of the IWPA group in suburban Jefferson.[47]

In turn, the German socialist press conceded a union shop to Typographia No. 9. In April 1882, *Die Arbeiter-Zeitung* complained that while it had bid twelve cents per 1,000 ems on a contract for city printing, the council had awarded the contract to *Die Neue Freie Presse*, which had bid twenty-five cents. Typographia No. 9 appears then to have subsidized the socialist press by working below scale on SPS publications. The bourgeois German papers resented that practice, as did the English Typographical Union No. 16. At a Trades Assembly meeting in fall 1885, its officers complained that "the *Arbeiter-Zeitung* is a socialistic sheet and the members of the International Typographical Union [ITU] are not permitted to work in its office." An investigative committee recommended that the only solution to the problem was to "induce" the *Arbeiter-Zeitung*'s employees "to return to Union No. 16 of the ITU."[48]

Compared to its editors, staff, and compositors, the readership of Chicago's socialist and anarchist press remains largely invisible. What little information we can recover supports three conclusions. First, the German-language papers clearly dominated circulation. Between 1880 and 1886, *Der Vorbote*, *Die Fackel*, and *Die Arbeiter-Zeitung* accounted for 80 percent of the movement's readers, with the Czech, Scandinavian and English readers splitting the remaining 20 percent. Second, much of that circulation was by subscription and delivered by newscarriers. *Die Arbeiter-Zeitung* and *Budoucnost* had an elaborate distribution network that included carriers, newsdealers, and the postal system for out-of-town readers. In contrast, the bulk of *The Alarm*'s circulation was of single issue purchases handled by newsdealers. Third, and to reverse Richard Ely's insight, their "respectable circulation" carried with it "advertising patronage", some directly addressed to party members.[49]

The publishing and circulation histories of those papers reflect the movement's growth. (see Table 5.2) German-language circulation increased from 13,000 in 1880 to 26,280 in 1886, an increase of 102 percent. Estimated Bohemian circulation grew from about 750 in 1883 to 1,500 in 1886 (up 113 percent); English from 2,000 in 1884 to 3,000 in 1886 (up 50 percent). The SLP's four papers had enjoyed a total circulation of 14,600 in 1880; the IWPA's seven papers enjoyed a total of 30,880 in 1886, an increase of 111 percent. Not only did circulation grow faster than population, but this discussion may underestimate readership, for it presumes that circulation equalled readership, that a paper was read by only one person.[50]

The decision to subscribe to one of these papers was a conscious one. The anarchist press did not entrap its readership. Each paper proclaimed its radical politics; the front page of *Budoucnost*, for example, carried the slogan "From agitation comes organization, from organization [comes] revolution!" Nor was the anarchist press the only ethnic press in Chicago. On the contrary, each paper had to compete with other foreign-language papers, some of which were long and firmly established. Thus, *Die Arbeiter-Zeitung* competed with four other German-language dailies, one established in 1848; *Der Vorbote* and *Die Fackel* competed with at least ten other German weeklies. *Den Nye Tid* was up against five other Scandinavian papers, both dailies and weeklies. Finally, *Budoucnost* and *Lampcka* had to share the Bohemian market with *Svornost*, founded in 1875, and at least one other weekly.[51]

Throughout the seventies and eighties Chicago's anarchist press simultaneously competed with an English-language labor press. Measured by either longevity or circulation the socialists and anarchists won that competition: *Der Vorbote*'s fifty-year run, from 1874 to 1924, was never equalled. In the 1870s the chief competition came from Andrew Cameron's *Workingman's Advocate*, which appeared in 1864 and died in 1877. Theirs was a peculiar competition; after an early and aborted German-language supplement, Cameron never mentioned the socialists in his paper; *Der Vorbote* never mentioned his name or paper. In late 1879 and early 1880, several Greenback papers (among them the *Anti-Monopolist*, the *Daily Telegraph* and the *Standard of Labor*) were issued to present the National Greenback Party to Chicago's workingmen. Like *The Socialist*, none survived more than a year.[52]

The second of the socialists' rivals appeared in March 1881 and survived for about two years. *The Progressive Age* was initially edited by two labor reformers who proposed "to wage relentless war on the grasping and soulless corporations and monopolies which threaten the very

Table 5.2 CIRCULATION OF CHICAGO'S ANARCHIST PRESS, 1880–1886

Paper	Circulation by Year						
	1880	1881	1882	1883	1884	1885	1886
Der Vorbote	5,000	6,000	6,500	7,000	7,115	8,000	8,000
Arbeiter-Zeitung	3,000	4,500	4,850	5,200	5,326	5,110	5,780
Die Fackel	5,000	5,000	7,150	9,300	10,035	10,000	12,200
Den Nye Tid	1,600	1,600	[2,000]	[2,400]	2,800		
The Alarm					2,000	3,000	[3,000]
Budoucnost & Lampcka				[750]	[1,000]	[1,200]	[1,500]
Anarchist							[300]
totals =	14,600	17,100	20,500	24,650	28,276	27,310	30,780
# increase		2,500	3,400	4,150	3,626	–961	3,470
% increase		+17.1	+19.9	+20.2	+14.7	+3.4	+12.7

SOURCES: N.W. Ayer and Sons (firm), *American Newspaper Annuals*, 1880–1886 (Philadelphia, 1880–1886); George P. Rowell and Co., *American Newspaper Directory*, 1880–1886 (New York, 1880–1886); Michael Schaack, *Anarchy and Anarchists*, (Chicago: F.J. Schule, 1889), 358.

NOTE: entries in brackets are of estimated or interpolated figures.

existence of the Republic." The Trades Assembly endorsed the paper in September 1881, agreeing to collect its subscriptions and provide funding. Soon after, the assembly bought the paper, staffed it with union men, and ran it as a joint-stock company. By 1882, the paper claimed 20,000 subscribers and may have been the nation's only labor paper owned and operated by a city's trade unions. That year the Knights of Labor's DA 24 extended an endorsement and it became, for a while, the order's official organ in the city.[53] When a new editor arrived and championed temperance, the Trades Assembly denounced the paper, withdrew its support, and started the short-lived *Western Workman* as its own.[54]

The third and last of the anarchists' competitors came from their former comrades in the SLP. Stung by the "kickers" control of the press during the fusion debate and the subsequent split in 1880, the loyal Germans began to talk of their own organ in December 1883. The discussion occupied the section for months. In March 1884 the Germans hoped "to annihilate the *Arbeiter-Zeitung* . . . to kill that paper so dead that one more issue will be about the last that will be seen ot it. Then there will be no more Anarchists, as there will be no public press to mislead and corrupt the minds of the uninformed."[55] Planned as a triweekly, the paper was organized on the customary shareholding plan, with "none but the faithful as stockholders." In May, the section established a subscription committee and a board of trustees. A fund-raising picnic was arranged, but the section lacked both picnickers and subscribers. When *Der Illinoiser Volkszeitung,* coedited by Julius Vahlteich and Heinrich Walther, appeared in May 1884 it had become a weekly and was issued from New York. A four pager, only the inner pages came from Chicago. Before the end of the first insolvent year, the Chicago section repudiated the paper when it fell into the hands of a "clique" that had usurped the Presse Komite and betrayed the party.[56]

The size and growth of the anarchist readership then was neither the result of entrapment nor the product of default. And it would be difficult to overestimate the press's importance to the movement. The Grottkau faction's control of the press had proven crucial in its fight with Morgan in 1880, and the SLP's effort to establish its own organ in the summer of 1884, again testified to its value. Papers were weapons that could be turned on both those within and outside the movement. They recruited, educated, politicized, and mobilized the movement's membership; they served as bulletin boards, both announcing and reporting the movement's meetings and club life.

The calendars of anarchist and union meetings, published weekly in

The Alarm or daily in *Die Arbeiter-Zeitung,* reflect the intensity of activity and the vigor of life within the movement. Club life and the press demanded time, money, and effort. After they were arrested in the wake of the Haymarket riot, Captain Schaack got some of the anarchists and their wives to describe the movement's effects. Johannes Gueneberg remembered the way his family "suffered while I was giving my time to Anarchy. I have now worked four weeks and made full time [wages]. This I have not done for the last two years." William Seliger's wife "related how she had lived in misery ever since her husband began to take part in the Anarchist meetings, and she stated that after [Louis] Lingg came to live in the house she had not seen a pleasant hour. She had often pleaded [with her husband] not to attend the meetings, or read any of the Anarchist papers, but to remain at home with her." Gustav Lehmann's wife remembered that "he would take the last cent out of the house and run to meetings every night." As Officer Schleuter led her husband away, Mrs. Ernst Hübner told him "if my husband had gone more to his shop and to work instead of running to meetings, you would not find my house in this shape. I am all broken up. I am sick, and now he is arrested. I suppose this is the last of our family."[57]

Chapter Six

DANCING SOCIALISTS, PICNICKING ANARCHISTS?

It is surprising to discover that the supposedly unwashed, wild-eyed, bomb-throwing anarchists held family picnics and went to dances. This chapter attempts to penetrate that contradiction by describing a "movement culture" in Chicago during the decade and a-half before the riot. At its simplest, the argument here is that between 1870 and 1886 the class-conscious memberships of the IWA, WPI, WPUS, SLP, and IWPA actively created and expanded a vital, militant, and socialist culture inside the city's working class.

Some contemporary observers, like Friedrich Sorge, were impressed with the movement's vitality and militancy:

Chicago experienced an extraordinarily energetic and effective propaganda campaign, carried on in public meetings held in halls and in the open, in which speakers of various nationalities and languages participated. Big parades and processions were held often, and every appropriate event in public life was used to shake up the people, the workers, and to bring them to a realization of the condition and also, certainly, to frighten the philistines and politicians. The

Chicago workers' festivities held in these days were wonderful events, and those held in the open drew crowds of 20,000 to 40,000 people.[1]

With Sorge's catalog as an outline, this chapter focuses on the creation of several cultural institutions and their roles in the history of the socialist and labor movements in nineteenth-century Chicago. If we now know that the movement was large and growing, and that it played an important role in Chicago's labor movement, we do not yet know how it grew or became important. We need to understand the cultural forms by which its ideology was created, manifested, and transmitted to complement existing scholarship on anarchist ideology.[2]

Six elements of that movement culture can be readily identified: singing societies, theater groups, dances and Stiftungfeste, picnics, and parades and processions. A sixth element, the annual commemoration of the Paris Commune, brought the others together, if only for one night each year. Three qualifications should be explicit here at the outset. What I am describing as a movement culture was *not* synonymous, numerically or institutionally, with working-class culture.[3] Rather movement culture, which tried to draw upon or from the larger class culture, was always smaller. The largest events the movement managed to schedule were parades: the largest, in April 1886, mobilized about 35,000 people, at a time when the city's population was about 800,000. Never exclusive, that culture served as a base for recruiting and maintaining a socialist membership. Second, while movement culture derived from the ethnic cultures within the movement and city, they were *not* synonymous. The socialist movement was too diverse and pluralist to have imposed any one ethnic culture on its membership. The First International, the SLP, and the IWPA drew upon a European political culture that was international and socialist. Third, while distinctly proletarian and socialist, the movement and culture sketched here was *not* unique to Chicago. Richard Oestreicher has described "the emergence of a subculture of opposition" embodied in "new working class institutions," which included concerts, balls, and demonstrations in Detroit during this same period.[4]

We should look first at two cultural institutions within the movement; then at three cultural events; finally at the relationships between movement and working-class culture on the one hand, and between working-class and bourgeois culture on the other. Beyond merely listing those cultural institutions and events, this chapter will penetrate and then "thickly describe" them.[5]

SINGING SOCIETIES

Music was important to Chicago's socialists and anarchists. The SLP opened its meetings with songs and the programs for anarchist social events included music. A "volunteer quartet sang a selection and T. J. Morgan sang a solo" to open one meeting; at another Morgan sang "an impromptu song on the Irish agitation, which he had evolved for the entertainment of his hearers." The movement could provide its own brass bands for parades, but it usually hired local orchestras for its festivals. Some of these were famous: The Great Western Light Guard Band, Johnny Meincken's Germania Orchestra, or the Hibernian Band. Because music was their labor, those musicians were paid for their performances, even when they played for the labor movement.[6]

Socialist festivals featured the performance of singing societies (Gesangvereine in German) whose members came from within the movement. The seventh anniversary of the Paris Commune in 1878 featured songs from the "Liedertafeln 'Vorwaerts' (deutsch) and 'Internationale' (skandinavisch)"; the eighth anniversary featured eight singing societies: Liedertafel Lassalle, the Socialistic Mannerchor of the Northside, the Schiller Liedertafel, the Freier Sangerbund, Liedertafel Vorwaerts, Liedertafel des Sozialen Arbeiter-Vereins, Liedertafel Internationale, and the Sennefelder Liederkranz. While those names suggest both ethnicity and political affiliation, it is impossible to discover much about their memberships.[7]

At least six singing societies affiliated with the IWPA in the eighties. The Socialistic Mannerchor split into two groups, one on the city's North side, the other on the Southwest; the Socialistic Sangerbund drew its membership from the South side; the Rote Mannerchor (Red Men's Choir) drew either from the Northwest or the center. In addition to a Scandinavian Workingmen's Singing Society, there was at least one Bohemian group, and probably an American one. They advertised their meetings, rehearsals, picnics, and concerts in the anarchist press, only irregularly in the bourgeois press.

Their performances were an integral part of socialist festivals. Workingmen's singing societies rejected the bourgeois pretensions of the ethnic Gesangvereine; originally social and fraternal, they became politicized in the 1870s and survived well into the twentieth century.[8] Their concerts were, aside from the radical press itself, the main conduit through which socialist poetry reached its intended audience. In a recent dissertation,

Carol Poore argued that the gesangsvereine had two explicit goals. The first "was that of enlightenment, to expose social contradictions and to invest the working class singers and their audiences with a sense of their just rights." The second goal sought to cultivate a specifically socialist aesthetic.[9]

In Germany, Gerhard Ritter has noted, "communal singing was part of the standard programs at many events, ranging from local gatherings to the annual social democratic convention, which after 1875 usually ended with the singing of the 'Workers' Marseillaise.'" In Chicago, as in Germany, "the function of the workers' songs lay not only in strengthening feelings of solidarity, satisfying emotional needs and expressing a protest against oppression; it also confidently proclaimed the certainty of victory. This purpose was served by militant and revolutionary songs often set to well-known patriotic tunes."[10]

The titles and lyrics of the songs in Chicago confirm Ritter's argument. The Commune celebration featured an original song, "Der Volker Frei-heitssturm," in 1882; twenty "unwashed musicians" sang another original piece, "Arbeit und der Arbeiter," at a rally in 1885. Carol Poore's survey of the musical archives of New York City's largest socialist singing socie-ties found the scores to 375 songs "including folk songs and about 50 humorous songs. Of the total, about 20 percent are political." *Die Freie Sänger*, a collection of the songs used by workingmen's choral societies in Germany, had about the same mix.[11] The following titles can be gleaned from accounts of Chicago's socialist festivals: "The Song of the Flag," "The March of Liberty," "The Seventh of May Song," "Home, Sweet Home," "The Federal Song," "The Last War," "The Huntsman's Plea-sure," "The Internationale," "The Marseillaise," and one described as "the workingmen's song, 'Pray and Work.'" Yet the size of that sample precludes rigorous comparison.

If that sample overrepresents German songs, Chicago's Germans had no monopoly on lyricism. Josef Pecka and Norbert Zoula, from *Budouc-nost*, wrote "a few revolutionary songs" that were "vigorous and clear." Pecka's *Sebrane basne* (Collected songs), published posthumously by his comrades, ran some ninety-two pages and the songs have been described by one historian as "the revolutionary rhapsodies of the down-trodden proletariat."[12] Marcus Thrane wrote songs in both Danish and Norwegian. In addition to Morgan's impromptu songs, W. B. Creech, "the socialist songster" or "the untamed troubadour," enter-tained English-speaking audiences; and according to Captain Schaack, "one Dr. McIntosh could always be depended on for grinding out any quantity . . . of doggerel for any occasion."[13]

The cacaphony of lyrics, sung in as many as six languages, must have been bizarre. The *Tribune* described it that way, noting that "those who couldn't sing the French words of the hymn swelled the chorus by humming inharmoniously." Yet it was the politics of the lyrics that distinguished those socialist singers from their bourgeois counterparts. The "political songs of the workingmen's choral societies were to be the battle hymns of the class-conscious workers' army; the choirs were to be the 'trail blazers and pioneers of the artistic cultural era that [would] accompany the advent of socialism.'"[14]

THEATER GROUPS

In addition to an original song, the program for the eleventh anniversary of the Paris Commune also featured the premiere of a four-act play, *Die Nihilisten* (The nihilists), written especially for the festival. Parts of its first act had been published in *Die Fackel* before the opening, and the following week the same paper proudly headlined the "Tremendous Success of 'The Nihilists!' The Commune Celebration a Genuine Peoples' Festival." "Indeed," remarked *Die Arbeiter-Zeitung*, "Chicago's socialists can look with pride at this great success."[15]

"Based on historical sources," the play memorialized the assassination of Czar Alexander I. It was written by Chicagoans, performed by Chicagoans, for an audience of Chicagoans. In the first act the nihilists are printing broadsides and discussing Russia's future after her liberation from Czarist tyranny. In the second act, the military and aristocracy have gathered to plan the suppression of the conspirators. The third act was destined to be prophetic for in it the nihilists have been arrested, their leaflets and printing press confiscated, and they await trial. Accused of treason, they address the court not only to accuse their accusers, but use the courtroom to explain how social injustice drove them to nihilism and assassination. In the final act the condemned, who are on their way to exile in Siberia, are rescued by armed comrades who announce the death of the hated czar.[16]

Repeated performances of *Die Nihilisten* were intended to serve several functions. "The first was didactic, to transmit historical information and to educate the audience about the nihilist movement." Ads described it as "a true illustration of the terrible struggle of our brave comrades in

Russia." The audience was then invited to compare its own goals with those on stage. Finally, the play was revolutionary and international political statement. While not great literature, this was compelling theater. What we know about its casting and staging suggests that the director sought community participation. Two of the roles were played by August Spies and Oskar Neebe, who would ironically recreate their roles four years later, in front of a real judge and a real jury. Women had major parts, especially in the court scenes before the czarist court, and members of the Lehr- und Wehr-Verein played the armed rescuers in the fourth act. This was most probably an amateur production.[17]

The anarchists's repertoire contained other works. In 1878 Gustav Lyser published a satire of the Hewitt Committee hearings on the current depression. The sketch, about the "Congress for the Muddling Up of the Labor Question," was subtitled "A Comedy at the Expense of the Proletariat," and featured an allusive dialogue between the "president of the investigating committee, whose business it is to appear half-witted," and an idealized Labor Leader, who champions the true interests of the people. It remains, as its translators have argued, "a forgotten piece of working-class literature," yet "it is impossible to establish whether Lyser's play was actually performed."[18] There were other, but unoriginal pieces. The Sylvesterfest [New Year's Eve Festival] in 1879 saw a two-act comedy, *Press-Prozesse, or The Daughter of the Public Prosecutor*. The 1883 Communefeier featured *Die Tochter des Proletariat;* a dramatic entertainment produced "the melodrama 'A Cross Wife'"; another that year saw "The Songs of the Musician"; and one in 1884 included the performance of "The Glove," described as "A Burlesque after Schiller." The 1885 Communefest included the "production of the Grand Play 'Labor and Capital' by Isenstein's Dramatic Troupe," and "the performance of a play entitled 'The Rich and the Poor: or Life on the Streets of New York City.'"[19]

Drama was not alien to the city's working class and encores of *Die Nihilisten* marked the process by which working-class theater came to Chicago. Indeed the *Arbeiter-Zeitung,* like the *Tribune* and the *Illinois Staats-Zeitung,* had a regular column that reviewed the offerings of the downtown theaters, and at least once *Der Vorbote* addressed the relationship between the socialists and the theater. In 1879 *Die Arbeiter-Zeitung* advertised the "Sozial-Dramatischer Verein": the SLP's membership was invited to try out for the cast of a two-act comedy [Lustspiel] to be performed at that years' Sylvesterfest. Of seven cast members, six can be identified as members of the SLP; the seventh, a Fraulein, may have been a party member's daughter or sister.[20]

In December 1879, the "Working Peoples' Dramatic Association," "composed of men and women who earn[ed] their living by some productive labor," proposed a cooperative theater "that is, after all salaries and expenses have been paid, 50 percent of the profits will be set aside for the purpose of furthering the objects of this Association, and 50 percent will be divided among the stockholders," who were to be "sober, moral and industrious" people. The prospectus proclaimed "the object of this Association shall be to present upon the stage plays, and operas that shall tend to elevate, educate, and advance the interests of the producing classes, and to carry on the agitation of the labor question through printed songs, poetry, and such other means consistent with the dramatic profession."[21]

Despite that promise, working-class theater in Chicago never enjoyed permanent organization before Haymarket. The German "Sozial-Dramatischer Verein" may have lasted until 1882; the English "Dramatic Association" for barely a year. However noble, the groups were not solvent. In 1884 and bolstered by the ongoing success of *Die Nihilisten*, one IWPA group was again reported "forming to start a theatrical society." Four years later, in September 1888, *Die Arbeiter-Zeitung* announced that "the dramatic club, [Die] Arbeiter Bühne, will open its third season . . . for the benefit of the Sunday schools of the Workingmen's Progressive Unions of the Northwestside."[22]

Proletarian theater was never the exclusive property of the German community. Amateur theater appeared in most ethnic neighborhoods at about the same time; later, when the immigrant community could support a professional theater, the working class began to set up their own dramatic groups. As early as 1866 Marcus Thrane organized a troupe that performed Norwegian, Danish, French, and German comedies, as well as several plays written by Thrane himself. "Even here his concern with social justice found expression, particularly in a later play— his best known—*Konspirationen*, which was based on the Haymarket Riot of 1886." Thrane's troupe generated enough interest to later found the Norske Dramatisk Forening. "For a few years this group of amateurs . . . brought to the American West an echo of the European theater. In fact, the world premiere of Ibsen's 'The Ghosts' took place in Chicago, in 1883," when it was still banned in Scandinavia.[23]

Bohemian amateur theatricals in Chicago date from 1863; by the late seventies, Czech workers had developed their own dramatic societies. There were at least two in the eighties: in 1880 the president of the "Tyl Dramatic Society" was an active member of the SLP's Bohemian section, and in 1885 Anton Hradecny, *Lampcka*'s editor, played the lead in a troupe founded by another party member. Bohemian audiences saw melodramas (*Orphan of the Wood*), classics (*Hamlet*), and political pieces (*Celebrated Cause*); and in 1883 they watched the Czech premiere of *Die Nihilisten*.[24] In 1882, *Skandinaven* announced that "the Danish community has finally agreed that its much discussed theatre, Folke Theatret [Peoples' Theatre] will be officially opened this week. The stock company attached to the theatre will produce plays by Ibsen, some German and English productions, and they will also rehearse a great many light operas." Given both custom and the Danish colony's size, Folke Theatret probably operated as a pan-Scandinavian troupe, performing in both Danish and Norwegian. In contrast, theatre for English-speaking Chicagoans had already been commodified as minstrel shows, melodramas, and musicales. When the Trades Council proved unwilling to invest in a cooperative theatre in 1879, there was not enough interest to sustain the Working Peoples' Dramatic Association.[25]

Nineteenth-century proletarian theatre seems pale compared to its twentieth-century offspring, but much of its experience has been subsumed as "immigrant theatre" without regard to its class foundation or political intent. Yet two historians of the Finnish-American theatre have convincingly argued that "working class immigrant theatre . . . must be understood as a significant part of Finnish-American [radical] activity." It was not unique to Finns. In Germany, workers' dramatic clubs, singing societies, and Bildungsvereine served as covers for political discussion and organizing during the period of the antisocialist laws.[26] In Chicago, during those same years, those organizations were always above ground. In the Arbeiter Bühne and its predecessors, Chicagoans enjoyed a workers' theater, with plays written by workers, acted and staged by workers, for audiences of workers.

DANCES AND STIFTUNGSFESTE

The fourth and last pages of *Die Arbeiter-Zeitung* and *The Alarm* carried ads for socialist dances and citywide festivals. In November 1884, *The Alarm* advertised no less than five, sponsored by the Cigar Makers' Progressive Union, the Carpenters and Joiners' Union, the Metalworkers'

Union, the Lehr- und Wehr-Verein Mutual Aid Society, and the IWPA itself. These citywide events drew upon the combined membership of the IWPA's groups, the Central Labor Union, and the movement's sympathetic following. Dances could celebrate any kind of occasion: the Fourth of July, Christmas, Maifest, Sylvesterfest, Mardi Gras; or important anniversaries like the death of Marx, Lassalle, or Tom Paine.[27]

These were eagerly anticipated opportunities to flee a home or boardinghouse, to dress up, to take the children, to see friends, to hear an orchestra or choir, and to dance until late into the night. Socialist dances were not unique to Chicago. Gerhard Ritter has described them in Imperial Germany, where evening entertainments

> were intended to fulfill the need of the worker [and his family] to escape from the burdens of everyday life, to find social contact and enjoyment, while strengthening the feelings of solidarity [within the movement]. They were carefully prepared, with lectures, choral singing, poetry readings, tableaux and short plays, occasionally with gymnastic displays, almost always ending in a grand ball. They had considerable publicity value which helped to attract workers still outside the organization; and at the same time they made a financial profit.

What was unique about the dances and balls in Chicago were the multiethnic dancers and dances: "Every variety of step might have been witnessed yesterday [night]. The 'Bohemian dip,' the 'German lunge,' the 'Austrian kick,' the 'Polish ramp' [sic] and the 'Scandinavian trot.' All these countries seemed to be represented, but it is safe to say that the native-born American, the Irishman and the Englishman were conspicuous by their absence."[28]

Another standard occasion for socializing was the *Stiftungsfest* (anniversary festival) held on the anniversary of the group's formation. These became annual balls: in 1884 the Cigarmakers held their second, the Metalworkers their third, the LWV their fifth, the German Typographical Union their twelfth. After studying similar events in Germany, Klaus Tenfelde has argued that "the annual foundation celebrations adopted from bourgeois club culture, which almost all workers' associations solemnly observed, were most important in helping to bind the members together and present themselves to the outside world." In Chicago the solemnity of those occasions may have been lost. *Die Arbeiter-Zeitung* anticipated one this way: "The Southside group celebrates . . . its foundation festival. The program includes speeches and song. The comrades

. . . are a jolly crowd and therefore we may expect a very enjoyable evening."[29]

Where dances and balls were citywide events, Stiftungsfeste were smaller, local ones. "The Socialist Club of the Southwestside held a pleasant meeting combined with dancing. The main points were serious and humorous lectures and plays of every kind. The Socialistic Sangerbund of the Southwestside did its full share. It seems that there exists no more fun and enjoyment anywhere than among the socialists as they only separated in the best of spirits early in the morning." While it is difficult to penetrate these events, the evidence supports three conclusions. First, they were frequent. There were twenty-six groups in Chicago, and at least one Stiftungsfest each month, often two. Second, these were small events held in the group's neighborhood halls: attendance ranged between 200 and 300. Gruppe Freiheit, for example, "held a festival . . . and realized the sum of $30 for the benefit of *The Alarm*." Since the price of admission had been announced at fifteen cents, we can calculate a turnout of at least 200 paying celebrants. Third, these festivals proved engaging and fun: they frequently lasted well into the morning hours, and it is rare to find socialists anywhere described as "a jolly crowd."[30]

Some festivals were more elaborate than others. *Die Fackel* reported in March 1884 that the members of one club had formed a theatrical society. And the programs for Gruppe Vorwaerts' Mardi-Gras, the "long-awaited Maskfestival," included a grand procession and a six-part tableaux vivant. *Die Fackel* announced the program this way:

First scene: Prince Carnival with his retinue on a carousel tour.
Second scene: Our Earth—and she is still moving.
Third scene: Deutschland, Deutschland, Uber alles!
Fourth scene: France, Allons enfants de la Patrie!
Fifth scene: Russia, I played with Scepter, crowns and stamps, now my people enjoy throwing bombs.
Sixth scene: England, God save the Queen and John Brown. After [the tableaux], the Ball!

If those "living scenes" aren't particularly vivid, if the humor seems lost on us, we should note the internationality of both the festival and audience. A Stiftungsfest was not a chore, but the celebration of the group's formation and continuing existence.[31]

The receipts of these smaller festivals provided sickness and death benefits. Gruppe Südseite reported, for example, that "a collection was taken up for the benefit of a sick comrade and also for the family of Stellmacher [in Vienna], which totalled $11.60. Besides $5.00 was allowed from the treasury for the benefit of a comrade's family which is in great need. It was resolved to hold an evening entertainment in the near future, combined with the bestowing names upon children." That last clause suggests something of the depth of both the culture and community created by the anarchist movement.[32]

In 1885, an ad for yet another "Grand Entertainment and Ball with Recitations arranged by the Second Company of the Lehr- und Wehr-Verein" promised "an anarchist christening of a little child." Beyond those announcements, I found three other reports of "anarchistic christenings": a brief mention of a double ceremony held by Gruppe Südseite, a rite for four children on the Southwest side, and this description of "einer dreifachen Kindertaufe" (a three-fold christening) of "neuen Weltbürgern" (world citizens) in November of 1883:

> Then the christening of the three children was performed in a socialist manner. These were the children of comrades Kaiser, Kiesling, and Dannenberg. Our old and trusted comrade Rabusch performed the christening and delivered a very beautiful and appropriate speech. Then he said: "I give you the name Carl Marx Kaiser, you the name Heinrich Ferdinand Kiesling, you the name Martha Sophia Dannenberg." After the christening there were more socialistic songs and poems, particularly by the young Gesangverein of the Southwestside; the festival was magnificent.[33]

That ceremony resembled more conventional ones. An "old and trusted comrade," not a cleric, performed the rite; he did so in Sachse's Hall, a saloon with meeting rooms, not in a church; and yet the ceremony was public, not in front of a congregation or parish, but in front of the parents' comrades. Pietist rituals were translated into a proletarian and secularist form.[34]

PICNICS

The picnic outing, a family and community affair, was a favorite occasion for the nineteenth-century labor movement. The SLP adopted the tradition in the 1870s and the anarchists continued to use it. *The Socialist* advertised "A Grand Picnic Combined with [a] Flag Dedication and Procession [for] all Military Organizations, Trades Unions and other Societies, arranged by the JaegerVerein," in June 1879. Later that month

3,000 people attended what Police Captain Schaack described as "a monster picnic" to fund an English-language paper. The SLP organized a three-day picnic to celebrate the Fourth of July. Peter McGuire and Ira Steward were the guest speakers, the year before George McNeill had come from Boston. In September, yet another picnic was the occasion for announcing *The Socialist*'s death.[35]

One picnic, in June 1879, turned into a melee. The Bohemian Sharpshooters, a working-class militia, had reserved Silver Leaf Grove, on the city's Southwest side, for a day-long picnic. By the time the band started to play for dancing, the grove had been invaded by "Irish hooligans." Armed and uniformed Sharpshooters attempted to remove the Irish, stones were thrown, and the Sharpshooters fired into the Irish after a Bohemian child was struck in the face by a rock. Police Officers Lacy and Hogan, "present at the picnic in citizen's clothes," arrested twenty-three of the Sharpshooters: only two were later convicted of assault. The LWV had scheduled another picnic that afternoon, and some Chicagoans feared the armed Germans might attempt to free their Bohemian comrades. Those fears proved groundless, but survived.[36] Both melee and fears reveal, as early as 1879, not just the hostility between Bohemians and Irish, but also the fearful relationship between the police and socialists.[37]

Even picnics could be elaborate. The program for the Volksfest on the Fourth of July 1879 included an appearance by the just-bailed Sharpshooters, a procession, and a concert by an orchestra and the movement's own Gesangvereine. According to the *Arbeiter-Zeitung*, "Last year's picnic is still in the memory of the people, and no doubt this year's picnic will be a great success." "The Great Picnic of the United Armed Organization is approaching," the same paper announced in June 1880, "a wonderful program is expected . . . Nature herself will decorate the park in full bloom. There will be no dearth of music and dance[:] the Lehr- und Wehr-Verein's excellent band is going to perform some beautiful pieces." *Die Arbeiter-Zeitung* advertised a "Great Excursion of the Armed Organizations of Chicago" on 1 August 1880. They left by train at 8:30 A.M. and were welcomed "by the clubs and workingmen of Milwaukee" with a concert that featured a local orchestra, the LWV band, and the massed voices of both cities' singing societies. The afternoon was taken up with a parade, the "grand picnic," exhibitions of military drill, and speeches in German, Bohemian; and English; the evening was devoted to a "summer night's festival and ball."[38]

We know more about anarchist picnicking during 1885. In May, the

CLU arranged "A Grand Picnic" combined with "a Summer Night's Festival"; the next month *The Alarm* advertised the "Fifth [annual] Picnic arranged by the Socialistic Mannerchoir of the Northside." An outing sponsored by the IWPA in July drew a crowd estimated between 2,000 and 3,000; later that month 1,000 people trekked to Indiana for the day. On Sunday, 5 September 1885, the anarchists called for a procession from Chicago, led by "fifty young girls with a banner above them reading 'American Corps,'" to Ogden's Grove, "where from three to four thousand people assembled." Again in September, to cap off the summer, *The Alarm* advertised another "Grand Excursion to Sheffield, Indiana."[39]

During the Haymarket Trial, the prosecution charged that these innocent family outings covered agitation and conspiracy. Schaack's book *Anarchy and Anarchists* has several pages of drawings of those picnics; rendered by an artist who was not an eyewitness, after the fact, and in the employ of the police, they are perhaps our only means to penetrate the (otherwise) idyllic image. One drawing depicts an anarchist selling books on explosives, another set of drawings show speeches, "getting inspiration"—from a beer-keg, and "experimenting with dynamite." Trial testimony supported the last charge.[40]

In July 1885 the Lehr- und Wehr-Verein "arranged a bivouac and prize shooting on the 16th of August in North Chicago Sharpshooters' Park." Both ad and event seem innocent, but the forces of order saw another opportunity for the forces of anarchy to drill with their weapons. Back in 1878, one socialist picnic had been "fancied by many nervous men and women" as "the signal for a Chicago imitation of the Sicilian vespers." "Captain Grund, of the Fourth Precinct, supplied the picnickers with a squad of twenty men under Lieutenant Baus and a sergeant to preserve order." Yet every policeman in the city was called to duty; "the incoming men were all retained in the stations, and the Lake Street squad, which usually gets the day off, reported." Even that was judged inadequate: the First and Second regiments of the Illinois National Guard were called to their armories for the day of the picnic. Nothing untoward happened.[41]

PARADES AND PROCESSIONS

Because its picnic sites were located outside the city limits, perhaps only for atmosphere, but also away from the eyes of the police, the movement arranged processions to move from a central rallying point (usually Market Square) to the picnic grounds. "With the smell of gin and beer, with blood-red flags and redder noses, and with banners inscribed with revolutionary mottoes, the anarchists inaugurated their grand parade and picnic yesterday." These were pageants, an opportunity to display banners, flags, wagon-drawn tableaux, transparencies, the armed might of the organized working class, and the size of the movement itself.[42]

The *Tribune* described one parade in April 1879 as "A Menace, Under the Thin Disguise of a Protest": "Never before in the history of civilized communities did 400 men, armed with breech-loading rifles and fixed bayonets, parade the peaceful streets of a great city in order, as they express it, 'to show the legislature and the people of Chicago What They Can Do!'" The next day the *Inter Ocean* asked in its headlines "What Does It Mean?" and the *Tribune* seemingly answered, "The parade of yesterday was a threat." It was aimed first, by the printers, at a new iron-clad oath that forbade membership in the union. The second protest was directed at some new amendments to the state's Militia Act. Two months earlier, the Illinois Assembly became alarmed by the existence of working-class paramilitary organizations, and investigated "the possibility of a dangerous Communistic outbreak in Chicago." In April, the Military Code was amended to forbid "any body of men" to "associate themselves together as a military company or organization, or to drill or parade with arms in any city . . . without the license of the Governor." That parade protested the bill's passage, two others would challenge its constitutionality.[43]

On 2 July 1879, Captain John Bielefeldt and ten members of the LWV were arrested as they drilled for the SLP's Fourth of July parade. The charges against the ten were dropped and a test case acquitted Bielefeldt on the grounds that the amendments were unconstitutional. The socialists celebrated with another parade: "the brass band of the LWV at the head . . ., followed by the [Irish] Labor Guard; then the grim-faced Bohemian Sharpshooters, who carried empty rifles; next the well-dressed [Jaeger Verein] with breech and muzzle-loaders; then the LWV in all its glory . . . finally came the furniture workers, with a band in its vanguard." The *Tribune* was obsessed with the marchers' numbers: "Labor Guards, 10; Bohemian Sharpshooters, 36; Jaeger-Verein, 116; Lehr und Wehr Verein, 236. Following these were the German carpenters', bricklayers', and shoemakers' Unions; the French section of the Socialist[ic Labor] Party, and a few representatives of the other sections." "Only 286 rifles" were displayed, surely there were more.[44] On 14 September 1879, Major Herman Presser, "riding on horseback, and in command" of about 400 men "armed with rifles and Presser with a cavalry sword," again tested the state law. Presser was arrested, convicted, and fined. His appeal to the United States Supreme Court took seven years; in January 1886, the court upheld both the conviction and law.[45]

That law banned armed parades, not parades as such. On 2 July 1880, the *Tribune* reported that the LWV had applied to the governor for permission to march on the 5th of July. He apparently gave it, for the *Arbeiter-Zeitung* boasted that "the military organizations marched out this morning with weapons and with colors flying, as previously announced. The streets through which the parade moved were richly decorated with flags and bunting." Indeed, after 1876 the Fourth of July became a standard occasion for a socialist parade, as did the first Saturday in September in the 1880s.[46]

Anarchist pageants in the 1880s were more confrontational. In November 1884, the IWPA protested the hypocrisy of the governor's annual Thanksgiving message. In freezing drizzle, men, women, and children cheered the unfurling of the Black Flag, "the emblem of Hunger," and sarcastically declared their thanks. *The Alarm* reported that some 3,000 people had turned out, despite the weather; the *Tribune*'s reporter saw "more than a thousand." In April 1885, the new Board of Trade building, "the Temple of Mammon" according to the anarchists, was opened with a gala celebration: The IWPA called for a counterdedication which "threatened a serenade and grand brick-throwing soiree." The crowd— "numbering perhaps 1,000" according to the *Inter Ocean*, more than 2,000 according to the police, 3,000 according to *The Alarm*—was deflected from their march by what the *Tribune* called "admirable police arrangements."[47]

These were not rag-tag marches but ordered and orderly processions. The *Tribune* described "the perfect order" of one; the equally hostile *Staats-Zeitung* judged another to have been "extremely peaceful." Each parade had an arrangements committee that appointed a chief marshal and his assistants, who were usually mounted on horseback; union flags or socialist banners identified many of the units. In August 1884, for example, the *Arbeiter-Zeitung* published a "Programm der Prozession" that organized the parade into divisions, told the marchers where to rally for each, and assigned them places within their designated units. When the *Times* reported on the April 1886 Eight Hour demonstration, it simply reproduced the procession order published in *Der Vorbote* or *The Alarm*.[48]

Friedrich Sorge recognized that these pageants would "frighten the philistines and politicians." A month before the Fourth of July processions in 1878 and in 1879 the *Tribune* headlined: "Fully Prepared—City Authorities Ready to Meet any Communistic Emergency," explaining there were "Fully 3,000 Well-Armed and Drilled Men on Hand for Action, Behind This is the Full Strength of Law-Abiding Citizens." Gun clubs volunteered their services to the sheriff and "the principal business-men" subscribed to equip 500 men with Springfield rifles. The Citizens' Association and "the military men . . . believe emphatically in eternal vigilance." The militia practiced its street-riot drill nearby as the IWPA marched on Thanksgiving Day 1884, and again when they protested the opening of the Board of Trade the next year.[49]

DIE COMMUNE FEIERN

The anniversary of the Paris Commune was celebrated as "The Dawn of Liberty" by Chicago socialists each March from 1872 through 1909. The fact that Chicago's multiethnic working class commemorated the Com-mune for thirty-seven years is extraordinary; yet it has been overlooked by too many historians.[50]

The history of Chicago's Communefeier is as fascinating as the festival itself. Many of the city's Germans eagerly awaited news of the Franco-Prussian War of 1870–71 and planned to celebrate the first major battle; only *Der Deutsche Arbeiter* denounced the rampant chauvinism. When news of that victory finally arrived, on 5 August 1870, about 2,000 people "gave vent to their feelings by thunderous applause." The *Illinois Staats-Zeitung* called the occasion a "glorious victory . . . the most glorious feat of arms recorded in modern history." A month later, when the news of the fall of Paris and the armistice reached Chicago, there was a second celebration and the *Staats-Zeitung* described a second patriotic outburst: "the word enthusiasm is only a weak description." In April and May 1871, the German community gathered for two more "peace celebra-tions." The program in Crosby's Opera House included the performance of singing societies, a "Jubilation Overture," and a lebende bilder which featured "the Goddess of Peace" who recited "a long, somewhat in-volved poem." At the end of May the German community, its Gesang-vereine, societies and leaders, paraded through Chicago's streets in another celebration of peace.[51]

Chicago's working class arranged its own commemoration in 1872; not of the military victory at Sedan (in August), not of the end of the war (in May), but of "the rising of the workingmen of Paris" in March. Where the 1871 peace celebration had been addressed by six men who were prominent Germans, the 1872 workingmen's festival featured five speakers, in three languages, all of whom were proletarian. They gathered with three declared objects: "the celebration of the anniversary of the establishment of Communism, the contradiction of the lies [about the Commune] circulated by the press, and to become acquainted with their fellow workingmen." The meeting was addressed in German, English, and Norwegian before turning to dancing. The *Tribune* described an audience "of about 400 . . . composed solely of workingmen, well dressed and well-behaved." The First International arranged the first, the WPI, the WPUS, and the SLP continued the event, but after 1881 the festival belonged to the anarchists. By 1876 the bourgeois press noticed the celebrations; three years later they moved to control what they perceived as the increasingly threatening nature of the Commune-ists and their festivals.[52]

Celebrated on March 18, the festival was an international commemoration of the Paris Commune of 1871 and the Revolutions of 1848. In 1875, "crayon drawings of Ferdinand Lassalle and General Blanqui" adorned the stage; the next year featured a living tableau of General Dombrowsky's death. In 1879, Gabrienne Davoust, a French-born veteran of the Commune, and Dr. Ernst Schmidt, a German Forty Eighter, were the featured speakers as "one hundred thousand people [came to] celebrate the anniversary of the first efforts for labor's emancipation." In 1880 English-born Thomas J. Morgan set "forth the objects and aims of the Paris[-ian] workingmen in their remarkable struggle for industrial freedom." The ads for the thirteenth anniversary explained that "forty thousand . . . were slaughtered in the streets of Paris for having dared to revolt against their capitalistic masters. American workmen should give honor to those who gave their lives that labor might be free." By 1884, the IWPA's Czech groups in Chicago were sponsoring "a Paris Communal"; the next year their festival attracted Bohemian trade union delegations. And in 1886, Albert Parsons, a native-born American of Puritan stock, had to explain that ill-health had forced "Madame Delescluz[e] . . . a participant in the Paris Commune," to cancel her appearance.[53]

What did the Communefeier look like? *Der Vorbote* described the festival in 1878: "After the excellent performances of concert pieces by the orchestra and the two singing societies, . . . tumultuous applause greeted [the speaker,] party comrade Paul Grottkau." Indeed, "the pattern of the celebration of the Day of the Commune was the same in 1908 as it was twenty-five years earlier: the central political speech (or play or tableaux vivant) was framed by traditional forms of the community's expressive and performative abilities: in music (orchestra, choir), recitation (poetry, song, instrument), acting (drama, comedy, tableaux vivant), gymnastics." The festivals became more elaborate each year.[54]

In the early seventies, they drew audiences of less than 1,000. In 1875, 2,000 were expected but a snowstorm kept all but 500 away. The crowds dramatically increased by the end of the decade, as the SLP used the festival to set off its spring election campaigns. Thus the 1879 commemoration, which was free to use the city's largest public hall, drew the largest audience. The always hostile *Tribune* reported "the main floor, the galleries, the platforms and stands,—in fact every foot of available space was covered with a dense mass of humanity; even the [proverbial] rafters under the roof were occupied." The *Times* estimated the attendance somewhere between 20,000 and 25,000 people; a bourgeois German paper, *Der Westen*, set it at 30,000; the *Tribune* between 30,000 and 40,000; and *The Socialist* ecstatically claimed 80,000 to 100,000 participants in the two-day affair. The program that night was to have featured an orchestra, acrobats from the Turnvereine, tableaux, beer, singing, and an exhibition of military drill in addition to a number of addresses, all before "the grand ball." But the building got so crowded that the program had to be curtailed: "It was not until an early hour in the morning could sufficient space be obtained to give to the celebrants to have a decent dance, which was the principal object for which they had come." Because the forces of order distrusted the socialists' willingness to maintain order, they garrisoned a National Guard regiment next to the Exposition Building. Their presence was noted and denounced in an angry letter to *The Socialist*. And the *Tribune*, which had called for a regiment whenever the communists met, questioned the ease with which they had rented and used the building.[55]

Banned thereafter from the largest public halls in the city, the movement made do with smaller, private halls. At the same time, a split within the SLP over strategy and another economic slump reduced the audiences. Thus the 1880 festival was held in Vorwaerts Turnhalle with a capacity of 3,000; the next year it fit in Greenebaum's Hall which only held about 1,500. The tenth anniversary (in 1882) featured an original song and an original play to an audience of more than 2,000. In February 1885, *Der Vorbote* published a letter complaining that "last year one [hall] wasn't big enough." Instead the IWPA scheduled two festivals in the Northside and Westside turnhalles. There were different programs for each and the advertisements in the *Daily News* and *Die*

Arbeiter-Zeitung pointedly suggested "Americans will prefer the Northside Turner Hall."[56]

Chicago's IWPA celebrated the fifteenth anniversary only six weeks before Haymarket. "The spacious hall presented an unwonted scene with its brilliant lights, crimson banners, beautiful mottoes and vast throng of revolutionary workmen and their wives and children," all "bent on doing honor to the martyrs to Liberty, Equality, and Fraternity," according to *The Alarm*. The program for the evening "consisted of a theatrical performance, speeches, singing, music and dancing." Madame Delescluze had to cancel, but Albert Parsons "spoke briefly upon the Paris Commune." He concluded by reading "a poem written by Mrs. Mary Miller, of the American group, when the band struck up the Marseillaise hymn and the enthusiastic audience joined in the refrain, 'Vive la Commune!' The floor was then cleared, the orchestra took up its position . . . and to the strains of soft and enchanting music, all entered heartily into the joys of the dance and the festivities of the hour until early morn."[57]

Chicago's anarchists were not alone in their celebrations. In New York City, the Société des Refugees de la Commune held a banquet and ball on March 18; across the Atlantic, European socialists held similar celebrations. In Britain, an international collection of anarchists in London, and the socialists gathered around H. M. Hyndman and William Morris, held annual commemorations. Starting in 1880, with the amnesty of the Communards, French socialists feted the Commune at the Mur des Fédérés. And in Germany, facing Bismarck's anti-socialist laws, their commemorations were profoundly political. While its bourgeoisie patriotically celebrated the military victory at Sedan, the German working class remembered the rising of Paris.[58] Chicago's festival began in 1872, with the first anniversary. Although it became a tradition for immigrants, Chicago's Commune festival was not an imported or immigrant tradition.

It is too easy to see Chicago's Communefeier as a German event. The audiences may well have been heavily German, but so was the city's population, and even this chapter tends to perpetuate that error with its overreliance on German sources. Yet from their beginning Chicago's Commune celebrations were multinational, multiethnic, multilingual affairs. The first anniversary was addressed by five speakers: three in German, one each in English and Norwegian. In subsequent years there were French and Irish speakers. Czech socialists initially sent delegations from their unions; by 1885 they sponsored their own "Paris Communal."

The most striking feature of contemporary accounts of these festivals is the emphasis they placed on the multiethnic character of the audiences. The *Times*, for example, listed "a lot of Poles, Bohemians, Germans, Hungarians, Laplanders [?], Siberians [?], Frenchmen and here and there an Irishmen" [sic]; the *Tribune* described that same audience as "a regular German-Scandinavian-Bohemian-American crowd, . . . a howling, whooping mob . . . such as only a Socialistic community could bring out or would tolerate."[59]

Precisely. In Chicago from 1872 to 1886, a socialist movement had organized within a multiethnic working class. Their annual commemorations of the Paris Commune tapped the resources of a movement culture that was alive and growing within the city's working class. With songs, plays, speeches, and dances, workers in nineteenth-century Chicago, seized upon the Commune as a landmark in the struggle for a genuinely democratic society.

MOVEMENT CULTURE

These events were cheap, respectable, and family oriented. Admission to a dance or festival never cost more than twenty-five cents; and was invariably quoted "For Lady and Gentleman." Socialist parades were orderly; indeed the incredulous *Inter Ocean* reported in 1878, "the people were conspicuous for their quiet and inoffensive bearing, and seemed, in truth, what they were, sober mechanics out with their families for a gala day." After the scare in 1879, anarchist picnics became commonplace and unremarkable. The *Herald* noted, "They enjoyed themselves much as any other band of picnickers largely composed of foreigners would have done, and went home in beery good nature."[60]

At the simplest level dances, festivals, and picnics served as fund-raising events with many organized to support the socialist press. The revenue from a June 1878 picnic was "used in starting the English Socialist paper, with an editor-in-chief whose wages are to be $5 a week and an occasional benefit picnic to carry him through." In December 1885 *The Alarm* advertised a

Grand Christmas Festival
with Great Raffle of Presents
Concert, Theatre and Ball
at
Vorwaerts Turner Hall,

West 12th Street,
on
Saturday Evening, Dec 26 1885
Arranged for the Benefit of the Socialistic Press
Admission 25 cents a Person

There were other causes. Picnics also paid legal expenses: for the arrested Sharpshooters and LWV; to seat Frank Stauber in the city council; and after the Haymarket Riot, for the imprisoned Martyrs. An 1882 festival raised money for the socialist Sunday schools; Gruppe Freiheit's "Humorous Evening Entertainment" in April 1884 was arranged, according to the advertisements, "for the benefit of the arms fund." That same year the LWV held "a benefit performance [presumably of military drill] for a comrade who has been ill for two years." Widows and orphans deserved support, and dances, festivals, and picnics were proven fund-raising events. The revenue went to propaganda (keeping the radical press solvent during a depression), to arms for the workingman's militia, and for sickness and death benefits. Most of the money stayed in Chicago, but some went as far as Copenhagen, Berlin, or Vienna.[61]

These two institutions and four events barely sketch something best denoted as a "movement culture." These six elements encompass a community in which a worker could live, dance, sing, picnic, and parade after work and outside the workplace; a community that tried to serve its members from the christening of their children to their funerals, even caring for their survivors. With outdoor events in the summer, and with indoor events throughout the fall, winter, and spring, Chicago's social-revolutionaries enjoyed a secular and class culture they had created for themselves.[62] Following Herbert Gutman, by "culture" I mean something more than the anthropological sense of tools or resources inherited, acquired, and renewed by each generation. "Culture is used," anthropologist Sidney Mintz has argued, "and any analysis of its use immediately brings into view the arrangements of persons in societal groups for whom cultural forms confirm, reinforce, maintain, change, or deny particular arrangements of status, power and identity."[63] This culture was consciously created and used in that its symbols, forms, and rituals were deliberately selected and deployed.

These events were intended to be didactic and uplifting: working-class theatre was consciously didactic, and the Gesangvereine hoped to fill both singers and audiences with a feeling of solidarity and a sense of mission. Social events were designed to recruit and sustain the membership. Movement culture created a bond, a sense of tribal unity, which proved reinforcing and inspiring to the membership. It cemented the body of true believers and provided a sense of a closed-off, nurturing, insular world. That bond produced and reinforced by a sense of pride in craftsmanship—of socialist songs well sung, of plays well acted, of pageants well staged. Thus, movement culture was itself a social product, one produced by the interaction of a socialist intelligentsia—Antonio Gramsci called them "organic intellectuals"—and the movement's active membership.[64]

Socialist culture drew upon the diversity of the movement's membership. Sylvesterfest, Carnival, Maifest, and Weihnachtfest were traditional festivals put to socialist purposes. The basic unit for building a class movement in late nineteenth-century Chicago had to be the ethnic group. Singing societies and theater groups operated as separate ensembles, for language was a real obstacle but could be overcome. In parades at the end of the 1870s the SLP's sections marched in units organized by ethnicity. A mass demonstration or picnic, in which the preceding parade was ordered by ethnicity, would be addressed by multiple speakers. There were separate Commune festivals by 1885 for German, Czech, and English-speaking audiences. The IWPA conscientiously sought to mold a class experience out of fragmentation.

Ethnic diversity within the IWPA only masked underlying class and cultural similarities. For if competing ethnic groups shared the experiences of immigration, urbanization, industrialization, alienation, and radicalization, these immigrants also shared similar organizations. Club life, singing societies, theater groups, and festivals were common cultural institutions that served as a basis for community events. The Turner Societies, for example, were not simply German; Chicago also boasted a Scandinavian Turner Brotherhood and the Bohemian sokols.[65] As gymnastic societies dedicated to the physical condition of their citizen-members, these three organizations cooperated. With socialists and anarchists as members and officers, all three came to be regarded as the "hotbeds of socialism."[66]

For all its attention to dances and festivals, the socialist and anarchist press reveals little about the shop culture of the movement's membership. Yet it must have resembled the kind sketched in Samuel Gompers' autobiography: small shops that employed the bulk of the movement's membership and that accommodated, even fostered, craft traditions and working-group intimacy. There must have been a great deal of "daily intercourse" between "fellow-workmen"; as Gompers described, "shop talk was generally on serious subjects, but often it ran the gamut of our personal interests." With their names appearing in the city's papers, anarchists were known and recognized in their trades, and they must have capitalized on "the educational value of the little forum[s] existing in each shop." Gompers remembered, "we subscribed to several labor papers for the shop," explaining that "while the rest worked, one of our members would read to us perhaps for an hour at a time," and every issue of *The Alarm* asked its readers to "Pass this paper to a friend."[67]

Other than Parsons's account—he had been "discharged and blacklisted" and then dragged from the *Times*'s composing room in 1877 for his public speaking when "the men threatened to strike then and there on account of the way I had been treated"—the *Autobiographies* record little about socialist or union organization at the point of production. George Engel read his first copy of *Der Vorbote* while working in a wagon factory where he "got acquainted with a socialist"; Michael Schwab's employer "had a friend" who "furnished [him] with socialistic papers"; and "while working at my trade alongside my colleagues", Adolph Fischer "tried to convince [them] of my ideas". Shop culture remains largely unreported, except in rare instances. During a lakefront speech in August 1884, "Dynamite" Dusey was "harassed by another stairbuilder who had been fired for opposing J. P. Dusey's politics at the shop."[68]

Where the experience of work proved alienating, the intersection of ethnicity and radicalism, of working-class and movement cultures, lay in the organization and use of leisure time.[69] Culture remained the social space most open to agitation, a space once radicalized that could function as a reservoir for socialist values and traditions. The movement drew upon ethnic institutions and events. There was nothing radical or political about picnics or dances, dramatic or singing societies, festivals or parades: all were older than the socialist movement. Old traditions and symbols were reactivated, revitalized, and radicalized. The organization of processions by craft and trade, for example, seems to reflect the survival of craft and guild traditions. The *Tribune* described the arrangement of an 1878 parade:

The Furniture and Upholsterers' Unions, pictureframe makers and carpenters followed, marching in fours with their trade banners, an occasional red flag, and many of the Stars and Stripes. The cigarmakers, numbering at least 300 men, the Wood Carvers' Association, with banner, Carpenters' and Joiners' Consolidated Union, and other trade organizations marched by in good time.

They were followed by a wagon bearing the legend, "Social-Democratic Print-ing Association." Some typecases and a miniature press were on board, and four or five printers, in black aprons and flat caps, distributed Socialistic circu-lars, which, by a flight of fancy, were assumed to have been printed on the road.

While manifestations of craft pride, an artisan identification, appeared, there were other symbols and traditions. Again the *Tribune* on that same procession: "The second [wagon] was allegorical; very much so. There was a pasteboard castle and a lot of men standing around, one with a hammer, with which he made feints of striking at the turret-topped erection, supposed to represent aristocratic tyranny. The motto on the wagon was 'Down with Monopolies.'" This parade was interspersed with other wagons that "were not [?] extra-ordinary for their decorations. The most noticeable was the French, bearing the motto 'Liberty or Death,' and mounted by a group of individuals clad in the crimson colors of the Commune." Other wagons featured other tableaux: the German Peasants' War, the American Revolution, and "the victory of the agrarian law—the figure of Despotism lying prostrate under the foot of Liberty." Beyond the rhetoric, and through the eyes of unsympathetic reporters, castles and despots were juxtaposed with monopoly: alien (i.e., Euro-pean) symbols shared wagons and transparencies with American ones.[70]

Some slogans were traditional: "All for One, One for All," "United We Stand, Divided We Fall," "No Masters, No Slaves," and "All Happy, None Rich, None Poor." Others proved disturbing. "The only objection-able feature about the procession," reported the *Inter Ocean*, "was the profuse display of the red flag, the emblem of revolution and bloodshed in the eye of the public." The black flag, "the emblem of hunger," was not unfurled in Chicago until 1884; by then the ratio between the red flag and the Stars and Stripes had reversed. Those flags, with their slogans and craft symbols (including the arm and hammer), became another source of pride. When the Jaeger-Verein unfurled a new flag in 1878, it arranged a dedication ceremony, inviting "military organizations, trades unions and other societies." In 1880, when Chicago's socialists planned a demonstration with their Milwaukee comrades, *Die Arbeiter-Zeitung* asked if "the various clubs will appear with their flags." And the red flag that Lucy Parsons had sewn in 1885 went with Albert to his grave in 1887.[71]

Beyond adaptation, the movement invented some of its own institu-tions and traditions. The Lehr- und Wehr-Verein was one such innova-tion. The "armed self-defense group was a unique response to specific

Chicago conditions. On the one hand, the liberal American Laws of association allowed for a kind of armed organization unthinkable under European, and especially German, conditions. In addition the Verein was the logical response to the situation where Chicago's ruling class, through the use of the police [and militia], brutally suppressed workers' demands. In a raw expanding city with weak institutions or order, self-defense organizations seemed the appropriate answer."[72] Where other strikers were forced to fraternize with state militia, those in Chicago had their own, even if the LWV never saw combat.

Again it would be wrong to dwell upon the wholly German composition of those groups: the LWV and the Jaeger-Verein were German, but there was a French section of the LWV, and it marched alongside the Bohemian Sharpshooters, the (Irish) Fifth Ward Labor Guards, and the English-speaking International Rifles. The "workingman's militia," as *Der Vorbote* styled them in 1875, reflected the ethnic composition of the city's working class. In turn, the militia created its own institutions and traditions: their own uniforms, constitution, officers, maneuvers, discipline, and flags. They served as guards at picnics and as doorkeepers at festivals and meetings; they turned out for parades, especially on the Fourth of July, and conducted funeral processions for fallen comrades.[73]

Movement culture then might be best understood with Eric Hobsbawm's notion of "invented tradition." A political culture that had both ritual forms and a symbolic nature, movement culture "sought to inculcate certain values and norms of behaviour by establishing a sense of continuity with the past and an obligation to maintain such continuity" in the present. The annual celebration of the Commune was clearly an "invented tradition" because its continuity with the past was largely "factitious."[74] With the exceptions of Gabrienne Davoust, a survivor, E. B. Washburne, the American minister to Paris, and (perhaps) a few veterans of the Prussian army, contemporary Chicagoans had little direct knowledge of the rising in Paris. The Commune had to be explained to them. Thus before each anniversary the radical press printed eulogies on "Die Geschichte der Pariser Commune"; at least one speaker commented on its meaning and continuing relevance. Louise Michel had been invited to speak in 1882, but "her mother's serious illness prevented her from sailing." Instead, *Die Arbeiter-Zeitung* translated and serialized her *La Misère*; in 1885 it published Prosper Lissagaray's classic *History of the Commune of 1871*.[75]

From the 1870s those within the IWA, WPI, WPUS, SLP and IWPA embraced a socialist critique that recognized a class of workers who might confront and then end the exploitation of men by men. They tried to share that critique, its vision, and its values among those with whom they lived and worked. With songs and theater, at dances, festivals, picnics, and parades, they sought to subsume ethno-cultural conflicts with (or into) a class culture. By the time of Haymarket, the anarchists had got no further toward that goal than a movement culture. To argue that "almost all [of] their institutions were modelled after similar efforts in Germany" is to miss both the internationality and the creativity of the movement.[76] What Chicago's socialists and anarchists had accomplished, between 1872 and 1886, was the creation, within the city's working-class communities, of a distinctly working-class and socialist culture, with its own traditions.

Antonio Gramsci appreciated "the importance of the 'cultural aspect,' even in practical (collective) activity": "An historical act can only be performed by 'collective man,' and this presupposes the attainment of a 'cultural-social' unity through which a multiplicity of dispersed wills with heterogenous aims, are welded together with a single aim, on the basis of an equal and common conception of the world." While critical, Friedrich Sorge, for one, was impressed with what he heard and read from Chicago. "It is the undeniably meritorious accomplishment of the Chicago anarchists to have brought to this marvelous mixture of all nationalities and language a certain order, to have created affinity, and to have given the movement at that time unity and goals."[77]

Out of the ethno-cultural, linguistic, skill, gender, and craft divisions produced by rapid industrialization, the anarchists were forging a class solidarity. One way to understand that achievement is to approach it culturally. With a program of events that were public and visible, socialists and anarchists nurtured a culture that was confrontational and aggressive. Both movement and culture were self-conscious and class-conscious. Most importantly, that movement threatened to infect the larger working class.

Chapter Seven

BAKUNIN NEVER SLEPT
IN CHICAGO

If European anarchism is identified with Proudhon and Kropotkin, American anarchism with Josiah Warren and Benjamin Tucker, and immigrant anarchism with Emma Goldman and Alexander Berkman, then the membership of Chicago's IWPA was not anarchist. I resist the common designation of Parsons and his comrades as "anarchists" because I share Henry David's view that "the various doctrines associated with the Chicago movement resist almost entirely being pressed into one of the familiar categories of revolutionary theory." The label "anarchist" is an awkward fit on Chicago's social-revolutionaries for it was given, not chosen. While historians have described their movement as "syndicalist," "anarcho-syndicalist," and "anarcho-communist," it should not be approached with twentieth-century labels. Instead, we might assume that its culture, thought, and ideology were in a process of change and development.[1]

There are two conventional approaches to the ideology of Chicago's anarchist movement. The first has focused on the *Pittsburgh Manifesto* or on a set of editorials culled from *The Alarm*. The second approach has taken *The Autobiographies of the Haymarket Martyrs* or Parsons's posthumous *Anarchism: Its Philosophy and Scientific Basis* as its *texte de explication*. Both approaches can be extensively criticized. First, *The Alarm* had one of the shortest lifetimes of all Chicago's anarchist papers. Its editorials appeared at the movement's height without revealing any of its ideological development: the period is simply too short. Second, it is difficult to use *The Alarm* for a discussion of ideology because the IWPA exercised very little control over its editorial policy. According to Parsons, "I not only did not write 'most of the articles,' but wrote comparatively few of them."[2] Third, editorials and manifestoes were produced by ideologues, the movement's intellectual elite, and their study presumes a unity between leadership and membership that ought instead to be investigated. Finally, one suspects that Parsons and *The Alarm* have been used so extensively precisely because they appeared in English. Further use would only perpetuate that convenience, and continue to ignore the movement's linguistic and ethnic diversity.[3]

THE PROPRIETY OF THE "ANARCHIST" LABEL

The etymology of that label is important. Throughout the 1870s the workingmen's parties in Chicago had been labelled "communist" by the bourgeois press. With the birth of the SLP in 1878 the press used both "communist" and "socialist" interchangeably, then the latter gained currency. Beginning in 1881, according to Albert Parsons, "the capitalistic press began to stigmatize us as Anarchists, and to denounce us as enemies to all law and government." In response "we began to allude to ourselves as anarchists, and that name which was at first imputed to us as a dishonor, we came to cherish and to defend with pride." In March 1885, C. S. Griffin, of the American Group, defiantly explained: "Anarchism is a nickname or reproach . . . given to us by our enemies . . . Anarchy means disorder and confusion. . . . In short, they will call you an anarchist. This is the way we got the name, and in default of a name that will describe us we have accepted the nickname, and now we call ourselves anarchists."[4]

Although the term became a badge of honor, the movement consistently preferred the adjective "socialist." Thus *The Alarm*'s subtitle identified it as "A Socialist Weekly" (after December 1884 as "A Socialist Fortnightly") never "An Anarchist Weekly." With one exception, the term never appeared in the titles or subtitles of any of the IWPA's other

Chicago organs. Indeed, the weekly meetings of the local IWPA groups published in *Der Vorbote* and *Die Arbeiter-Zeitung* were always reported under the headline "Sozialistische Versammlungen," never "Anarchistische Versammlungen." There was a "Sozialistische Mannerchor," and a "Rote Mannerchor," not an "Anarchistische" one. The exception is, of course, *Der Anarchist*, which broke with the SPS because it was insufficiently radical.[5]

The movement had three opportunities to clarify its platform. The first came in October 1881 when the radicals first split form the SLP and founded the Revolutionary Socialistic Party in Chicago's Turner Hall. The second came in April 1884 when Alexander Jonas came to address the thriving IWPA and the moribund SLP. Both offered the "anarchists" a chance to differentiate themselves from the electoral socialists. Beyond the rhetorical flourishes the anarchists could not or did not clarify their positions: the Turner Hall Congress actually endorsed the ballot to prove its futility. To their mutual consternation the SLP and the IWPA could find no major differences beyond a "few clauses of a reactionary coloring." The third opportunity came a month after Jonas left when Johann Most and Paul Grottkau debated the difference between "anarchism" and "communism." If the first two opportunities could have clarified the ideological difference between the IWPA and the SLP, this debate should have clarified the distinctions within the IWPA. Despite the oratorical skills of two brilliant minds the debate was a draw. Most stood by the Pittsburgh Manifesto and Grottkau confessed that he had never acknowledged its authority.[6]

Adolph Fischer argued in his "Autobiography" that "the 'IWPA.' is the representative organization of the communistic anarchists. Politically we are anarchists, and economically, [we are] communists or socialists." And Johann Most, the personification of immigrant anarchism, told the *Tribune* in 1882, "I entertain the views of the Carl Marx school of agitators, but advocate the practice of the Anarchist." This left it up to C. S. Griffin, one of the IWPA's few Anglo-Americans, to state the obvious: "We confuse ourselves and all others by indiscriminately calling ourselves Socialists, Communists, Nihilists, Anarchists and Internationalists; and it is quite time we had our fixed name and our clear platform." Griffin was dissatisfied with the Pittsburgh Manifesto and argued for a new and different statement. Michael Schwab remembered August Spies's response: "The Pittsburgh program is secondary, our program is the "Communist Manifesto!"[7] Between July 1885 and May 1886 the movement never got around to fixing its name or clarifying its platform.

FOUR THREADS IN THE CLOTH OF IDEOLOGY

> I follow four commandments. Thou shalt deny God and love Truth; therefore I am an atheist. Thou shalt oppose tyranny and seek liberty; therefore I am a republican. Thou shalt repudiate property and champion equality; therefore I am a communist. Thou shalt hate oppression and foment revolution; therefore I am a revolutionary. Long live the social revolution!
>
> —Johann Most
> *Die Freiheit*, 15 July 1882

It is difficult to assess Johann Most's impact on Chicago's anarchists. For Chester Destler, Most's arrival "galvanized" an otherwise moribund movement in the United States.[8] *The Alarm, Die Arbeiter-Zeitung,* and *Die Anarchist* reprinted articles from his *Die Freiheit,* and he visited the city on three agitational tours. If Most did not have the influence Destler claimed, his creed serves now as a convenient catalog of four threads in the cloth of anarchist ideology: atheism, republicanism, communism, and revolution, although I want to consider those elements in a slightly different order. And to anticipate, the argument here is that Chicago's anarchists can be best understood as revolutionary socialists, the self-conscious heirs of the failed bourgeois revolutions of 1848.[9]

The Anarchists Were Political Republicans
The year 1848 had been "the springtime of the peoples": an awakening of republicanism and hope. When they failed, Chicago received many of "the refugees of revolution," not just Germans, but also Czechs and Scandinavians. The *Illinois Staats-Zeitung* denounced those Forty Eighters who "came over here to America, their heads filled with world messianic dreams," explaining that too many had become "enthusiastic and reckless representatives of socialism."[10]

The IWPA mingled two republicanisms: an indigenous, Anglo-American one, the other immigrant, almost "alien," and European. This mixture may have sacrificed coherence for cogency. Born in different places, under different conditions, the two were not identical; yet they shared similar notions, heroes, conceptions, and vocabulary. Both Anglo-American and European republicans believed in limited government, with a mixed and balanced structure, and in the sovereignty of the people. Both native and immigrant republicans embraced as first principles the notions that property ought to be widely dispersed, that antimonopoly vigilance was imperative, and that luxury was not just a sign of wealth but of the corruption of the republic. Both shared what Eric Foner has described as "a passionate attachment to equality (defined not as leveling of all distinctions, but as the absence of inequalities of wealth and influence), a belief that independence—the ability to resist personal or economic coercion—was an essential attribute of the republican citizenry, and a commitment to the labor theory of value, along with its corollary, that labor should receive the full value of its product."[11]

Republicanism pervaded the movement's thought but was most visible in its conception of civil society and of citizenship. In 1878 *The Socialist* argued: "With us there is no necessity for an appeal to arms involving a bloody revolution. We have a Declaration of Independence and a Constitution, and under them we have the right, now enjoyed for a century, of promolgating [sic] our ideas and of establishing a party in support of them." The socialists presented the Lehr- und Wehr-Verein as a civic organization. In defending the verein, *Die Arbeiter-Zeitung* quoted from its charter: "The Society's duty is to develop mental and physical qualifications of their members, and thus enable them to exercise their duty as good citizens, that the member should get acquainted with the law, and political economy and practice military and gymnastic drilling." Citizenship carried with it obligations, "the duty" of "good citizens."[12] The verein presented itself as a popular militia, composed of workers and organized as their defense against the "servile militia" of the bourgeoisie. As Conrad Conzett explained, "It is our duty to train ourselves in order to be able to lead the coming uprising of the people in such a way that the victory of the oppressed cannot fail." With its roots in 1848, the verein could still claim the legacy of 1776. In parades, some of its members dressed "in Continental style" and carried placards emblazoned "Give Me Liberty or Give Me Death"; its wagons bore the placard "1876."[13]

Both socialists and anarchists believed that workers were citizens; in turn, their notion of citizenship underpinned their conception of the republic. In 1879 and 1880, at election time, *Die Arbeiter-Zeitung* argued that any worker who failed to vote was unworthy of that privilege. Yet citizenship was never conceived in nationalist or chauvinist terms. Indeed, the children of IWPA members were welcomed as "neue Weltburgern," citizens of the world. In the wake of electoral failure and fraud, many abandoned their faith in the ballot as *Der Vorbote* contrasted "Reformschwindel und Revolution." A year later Lizzie Swank considered "Election Day":

The American citizen has walked boldly up to the polls, deposited a piece of paper in a box, gone back to 12 hours work, a shanty and a crust of bread, and thus demonstrated to the world his glorious freedom and independence! Perhaps his vote counted, perhaps not, for all he had to vote about, it does not matter. He was offered a choice between two sets of men, of whom he knows nothing, nominated he does not know how, or why, or by whom, and actuated by one and the same principle—to get there.[14]

The anarchists argued that the aristocrats and monopolists had perverted the political process with their greed. They rejected "what may be termed the American theory of government": "the theory that each voter is a sovereign of the Republic; that on election day at the ballot-box the rich and the poor, the wage-class and the capitalistic class are upon a level of equality; [and] that the ballot of the propertyless is as potential for enacting law as is that of the property-holding classes." In 1879, socialists protesting the new Militia Bill passed out leaflets as they marched. One of them was headed, "Eternal vigilance is the price of liberty! Citizens, stand by the Constitution of your country! The militia bill is the product of a conspiracy to overthrow the republic, that has been cemented by the blood of our forefathers, and to dragoon the working people of Illinois into abject submission." The last banner in the procession repeated the warning "Citizens, Wake Up to the Situation and Save the Republic." Two years later John Blake told the Chicago Labor Union, "We have political freedom, but now we will assert our industrial freedom by a central council of amalgamated trade and labor unions that will place us in a position to offer a united front to the business community." By 1884, John Keegan, a young Irishman active in the IWPA's American Group, argued at the Lakefront "This is not a republic and never will be until the present industrial system should be abolished."[15]

The Anarchists Were Economic Socialists

One of the speakers at the celebration of Turn-Verein Vorwaerts's fifteenth anniversary complained: "Although we are living under a republican form of government (a government by the people!) much is left to be fought for. Merely existing is not satisfying, we are desirous of higher ideals. We strive for a socialist state based on righteousness, truth and humanity." Because the conflict between virtue and commerce had corrupted the American republic, these Chicagoans broke with Anglo-American republicans and bourgeois political economy. The system of private property had destroyed the republican promise and brought with it wage slavery. "Those who believe they have equal rights," advised *The Socialist*, "should walk, after work, through the fashionable avenues," whose residents had bought the workingman's rights because they owned both his labor and their capital. When Frank Stauber was denied a seat in the City Council, *Der Vorbote* charged "that the holiest institution of the American people, the right to vote, had been desecrated" and became "a miserable farce and lie." "'Practical politics'," concluded *The Alarm*, "means the control of the propertied class. Politics and poverty, like oil and water, won't mix."[16]

Svornost's editor argued in 1880 that socialism would counteract the political power of "the capitalists, railroad kings, industrialists, land speculators, and monopolists." Capitalism was worse than slavery, charged Frantisek Zdrûbek, for "the slaveowner had to provide for the welfare of his slave. . . . The employer, however, had no regard for his employee and was not concerned about the wages he paid him." The solution, believed Zdrûbek, could not come through cooperation with the existing parties, but through "labor cooperatives and direct social change . . ., for socialism promised prosperity to all who wanted to work."[17]

Anarchist oratory and editorials were replete with phrases like "the abolition of slavery" and the "emancipation of the working class." In his first Chicago speech, Paul Grottkau linked the two: "whereas the Americans had evinced a spirit of liberty in ransoming the Negro," Grottkau could barely "entertain a hope that eventually the rights of the white laboring men would also be respected." Five years later, Albert Parsons almost presented the IWPA as a vanguard party, arguing: "The International is a labor organization composed of people who are devoting their time, their energy, their money and their lives to bring about the abolition of economic slavery and the complete emancipation of the working class from the tyranny of capital." "State Socialism," he argued "is the natural production of the age. It is the end of republican government. It is the complete union of all in one, and one for all alike."[18]

What kind of socialism? In short, all kinds. In the ranks of the SLP, the RSP, and the IWPA we can find Owenites, Blanc-ists (and Blanquists), Lassalleans, Marxists, even a few Bakuninists, as well as former enthusiasts of both cooperation and greenbacks. Some had been active socialists before emigration. Louis Pio and Alfred William Hansen were among the founders of the Danish Social Democratic party. While Ladimir Klacel and Vojta Náprstek were Forty Eighters, the later Czech emigrants, including Josef Pecka, Norbert Zoula, and Jacob Mikolanda, were early members, if not the founders, of the Czech socialist movement. Paul Grottkau, Gustav Lyser and Louis Lingg had joined Lassalle's Allgemeine Deutsche Arbeiter Verein; Julius Vahlteich had been Ferdinand Lassalle's private secretary and an SPD delegate in the German Reichstag. Dr. James Taylor, of the American Group, proudly told the Haymarket jury that he had learned socialism from Robert Owen, Robert Dale Owens' father. As Frank Hirth explained in 1879:

> The present labor movement is international in scope and in fact. It was not so originally. It began in France, in 1793, through Babeuf and his comrades, and was Communistic and Centralistic. . . . The movement stopped, till in 1823 St. Simon and his school re-enlivened it. . . . Much of this tendency was continued in the Communist systems of Cabet and his Icarians, and of Fourier.[19]

Others remained ignorant of socialism until they got to America, and Chicago in particular. Thus August Spies wrote in his "Autobiography" that "when I arrived in this country I knew nothing of Socialism, except what I had seen in the newspapers." Although he arrived in Chicago in 1873, "I think it was in 1875, at the time the 'Workingmen's Party of Illinois,' was organized [that] upon the invitation of a friend, I visited the first meeting in which a lecture on Socialism was delivered." For George Engel "Chicago is the first place where I heard something of socialism for the first time in my life." In 1874 a socialist "showed me a newspaper, *Der Vorbote*. . . . I found the paper very interesting and saw that it contained great truths. I was delighted. In it was an advertisement of a meeting held by the "International Workingmen's Association." . . . I went to the meeting." Oskar Neebe heard his "first communistic speech and that all men are equal" at New York's Commune in 1872, but did not join the communists in Chicago until 1877. Socialism meant the abolition of both private property and the wage system, and its replacement by a system of cooperative production and distribution. If the movement debated the finer points of theory at all, it shared a passionate opposition to the capitalistic system.[20]

The invitation to the Pittsburgh Congress that founded the IWPA in 1883 had advertised it as a "Congress of North American Socialists," and left the definition of "socialist" to the reader. Throughout its history the IWPA sought to be an inclusive, rather than exclusive, association. Despite its affiliation with the Black International, the IWPA was unaware of the Marx-Bakunin fight, it cared little for the split between Marxists and Lassalleans, and it tried to coexist with individualist anarchists. That coexistence, Chicago's association with San Francisco's International Workingmen's Association, and the offer of reconciliation with the SLP just after the Pittsburgh Congress all suggest that socialist theory had not yet hardened into schools and sects, indeed socialism was still fluid. As a consequence of that fluidity, Chicago's socialists seem eclectic. The books and writers they read, and urged others to read, reflect that diversity. The IWPA recommended Marx, Engels, Bebel, and Liebknecht to German readers, and Most, Bakunin, Hyndman, Reclus, and Gronlund to readers of English.[21]

This is clearest in Parsons's posthumous work *Anarchism: Its Philosophy and Scientific Basis As Defined by Some of Its Apostles*. It is divided into two parts. The first offered an outline of American history to 1886 and a discussion of the origins and development of capitalism in Europe. Asserting that capitalism is but one of a succession of class societies, Parsons reproduced an eighteen-page section from *Capital* (Chapter 19: "The Transformation of the Value of Labor-Power into Wages"), followed by an eight-page extract from the *Communist Manifesto*. The second part of the book extracted the speeches of the eight Haymarket Martyrs, followed by a number of essays by Kropotkin, Reclus, and others offering anarchist critiques of the state and descriptions of postcapitalist society. This is not eclecticism, but rather the reflection of a movement still sorting out and developing its thought and strategy.[22]

The Anarchists Were Social-Revolutionaries
The anarchists broke with the SLP over the strategy for achieving socialism, not the goal. The necessity for and inevitability of a social revolution became a third article of faith. In 1884, the Progressive Cigarmakers, Die Metall-Arbeiter Union, and the Central Labor Union proclaimed their belief "that the only means whereby the emancipation of mankind can be brought about is the open rebellion of the robbed class in all parts of the country against the existing economic and political institutions." There was, as Henry David noted, an "annoying vagueness" about the anarchists' notion of revolution. For Parsons, it meant "the time when the wage-laborers of this and other countries will assert their rights—natural rights—and maintain them by force of arms. The social revolution means the expropriation of the means of production and the resources of life." And as David noted, "it rarely occurred to the leaders of the movement to clarify the meaning of the term 'social revolution' for the benefit of themselves and their followers."[23]

There was no ambiguity about the weaponry to be used. Articles headed "Dynamite," "Assassination," "Explosives," "Bombs!" "War with All Means," "Streetfighting," and "How to Meet the Enemy," which appeared in *The Alarm, Die Arbeiter-Zeitung,* and *Der Vorbote* from 1884 through 1886, are infamous. Many reappeared, first as evidence in the Haymarket Trial, then in contemporary and sensational histories of anarchism, still later in scholarly accounts. Their uncritical repetition has become a hallmark of anarchist scholarship and exaggerated the "cult of dynamite." According to *The Alarm,* "one dynamite bomb, properly placed, will destroy a regiment of soldiers." Wage slaves were urged "to start a manufactory of hand grenades"; "Instructions Regarding its Use and Operations, precautions in handling and storage" were available at *Die Arbeiter-Zeitung*'s offices.[24]

The cult centered around *Die Anarchist,* Engel, Fischer, Lingg, and Gruppe Nordwestseite, who had condemned *Die Arbeiter-Zeitung* as insufficiently radical. Twenty years after his pardon Oskar Neebe was still "indignant at the 'defense' literature that made the victims bleating lambs. They were emphatically brave soldiers, and Engel was an out-and-out militarist." Johann Most's meticulously researched pamphlet *Revolutionare Kriegswissenschaft* became their bible. The English translation of its title page accurately describes its contents: *The Science of Revolutionary War: A Manual of Instruction in the Use and Preparation of Nitroglycerine and Dynamite, Gun-Cotton, Fulminating Mercury, Bombs, Fuses, Poisons, etc.*[25]

The "Intransigents," as Paul Avrich has labelled them, came to embrace the propaganda of the deed and to use it as a theory of radicalization. The *attentater* was to be a revolutionary sacrifice; his *tat* would revenge the working class, frighten the bourgeoisie, result in his own martyrdom, and then serve as propaganda for the movement. The propaganda of the deed was conceived as a sympathetic and symbolic act of violence. By attacking a representative of the oppressors, the intransigents expected to focus the nation's attention on oppression and then trigger a series of *attentats* that would inevitably culminate in revolution.[26]

Most of this was talk, "bomb-talking," as Floyd Dell perceptively called it. "Why then did these men talk dynamite?" Dell asked as he caught one side of the phenomenon: "It was done partly to attract attention to their real beliefs—it was a way of shocking the public into attention. So desperate a means of securing an audience is only taken by a small faction—it is a sign of weakness." George Schilling thought it more dangerous than desperation and weakness. In a remarkable letter to Lucy Parsons in 1893 he argued the open espousal of physical force—especially when advocated by foreigners—as a remedy for social maladjustments can only lead to greater despotism. When you terrorize the public mind and threaten the stability of society with violence, you create the conditions which place the Bonfields and Garys' in the saddle . . . Fear is not the mother of progress and liberty but oft times of reaction and aggression."

Speaking of the martyrs, and to Parsons' widow, Schilling maintained "They worshipped at the shrine of force; wrote and preached it; until finally they were overpowered by their own Gods and slain in their own temple."[27]

While Chicago's anarchists revelled in bomb talking, the propaganda of the deed remained a recessive characteristic within the anarchist movement. If two of Chicago's IWPA groups published *Die Anarchist*, twenty-four supported *Die Arbeiter-Zeitung*. The majority of the movement never embraced the *attentat*, nor did they ever denounce those who had. The best explanation for that failure must lie in their recognition that force would be required in the future. Instead the movement pointed to five revolutions, three within their lifetimes, as social revolutions. They were farthest removed from the American Revolution, but they celebrated Tom Paine's birthday annually, and venerated George Washington enough to place his portrait next to Ferdinand Lassalle's at other celebrations. They quoted Jefferson and the Declaration of Independence in the Pittsburgh Manifesto. The French Revolution of 1789 was almost as distant, and the anarchists chose to remember Gracchus Babeuf and "Die Baboeufisten" as heroes.[28]

The symbols of the American and French revolutions penetrated to the rank and file, which used them in public demonstrations. We have already noted some: the French and German tricolor flags, the Lehr und Wehr-Verein's affinity for the revolutionary militias, and the arm and hammer. Within the same parade one banner proclaimed Patrick Henry's words "Give Me Liberty or Give Me Death," and another bore the legend "Liberté, Egalité, Fraternité." Other processionals carried banners with slogans like "Not to be a Slave is to Dare and Do!" which was attributed (on the banner itself) to Victor Hugo. The slogan "Vivre en Travailleur ou Mourir en Combattir," first seen in the Lyon *journées* in 1830, showed up in Chicago during the unemployed demonstrations in 1873 as "Work or Bread." It reappeared during the great railroad strike of 1877 as "Life by Labor or Death by Fight"; a year later, in an SLP procession, the same slogan had become verbose: "Without Bread We Cannot Live. Bread is

What We Wish, and for Bread We Will go unto Death." When the police raided *Budoucnost*'s offices they found the Czech equivalent emblazoned on a shield: "Working to Live or Fighting to Die."[29]

The two most important revolutions for Chicago's anarchists—1848 and 1871—were linked as "The Dawn of Liberty" in broadsides for the Commune festival in 1879. After 1871 the Paris Commune became the model for social revolution. In William Holmes' words, the Commune had been a revolt against "the iniquitous political, industrial and social systems which then prevailed, and under which we still suffer. It was the complete overthrow, for the time being, of all existing institutions, and an attempt to found a social and industrial republic upon the inherent rights of man." It became "a remarkable struggle for industrial freedom," "the rising of the French working people," a revolt of the profoundly oppressed against their capitalist masters. The Commune redefined the socialist mission. "All the French and German communists wanted during the dark days of '48 and '71 was to establish a self-governing Republic, wherein the working-class—the masses—would partake of the civilization which their industry and skill had created." Each March, from 1872 through 1886, the movement honored "those who gave their lives that labor might be free." From the two Communes they chose to celebrate August Blanqui, General Dombrowski, Charles Delescluze, Prosper Lissagaray, and Louise Michel.[30]

The Great Upheaval of 1877 loomed as the fifth and most recent revolution, one within their own experience. In April 1878, Parsons argued "The Social Revolution began last July. The issue is made and sooner or later it must be settled one way or another." Lizzie Holmes remembered that it "brought out the vague lines between classes distinctly, and forced every thinking man and woman to take a stand on one side or the other." Although the Upheaval was never celebrated, it stood for the anarchists as proof of the revolutionary potential of the working class, and promised an American Commune. The great railroad strike had produced a mass strike and armed struggle, but it was not a revolution. And Chicago's anarchists "misread the meaning of 1877," for as Richard Schneirov noted, "the upheaval was as much a transitional mode of struggle as it was a harbinger of things to come."[31]

Finally, there was more than a streak of revolutionary romanticism in all their discussions of revolution and armed struggle. During a violent strike in 1875, John Simmens prophesied a "proletarian revolution within a few decades." The waiting period seemed brief, the glorious revolution just around the corner, needing but a single spark. The capitalist system was in crisis and on the verge of collapse. Many had convinced themselves of "an already approaching revolution," which "promises to be much grander than that at the close of the last century"; and Parsons spoke fondly, "We see it coming. We predict it, we hail with joy!" "Tremble, oppressors of the world!" proclaimed the Pittsburgh Manifesto. "Not far beyond your purblind sight there dawns the scarlet and sable lights of the Judgement Day." For some revolution meant the millenium.[32]

The Anarchists Were Atheists and Freethinkers

Most anarchists expected it would be a godless millennium. E. A. Stevens, the president of the Chicago Liberal League and an active member of both the SLP and the Knights, wrote to the Detroit *Labor Leaf* a week after the Riot: "The authorities are making a point against them that they do not believe in God. The police are principally Irish Catholics, and were glad to have a pretext to make the attack."[33]

At a time when the rhetoric of the American labor movement was couched in evangelical Protestantism, and the Knights of Labor in Chicago enjoyed close ties to the Roman Catholic church, the anarchists rejected both the symbols and content of Christianity. This rejection alienated not only the police and clergy, but also many in the labor movement, especially the Knights. We should not be confused that "conservative trade unionists and radical anarchists and socialists . . . often appealed to Christianity for its sanction." On the other hand it is clear, as David Montgomery has argued, that "the deepest line of division within the working class . . . was that of religion."[34] Yet both insights underestimate the complexity of the situation in Gilded Age Chicago where Protestants and Catholics confronted a third group of atheists and freethinkers found in Scandinavian, Bohemian, German, and even native-born neighborhoods. Not only were these ethnic freethinking groups aware of one another's presence, but they frequently cooperated. Let us look first at the Czechs, then at the English-speaking liberals.[35]

When the Congregational Club and the Chicago Missionary Society met in May 1884 they were dismayed at the heathenism in the immigrant and working-class neighborhoods. Reverend Emrich reported good work among the Germans and Scandinavians, where the club was "giving spiritual help and urging them to come into the church," but the situation was worst in the Bohemian neighborhoods on the Southwest side. "Among these people," the Reverend E. A. Adams conceded, "there were a few Lutherans, but the majority were freethinkers, atheists, and communists." Free thought pervaded Chicago's Bohemian community, where it had been introduced by immigrant Forty Eighters and sustained through the radical press. Indeed *Svornost,* a daily established in 1875, became the country's largest free-thought paper and the city's leading Czech paper. C. F. Gates, the president of the Missionary Society, reportedly spent $2,000 a year "to spread the blessing of Protestant Christianity among the Bohemians."

> We can see swarms of children running wild in the streets. We can see crowds of men leaving their dwellings and going to the meetings, to listen to instigative speeches of the communistic and socialistic leaders. The only things they learn at these meetings is to fight against God and the Church, against the law of possession, against the family's rules and social connections. When we consider, that their votes . . . have the same worth as ours we will understand the big value of our undertaking to penetrate those crowds with the Light of the Holy Gospel.[36]

Czech free thought became so pervasive and survived so long precisely because it was organized and even institutionalized. The Bohemian Freethinkers in Chicago (Svobona obec Chicagu) was founded in September 1870; in April 1878 it received a state charter as a corporation with Frantisek Zdrûbek as its minister. The society maintained schools and libraries, organized children's programs, and sponsored lectures, musical and cultural programs for families; Zdrûbek himself proposed the idea of establishing the Bohemian National Cemetery.[37] The Bohemian rationalists were deists and profoundly anticlerical, opposed to the established church and its dogma. In the Bohemian community free thought had long been related to political radicalism and hence to socialism. Forty Eighters, like Vojta Náprstek, Lev Palda, and the ex-monk Ladimir Klacel, combined free thought and a European republicanism with proletarian demands. Their socialism was communal, Fourierist, and utopian rather than Marxist.[38]

The link between socialism and free thought became explicit in Pilsen. Lev Palda, a freethinker, published Chicago's first Czech-language socialist paper, *Narodní noviný* in 1870. By late 1873, there were three sections of the International Social and Political Workingmen's Association in the city; three years later Palda and Martin Baumrucker served as delegates to the WPUS's founding congress. Politicization came in the wake of the Upheaval of 1877, in which the largely unskilled Bohemians were prominent. That fall the Sixth Ward's Fourth Precinct, the center of both the lumber district and the Czech colony, overwhelmingly supported the SLP.[39] Two years later, during Ernst Schmidt's mayoral campaign, Citizen Vytacil moved "that *Svornost* be made the official publication of the Bohemian workingmen. The motion was unanimously accepted as excellent." Two days later the paper returned the recommendation when it endorsed the SLP slate as "honorable, educated" candidates. In an editorial, "After the Battle," *Svornost* threatened to "publish the names of all those who worked for our side and the names of all who were against us." With Zdrûbek's endorsement of its candidates, platform, and party, socialism became respectable. With the decline of the SLP and the arrival of a new set of editors, many in Pilsen affiliated with the IWPA.[40]

The SLP's English section and the IWPA's American groups contained the most tolerant atheists within the social-revolutionary movement. *The Socialist*'s original editor had been fired in 1879, in part for "his abuse of various forms of religion and religious teachers of the past and present." In its short life atheism never dominated the paper. It was there, in sentences and paragraphs, but never at editorial length. Rumors of "religious differences" within the SLP had surfaced in April 1879. The participation of the Irish was at stake, and according to one report they "were disgusted with the infidelity and materialism that were constantly forced upon them; and that an open rupture was eminent." Yet the *Times* quoted George Schilling to the effect "that there were in the ranks of the socialists materialists, infidels, orthodox religionists, Catholics and Spiritualists." "We all get along well enough together," he continued, "for religion is something that is never under any circumstances touched upon." The headlines that "Religious Questions [were] Raising a Rumpus in the Socialistic Party" were true: after 1880 the Irish membership declined dramatically.[41]

By 1881 and with the ongoing decline of his party, T. J. Morgan could be more conciliatory. At one meeting of the Chicago Labor Union he "declared that Socialism was more of a church society for the propagation of social and religious ideas" than a political party. In March 1882, under George Sloan's leadership, the SLP began to call itself "a socialistic church." According to the *Inter Ocean*, "They adopted a creed which provides for the reconstruction of society on a socialistic basis, and has very little to do with religion. Mr. G. M. Sloan, the founder of the self-styled church, wishes it to be the refuge of all religions. . . . The audience consisted mostly of dissatisfied Socialists who hope by calling their meeting a church, to revive interest in Socialism." Morgan's comparison was apt, though Sloan's creed was strained: there were affinities between socialism and organized religion. Many of Chicago's socialists spoke of their "conversions" and their new moral and spiritual "convictions." In 1879 Alzina Stevens "was supposed to read a paper on 'What Part of the Labor Question Socialism does not include'" to a meeting of the Working Women's Union. Instead she "confessed that her study of the question had resulted in her acceptance of Socialism as the only means of salvation from the horrors of our present society and industrial system. The confession was received with a generous welcome by the socialistic portion of the audience, embracing fully two-thirds of the whole number."[42]

Chicago's Christians and socialists antagonized one another. In June 1878, the *Tribune* devoted a full page, "From the Pulpit," to four sermons on communism; despite German and Bohemian affection for beer, one connected anarchy and the demon rum. *Skandinaven,* a pious Norwegian weekly, advised *Den Nye Tid*'s editors and readers to forget their politics and propaganda "and think more of salvation, and of the brotherhood of man." If the clergy misunderstood the city's socialists and anarchists, they in turn outraged the church. They desecrated the Sabbath, attacked both religion and property, and they despised temperance. Yet some of the confrontations between middle-class Protestant reformers and the anarchists were humorous. At least twice the anarchists had to share the Lakefront with "a white-tied representative of the YMCA" and with "a chorus of silver voices" from the Salvation Army. The anarchists won both contests, even against the Army's brass instruments.[43]

As the Eight Hour Movement picked up enthusiasm, some of those Protestants invited the dreaded anarchists to explain themselves. The West Side Philosophical Society invited Albert Parsons to speak in march 1885. George Schilling remembered it as "one of the most eloquent, cutting, and defiant speeches I ever heard." Later that year August Spies was invited to speak to another meeting of ministers, but not to their congregations. While the ministers could sympathize with his discussion of "universal cooperation," they became upset when he suggested that "the family would be the child of the community," and disgusted when he mentioned "free love."[44]

Albert Parsons was convinced "there is but one God—Humanity. Any other kind of religion is a mockery, a delusion, and a snare." Both socialists and anarchists were active in the English-speaking equivalent of the immigrant freethinking groups, the Chicago Liberal League: Philip Van Patten, George Sloan, Lizzie and William Holmes, Marcus Thrane, and

William Gorsuch, to name only a few. The ex-Methodist minister, Samuel Fielden, admitted he was "more or less prominent in the society, . . . being elected financial secretary, vice-president, and delegate to the national congress held at Milwaukee in the fall of 1884." Another member remembered the socialists as "unyielding in their opposition to the church [any church], they pointed to the contradiction between a religion that taught that all men were brothers and an economic system that organized them as masters and slaves." The league, which had initially welcomed them, eventually barred the anarchists for being too disruptive and too political.[45]

The confrontations between the irreligious anarchists and The Noble and Holy Order of the Knights of Labor remained humorless. Throughout its history, and especially in Chicago, the Knights were led by a group of men who were Irish and Catholic. As early as 1882, the Grand Master Workman, Terence Powderly, denounced the "atheist socialists" in Chicago as "liars" and "enemies to the labor movement." One Knight wrote Powderly asking "Can a member be expelled . . . for not excepting [sic] the orthodox religion or the inspiration of the Bible?" Another declared: "I can not, either as a Catholic or as a true friend of my class, lend myself to or become an advocate of the teachings of a Carnot, a Danton, a Robespierre, a Most or a Louisa [sic] Michel."[46] That atheism was a chasm between the anarchists and the order is clear in an exchange published in the *Knights of Labor*. The occasion was a review of Richard Ely's *The Labor Movement in America*, in the course of which "the reviewer makes some unfair remarks about the IWPA, as well as flagrant misstatements of facts." Writing from his jail cell, Albert Parsons asked to make some corrections. "'Your reviewer says that when 'God is left out of any movement, there is very little of it left,' but nevertheless, the IWPA still insists that the labor movement is in fact capitalistic as long as the supreme, absolute right of man over himself is 'left out of it.'"[47]

The chasm deepened as both organizations prepared for the inauguration of the Eight Hour Day. George Schilling, who "had repudiated [his] former belief—State Socialism—and defended competition and the institution of private property," took charge of arranging the joint Knight and Trade Assembly rally. He scheduled the meeting in the Cavalry Armory for a weekday (i.e., working) night, envisioning "a grand Eight Hour Jubilee." Such a meeting, he thought, should be "entirely in the hands of the preachers." Schilling had convinced himself, the Knights, and the Trades Assembly that "a manifesto from the leaders of religious thought in Chicago would be more powerful in inaugurating the Eight Hour System than any statutory law." During the preparations one assembly delegate proposed to invite the CLU, "provided they consent to lay aside the red flag of communism and carry only the star-spangled banner." The proposition was tabled. A week later the armory was filled and at least 7,000 men were turned away at the door. The speakers' platform was sprinkled with the city's religious leaders. There were no ministers in attendance at the CLU mass demonstration two weeks later on Easter Sunday. None marched in the procession, none followed in the crowd, none spoke at the Lakefront. Rather they were in their pulpits, or serving communion, or at home enjoying Easter lamb.[48]

Atheism and free thought intertwined in the nineteenth century, especially in the eyes of the faithful. Not all freethinkers were socialists, but most socialists were freethinkers.[49] Atheism and free thought cut two ways in the Gilded Age. On the one hand, freethinking organizations (like the Skandinavisk Fritaenkere Forening or the Bohemian Svoboda obec Chicagu) were breeding grounds for socialism; in Richard Schneirov's words, they "provided a congenial environment for socialism to thrive and develop." Reverend Adams, a contemporary, put it succinctly: "The result of atheism always must be anarchism." On the other hand, atheism divided the city's labor movement by separating socialists from other immigrants, and from the native-born. Protestants and Catholics, pietists and ritualists, may well have divided at election time, but they shared an intense hatred of the godless.[50]

Adams was not alone in seeing that connection. In 1844, Marx asserted that the "criticism of religion [was] the premise of all criticism."[51] Beyond the organizational nexus, atheism was already political when it immigrated to America. Free thought became political in Europe when it confronted the established church. For Marcus Thrane in Norway and Lev Palda or Ladimir Klacel in Bohemia, anticlericalism served as a preliminary critique of not just the church but also the state. It was antihierarchical; it was egalitarian because it refused to recognize any Supreme Being, focusing instead on man. Moreover, free thought was materialist; by refusing to yield to another world, it concentrated on this world. Its ethics and morality flowed from that materialist egalitarianism. And while Americans enjoyed a constitutional separation of church and state, and many immigrants clung to their ethnic parishes, these radical immigrants brought a political antagonism to religion and to the state into a society and culture where that antagonism was utterly inappropriate.

BAKUNIN NEVER SLEPT IN CHICAGO

> . . . in this country, above all countries in the world, is Anarchy possible. . . .
> In those strong European governments . . . they strangle Anarchism or ship it
> here. Everybody comes to our climate; everybody reaches our shores; our
> freedom is great—and it should never be abridged—and here with that
> freedom, with that great enjoyment of liberty to all men, they seek to obtain
> their end by Anarchy, which in other countries is impossible. As I said, there is
> one step from republicanism to Anarchy.[52]

There were at least three other threads in the cloth of this movement's
ideology. One was a precocious feminism evident in Lizzie Swank's
articles on "Factory Girls" and the prominence of women in the American Groups. The IWPA remained uninterested in women's suffrage,
indeed the anarchists "offered no path to combat their oppression—
except the social revolution, which would somehow solve all problems."
An ambiguous position on racism formed a second. While Chicago's
anarchists applauded Riel's Rebellion in Canada and supported the
American Indian, their positions on anti-Chinese activity and towards
American blacks remained ambiguous—"at best fuzzy about the very
existence of racism" in Paul Le Blanc's judgment. A third thread denounced chauvinism, as *The Alarm* maintained that "Real internationalists
despise and loathe the name and spirit of Nationalism." And yet four
major threads can be easily discerned within the fabric of anarchist ideology: republicanism, socialism, revolution, and atheism.[53]

If the two Russians Mikhail Bakunin and Peter Kropotkin epitomized
nineteenth-century anarchism, then Chicago's IWPA was not anarchist.
Indeed the only Chicagoan in any way affiliated with the IWPA who had
met Bakunin was Dr. Ernst Schmidt. They met, only briefly, in St. Louis
in March 1861, the month before the start of the Civil War.[54] Beyond the
continuities of membership and organization lay an ideological evolution,
one best understood as a transcendence of nineteenth-century republicanism. This was not an evolution from socialism to anarchism but from
republicanism, through electoral socialism, to revolutionary socialism.
However unscrupulous he may have been, State's Attorney Julius
Grinnell understood that there was but "one step from republicanism to
Anarchy."

Republican images pervaded socialist and anarchist rhetoric. The
republic depended upon the independence of the citizenry and its active
involvement in society. Capitalist development, as some of Chicago's

radicals saw it, had destroyed independence and liberty and the concentration of wealth had corrupted the republic. Greed had perverted the political process and concentrated power in the hands of the few. "He who must sell his labor power or starve will sell his vote when the same alternative is presented. Our political institutions are but the reflex of the economic, and our political reformers should learn that the workers are not poor because they vote wrong, on the contrary, they vote wrong because they are poor." Despite rampant vote fraud, these anarchists did not completely reject the electoral process until 1882.[55]

They had already broken with republican political economy when they identified private property as the cause of corruption, economic depression, and social revolution. "Private property in the resources of life—the means of existence—is sanctified by the Church, made legal by the Constitution, enforced by the law, backed up and maintained by the army, navy, and police of the bourgeoisie." That identification was an irreconcilable breach with the republican notion that liberty and property were entwined. Anarchists argued that the concentration of private property had corrupted the republic, and that a free society must be based on the cooperative organization of production.[56]

And they broke with republican notions of the state and social evolution by embracing revolution. As socialists they had viewed the state as socially neutral and politics as mere electioneering. For anarchists, the state was not neutral and politics extended far beyond elections into the workshop and factory. Social revolution, on the model of the Paris Commune, promised to reestablish the republic. The Pittsburgh Manifesto thundered that "the political institutions of our time are the agencies of the propertied class" and that "their mission is the upholding of the privileges of their masters." The ultraradicals, those Paul Avrich has labelled the "Intransigents," rejected the legitimacy of any form of government. The majority within the movement seemed unconvinced by such arguments. Both envisioned the "destruction of the existing class rule, . . . [and] the establishment of a free society." Convinced that the ruling class would "never resign their privilege voluntarily . . . there remains but one recourse—FORCE! Our forefathers have not only told us . . . that force is justifiable . . . but they themselves have set the immemorial example."[57]

Irreligion served as a fourth thread in their ideology. English-speaking marchers carried banners emblazoned with "No God, No Master," Germans carried "Neider mit Thron, Altar und Geldsack," the Czechs "Zadný bůh Zadný pan." Few attended any church, even fewer believed; most subscribed to Bakunin's denunciation of God and State. Free thought and atheism contributed to anarchist conceptions of liberty, equality, and fraternity, and to the assault of both property and authority. Their lack of faith might have been tolerable, except that the Knights of Labor were deeply pious, the city's working class was still engaged by Protestant revivals, and the anarchists delighted in both blasphemy and sacrilege.

Finally, the movement's ideology, like its culture, reflected the dynamic interaction of ideologues and membership, and must be understood as part of a larger cultural system.[58] The active membership hired its editors and between 1874 and 1886 fired at least ten of them. If the Martyrs moved ideologically from socialism to anarchism, the active membership seems to have moved from republicanism, through parliamentary socialism, to revolutionary socialism. And the movement expressed that ideology culturally. While our understanding of their ideology has relied on editorials and manifestoes, each of these four threads was woven figuratively into the banners carried by the rank and file. Socialist singing societies, theater groups, dances, picnics, parades, and festivals tried to promote a sense of solidarity and mission within the active membership, which then offered its abilities and services to the sympathetic following within the city's working class.

PART THREE

The Haymarket Riot and Afterwards, 1886–1900

Anarchy is on trial. Little did it matter who the persons were to be honored by the prosecution. It was the movement the blow was aimed at. It was directed against the labor movement, against Socialism, for today every labor movement must, of necessity, be Socialistic. Talk about a gigantic conspiracy! A movement is not a conspiracy.
    —Michael Schwab

Chapter Eight

EIGHT HOURS, RIOT, AND REPRESSION

The size, growth, composition, organization, culture, and ideology of the anarchist movement form the background for understanding the Haymarket Affair. That movement was both large and growing at the time of the riot and had organized around a vital, militant socialist press; an active, democratic club life; and an ominous federation of "progressive" unions. Movement culture expressed an ideology that transcended artisan republicanism by becoming collectivist, solidaristic, and communitarian as it embraced revolutionary socialism. In sum, the anarchist movement threatened to assume the leadership of the city's working class.

This chapter focuses on the riot's immediate foreground, the organization and agitation of the Great Upheaval of 1885–86, in which the IWPA and the Central Labor Union played the central role. We need to look first at the unprecedented mass movement to establish the eight-hour working day. Then, we can briefly review the riot in Haymarket Square the night of 4 May 1886. Finally, we need to understand the trial and the executions of the Martyrs as part of a much wider program of repression, one which began before and continued beyond the legal proceedings, beyond the executions, and well into the 1890s.

This is familiar ground, and it is not my intention to reconstruct either riot or trial at any length; that project has already been done by competent historians. The point instead must be to understand that the Haymarket Affair offered an opportunity to try eight prominent anarchists as criminal conspirators, and to bring the full weight of civil authority against the most radical organization within the city's working class. Finally, we need to assess the impact of repression on the movement as a whole.

THE EIGHT HOUR MOVEMENT

The year of 1886 was a year of great activity in the labor movement. The Knights of Labor had had a previous convention and resolved to engage in an effort to establish the eight-hour day. In May, 1886, and some months before, they had entered into an agitation to accomplish their purpose. There was no knowledge of that movement in our group at all; information about it was distributed through the American and German press, but since we could read neither German nor English, . . . we knew nothing of that movement; but it was in the atmosphere and it seemed to have crossed the border of our settlement, because in the months of February and March there was quite a lot of dissatisfaction among our people about the prices paid for work.

That description comes from Abraham Bisno, a twenty-year-old Russian-born Jewish sewing-machine operator, who had arrived in Chicago in 1882 and joined the Eight Hour Movement four years later. The earliest meetings of the Jewish garment workers were "very cleverly" arranged by someone unknown to them. "There was a great tumult[,] everybody was talking and nobody knew quite what this thing was about." A Knight appeared at a second meeting and signed the workers up. According to Bisno, "All I then knew of the principles of the Knights of Labor was that the[ir] motto . . . was, 'One for All, and All for One.' I think they did require us to pay in a dollar per man . . . and [then] we were all initiated with great ceremony."[1]

Bisno was mistaken. The Knights were not the driving force behind the eight-hour day, nor was the Trades Assembly, nor the Central Labor Union. Two years earlier, in 1884, at a convention in Chicago, the Federation of Organized Trades and Labor Assemblies had ordained 1 May 1886 for the inauguration of the eight-hour day. Both ordination and inauguration died for lack of interest. In the fall of 1885, however, the movement was reborn by the unskilled and unorganized. Their "dissatisfaction," in Bisno's words, deepened and organization spontaneously appeared. Indeed, the organized and skilled found themselves drawn into a movement they had not started and long disdained.

Although it had hosted the federation's convention, Chicago's Trades Assembly neither endorsed the eight-hour demand nor established an eight-hour committee until October 1885. Two months later, and six months before May Day, only eleven of the Assembly's twenty-five member unions had endorsed the movement for shorter hours. The assembly was more concerned with fighting the introduction of new machinery, and with fighting the dilution of craft skills by female, child, unskilled, and prison labor. However beleaguered, Chicago's skilled and organized workers could not get enthusiastic over shortened hours. Because they treated the relations between labor and capital "from a conservative point of view," and because they recognized the reality of intercity competition, the assembly held that eight hours was unwinnable.[2]

While the anarchists and socialists scurried from meeting to meeting, *The Alarm* complained in January that "the Trade and Labor Assembly has done but little or nothing."

> Thus far the only large mass-meetings in behalf of the "Eight Hour Movement," have been held by those who have been accused of being opposed to the movement—The revolutionary Socialists, Anarchists, Internationalists, or whatever you may call the "ignorant foreigners" who follow the red flag and proclaim that wage-slavery is the curse of this age.

Two weeks later Albert Parsons explained: "The Trades Assembly has so much to do in other directions that they don't get time to bother with such little things as the Eight Hour Movement." The Knights of Labor were similarly unenthusiastic. In March, the Order's Grand Master workman released his "secret circular" which disavowed the eight-hour strikes, refused to charter new assemblies for forty days, and counseled against both strikes and boycotts.[3]

Until Haymarket, the anarchists remained ambivalent towards the Knights. When Powderly appeared to concede to Jay Gould on the Southwest strikes in March 1886, *Der Vorbote* labelled him a "monarchical, outdated labor leader" who "might have been of use a thousand years ago." "The Knight of the rueful countenance" became "Pope Powderly I," the head of "the established Catholic Church of modern times,"—"an arrogant, ambitious ignoramus." The Knights became "muddleheads and men of simple belief who do not understand their position in society and don't know anything about economic laws." In April, *Der Vorbote* cautioned a new union against "the haphazard step" of joining the Knights, recommending instead an "independent" course.[4]

While the German newspapers attacked, the American Groups and their paper cooperated with the Knights. In March, *The Alarm* reported that an attempt "to create ill-feeling between the Socialists and the Knights" had "proved a dismal failure." During a meeting of the American Group "a laborer in the audience rose and inquired if he could join the Knights of Labor as he had come to the meeting for that purpose." The chairman, according to *The Alarm*, "informed him that the Knights of Labor was a secret organization and that the International was not, and he would have to go to some Knight . . . Assembly in order to join it." Instead of denouncing the Noble Order, the chairman merely directed the man down the street. *Der Vorbote* hoped the Eight Hour Movement would "lead the Knights in the right direction toward radicalism." Despite their vicious criticism of the local and national leadership, Spies and Schwab argued "their demonstration of power is a very favorable development." Although Spies had approached Bisno and the Jewish tailors, the anarchists were not disturbed when they joined the Knights. Oskar Neebe remained adamant that "hundreds of our speakers [spoke] to workingmen to organize themselves, no matter in what form as unions or Knights [arguing] that in organization lay their strength." As the anarchists organized, they "did not assail" the Knights, "on the contrary, [they] applauded them."[5]

Neither the IWPA nor the CLU was initially enthusiastic about shorter hours. "We do not antagonize the eight hour movement," *The Alarm* explained, "viewing it from the standpoint that it is a social struggle—we simply predict it is a lost battle." Asked why the IWPA did not support the Eight Hour Movement, *The Alarm* answered, "Because we will not compromise." Other anarchists were less adamant. At a CLU meeting in the Bohemian Turner Hall in December Josef Pecka judged the movement a good one "as it afforded an opportunity to spread revolutionary ideas." Confronting the groundswell of a mass movement, the anarchists moved to join it that fall.[6]

On the eve of the Great Upheaval, Chicago's labor movement contained three different organizations, with different memberships and organizations. That fragmentation was typified by the 1,381 production workers in McCormick's reaper works. The Knights claimed 750 members among them, the Metall-Arbeiter Union (which belonged to the CLU) 250, and the Molder's Union (which belonged to the Trades Assembly) 10; the remaining 300 were nonunion men. The Trades Assembly remained a conservative body composed of skilled and organized Anglo-Americans.

The Knights were organizing both skilled and unskilled, male and female, under an Irish-American leadership. The CLU had been organized by skilled European immigrants, but in the heat of the movement for shorter hours, would push hardest for the organization of the unskilled and previously unorganized.[7]

As the winter of 1885–86 set in, the CLU found itself caught up in the Great Upheaval, and the IWPA followed. Before the end of the year the two organizations scheduled weekly, then almost daily meetings. From the Deering reaper works on the far North side, to a hall outside of Pullman on the far South side, its speakers addressed workingmen and -women in German, English, Czech, Norwegian, Danish, and Polish. Their agitation penetrated at least one community, the Polish, which had been ignored by previous organizing campaigns. As late as January 1886, the *Times* reported, "The Poles and Bohemians are absolutely without any organization; except so far as their inborn sympathy with socialistic ideas has impelled them to join army military companies." Led by the CLU, "the Polish and Bohemians have finally begun to organize."[8]

The pace became even more frenetic in the last months before May 1. Established unions within the CLU, like the International Carpenters and Joiners, composed of Germans and Bohemians, continued to grow. In April, Die Möbel-Arbeiter Union claimed 1,600 members in its four branches. Existing unterstützsungvereine, like those among the German and Bohemian bakers, led by Mathias Schmeidinger, and among the German butchers, led by Thomas Florus, became unions and joined the CLU.[9] Under the eight-hour banner, other wholly new unions organized. In March, the brewers, with 400 members, joined the CLU. In April, the IWPA and the CLU called a mass meeting to create an Unskilled Laborers Eight-Hour League and about thirty men signed up at the first meeting. The Butcher Clerks' Union took the lead among the grocery clerks, organizing 250 members almost immediately. And on the night of May 4, Samuel Fielden, Lucy and Albert Parsons were late to the protest meeting in Haymarket Square because the American Group had been working, like the Working Women's Union seven years earlier, to bring organization to the city's sewing girls.[10]

Die Lumberyard Arbeiter Union was one of the newest unions. The Irish dockworkers in the lumber district had organized in the 1870s, but the Bohemian yardworkers, who had struck in 1876 and were prominent in the 1877 Upheaval, had never enjoyed any permanent organization. It came only with the Eight Hour Movement, and, like the Jewish tailors, only in the last weeks before May 1. The *Tribune* reported that "the majority of the men who are employed in the lumberyards and representatives of the rabid branch of the Anarchists and Socialists." Of ten officers elected by the new union, five were members of the IWPA, including the vice-president, the Bohemian-language secretary, and all three delegates to the CLU. The union's growth was meteoric: "About 60 new members joined the union, which now contains about 3,000 in the German branch and 2,500 in the Bohemian. Night before last 400 joined." The *Tribune* ominously noted: "The Lumber-Workers['] union is not a branch of the Knights of Labor[,] but of the notorious Central Labor Union."[11]

The unionization campaign that accompanied the Eight Hour Movement was frenzied. Under the heading "Stadt Chicago," *Der Vorbote*'s last page was filled with the announcements and reports of union meetings. The 21 April 1886 issue, for example, reported meetings of Die Möbel-Arbeiter Union; a mass meeting just outside Pullman where the Metall-Arbeiter Union gained fifty new members and Die Möbel-Arbeiter Union No. 3 initiated seventy-five; the Linseed Oil Arbeiters; die Maurer [masons]; tanners, butchers (with forty-five new members); carpenters (fifty-four new members in two locals); saddlers ("fifty neue Mitglieder"); and Die Metall-Arbeiter Union, which gained ninety-six new members for a total "uber 900." According to the *Tribune*, the Passementerie Workers' Union added "25 new members, mostly girls," the shop tailors were organizing and about seventy joined, and the wagonmakers union had decided to affiliate with the CLU.[12]

Each of the city's three labor organizations grew in the Great Upheaval. The Trades Assembly reported some twenty-five member unions in October 1885; five months later there were fifty. The CLU had eight founding unions in February 1884; two years later it had twenty-four, including the eleven largest unions in the city. One month before the riot, *Der Vorbote* estimated the Assembly at 20,000 members; a week before the bomb it claimed 28,000 for the CLU.[13] Despite long-standing fears of "mushroom growth" and Powderly's secret circular, the membership of the Noble and Holy Order continued to grow. Indeed if DA 24 obeyed the circular, DA 57 did not. At the end of March 1886, the *Tribune* counted about twenty-six local assemblies and 5,000 Knights attached to DA 57, and "about the same membership" in DA 24, for a total of 10,000. In June 1886, the Illinois Bureau of Labor Statistics reported about 18,000 Knights in Cook County; in July the Knights's *General Assembly Proceedings* reported a total of 22,592 affiliated with the city's three DAs.[14]

The contrasts could not have been plainer than in the juxtaposition of Chicago's two Eight Hour demonstrations in April 1886. The first was scheduled by the Knights and the Trades Assembly and held in the Cavalry Armory on a Saturday night. Of thirty people who can be identified in the platform party, 60 percent had Irish surnames; another 26 percent came from Britain; no more than 14 percent were immigrants from continental Europe. The Knights claimed sixteen representatives, the Assembly eleven. All of the evening's speakers, including the Protestant ministers and the head of Chicago's Clan-na-Gael, spoke in English. Their speeches were fervent but cautious, almost conciliatory. According to the *Tribune:*

> Workingmen were called upon to organize and to join the Knights of Labor; to abstain from whiskey-drinking and prepare themselves for the 1st of May . . . [when] the clink of the hammer and the turn of the wheel should stop and the fires be drawn resolutely. . . . They were to ask for eight hours of work and eight hours' pay; . . . and the justice of their demand would assure its realization.

Two weeks later the CLU and the IWPA arranged a second eight-hour demonstration that the *Tribune* dismissed as "Mainly Communistic." It drew from 10,000 to 15,000 marchers, male and female, who gathered in Market Square and then wound through the Loop led by seven bands. A great crowd accompanied the marchers, who divided towards two speaker stands, one for English and Germans, the other for English and Czechs. This second demonstration was multilingual, as were the speakers. The ministers were absent, for the procession and rally had been scheduled on Easter Sunday. The red flag far outnumbered the Stars and Stripes; where the Knights and unionists sang "My Country 'Tis of Thee," the anarchists and their followers sang the "Marseillaise." While those in the Armory petitioned for an eight-hour day, those in the streets demanded shorter hours with no reduction.[15]

There was a strident difference between the two organizing slogans, the Knights and unionists calling for eight-hours' work at eight-hours' pay, the anarchists and CLU demanding eight-hours' work for ten-hours' pay. The first was presented respectfully, almost deferentially; the second was brazenly, defiantly, demanded. The first conceded to the reigning notions of political economy; the second utterly rejected them. If the anarchists had initially disdained the Eight Hour Movement, historians, not contemporaries, faulted and discounted them. As they organized during 1885–86, Chicago's workers enjoyed the luxury of choosing from among the established trade unions, the reformist Knights, and the revolutionary CLU, all of which offered organizers. That many chose to follow the anarchists and the CLU does not mean they chose anarchy or revolution. By May 1,

47,500 workers had already won shorter hours, many at a higher wage; on May Day an additional 62,500 struck, including the building trades, cigar-makers, freight handlers, lumber shovers, furniture and garment workers. According to the state Bureau of Labor Statistics, 16,000 of the 19,000 workers surveyed had demanded eight-hours' work at ten-hours' pay.[16]

On May Day, the *Tribune* published an interview with an otherwise unidentified anarchist who compared the organizing campaigns of the two major competitors:

> The German and Bohemian workmen are thoroughly organized and armed and will fight to achieve their end. The brewers, malters, butchers, and bakers have already achieved their eight hour day. The Knights of Labor are principally American and Irish; they don't train with the Germans and Bohemians. And we can't get them to do aggressive work in the movement[:] they hang back and take what they can get, while the Germans and Bohemians go out and get what they want.[17]

Beyond their organizational and agitational skills, the anarchists and the Central Labor Union brought a sense of militancy to Chicago's Eight Hour Movement, giving it a confrontational edge.

THE HAYMARKET RIOT, TRIAL, AND EXECUTIONS

That edge reinforced the shadow of 1877. Nine years before Haymarket, Federal troops who had campaigned with General Custer fought Bohemian and Irish workers in "The Battle of the Halsted Street Viaduct." That afternoon police had charged into the Westside Turner Hall and, in the course of breaking up a negotiating session of furniture workers and their bosses, killed one worker and wounded others. After being fired from the *Times,* Parsons went to speak in Market Square that night and remembered in his autobiography "over 100 policemen charged upon this peaceable mass-meeting, firing their pistols and clubbing left and right." For three days that July men, women, and children had taken the streets, closed the city's factories and workshops, and fought not only police but state militia and two Army regiments. About thirty workingmen had been killed, another 200 wounded. The police were undermanned, practically unarmed, and so ill equipped that Marshall Field, a leading merchant, lent the department his delivery wagons for transportation. Led by the Board of Trade, the city's business elite had formed a Veteran's Corps and a Citizen's Patrol. The police proved so ineffective that the militia and cavalry had to be summoned.[18]

The socialists had long been identified as troublemakers. During the 1877 strike, the mayor and a group of businessmen threatened Parsons in the police chief's office, advising him to leave the city. In March 1879, the militia had been garrisoned next to the Commune festival in the Exposition Building; a month later the state legislature outlawed the Lehr- und Wehr-Verein and revitalized the state militia. As recently as July 1884, nineteen-year-old Wilhelm Spies, the youngest of August Spies's brothers, had been fatally gut-shot by an Irish cop while defending a drunken friend from arrest. If plainclothes detectives had shadowed socialists since 1877, the first Pinkerton agent did not infiltrate the anarchist movement until December 1884. He was not alone: John Dusey recognized and "scolded" four Pinkertons at a lakefront meeting in July 1885.[19]

There were more recent incidents of what had become routine police violence. The most brutal came in the first week of July 1885 during a citywide streetcar strike. Led by an as yet unknown lieutenant, John Bonfield, twenty-five officers mounted a train's first car and towed a second for prisoners and a third for their reinforcements along the Madison Street line. Anyone who blocked or passed the train was clubbed, anyone who shouted "scab" or "rat" was similarly treated, and Bonfield earned the nickname "Blackjack." The track was slowly cleared and more than 150 arrested, including sixty-five strikers and two groups of jeering bystanders. Such brutality was unprovoked and widely denounced by all sections of the community; yet it was also effective and the strike collapsed. The Trades Assembly called for Bonfield's job, but Mayor Harrison deferred. Most importantly the strike marked a new, and unauthorized, aggression by the police.[20]

As May 1 approached, the forces of order prepared with the Police Department as the first line of defense. Between 1880 and 1883 it had grown from 473 to 637 men; by 1886 it had been expanded to just over 1,000. While they were not officially armed, a few relied on their nightsticks. The department recruited the native-born, British, and Irish, and did not hire its first Bohemian, for example, until 1882. The department was not fully trusted by the city's manufacturers. In 1882 it had failed to intercede during a streetcar strike; in 1884 the firm of Cribben and Sexton had been forced to hire Pinkertons when the department failed to control strikers. The most recent scandal had revealed that an officer had refused to order his men to break up a strike by boxmakers in the winter of 1885–86.[21] Behind the force stood a larger group of police "extras" and "specials," reinforced in turn by an expanding militia. If the Lehr- und Wehr-Verein was training in the basements of their meeting halls, another rumor had Marshall Field's clerks armed and drilling in his company's warehouses. The Citizen's Association supported the expansion of both the police and the militia; the Commercial, Union League, and Chicago clubs preferred a nearby garrison of Federal troops but continued to patronize the National Guard's officers and armories.[22]

The Haymarket riot can best be understood then in a context of suspicion, hostility, and fear, for the Eight Hour Movement reawakened the terror of 1877. For a decade and a half, Chicago's communists had annually celebrated, even invoked, the specter of the Paris Commune. In January 1885, during another of the city's recurrent red scares, the state militia put "a voluntary guard" on the First Regiment's Armory to protect it from a possible attack by the Lehr- und Wehr-Verein. When the attack never materialized, the *Inter Ocean* interviewed several members of the LWV and of the Jaeger Verein; two weeks after those rumors first appeared, the *Daily News* headlined "No Cause for Alarm."[23]

Those fears multiplied in the Great Upheaval. The First Infantry Regiment "satisfactorily performed" its street-riot drill on Thanksgiving Day 1885. The next month "an infernal machine" was found on a judge's doorstep, obviously placed there by "an insane freak of some socialistic crank." In January 1886, stories, emanating from New York, reappeared "regarding a socialistic outbreak in Chicago." The *Tribune* responded with an editorial calling for "A Regular Army Garrison in Chicago" which could quell "the dangers of riot and insurrection." In March, Charles Bodendeick, a member of the American Group, frightened another judge "by calling at his house late at night and demanding $25;" bound by a $1,500 bond, "the defendant exclaimed: 'I am a socialist, and am proud of being one.'"[24]

The forces of order expected the worst as they planned for the inauguration of the eight-hour day. Two days before the CLU's procession and Lakefront demonstration, the First Cavalry Regiment performed another exhibition drill and dress parade for the Commercial Club. Three days later the First Infantry Regiment held its annual inspection and the same club, led by Philip Armour, subscribed more than $2,000 "to furnish the regiment with a good machine gun, to be used by them in case of trouble."[25] The anarchists did nothing to calm the city. From February 1885 through March 1886, *Die Arbeiter-Zeitung* reportedly advertised free rifle instruction to workers at Smrz's Hall on Clybourn Avenue; the IWPA's English and German organs had issued directions for making and using dynamite; *The Alarm* published diagrams on street fighting and how to attack a Gatling gun. Military rhetoric permeated every discussion of the labor movement and class relations. On May Day, *Die Arbeiter-Zeitung* called:

Bravely forward! The conflict has begun. An army of wage-laborers are idle. Capitalism conceals its tiger claws behind the ramparts of order. Workmen, let your watchword be: No compromise! Cowards to the rear! Men to the front! The die is cast. The first of May, whose historic significance will be understood and appreciated only in later years, has come.[26]

May 1 came and nothing untoward happened. Expecting, even predicting "trouble" and "violence," the bourgeois press waited. When an anarchist let slip that "Herr Most" was expected that afternoon, the *Tribune* sent its reporter to police and military headquarters. Police Chief Frederick Ebersold had "no intimation that there is to be any great amount of trouble" and dismissed "all this talk of police reserves, police preparations and special orders" as "nonsense." On the other hand, "the arms and ammunition of the regiment were in readiness for immediate use" at D Battery's armory. At the First Infantry Regiment's new armory and headquarters, "extra men were in charge" but there were "no extraordinary precautions." If the police remained resolute, and the militia stood ready, the *Tribune* reassured its readers that a Gatling gun had been bought and would arrive that very night. Chief Ebersold, Inspector Bonfield, and the precinct captains quietly met "in consultation" the second day, but all the press could report was that "the police will be disposed about the city . . . and others will be held to act at a moment's notice. The entire force will be on active duty." The Knights, the Trades Assembly, and the CLU met, separately of course, and went over strike reports. That night the Assembly held a "slimly attended" Eight-Hour Ball at Battery D's armory.[27]

The Trades Assembly held another "protracted" meeting on Monday, May 3. A resolution from the floor recommended "the formation of an Executive Board, composed of representatives of all trades," which would have meant not just recognition of the CLU, but outright cooperation at least for the Eight Hour Movement. R. C. Owens, from the carpenters' union and LA 1307, seconded the resolution, arguing that such cooperation was both timely and essential to success. The vulnerable Andrew Cameron, former editor of the *Workingman's Advocate* and one of the oldest of Chicago's labor reformers, took the floor to denounce any notion of cooperation:

> I am one of those who do not think it a crime to be an American, or worse than murder to speak the English language. I am opposed to any movement toward joining with those who carry the red flag of Socialism [from] Europe to the democratic-republicanism of America. The Trade Assembly will be certainly smirched if it takes on such a responsibility.

Additional denunciations followed, echoing Cameron's lead, and the resolution was allowed to drop.[28]

That same afternoon the lumber shovers invited August Spies to address a strike meeting. Attended by more than 5,000 from the union, the meeting was held a block from McCormick's plant, and attracted about 500 of the strikers there. At shift's end, the strikebreakers started to file out, and Spies's audience left to jeer the scabs. A police detail arrived unexpectedly, fired on the strikers, and then charged; at least two strikers were killed, five or six wounded, and others injured. Spies rushed back to his office, dashed off the "Revenge Circular," and handed it to the composing room foreman.

Only 200 or 300 of the 20,000 handbills carried the word "Revenge" as they announced a mass meeting that evening to protest the latest police outrage. And however durable, the label "the Haymarket Riot" is wrong on two counts. Based on the CLU's turnout a week before, the meeting's planners expected a crowd of 25,000 and originally chose Market Square. When someone objected that it was "a mousetrap" with few exits, the site was changed to the Haymarket Square. When the crowd never materialized, the event did not take place in Haymarket Square, but in an alley off the square. Second, it was the police, not the crowd, who rioted. The meeting was called for 8:30 P.M. but none of the speakers was present and runners were sent to find them. Mayor Harrison stopped by to measure the crowd, judged it "tame," concluded that "nothing had occurred yet, or looked likely to occur to require interference," and suggested that the reserves at the Desplaines Street Police Station be sent home.

Spies spoke first, then deferred when Parsons, his wife, children, and Fielden finally arrived. Parsons spoke for almost an hour, then introduced Fielden who spoke for about ten minutes. Threatened by rain, the meeting was about to break up when the police arrived. "In the name of the people of the state of Illinois," Captain Ward intoned, "I command this meeting immediately and peaceably to disperse." When Ward repeated the order Fielden replied, "We are peaceable." A moment later the bomb exploded. Chaos ensued; then the police reformed, opened fire, reloaded, and fired again. There may have been some return fire from the fleeing crowd, then all was quiet.

Who was in the square that night? We can identify only eighty-two in a crowd estimated between 600 and 3,000. This is not, however, a random sample and there is little reason to believe it representative. About a third of the sample were marked by the riot: sixteen were shot that night, four more got clubbed, four arrested, four died. We know the ages of only seventeen, with a mean of thirty-five years old; we know that twelve in the crowd had been city residents for an average of eleven years. One victim was visiting from Indianapolis, but the majority had addresses within eight blocks of the square. All three of the speeches that night were in English, but 60 percent of the crowd had German surnames; about 10 percent English; another 10 percent native-born; the remaining 20 percent were split among Bohemians, Poles, Swedes, and French. Drawn from the surrounding neighborhood, the crowd was composed of "workingmen of all beliefs and views," just as Spies described them; and shoemakers comprised the single largest occupational group.[29]

We have much more accurate information on the police contingent commanded by Lieutenants Ward and Bonfield. They were "all select men, the flower of the Central Detail", "a company of giants," according to the department's official historian, and each carried two loaded revolvers. Mathias Degan died instantly; officers Mueller, Barrett, Flavin, Sheehan, Redden, and Hansen died later; up to seventy others were injured, most by police bullets, most shot in the back. The detachment had a mean age of 33.5 years. Four of the officers had been with the department for only fourteen days; two had served seventeen years; overall they had a mean of five years of service. A microcosm of the department, Captain Ward's squad was an Irish-American unit: fully 40 percent had been born in Ireland, 24 percent were native-born, 22 percent in Britain, and the only Pole, Charles Dombrowski, "disgraced his uniform by fleeing."[30]

The bomb thrower's identity remains a mystery. The grand jury indicted Rudolph Schnaubelt, who figured as the bomber throughout the trial, but the evidence remains inconclusive. There are two schools for speculation. One holds that the bomber was an agent provocateur. Parsons maintained that the bomb was thrown "to break up the eight-hour movement, thrust the active men into prison, and scare and terrify the workingmen into submission." Eight months later the *Arbeiter-Zeitung* still had "every reason" to believe that the bomb was thrown by a police agent. If Henry David failed to identify the bomb thrower after weighing the evidence against eight suspects, Paul Avrich has argued more recently that it was thrown by someone inside the movement. In 1984, Avrich's best guess identified George Schwab (no relation to Michael), "a German shoemaker and ultramilitant." In 1986, he proposed a new candidate, George Meng, "a German anarchist, a 'self-determined' militant in the Chicago groups, a known figure in the movement." Without some startling new evidence the mystery will apparently endure.[31]

REPRESSION

On Wednesday, 5 May 1866, the day after the riot, the police regrouped and struck back. Armed, but without a warrant, they charged into *Die Arbeiter-Zeitung's* offices and arrested everyone they found: August Spies, Michael Schwab, Adolph Fischer, and the entire staff of reporters, compositors, even the printer's devil. The police returned, arresting a few more, confiscating manuscripts, type, galley proofs, the library's books, the paper's records and such. That afternoon Blackjack Bonfield led the detachments that closed both Zepf's and Greif's halls on Lake Street. The next day, May 6, the police raided and closed *Lampcka* and *Budoucnost's* offices, where they again confiscated manuscripts, back issues, records, and a dozen banners. They also netted three anarchists (Jakub Mikolanda and Vaclav and Hynek Djmek) and a list of the paper's subscribers. The Djmek brothers were promised money and jobs to turn state's evidence; both refused and were eventually released. Within two weeks the police had raided each of the IWPA's known and suspected meeting places, more than fifty in all.[32]

Throughout their investigations the police followed State's Attorney Julius Grinnell's advice to "Make the raids first and look up the law afterwards!" More than 200 men and women were arrested in their homes, at work, and in the streets. The police arrested Henry Spies because of his last name, and William Boege when he bragged about the riot in a saloon. Martel Obermann was pinched carrying a half-empty revolver, and George Dietz, a cabinetmaker, had a breechloader, cartridges, bullet molds, bulk lead, and several hundred copies of the *Arbeiter Zeitung*. Captain Schaack proudly published his versions of the interrogations of about seventy prisoners, revealing in the process that many were denied counsel, food, water, and medical treatment.

The program of repression was never selective. The day after the riot, Inspector Bonfield met with a group of freight handlers "and advised them to avoid assembling in crowds upon the streets, and especially not to march in procession. He gave them a lot of good advice about avoiding even the appearance of evil, and withdrew." Some never heard the advice. The same morning 600 Jewish tailors marched from their ghetto towards the garment district; "patrol wagons came in on us from all sides . . . hundreds, probably thousands of policemen were unloaded in very short order . . . every policeman had a billy and they began to chase us and beat us unmercifully." Yet, as Abraham Bisno remembered, "None of us were arrested, none of us had time to do anything that would warrant an arrest."

After May 1st, 1886 [sic, May 4th] picketing became absolutely impossible. The police arrested all pickets, even two or three. The attitude on the part of the police was practically the same as though the city was under martial law. Labor unions were raided, broken up, their property confiscated, the police used their clubs freely. Arrests were made without any cause, and the life of a working man was not quite safe when out on strike.[33]

Some, of course, fled immediately. *Lampcka*'s editor and publisher, Anton Hradecny, left Chicago Tuesday or Wednesday night but returned to give himself up on the Tenth. John Henry ran to St. Louis; Balthaser Rau ran to friends in Omaha, Neb., only to be arrested (without a warrant) and returned to Chicago. After being twice arrested, Rudolph Schnaubelt shaved off his beard, and chose flight, telling Sigmund Zeisler: "I believe it would be better for me to get out of Chicago for a time." He never returned. Albert Parsons, the most famous fugitive, fled first to William and Lizzie Holmes's house in Geneva, Ill., and then hid out in Waukesha, Wis. Others went underground within the city. William Seliger ran to a comrade's home in Lakeview but was later turned in by his own wife. The Seliger's boarder, Louis Lingg, hid out with two friends on the South side only to be tracked down when he sent for his tools. As late as August, the *Tribune* reported that Hendrich Sever, Solene Henri, and Justus Mont, all "parties to the Haymarket tragedy," had been traced to Ottawa (Illinois or Canada?) and that extradition was being arranged.[34]

On May 5 the coroner's jury ruled that Officer Degan's death had been murder and charged all those then in custody with its responsibility. A grand jury was empaneled on May 17, conducted its investigation without a trace of secrecy, and dutifully presented an indictment on June 5 which concluded by thanking "the police force [whose] heroic bravery [had] saved this city from a scene of bloodshed and devastation equal to or perhaps greater than that witnessed by the Commune of Paris." The indictment named thirty-one men: the eight Martyrs, Schnaubelt, and twenty-two others who never stood trial. All but Schnaubelt and Parsons were already in custody.[35]

Their trial became the most prominent manifestation of repression. We need not dwell on it at any length, yet some points deserve our attention.[36] It was a long trial, lasting two months from jury selection to verdict; the transcript ran to 8,000 typed pages. Fully 981 talesmen were examined for the jury, and as the bailiff guaranteed, the defense exhausted its peremptory challenges. In the end, the prosecution managed to pack the jury with men who freely admitted their prejudice. The presiding judge, Joseph Gary, was grossly biased and consistently ruled against the defense. The defense team was inexperienced: Moses Salomon and Sigmund Zeisler were immigrant labor lawyers, only recently admitted to the bar; they were joined by Captain William Black, a corporation lawyer.[37]

Led by State's Attorney Julius Grinnell, the prosecution charged the defendants as accessories to Officer Degan's murder, having incited "a person or persons unknown" to commit the act. In exchange for immunity, Gottfried Waller and Bernard Schrade testified that Engel and Fischer planned the bombing in Zepf's Hall. William Seliger testified about Lingg's bomb making, and Engel's peculiar furnace was introduced along with the chemical analysis of the bomb fragments. Two reporters, Harry Gilmer and M. M. Thompson, swore they saw Schnaubelt throw the bomb. Additional testimony placed Fielden, Spies, and Parsons in the square that night. The evidence against Neebe remained especially thin: he owned stock in the *Arbeiter-Zeitung* and had been arrested in its offices, he read the "Revenge Circular," was a member of the IWPA, and owned a pistol, sword, breech-loading rifle, and red flag. Perhaps the most damaging testimony was read to the jury from *Die Arbeiter-Zeitung* and *The Alarm* in order to illustrate their revolutionary content, inflammatory rhetoric, and criminal intent. The core of the prosecution's case lay in conspiracy, not murder.

Led by Captain Black, the defense probably erred by basing its case on the evidence and the charges. The eyewitnesses contradicted themselves and each other. Neither Gilmer nor Thompson was particularly reliable; Seliger, Waller, and Schrade admitted they had received money, jobs, and immunity for their testimony. The state had offered no proof that any of the defendants had thrown the bomb, indeed the state failed to connect its general conspiracy theory with the meeting in Zepf's Hall. The defense hammered at testimony and evidence, discounting the conspiracy, convictability, and manifest guilt of the defendants. In his closing remarks Grinnell explained the obvious: "Law is on trial. Anarchy is on trial. These

men have been selected, picked out by the grand jury and indicted because they were leaders. They are no more guilty than the thousands who
follow them. Gentlemen of the jury; convict these men, make examples of
them, hang them and you save our institutions, our society."[38]

On August 20 the jury announced that all of the defendants were guilty
as charged. With the exception of Neebe, who received fifteen years, all
were sentenced to death. Captain Black appealed to the Illinois Supreme
Court for a writ of error and the executions were postponed. A year passed
before the final appeal to the United States Supreme Court failed and the
date of execution set. On 10 November 1887, Governor Oglesby com-
muted Fielden and Schwab's sentences to life imprisonment. At nine
o'clock the next morning the law was avenged: Lingg committed suicide;
an hour and a half later Engel, Fischer, Parsons, and Spies were hanged.[39]

The red scare continued unabated outside the courtroom. Captain
Schaack supplied the commercial press with a steady diet of raids, arrests,
and interviews. Secret "anarchist arsenals" were still being discovered, in
basements, and under sidewalks, throughout July and August. More than
a week after the trial had ended, the police were reportedly prepared to
move on the Bohemian anarchists who haunted the Sixth Ward. A second
round of grand-jury indictments was repeatedly threatened but never
produced. Suppressing anarchy became a big business. By May 18, responsible citizens had contributed $67,445 to a fund for the families of
officers killed or injured in the square. Schaack used a different, larger fund
to hire Pinkerton detectives, and Melville Stone, editor of the *Daily News*,
paid for still others. One contemporary questioned Schaack's zeal:

> He saw more anarchists than vast hell could hold. Bombs, dynamite, daggers,
> and pistols seemed ever before him; in the end, there was no society, however
> innocent or even laudable, among the foreign-born population that was not to
> his mind engaged in deviltry. The labor unions, he knew were composed solely
> of anarchists, the Turner societies met to plan treason, stratagems, and spoils;
> the literary guilds contrived murder; the Sunday schools taught destruction.
> Every man that spoke broken English and went out o'nights was a fearsome
> creature whose secret purpose was to blow up the Board of Trade or loot Mar-
> shall Field's store.[40]

Police Chief Ebersold, who proved unwilling to restrain him at the time,
tried much later to disown his subordinate.

> Captain Schaack wanted to keep things stirring. He wanted bombs to be found
> here, there, all around, everywhere. I thought people would . . . sleep better if

they were not afraid their homes would be blown to pieces any minute. But this man, Schaack, . . . wanted none of that policy. . . . After we got the anarchist societies broken up, Schaack wanted to send out men to organize new societies right away. . . . He wanted to keep the thing boiling, [to] keep himself prominent before the public.[41]

The police had help investigating anarchy. According to George McLean, "the most sensational evidence" to come out of the trial "was that of Detective Andrew C. Johnson, of the Pinkerton Agency, . . . who was detailed in December, 1884 by his agency, which had been employed by the First National Bank to furnish details of the secret meetings which it was known were being held by revolutionary plotters at various places throughout the city." Masquerading as a cabinetmaker, Johnson had infiltrated the American Group in February 1885 and joined its armed group. Although William Holmes later insisted that the "spies" were "generally known," both Parsons and Charles Bodendeick had vouched for Johnson.[42] Johnson's testimony was sensational, if not wholly manufactured, but Holmes mentioned "spies," for Johnson was not alone. As soon as he got the case Captain Schaack

at once employed a number of outside men, choosing especially those who were familiar with the Anarchists and their haunts. The funds for this purpose were supplied to me by public-spirited citizens who wished the law vindicated and order preserved in Chicago. I received reports from the men thus employed from the beginning of the case up to November 20, 1887. There are 253 of the reports in all, and a most interesting history of Chicago Anarchy do they make in themselves.

For eighteen months after the riot, Schaack "had at least one man present" whenever the dreaded anarchists met: "Before midnight I would know all that had transpired at meetings of any importance." Once Schaack ordered his officers to listen through a hole cut in the floorboards; another time they hid under the floor of the stage in Thalia Hall. Some of this could be amusing: two spies, both in Schaack's employ, denounced each other to the Captain. Yet undercover work also proved dangerous: one agent barely avoided disclosure by denouncing a legitimate member; Schaack also reported that another of his detectives was "betrayed by beauty" and mysteriously drowned by a female anarchist.[43]

Cheered on by an adoring press, the police continued both surveillance and repression long after the trial and executions. In September 1886, State's Attorney Grinnell announced he was ready to prosecute the Bohemian anarchists who had been arrested in May and still sat in jail. Al-though all were convicted, their trials were reported as the beginning of a detailed investigation of anarchism in the heathen Czech community. The day before the executions a judge restored the indictments of nine-teen anarchists and issued the appropriate warrants "as a precautionary measure." None, however, was ever used.[44]

The city's reaction to the entire affair split along complex lines. The English-language press universally denounced the riot, the conspirators, the defense, the appeals, and the foreign-born in general. The *Staats-Zeitung* labeled the anarchists as "the worst enemies of the Germans" but noted the "deplorable fact that most of them bear German names [and] that many talk no other language but German." Led by *Svornost*'s editor, "reputable Bohemians" disclaimed any connection with or sympathy for the dreaded anarchists. The *Times* quoted a similar resolution issued by a meeting of "reputable Polish residents: "Our nationality is moved by motives only of good citizenship . . . [we] have always denounced[,] in no measured terms[,] communism, socialism, and anarchism."[45]

Yet others, less respectable perhaps, rallied to support the accused, the convicted, and the condemned. A committee, drawn from the CLU, but headed by Dr. Ernst Schmidt, collected funds for the defense and appeals. Most contributions were under a dollar, yet the committee raised more than $40,000. After the trial, and when the appeals failed, the defense committee became an Amnesty Association and expanded its base.[46] The movement tried to provide for the Martyrs' families. When Oskar Neebe's wife died in March 1887, the movement arranged both wake and funeral. A month before, *Der Vorbote* had published the initial call and the constitu-tion of the Pioneer Aid and Support Association, which would care for the martyr's widows and orphans. The association arranged frequent benefits to raise money. One, in January 1889, was described by the *Staats-Zeitung*: fully 7,000 people came to a concert sponsored by twenty clubs, "mostly singing and athletic." It was "a cheerful gathering and . . . all enjoyed the skillful performances" of 200 singers and fifty-odd gymnasts. Beyond honoring the Martyrs, such family support had long been a feature within the movement.[47]

The forces of order chose to see any defense activity as proof of anar-chism. Noting that both Christian and August Spies "had been members for years," the Aurora Turn-Verein contributed $100 to the defense fund in July; their continued support later rebounded. Two years later the Sozialer Turn-Verein had to deny, in the pages of the rabid *Saats-Zeitung*, that it had glorified anarchy or insulted the American flag. The national Turn-

Verein, which had removed the word "sozialistische" from its name in 1856, broke its affiliation with the Chicago Turngemeinde in June 1887 over its repeated requests to support the Martyrs. The red flag remained an issue. During the November 11 memorial meeting in Vorwaerts TurnHall in 1891 "Lt. Gibbons, followed by a squad of policemen in civil clothing" mounted the speakers' platform to demand that the American flag be raised among the red ones. Then in May 1892, Julius Vahlteich was expelled from the Turngemeinde "for anarchistic speeches" in its halls.[48]

Organized repression continued long after the executions. In July 1888, the police trotted out still another conspiracy when three Czech anarchists, John Hronek, Frank Chleboun, and Frank Capek, were arrested and charged with plotting to assassinate State's Attorney Grinnell. Hronek was convicted and sentenced to twelve years in prison on Chleboun's bargained testimony. Two months after their trial, Charles Bodendeick was arrested and held incommunicado for twelve days, charged with "manufacturing dangerous explosives and conspiracy to destroy city hall." He never went to trial, but Captain Bonfield reportedly told him "to immediately leave the country as he was liable to arrest in every city and town in the United States."[49]

A year after the executions some of the more naïve anarchists reorganized as the Arbeiterbund and foolishly published their constitution in *Der Vorbote.* The police quickly raided their earliest meetings and Mayor Roche argued that the city's ordinances gave him the authority to suppress any meeting that he considered revolutionary or otherwise illegal. Arguing free speech and assembly, the anarchists took the case to court, managing to get it before a judge who had originally been elected by the SLP (in 1879) and more recently reelected by the United Labor Party (in 1886). He ruled in their favor, arguing: "Anarchists have the same rights as other citizens to assemble peaceably for the discussion of their views; . . . in no other city of the United States except Chicago have the police officials attempted to prevent the right of free speech on such unwarranted pretenses and assumptions of power, and . . . it is time to call a halt." Although the *Tribune* published the Bund's constitution and listed the names of its "secret agitation committee," *Die Arbeiter-Zeitung* still rejoiced in the decision with a story headlined "Chicago Vanquished!"[50]

In September 1888, *Die Fackel* charged Schaack with nepotism, moonlighting, and possession of a $75,000 fortune. Considering the source, nothing came of the story. Then, sixteen months later, during a messy divorce case, the wife of one of Schaack's detectives charged that her husband and his boss had robbed prisoners, received stolen goods, and committed extortion. When *Die Arbeiter-Zeitung* published the story, its editor found himself arrested and charged with criminal libel, despite the fact that he had only commented on an article that originally appeared in the *Times*.[51]

The police continued to harass the annual commemorations of November 11 and to raid anarchist haunts. As the marchers came back from the cemetery in 1888, they were accosted and ordered to remove their red lapel ribbons. That year the bakers' union chose to hold a secret memorial, but the *Staats-Zeitung* still reported it. The harassment and surveillance did not stop when Schaack and Bonfield were suspended and later dismissed from the force in 1889. A prominent site for both the SLP and IWPA, Thomas Greif's Hall at 54 W. Lake Street remained a meeting place for anarchists, socialists, and unions past the turn of the century. The police raided it several times in the weeks after the riot and irregularly thereafter. The last two raids apparently came in April and November 1891, the latter occasioned by the semiannual business meeting of the Arbeiter-Zeitung Publishing Company's stockholders.[52]

In January 1892, the *Herald* charged that the most recent raid on Greif's Hall "was simply a scheme to show men who had been putting up money to keep down anarchist movements that the followers of Parsons and Spies were not yet dead." An anonymous group of businessmen had reportedly raised an annual fund of more than $115,000, instructing the police: "Use this money as you may find best, the object being to crush out anarchy." In October 1891, they closed their books; $487,000 had been spent since May 1886, and although $57,670 remained on hand, nothing had been spent in the past year. The *Herald* charged that the last raid had been staged to reopen the fund.[53] The surviving elements of the anarchist movement still had police shadows as late as September 1895. When 3,000 of them assembled at Hahn's Garden there were fifty plainclothes policemen on the grounds and another fifty in uniform held in reserve a block away. "All these numerous peace guardians gave the harmless picnic more the appearance of a serious affair of state," yet according to *Die Abendpost*, a bourgeois German paper, the "picnic was absolutely peaceful."[54]

In addition to surveillance by Pinkertons, the department's own detectives, and Schaack's "privates," Chicago's anarchists were watched by Imperial German police agents. "According to the press in Berlin at the beginning of 1890 a man named Heinrich Danmeyer or Dammeyer, who had been regarded as a wide-eyed socialist or anarchist, was revealed to be a police agent in Chicago. He was considered to be one of the most 'raging' of the anarchists, . . . the most outstanding of the leaders of the [Arbei-terbund], . . . of the Freethinkers' Association and . . . of the Karl Marx Assembly. Danmeyer had been in the pay of the police since at least 1886 and had called for the assassination of [the] police, state['s] attorney and judge connected with the Haymarket Trial."[55]

Surveillance of German emigré radicals began in 1878 after an assassination attempt on Kaiser Wilhelm I. An adjunct to Bismarck's anti-socialist laws, it aimed at preventing emigrés and their literature from returning to the Reich. And an editorial in the *Inter Ocean* ten days after the riot reported a communication from Baron Schaeffer, an Austrian minister, to the American secretary of state asking his help in stopping the return of exiled Czech radicals. German surveillance continued until World War I. In Chicago, two agents submitted their reports to the consular staff, and two more agents were hired through the Pinkerton Agency. In 1902, those agents prepared a list of Chicago's "anarchists" for the Reichschancellor. Of the 145 names listed, forty appear to have been active in the IWPA before the Haymarket riot. The majority of the people only became "dangerous" after the riot, but 27 percent of the total were long-time activists.[56]

Although we can chronicle the program of repression organized by the civil authorities, we know little of the private sector's program. Immediately after the riot, the *Times* had screamed that "public justice" demanded "that no citizen shall employ or keep in his service any person who is a member of such . . . [an] . . . association of conspirators and assassins." Just as quickly, the Chicago Furniture Manufacturers' Association pledged not to employ "any communist, anarchist, nihilist, or socialist, or any other person denying the right of private property." *Die Möbel-Arbeiter Journal* reported that those resolutions made it "impossible for members of the union to find employment." Surely there were other resolutions, and with the names, addresses, and descriptions of alleged, accused, and suspected anarchists widely circulating, the program must have been effective.[57]

The city's business community supported the forces of order and the program of repression. They raised one fund for the families of the police officers who died or were injured in the square. Even before the trial verdict a citizen suggested that another fund reward the jurors. Still another, raised and directed by the Citizen's Association, not only paid for Pinkerton detectives but also supplemented police salaries. In 1889, the Commercial Club bought land thirty miles north of Chicago and donated it to the federal government for a garrison because Marshall Field felt safer with the troops at Fort Sheridan "instead of a thousand miles away, like

Fort Laramie or Fort Riley."[58] If the whole program remained uncoordinated, with detectives, "privates," Pinkertons, and German agents crossing each other and reporting to different superiors, it was nonetheless effective.

Repression affected all three levels within the anarchist movement. The trial decimated the leadership by convicting the combined editorial staffs of *The Alarm*, the Socialist Publishing Society's three papers, and *Der Anarchist*. Although he escaped the first indictment, a second trial subsequently convicted Jacob Mikolanda, from *Budoucnost;* and Anton Hradecny closed down *Lampcka*. The raids, arrests, and harassment similarly affected the active membership. Expelled from the Knights of Labor, many were also fired from their jobs and found it difficult to get employment. Reputations and friendships gained before the riot haunted many for years. And repression hit at the movement's sympathetic following. The raids on Greif's Hall and *Budoucnost's* office confiscated two different subscription lists and the police assured the commercial press that every name would receive special attention.

The anarchist revolutionaries reacted to such harassment in a most peculiar and ironic way. Arguing freedom of speech and assembly, some turned to the law and the courts for protection. The core of the Haymarket defense committee did not rest with the convictions, the appeals, the executions, or the pardons. On the contrary, they kept busy well into the 1890s. In the last half of 1888, *Die Arbeiter-Zeitung* regularly reported the activities of "The Chicago Workers' Legal Aid Society," which had been formed to defend Hronek, Chleboun, and Capek. The profits of an evening entertainment in October were "to be used for the defense of those Bohemian workers who were spotted by Bonfield, the bloody Haymarket slayer, as his latest sacrifices." The society became more than an ad hoc organization, for its services enjoyed a frequent, if not constant, demand. In 1896, the Chicago Socialist Trade and Labor Alliance announced the founding of the Alliance Bureau of Law. Staffed by T. J. Morgan and Paul Ehmann, among others, the bureau was "designed to furnish a convenient and reliable institution to which working people may safely apply for free advice and assistance in all legal and business matters."[59]

The breadth and duration of repression affected the movement in two different ways. According to Henry David, "In the decade after 1887, Chicago witnessed a more active, widespread, and intelligent discussion of revolutionary doctrines and labor theories than ever before."[60] On the other hand, repression fundamentally subverted the movement's energies and organization away from revolution and the working class and towards its own survival. The activities of the defense committee, Amnesty Association, Arbeiter Rechtsschutz-Verein, Personal Rights League, and the Alliance Bureau of Law were altogether different than the activities of the IWPA. Although the new organizations still depended on festivals, picnics, and dances to raise funds and solidify their members, mere survival replaced agitation.

Chapter Nine

MARTYRS AND SURVIVORS

The Haymarket Affair continues to overshadow the history of Chicago's anarchist movement. Yet few of the dreaded anarchists were even in the Haymarket Square that night: if thirty-one were indicted, only eight actually stood trial, only five died on November 11. When the story ends with four executions in 1887, or with three pardons in 1893, we seem to have lost the movement behind the Martyrs. The movement's rank and file did not conveniently evaporate or otherwise disappear. The anarchists played a crucial role in the United Labor Party's electoral efforts in 1886 and 1887. Beyond those two campaigns, what happened to the movement's membership, to its press, clubs, and culture? To answer these questions we have to return to those who survived the executions, to the rank and file, and to the collective biography assembled in chapter 5. Then we can consider the movement's two central institutions, its newspapers and club life; both survived the affair. Finally we have to understand the changes in movement culture after Martyrdom.

To anticipate, some of the IWPA's members left Chicago, never to be heard of again; others died before the century's end, many of them suicides; still others dropped out of both the socialist and labor movements altogether. But many stayed on in Chicago and continued to participate and contribute to both movements. Reflected in the survival of old traditions, in the growth of new organizations, and in the activity of aging radicals, their presence is clearly the most important continuity.

THE SURVIVORS

On 26 June 1893, Governor Altgeld unconditionally pardoned Samuel Fielden, Michael Schwab, and Oskar Neebe, who returned to Chicago as celebrities. Schwab rejoined the *Arbeiter-Zeitung*'s staff and spoke to the memorial meeting at the Waldheim gravesite that November. Two years later, he opened a shoe store on the Northwest side. It failed, and by spring 1898, when Emma Goldman visited, Schwab had tuberculosis. He died that summer and was buried at Waldheim Cemetery. Fielden picked up as a teamster again, then moved to Colorado and became a rancher on inherited land. Almost seventy-five years old, he died there in February 1922, and is the only Martyr not buried at Waldheim. Neebe soon married a comrade's widow and took over her stockyards saloon and remained active in both the brewers' and bakers' unions well into the twentieth century. Neebe flirted for a time with Populism and Chicago's labor-oriented Peoples' Party in the mid-nineties but returned to the socialist ranks and attended the 1907 convention of the Industrial Workers of the World. He died in April 1916 at the age of 65.[1]

If Lingg committed suicide; if Engel, Fischer, Parsons, and Spies were hanged; and if Fielden, Neebe, and Schwab were later pardoned, what happened to the remaining 715 members of the IWPA identified in chapter 5? The editorial staff of *Budoucnost,* for example, all but disappeared. "Norbert Zoula died in California [in 1886] of tuberculosis, 'the common malady of the proletariat,' a newspaper commented at the time," and, according to Tomas Capek, he died in utter want, deserted by his comrades. Josef Pecka stayed on in the city, editing *Práce,* later working on its successor. He died there, in 1897, only forty-eight years old. Arrested the day before the riot, Jacob Mikolanda was sentenced to six months in the county workhouse. When he got out, he wrote for the *Právo Lidu,* a Chicago weekly reportedly more moderate than *Budoucnost,* and died in Cleveland in 1907.[2]

Many had fled the city in the wake of the riot. Sam Goldwater, for example, went to Detroit where he rejoined the Knights, and became a leader of the Workingmen's Ticket in 1886, president of the Trades Council in 1888, president of the local cigarmakers' union, an organizer for the Michigan Federation of Labor, vice-president of the cigarmakers' union, an alderman in 1894, and an unsuccessful Democratic mayoral candidate in 1895 before he died in 1898. Released by the police, a beardless Rudolph Schnaubelt left Chicago on May 7 and travelled through Canada. Then he took a ship to London, where he stayed for almost a year, and still fearing arrest, he embarked for Buenos Aires. A machinery manufacturer there, he prospered, married, fathered three and died. After testifying as a state's witness, Gottfried Waller was attacked by his ex-comrades in a Chicago saloon in October 1886. According to his sister and sister-in-law, he was finally shipped to Germany by the police, and by December 1887 lived in Hamburg under an assumed name. Peter Petersen wrote from Minneapolis in 1889 to announce he was then editing *Det frie Ord*, which he described as a socialist paper. With few exceptions those who fled seem irretrievable.[3]

All but a few stayed away. Balthasar Rau, one of the exceptions, returned, became a foreman and stayed on at least through 1900. F. A. Kalbitz stayed on in Chicago for a few years, but represented the Mount Holyoke, Mass., section at the SLP's national convention in 1893. He returned to Chicago the next year and ran as an SLP aldermanic candidate. And Paul Grottkau came back from Milwaukee to open a photographic studio in 1888. At some point he moved west and worked on *Die Kalifornia Arbeiter-Zeitung*; at his death, in 1898, he was working as an organizer for the American Federation of Labor.[4]

In the fourteen years from 1886 to 1900 at least thirty-six anarchists died and the city directories record their wives as widows. Many of those deaths were natural, but at the Socialist Party's founding convention in 1901, T. J. Morgan remembered:

> Some of these men committed suicide. The editor of our Socialist paper committed suicide. John McAuliff, one of the best agitators we have had[,] blew his brains out. Leo Milebeck [sic], one of our best representatives, cut his throat. William Kem[p]ke, our German agitator, took the morphine route; [Frank] Hirth, a cigarmaker and editor of the first Socialist paper we had, poisoned himself in Detroit. . . . Their eagerness, their enthusiasm carried them beyond the bounds of reason, and they shattered our Socialist movement into fragments.

Morgan's body count remains incomplete. In July 1880, forty-year-old Thomas Rollinger, a coal agent and seven-year resident of Chicago, chose morphine; Emil Neudeck, a carpenter, shot himself in 1885; Louis Lingg blew his jaw off in his jail cell in 1887. Of the 723 anarchists identified in chapter 5, at least thirty-six were dead by 1900: four were hanged by the state, eight suicides, the remaining twenty-four of presumably natural causes.[5]

What of their survivors? In 1890, that is four years after the riot, 277 of the 723 (40 percent) were still Chicago residents. Of them, 152 (55 percent) remained in the city a decade later in 1900, a typical persistence rate. Despite repression and depression, more than a fifth of those who had been active in the IWPA during the eighties were still city residents and listed in the city directories at the turn of the century.[6] Those who stayed in Chicago seem to have prospered, and the data is presented in Table 9.1. The largest occupational group continued to be the ubiquitous "laborer," and the construction industry and the building trades (carpenters, painters, masons) maintained their predominance. In 1900 as in 1870, skilled and semiskilled workers continued to dominate these samples of the movement's membership.[7]

Those at the bottom of the social ladder experienced the greatest mobility. At the bottom, almost 30 percent of the IWPA's membership had held unskilled jobs in 1870, that percentage steadily dropped, to 19 percent in 1880, then to 12 and 11 percent in 1890 and 1900 respectively. Semiskilled employment started at 22 percent of the sample in 1870, jumped to 26 percent in 1880, then dropped off to one-fifth of the sample. If the size of the skilled contingent held steady at more than one-third of the group, low-white-collar employment expanded from about 17 percent in 1870 to 30 percent in 1900. White-collar employment saw no significant expansion over the same time period.

Table 9.1 also compares the social mobility of the IWPA's membership to that of Chicago's population. Between 1870 and 1900 the IWPA's occupational index rose from − 0.65 to − 0.06 while that of the city's population barely dropped from − 0.22 to − 0.17: those who survived Haymarket moved up a social ladder that had not dramatically changed in thirty years. The maturation of the city's economy and the on-going processes of industrialization are evident, and the ex-anarchists fared better than the general population. If most survivors held the same occupation in 1880 and 1900, the most frequent patterns for mobility within the movement saw skilled workers become self-employed as unskilled workers became semiskilled. Thus, all of those listed as shop- and saloonkeepers in 1900 had been skilled workers in the 1880s.[8] As Abraham Bisno later remembered, "There was a continuous migration from the group I worked with [the needle trades] into the avenues of [the] profession[s], manufacturing, and

Table 9.1 OCCUPATIONAL MOBILITY OF
CHICAGO'S IWPA MEMBERS, 1870–1900

Level	1870	1880	1890	1900
High white collar	0%	1%	2%	2%
Low white collar	17	18	24	30
Skilled blue collar	31	36	42	40
Semiskilled blue collar	23	26	19	18
Unskilled blue collar	29	19	12	11
Totals =	100%	100%	100%	100%
N =	48	248	264	148
Occupational Index =	− 0.65	− 0.44	− 0.15	− 0.06

OCCUPATIONAL STRUCTURES OF CHICAGO'S IWPA AND
POPULATION, 1870 AND 1900

	IWPA		Chicago	
Level	1870	1900	1870	1900
High white collar	0%	2%	8%	8%
Low white collar	17	30	20	23
Skilled blue collar	31	40	36	31
Semiskilled blue collar	23	18	13	19
Unskilled blue collar	29	11	23	19
Totals =	100%	100%	100%	100%
N =	48	148	1,143	548
Occupational Index =	− 0.65	− 0.06	− 0.22	− 0.17

SOURCES: (IWPA) Chicago city directories, 1870, 1880, 1890, 1900; (Chicago) Edward Bubnys, "Chicago, 1870 and 1900: Wealth, Occupation and Education" (Ph.D. diss., University of Illinois–Champaign, 1978), Table 4.3, p. 72.

merchandising." When his union excluded employers, Bisno dissolved his own shop and was repeatedly offered business opportunities in the nineties: in clothing, furniture, and real estate.[9]

There were few big success stories. A bookkeeper in 1870, a tinner in 1882, Fritz Reuter set up a building, loan, and homestead association (partnered with two former SLP members) in 1890, only to die three years later. "The most significant avenue for social advancement" open to workingmen and ex-anarchists remained "party politics" and in Chicago that meant the Democracy. Trained as a typesetter and reporter on the *Arbeiter-Zeitung*, Henry Bonnefoi had jumped to the Democratic *Neue Freie Presse* just before Haymarket. In 1890 he edited and published the *Lake View Tribune* while serving as the local post office superintendent, and in 1900 the city directory listed his occupation as justice of the peace.[10]

That the anarchists stayed in Chicago and climbed at least one step up the social ladder confirms that they survived the Haymarket Affair. Neither persistence nor mobility are as interesting as the continued activities of the IWPA's membership. Not only did the survivors far outnumber the Martyrs, but they left a record we need to examine.

THE ANARCHISTS AND THE UNITED LABOR PARTY

In fall 1886 the IWPA and the SLP joined the Knights of Labor and some of the trade unions in an independent labor party. Using a name coined by the Trades Assembly in the early 1880s, the United Labor Party (ULP) resembled the Eight Hour Movement more than it did the old SLP. The ULP was a coalition, or perhaps a confederation, of groups and individuals: Knights, unionists, socialists, greenbackers, single-taxers, and anarchists. The two labor parties of the decade, the Socialistic and United, beg to be compared.[11]

A day after the Haymarket verdict, 250 delegates from a cross section of Chicago labor organizations met in Greenebaum's Hall, and called for a "labor federation" that would enter the fall county elections. That federation endorsed the idea of a full slate and then appointed a Committee of Twenty-One to arrange a nominating convention the next month. The following month the various factions jockeyed for position. Richard Powers and Charles Rowan, of the Trade Assembly, wanted only to endorse candidates from the two regular parties, but on the convention's eve the oldest unions endorsed political action. According to R. C. Owens of the carpenters, the movement emanated "from the Knights of Labor and was . . . a bonafide movement of organized labor." The CLU was expected to "be solid for a straight ticket" and would "oppose any candidate who has taken a stand against the anarchists."[12]

The day before the convention the Committee of Twenty-One, led by T. J. Morgan, decided that credentials would go only to workingmen— "bonafide" representatives of Knights assemblies and trade unions. When the convention opened, Charles Dixon was elected chairman by a two-to-one margin over M. B. McAbee, of Typographia No. 16, and Morgan then "climbed on a table, was recognized by Dixon, and called for adjournment," noting that almost a third of the 560 delegates were without proper credentials. Claiming to represent 19,000 union men, the "McAboodlers" withdrew, reconvened as the Cook County Labor League, and endorsed a mixed slate of men who were already candidates of the Democratic and Republican parties. If the league was not a Democratic front (and its endorsement of several Republicans confutes the charge), it remained, as dominated by Irish-Americans, as the Workingmen's Industrial Party of 1878, and all of its ten candidates were English-speaking.[13]

The bourgeois press did not know what to do with the ULP. On the one hand, they denounced it as an anarchist front and decried the presence of known socialists; on the other, the Knights had already purged some of the anarchists from its ranks, and the press recognized the party's earnestness. Fearing that the "reds" might actually mobilize an insurgent working class and capture political power, the press repeatedly analyzed the registration figures in October. On the 24th, the *Tribune* estimated that the ULP would draw about 15,000 votes: 6,000 from the Democrats, 5,000 of the old socialist votes, and 4,000 from the Republicans. In fact the ULP polled almost 25,000 votes, about 27 percent of the total; the Democrats about 31 percent; and the Republicans swept the election with about 42 percent. Seven of the ULP's candidates were elected to the state's General Assembly, one to the state Senate, and five of the six judges endorsed by the party were successful. The Labor League's best candidate polled all of 1,779 votes, not even 3 percent of the total, and ran a sad fourth, and the league evaporated. Although the ULP failed to capture a single county office, it pulled so many votes away from the Democratic party that the Republicans won big.[14]

Ignoring the SLP, the *Knights of Labor* declared: "No party ever polled so large a vote, nor made itself so generally felt at so young an age as the United Labor Party." The ULP immediately turned toward the spring's mayoral contest when Carter Harrison would seek his fifth term and fourth reelection. His first and not unexpected step was to offer patronage appointments to some of the ULP's leaders. Under Morgan's leadership the party avoided that trap only to confront the threat of fusion. Despite a membership pledge that dismissed the regular parties as corrupt, both Democrats and Republicans continued to court the party's members and leaders. On 26 February 1887, more than 450 delegates convened for the ULP's second convention. All but a handfull were workingmen, three-quarters were Knights, no more than 10 percent came from the SLP or the IWPA. They hammered out a platform and then nominated a full slate of candidates.[15]

When fusion came it was against, not with the ULP. Two days after its convention, Carter Harrison advised the ULP: "What they ought to have done was to have selected some man who was in favor of granting justice to the laboring man, but who was not of them, for Mayor. It would make no difference whether the man was a Democrat or Republican—he could not well be a Republican, because that party is made up of the rich and monopolistic class, while the democratic party is the party of the people." When the ULP rejected his unsolicited advice, Harrison urged his own party to fuse with the ULP; when that failed, Harrison declined his party's nomination barely a week before the election. Without a standard bearer, the Democracy fused with John Roche's Republicans.[16]

An editorial in the Democratic *Times* just before the election argued "the issue that is joined is simply a question of public safety;" one of John Roche's campaign broadsides offered a choice between the red flag and the Stars and Stripes, promising "If I am elected Mayor there will be no red flags carried in the streets of Chicago." The Republican *Tribune* was more specific: "They [the United Labor Party] want to control the police force so that they can throw bombs with impunity, the fire department so that they can ravage and burn without having their work of anarchy arrested, [and] the machinery of taxation so that they can confiscate property by form of law and throw the revenues of honest enterprise into a common pool for plunder." The ULP's platform did not, in fact, address the police or fire departments, but it did promise equal property assessments and "taxation to the full limit of the law." Six of the planks in the platform promised to redistrict the city and reorganize the City Council, prohibit the sale of public land, establish the eight-hour day for municipal employees, abolish the contract system, and provide ample public education to the city's children. None of these was a new demand. Two newer planks dated from the SLP: municipal "ownership and operation" of "local means of transportation" and of gas, electric light, telephone, and telegraph companies.[17]

Both platform and party were decisively defeated that April. Robert Nelson, the ULP's mayoral candidate, lost by almost 28,000 votes to Republican John Roche: Nelson polled 23,490 (31 percent), Roche 51,249 (68 percent). The ULP won but one aldermanic seat, in the Irish-American Fifth Ward, and the Republicans won thirteen of the eighteen aldermanic contests. Had the ULP succeeded, the Knights would undoubtedly have claimed the credit; when it failed, they denied any responsibility. Such a catastrophic defeat brought mutual recriminations. Despite T. J. Morgan's boast that "the controlling power" within the ULP rested with the social-ists, despite the *Tribune*'s judgement that Morgan had "bossed" the ULP's conventions "from first to last," despite the *Knights of Labor*'s decision to lay the defeat at the feet of the "ultra-radical, fire-eating leaders," and despite the *Times*'s battle cry "Remember the Haymarket!" the ULP was neither an anarchist nor socialist party.[18]

The relationships among the socialists, the anarchists, and the United Labor Party remained complex. The day after its first convention, the CLU had endorsed the idea of a labor ticket. According to its secretary, barely 9,000 of the CLU's 16,000 members were voters, but "every effort [would] be made to induce the remaining 7,000 to take out naturalization papers and become qualified voters." *Die Arbeiter-Zeitung* endorsed the party and offered a daily column to the Committee of Twenty-One. The CLU subsi-dized the ULP: it taxed its membership two cents each, and Cigarmakers Local 15 (the former Progressive union) voted an additional twenty-five-cents-a-head assessment.[19] The Knights made no such effort: one local assembly taxed its members; one other voted a $50 contribution, but withheld payment when Powderly disapproved. Indeed, as Richard Schneirov noted, "the Knights did little beyond supplying the ULP with its candidates and platform."[20]

If less than 10 percent of the ULP's delegates came from the SLP and the IWPA, fully one-third of its leadership was (or had been) so affiliated. Thus Wilhelm Stahlknecht (of Die Möbel-Arbeiter Union), Mathias Schmeidin-ger (president of the German bakers' union), and Gustav Belz (secretary of the CLU and president of Die Metall-Arbeiter Union) sat on the original Committee of Twenty-One. In addition to the anarchists, eight more members of the committee had been (or still were) members of the SLP, including Schilling, Morgan, Paul Ehmann, and Frank Dvorak. Anarchists served on the party's speakers committee and as ward captains. If the radicals did not appear as candidates, they were still important: socialists and anarchists served the ULP so prominently and effectively because they possessed precisely the skills the party needed.

As in chapter 3, ecological regression across the city's 339 precincts, with ethnicity as the independent variables and the vote for ULP as the dependent variable can be used to define their relationship (see Table 9.2). Splitting the precincts between the native- and foreign-born reveals the strength and direction of the correlations, and the table also shows the change between the fall of 1886 and the spring of 1887. In that period, the Germans fell away from the ULP just as both the Irish and the Bohemians were increasingly involved. Within five months, as Schneirov has concluded, "the ULP had changed from being a labor party with a slight German bias, to one with more than a slight Irish bias."[21]

In April, the *Tribune* had noted that "the Scandinavians, Bohemians, and Poles probably absented themselves largely from the [voter's] registry through apathy." Despite the party's citizenship committee, there was no significant increase in voter turnout between fall and spring, and Robert Nelson ran well ahead of the party's aldermanic candidates. Thus the "one big catch" in the second contest, as Richard Schneirov put it, was the reality of vote splitting. Not only did the ULP fail to attract native-born and

Table 9.2 CORRELATIONS OF THE UNITED LABOR PARTY VOTE AND THE NATIVITY OF REGISTERED VOTERS, FALL 1886 AND SPRING 1887

[Precinct-level data, Pearson's, r^2]

Birthplace	Fall 1886		Spring 1887	
	r	r^2	r	r^2
Native-born	− .733	.537	− .830	.688
Foreign-born	+ .733	.537	+ .830	.688
Germany	+ .433	.187	+ .222	.049
Bohemia	+ .289	.083	+ .412	.169
Ireland	+ .248	.061	+ .505	.255
Poland	+ .213	.053	+ .183	.033
Norway	+ .103	.010	+ .113	.013
All other	− .256	.065	− .151	.022

Source: (election returns) Chicago *Tribune*, 3 November 1886, 1; 7 April 1887, 3; (nativity of registered voters) Lars Nelson, *Statistics Showing by Wards and Voting Precincts* [sic] *The Original Nationality of the Voters of Chicago* (Chicago: By the author, 1887).

English-speaking voters, but while Irish precincts were willing to follow Nelson, they would not desert their old ward loyalties.[22]

The mayoral elections of 1879 and 1887 marked an era spanned by the four terms of Carter Harrison's Democracy. The SLP's 1879 campaign contributed to his first victory; the ULP's 1887 campaign compelled him to withdraw. Both elections featured a labor party, the first Socialistic, the second United; their platforms were remarkably similar; and both parties tapped the same neighborhoods and wards.[23] The contrasts are more important. Ernst Schmidt captured 11,818 votes in 1879, Robert Nelson polled 23,490 eight years later. In that time population grew by 83 percent, but voter registration rose only 30 percent. Although the labor vote had doubled, neither party attracted the native-born or English-speaking. The correlation of Bohemian voters and the labor party remained unchanged, but those for Scandinavians and Poles had been halved. The most remarkable changes were those in German and Irish voting units. German wards had strongly supported the SLP in 1879 ($r = +.93$), but the correlation for German precincts and the ULP dropped to $+.22$ in 1887. Over the same period the Irish correlation rose from $+.15$ to $+.50$ (see Table 9.3).

The Germans and Irish remain central to our understanding of both labor parties. Had the two largest immigrant groups voted together in either year things might have turned out differently. Two months before the fall 1886 elections, the *Tribune* interviewed Tommy Ryan, once prominent in the SLP and founder of the Irish Fifth Ward Labor Guards, which had marched with the Lehr- und Wehr-Verein. Ryan had not been to a "Socialistic meeting for five years," but was excited by the ULP's prospects. It offered him a chance to "smash the party" that had "insulted" the workers with the class justice of the Haymarket Trial and the brutal death of Terrence Begley during the packinghouse strike. Six months later Ryan was dissatisfied with the ULP's original nominee for his Fifth Ward, and he sided with the Irish Knights against the German socialists in the fight. In the end the original candidate ran and even won. The Irish and Germans could not vote together.[24]

THE ANARCHIST PRESS AFTER HAYMARKET

Despite repression, the anarchist press did not disappear. The strongest, the Socialist Publishing Society's three papers, reappeared first. Although the galleys were set and ready to go to press on the Thursday after the riot, no shop in the city would print it. Oskar Neebe then secured new officers in the Westside Turner Hall, and the society finally bought its own printing

Table 9.3 CORRELATIONS OF PARTY AND THE NATIVITY OF
REGISTERED VOTERS: THE MAYORAL ELECTIONS OF THE SLP
(1879) AND THE ULP (1887)

[Pearson's r, r²]

Birthplace	SLP, 1879[a]		ULP, 1887[b]	
	r	r^2	r	r^2
Native-born	− .845	.713	− .830	.688
Foreign-born	+ .845	.713	+ .830	.688
English-speaking[c]	− .924	.853	− .589	.348
Non-English-speaking[d]	+ .924	.853	+ .589	.348
Germany	+ .931	.867	+ .222	.049
Bohemia	+ .423	.179	+ .412	.169
Poland	+ .411	.169	+ .183	.033
Norway	+ .203	.041	+ .113	.013
Irish	+ .147	.022	+ .505	.255
All other	+ .250	.063	− .151	.023

Sources: Tables 3.1 and 9.2, above.
[a]Based on ward-level data.
[b]Based on precinct-level data.
[c]"English-speaking" = Native-born, Canada, England, Scotland, Wales, and Ireland.
[d]"Non-English-speaking" = all others.

press. *Die Arbeiter-Zeitung, Der Vorbote,* and *Die Fackel* resumed publication
on Saturday, 8 May 1886. Despite the mayor's promise to suppress any
"inflammatory material," Spies and Schwab continued to write "the principle [sic] editorial matter" from their jail cells. They did not give it up for
more than a year, when a new set of editors, including Joseph Dietzgen,
Gustav Belz, Albert Currlin, Jens Christensen, and Simon Hickler, succes-
sively filled the position.[25] A socialist, indeed one of Marx's few American
correspondents, Dietzgen resigned his position on *Der Sozialist* in New
York, offered his services to the SPS in June, and edited *Die Arbeiter-Zeitung*
for almost two years until he died in April 1886. Albert Currlin, a major
figure in St. Louis's 1877 general strike, stayed a bit longer. They shared
editorial responsibility with Belz, president of the metalworkers' union

and secretary of the CLU. Christensen and Hickler took over after Belz's untimely death in October 1888, and managed the three papers through the nineties.[26]

Although the type, layout, features, and advertisers remained the same, the papers did change. They continued to cover the labor movement, but with a bit less urgency, and much less theory. The relationship between the press and the organized labor movement changed too. Die Möbel-Arbeiter Union got its own paper (*Die Möbel-Arbeiter Journal*, published in New York) as did the bakers (*Chicagoer Bäcker-Zeitung*); yet both unions stayed close to the Socialist Publishing Society. In November 1886, the CLU expressed concern about the new editors; in 1888, it briefly issued its own paper. As late as 1924, with a circulation of about 8,000, ownership still rested in the Zeitung Publishing Co., the Central Committee of the Socialist Party, Brewery Workers Union, Beer Bottlers Union, and the Bakers' and Confectionary Union, No. 2.[27]

Budoucnost was reincarnated, almost as quickly, as *Práce* [Labor], which grew out of a boycott of the city's largest Czech daily. Still a four-page weekly, and again edited by Josef Pecka, it was issued from the same little basement office. Both papers first appeared as dailies, then became weeklies, but the former was an anarchist paper, an official organ of the IWPA; although edited by an anarchist and printed by others, the latter was a labor paper funded by local Bohemian unions.[28] The Bohemian carpenters in Local 54 provided capital and a publication committee although "few had the ability to discuss the financing of the publication." They turned to the woodworkers' and painters' unions, promising "to make it the publication of all labor groups, to be supported by all labor groups, so that it would continue to function on a permanent basis." At one point the carpenters even considered its outright purchase, but with a membership of under 250 and a treasury of $400 the deal fell through. "A great many difficulties arose" between its publisher and printer and "All locals were requested to contribute to the support of this publication, and all members instructed to purchase and read it, to pay up an advance subscription." The CLU twice extended its financial support, to no avail; the carpenters pulled out and eventually banned discussions of the paper. *Práce* died in July 1887, leaving "bad feelings and hot blood amongst the [union's] members, in some for years, in some forever."[29]

Joseph R. Buchanan moved his *Labor Enquirer* from Denver to Chicago in spring 1887, just in time for the ULP's mayoral campaign. From its first issue both editor and paper were out of place. Buchanan simultaneously held membership cards as an organizer for the International Workingmen's Association and as the District Master Workman of the Knights' DA 89 in Denver. With a foot in both camps (like Parsons), he was misunderstood by both. Buchanan had been invited by one group of Knights only to discover that the *Knights of Labor* had already appeared, another rival was about to appear, and Buchanan was penniless. The *Chicago Labor Enquirer* appeared on 23 February 1887 as a biweekly and a brother printer assured him that it was "the neatest paper ever issued in Chicago." Yet the paper was insolvent, the post office refused to deliver it, and news carriers were warned not to touch it. After the ULP's campaign Buchanan cut back to a weekly, and the carpenters' union gave enough money to "make *The Enquirer* free of debt." At one point, early in 1888, a press association planned expansion, but the subscription list "was never more than one twentieth of what it should have been." Buchanan again cut his staff and set his own type.[30]

Then "something strange and disagreeable happened." Buchanan had joined the American section of the SLP, "the only Socialistic organization in Chicago." In fall 1888, he was summoned to appear before the section to show cause why he should not be expelled on the charge of selling out to the Democrats. William Holmes complained that the *Enquirer* "never took a square stand on any great principle. While at heart its editor was a revolutionary socialist, the *Enquirer* could never be called a socialistic paper. It advocated radical reform in a vague sort of way that left the reader in considerable doubt." From New York, *Der Sozialist* warned that Buchanan had withdrawn "from the control of organized labor." In August 1888, he dismissed his staff and sent his paper's obituary and subscription list on to Henry George. The next day Buchanan sent a letter of resignation to the SLP. It was returned, for "eight men and two women—not one of whom was American born" had already expelled him from the party.[31]

The Alarm reappeared in November 1887, eighteen months after the riot, six days before the executions. A four-page weekly like its namesake, it survived for twenty-two months, through January 1889, although it was published in Chicago for only the first five months. The new editor, Dyer Lum, was familiar in Chicago. He was a Knight, and a member of both the SLP and later the IWPA; he had edited a vaguely anarchist paper, *Lucifer: The Lightbearer*, in Kansas, and had been a frequent contributor to the first *Alarm*.[32] Against August Spies's advice, Lucy Parsons and Sarah Ames invited Lum to edit the new paper. Spies feared competition with Buchanan's paper and urged Gustav Belz to warn the CLU out of supporting the paper. With Lizzie Holmes returning as the assistant editor, the new *Alarm* looked like the old; but Lum was not Parsons. He highlighted free thought, disdained the ULP, all but ignored the labor movement, and addressed *The Alarm* to a shrinking readership. After moving to New York, a single column, on the third page, carried "Our Chicago Letter." The second *Alarm* had changed.[33]

Two new German papers appeared after Haymarket. The first remains as much a cipher as *Den Nye Tid*. The *Arbeiter Stimme* (Workers' voice), described by William Holmes as "the official organ of the Central Labor Union," was expected to appear in February 1888. "It will be a weekly," he reported to *The Alarm*, "and 25,000 copies are to be guaranteed for five weeks at least." The *Arbeiter Stimme* appears to have been the CLU's German-language competitor to Trades Assembly's new English-language *Record*; we know nothing however, about its editors, editorials, circulation, or even its history (if any) beyond those five issues.[34] Almost nine years after its demise in 1885 the German section of the SLP in Chicago reactivated *Der Illinoiser Volks-Zeitung*. Subtitled "Den Interessen den Arbeitenden Volkes gewidnet," and published by the Deutscheverein Druckerei with a Typographia No. 9 union label, it appeared in March 1893, with an enlarged format and a new title, the *Chicago Echo*.[35]

Fourteen years after *The Socialist* folded, the SLP's English-speaking section issued its second organ. An eight-page weekly, *Chicago Labor* was not even printed in Chicago, but in St. Louis, and only the last page carried local news. In sixteen months, from August 1893 to December 1894, the paper went through at least three local editors, including John Glambeck, the section's Danish organizer, and J. Hubert de Witt, who described himself as a "young, brilliant and energetic young man." Local reports were buried on the last page, jammed between local ads. Before reaching them, a Chicago reader had to wade through the SLP's national platform, reports from the New York sections, and national ads. After sixteen months Chicagoans wanted their own paper, which they finally got in July 1896.[36]

Socialist papers in the Progressive Era built on foundations laid in the Gilded Age. It is not clear precisely how the Haymarket Affair affected the socialist press. The SPS continued to issue three papers: if the editors changed frequently the type, articles, news, and advertisers did not. *Die Arbeiter-Zeitung*, *Die Fackel*, and *Der Vorbote* looked the same in 1900 as they had in 1880 or 1886. The ads for the LWV no longer appeared, the stories about dynamite were gone, but all three maintained their militant commitment to the labor movement. The experience of the non-German socialist papers was not much different. None survived as long, but the gaps in their publishing history were never glaring. In the Czech community *Práce* took over for *Budoucnost*, then *Denni Hlastel* (Daily announcer) appeared; when it was perceived as too conservative, *Spravedlnost* (Justice) came out. Although *Den Nye Tid* died in 1884, *Revyen* appeared a decade later, competed with the more radical *Arbejderen* from 1896 to 1900, and survived almost thirty years. Chicago's first Polish socialist weekly, *Nowe Zycie* (New life), appeared from 1889 to 1896, the second *Gazeta Robotnicza* (Workers' newspaper) in 1896. If the English-speaking socialist press experienced chronic bankruptcy, a new paper, with a new name and editors always appeared. The effort in founding and maintaining a multilingual press was apparently justified.[37]

ANARCHIST CLUB LIFE AFTER HAYMARKET

Where the press survived, even grew in circulation, the edifice of anarchist organization vanished in the wake of the riot. At the end of July 1886, barely two months after the riot, the *Tribune* reported: "As to the effect of the Anarchist Trial upon Anarchists in general, Joseph Gruenhut said yesterday that it was 'driving them together like wax,' and that their numbers were increasing instead of diminishing." Despite the *Tribune's* best effort to qualify its source—not only was he one "who ought to know," but "his knowledge . . . is unimpeachable"—Gruenhut had (perhaps unwittingly) played into the hands of the hysterics. The movement had closed ranks, but there is no evidence that its numbers increased. On the contrary, *Die Arbeiter-Zeitung* stopped listing the meeting times or places of the Chicago area's IWPA groups, as did *The Alarm* when it reappeared. It would have been foolhardy.[38]

If the label "anarchist" maintained currency in the commercial press, the name of the IWPA all but disappeared from the radical and labor press. Thus the *Tribune* reported in September 1886 that "Anarchist groups continue intact; [they] meet weekly but they are rather tame, as the members are not sure of their fellows." The German abbreviation IAA, appeared only twice in the pages of *Der Vorbote* after Haymarket. The first was in an open letter, "An die gruppen der IAA in den Vereinigten Staaten von Nordamerika," which reported that the association had reformed, declared its continued loyalty to the Pittsburgh Manifesto, and then endorsed the ULP's candidates. Three years later, in 1890, the initials reappeared in the headline of an article announcing the organization of a group among Chicago's Russian Jews.[39] There was one attempt, in November 1886, to reorganize the remnants of the Lehr- und Wehr-Verein and its announcements continued to appear until April 1887. But according to Christine

Heiss, after that date "information on the association peters out, with no official reference concerning its dissolution." That did not come until 1920, but because the verein failed to submit yearly reports or to pay a yearly fee it had forfeited its legal existence as early as 1901.[40]

When Joseph Buchanan arrived in early 1887, the SLP was "the only socialist organization in the city." In its seven-part series, "Geschichte der Arbeiter Bewegung Chicagos," serialized in May and June 1887, *Der Vorbote* never spoke of the IAA in the present tense, only in the past. Then, at the end of 1887, Joseph Dietzgen wrote an obituary for the name, asking "Ist der Anarchismus todt?" and answering in the affirmative. Only after Dyer Lum had moved to New York did the name appear in *The Alarm*. Two years after the riot, Lum still received "many inquiries" about the IWPA and requests for membership cards. From New York he advised:

> The idea of the International *was* to unite the workers of all lands and to instruct as well as to solidify. . . . Our work during the present transitional period is largely an educational one, and wherever "two or three are found gathered together" with earnest minds, there the spirit of the social revolution will be in the midst of them. Come together at stated intervals, select some revolutionary literature for reading and discussion; try to animate the lukewarm and secure their interest; make yourselves apostles of the new abolition with or without formalities, and if an English-speaking group, correspond with this office. . . . Organize your groups and social clubs and *The Alarm* will give you Sunday or other day lessons for study. All can work to this end and do much to revive hope, encourage [sic] weakness and strengthen devotion.[41]

With the IWPA's demise many of its members had fled into the Turnverein, "where ethnicity was used as a more or less effective shield against further encroachments" by the forces of order. Before Haymarket, anarchists had been members and officers, and the day after the riot the Westside Turnhall became *Die Arbeiter-Zeitung*'s new offices; during repression the Turnverein served as a front by providing halls, audiences, and support. Yet Julius Vahlteich and some others recognized that "the Turner Association cannot be a socialist organization in the real sense of the term," and they tried to push it in a more "progressive" direction. However useful, the Turnverein proved a dangerous refuge and Michael Schwab later argued that those who had remained undercover "became philistines. The Turner clubs have become somewhat more radical, but the price paid for this, i.e. stifling the growth of the socialist associations, was too high."[42]

Many of the anarchists returned to the ranks of the SLP. Some trickled back after the ULP's 1886 and 1887 campaigns, then membership reached a plateau and fell off. In February 1891, the city advertized only two sections; two years later the SLP reorganized with seven sections in Chicago and one in suburban Englewood. In March 1894, the party's official organ listed a total of eleven groups: two American [i.e., English-speaking], one again headed by T. J. Morgan, the other in Englewood; two German groups, including one in Lakeview; three Danish groups; one Bohemian group in the eighth, ninth and tenth wards; a Jewish group; and Karl Marx Groups Nos. 1 and 2. Another American group formed in April, and a new Danish group, the fourth one, in August. In September the "Bohemian-Slavonic Socialist Labor Clubs of the 7th, 8th, 9th and 10th Wards, claiming a membership of 10,000" applied for a charter; a month later a fourth American group was organized in West Pullman.[43]

Club life in the middle of the 1890s remained substantially unchanged from a decade before. It was still based on language branches and still tied into the associational network within the city's immigrant neighborhoods. The clubs met in the same halls, featured the same kinds of lectures, discussions, and debates, and offered the same services. John Glambeck, editor of *Chicago Labor*, and organizer of one of the Danish sections, explained: "During the last fifteen years [i.e., since 1879] the Socialist Labor Party of this country has not been an active party, but a school of socialism where the most advanced men and women could meet and educate themselves in the aims and objects of the modern labor movement." In May 1894, Danish Section No. 1—comprising some 60 members—"decided to establish a free reading room. . . . The Committee [was] instructed to find a suitable place not connected with a saloon." Beyond the usual books, the group "subscribed to *Social Demokraten, Ravnen* [both from Copenhagen], *Den Danske Pioneer,* and *Chicago Labor.* In American Group No. 1, Michael Britzius lectured on "The Aims and Progress of Socialism" and "Die politischen Interessen der Gewerkschaften," T. J. Morgan asked "what is Socialism?" William Snyder analyzed "Business Depressions," and Paul Ehmann spoke on "The Philosophy of the Labor Movement." Danish Group No. 2 had "an eloquent woman for its orator" at one meeting; at the next, Comrade Anderson "gave a brief history of the growth of the Social Democrats in Europe." In the Jewish section, Frau Iralowicz [sic?] lectured on "Die Stellung des Sozialisten zur Frauenfrage." Both Oskar Neebe and Samuel Fielden lectured frequently, and when Chris Meier, the "well known Chicago socialist," was appointed an election commissioner, the party's paper proudly noted he had "been identified with the SLP for the last twenty years."[44]

The clubs continued to offer the same services they had a decade before:

concerts, gala balls, picnics; the same celebrations of Stiftungsfesten, of Lassalle's birthday, May Day, and the Paris Commune. Those events still served as the party's major revenue source; a picnic ad in the summer of 1894 proclaimed, "We must have our own press!" And the Socialist Lie-dertafel, now a citywide chorus, was still "willing to donate its services to the different sections and no doubt will be a great aid in attracting people to agitation meetings."[45] Beyond the survival of the German and American sections was the rebirth of socialism in the Scandinavian community and its birth in the Jewish colony. We turn briefly to consider each.

Norwegians and Danes had been active in the WPI, the WPUS, and in the SLP during the seventies and eighties. In 1881 and 1883 their branch had sent delegates to the Chicago and Pittsburgh congresses of the RSP and the IWPA, and a Dano-Norwegian paper, *Den Nye Tid*, had been an important party organ from 1878 through 1884. But Scandinavian socialists became mysteriously invisible for the next six years. Sometime in spring 1886, the Pinkerton agent who had infiltrated the American Group approached Albert Parsons about starting a new paper and Parsons reportedly replied, "Yes, it is a good idea . . . we must have the Scandinavians with us."[46]

They returned to the socialist ranks in the nineties as pan-Scandinavian groups, uniting Danes, Norwegians, and Swedes. By 1895, the Norwegians had their own organ, *Revyen;* in 1896, the Danish groups organized the Arbejederen Publishing Association and issued *Arbejederen*. In February 1899, *Revyen* reported: "A new club, Skandinavisk Diskussionklub Fremad, has been founded. Its aim is to spread culture and information among Skandinavian workers. There are to be lectures on science, economics, history, politics and literature. The Club also asks everyone who has books which he does not want to keep to give them to the library." Two years later, the oldest of these clubs decided "to dissolve and join the English[-speaking] socialists in the wards where the members live. The members of the Scandinavian section were living too far apart to attend the meetings regularly." The same strategic debates surfaced again and again. In 1904, the Skandinavisk Socialdemokratiske Sygeforening (Sick benefit society) met to discuss the expulsion of the 28th Ward branch from the party. "Most of the members of the branch are not satisfied with the socialist platform adopted by the National Convention;" according to *Revyen*, "they find it too tame and not radical enough."[47]

According to Philip Bregstone, the Haymarket tragedy "was the forerunner of the radical movement among the Jews of Chicago. One of the results was 'The Jewish Workingmen's Educational Club' (JWEC), with club rooms at 450 S. Canal Street founded in 1888. It was there that the Jewish labor movement, Jewish radicalism, socialism and anarchism in this city first saw the light of day." As in the other groups the club established a library, conducted lectures, and encouraged public speaking. Eastern European Jews, not Germans, dominated the JWEC. Russian-born Bisno and his friends understood spoken German and it was August Spies who first presented a socialist critique to the group. Spies's argument "struck me like lightning . . . we are disinherited, the property of the country does belong to the rich; all we get out of it is a bare living for very hard work; . . . we ought to all unite, all the working people from all trades, and support what he calls the labor movement."[48]

The JWEC survived from 1888 to 1892, and although its membership constantly changed, there were about 200 dues payers, and a cadre of fifteen "ring leaders." Two groups appeared within the membership: one headed by Peter Sissman and Abraham Bisno that was social-democratic, the other, headed by Drs. Nahin and Knopfnagel, that "followed the doctrines of Bakunin and Krapotkin." Although the club dissolved in 1892, it produced two heirs: the cloakmaker's union, headed by Bisno, which became the city's first Jewish trade union in 1889; and the Lassalle Political Club, founded three years later, "a purely social democratic organization," headed by Bisno, Sissman, and the brothers Tuvim, which later affiliated with the SLP and the Socialist Trades and Labor Assembly.[49]

The Scandinavian and Jewish socialists stayed with the movement through to World War I. Although both continued to grow, they followed different paths. In the last half of the 1890s the Jews joined the Socialist Trade and Labor Alliance; the Scandinavians went first with the SLP, then the Socialist Party, finally, in 1905, with the Industrial Workers of the World.

MOVEMENT CULTURE AFTER HAYMARKET

With its two central institutions, its press and club life, intact, even growing, it is not surprising that the movement culture described in chapter 7 also survived. See, for example, this brief account:

> The Carl Marx Club arranged a social gathering last Saturday . . . which was well attended. A fresh socialistic atmosphere was evident, and the evening was spent in chummy comradeship. The socialistic party, and its ever-increasing political influence, was the subject for discussion and the comrades agreed that the day has now come, when we must all go out and in a short time Chicago, the State of

Illinois, indeed the whole world, will be ours. [After singing and dancing] the comrades parted about 3 o'clock in the morning.[50]

In the 1890s and by the first decade of the twentieth century movement culture had changed subtly, almost imperceptibly. Yet it may not have changed fast enough, for the movement failed to attract a second generation, and some of the first dropped away.

Movement culture continued to commemorate the same events. Thus, Julius Vahlteich, Ferdinand Lassalle's secretary in the 1860s, gave the central speech in April 1894 when the Debattir Club No. 2 celebrated its hero's birthday. In October 1894 *Chicago Labor* advertised the

2nd Anniversary
Concert and Ball
of
The Karl Marx Club No. 1
Section SLP
Sunday, 21 October 1894
at Ruehl's Hall
220 and 224 W. Twelfth Street
Tickets—10 cents

Five months earlier the Jewish section held its fourth annual "grand ball." During the summer, each group scheduled a picnic and invited all of the others. Picnics, dances, concerts and festivals in the 1890s continued to serve as fund-raising events just as they had one and two decades before.[51] The movement's old heroes—Tom Paine, Karl Marx, Ferdinand Lassalle—were still remembered annually. May Day, Labor Day, and the 11th of November became new events that coexisted with the older traditions. Marcus Thrane wrote his best-known play, *Konspirationen*, based on the Haymarket Affair, and there were Polish performances of *Nihilisci*, based on the assassination of Czar Alexander II. In May 1889, the Central Labor Union, the Socialist Publishing Society, and the Arbeiterbund arranged a centennial festival for Bastille Day, inviting Serge Schevitsch from New York and Robert Reitzel from Detroit as the German speakers, Robert Swallow, Lucy Parsons and T. J. Morgan in English, Jakub Mikolanda in Czech, and Jens Christensen in "the Scandinavian language." *Der Vorbote* reported more than 8,000 people came.[52]

Chicago's socialists continued to celebrate March 17 as "The Day of the Commune," at least through 1910. In 1889, "Die 18. Jahresfeier der Pariser

221

Commune," jointly sponsored by the SPS and the CLU, was commemorated by an English-speaking audience in Vorwaerts Turnhalle and by a German audience in Yondorf's Halle on the West side. The festival continued to spread from Chicago. The next October *Der Vorbote* reported that a new organization, the "Bohmischen Arbeiter Bildungsverein," was planning a national commemoration. In 1894 a "special Commune edition" of *Chicago Labor* outlined its history on the first and second pages, editorialized on the fourth, and advertised the Chicago festival (among others) on the last.[53] As Klaus Ensslen and Heinz Ickstadt have argued, and as we noted earlier, "the pattern of the celebration of the Day of the Commune was the same in 1908 as it was 25 years earlier." The programs continued to feature addresses, songs, music, dance, and theater. And the festival continued to be an international celebration. In addition to English, German, Norwegian, and Czech, new speakers used Danish, Swedish, Yiddish, and Russian for the increasingly varied audiences of the 1890s.[54]

The seventies and eighties had been "the heroic age" for socialist movement culture in Chicago. While the institutions survived, and despite reactivated and invented traditions, enthusiasm and vitality waned. With repression and time, movement culture shrank rather than collapsed, becoming melancholy and private. In 1909, *Die Arbeiter-Zeitung*'s editor confessed: "In the grave of time, the pain and fury about the misdeed of those ruling in 1887 have become corrupted to sweet nostalgia. . . . Whoever has his eyes on the whole must admit that, generally speaking, the cause of revolution has progressed beyond the stage it had reached when Spies and his friends were murdered." The decline in movement culture was relative, not absolute, for socialist audiences continued to grow, more slowly than the city's population to be sure. The crowd of 30,000 to 40,000 that had celebrated the Commune in 1879 was never seen again. Gesangvereine or theater groups performed for smaller, older audiences. Instead of recruiting new members, the movement's institutions and traditions only served to sustain old ones. By the end of the 1890s, the dramatic groups had disappeared, although the singing societies survived. One indication of the movement's shrinkage lies in the utter disappearance of its parades and processions. Compared to those sponsored and arranged by the SLP in the seventies or the IWPA in the eighties, those of the nineties became fewer and smaller. They no longer frightened "the philistines and politicians," nor shook up "the people, the workers," as Friedrich Sorge had put it earlier. Once a demonstration of the vitality of a confrontational and mass movement, when the socialists ceased to parade they became less visible. Despite its declining audiences, declining visibility, and the "corruption of sweet nostalgia," movement culture had not yet become as "fossilized" as Ensslen and Ickstadt make it out to be. Paul Buhle, for example, remains convinced that Chicago's German socialists were there at the "origins of left culture in the United States" and has convincingly argued that "when scholars analyse German-American radical culture in the late nineteenth and twentieth centuries, they are . . . studying the earliest and formative pattern of a far larger movement."[55]

The movement's leadership had been summarily executed in 1887, and the active membership had to endure almost ten years of repression. Those who had comprised the sympathetic following before the affair learned quite quickly that to associate, much less identify, with the anarchists risked perhaps too much. "Despite the buffeting it received at the hands of the police and the press," in Henry David's careful judgement, "the revolutionary movement in Chicago was not destroyed."[56] Its press, clubs, and culture survived. And yet anarchy seemed to fade away: not *because* of the riot or repression, not *because* of the Haymarket Affair, not even *after* the executions. It faded when it merged into later movements, including the American Federation of Labor, the Socialist Party, and the Industrial Workers of the World.

Chapter Ten

EX-ANARCHISTS
IN THE GAY NINETIES

By all accounts, save this one, Chicago's anarchist movement tragically ended in November 1887 with one suicide, four executions, and three prison terms. Our story is not finished, for there are still some loose ends to tie up before we can conclude. In chapter 9 we abruptly left the Eight Hour Movement in May 1886; we need to return and trace its denouement after the Haymarket Affair and in the 1890s. In chapter 3 we traced the Socialistic Labor Party's electoral struggle; we need a similar sketch. And finally, we need to return to chapter 2's discussion of dual unionism, to the conflict between socialist and nonsocialist trade unions, and to the apparent triumph of "pure and simple" unionism in the 1890s.

THE EIGHT HOUR MOVEMENT AFTER HAYMARKET

As Selig Perlman suggested almost seventy years ago, the Eight Hour Movement "assumed larger proportions in Chicago than elsewhere in the country and the outcome would have been proportionally successful, had it not been for the tragic event on the fourth" of May. As early as May 2, the Eight Hour Association felt it had lost control of the movement; that same day the Trade and Labor Assembly discussed abandoning its demands. The bomb exploded before either could abdicate. Three weeks later the *Knights of Labor* advised its readers to "settle your difficulties the best you can and return to work"; on June 5 it conceded "the general failure of the eight hour movement." Beyond the reckless demand of eight-hours' work for ten-hours' pay, George Schilling, who had successfully led the packinghouse workers, saw intercity competition as the central problem: "we did not 'paint the town red' as we would have done if the other cities had stood by us. Chicago can lead the country, but it cannot leave it."[1] Chicago's movement seemed doomed when other cities failed to follow its bold lead. The bomb exploded in Haymarket Square, not within the Eight Hour Movement. Indeed, some unions managed to hold out against stepped-up employer resistance and public repression. The packinghouse workers, cigarmakers, machinists, most in the building trades, and many of the retail clerks, for example, retained the eight-hour day. Other trades—including the furniture and garment workers, the bakers, and the brewers—claimed only partial victories. By the end of 1866, however, only 15,000 of the 80,000 workers who had struck in May still retained the short day.[2]

One has to wonder what might have happened if the police had not rioted, or if the bomb had not been thrown on May 4. Without martial law, without the police reaction, what would have happened in Chicago in the rest of May? Everything we know about the anarchists and the CLU suggests that they would have assumed the leadership of the Great Upheaval, especially when they heard of the Eight Hour Association's vacillation or the Trades Assembly's defeatism. Given the uncontrollable enthusiasm of the unskilled, the unmistakable signs of employer resistance, and the unbridled hostility of the police, one suspects that a confrontation, if not a riot, was inevitable. Had the police not marched to the Haymarket on the night of May 4 they would certainly have attacked within the month. However fascinating, counterfactual history is simply not as interesting as what actually happened.

The police did riot and the bomb did explode. Few within the city and its labor movement dared to offer any sympathy to the anarchists. The *Knights of Labor* disclaimed any "affiliation, association, sympathy, or respect for the band of cowardly murderers." Typographical Union No. 16 judged those responsible to be "the greatest enemy the laboring man has," and offered a reward for the bomb throwers; DA 24 and the Trades Assembly used similar language in a joint statement. Yet none of those denunciations differed from the ones that had appeared from 1884 to 1886: the bomb and riot may have been shocking, but they were not unexpected.[3]

Chicago's first Eight Hour Movement came in 1867, the second in 1879, the third in 1886. With each repetition the movement grew in size, influence, and power but not success. With the blame for the most recent failure firmly laid on the anarchists, the organized labor movement prepared for a fourth effort in 1890. Samuel Gompers recommended the issue to the AFL's 1888 convention which chose 1 May, 1890 for the inauguration of the eight-hour workday and threatened to strike for its enforcement. Within the Knights, both Powderly and the *Journal of United Labor* preferred the "Norton plan" which promised to phase in half-hour reductions until eight hours was reached. At its 1889 convention the SLP approved the movement as "the most radical reform possible under the present system." At the highest levels then unionists, Knights, and socialists favored reduction, but they disagreed over tactics and timing. Only the United Brotherhood of Carpenters pushed the issue, and by May 1890 they had assumed de facto leadership, both nationally and in Chicago.[4]

The movement was emasculated. The AFL voiced an ongoing demand, then strategically retreated, at first recommending the issue to its affiliates, then urging it only where it could gain success. In the end that meant not the building trades, just the carpenters. The Knights disdained a general strike, but promised to "lend their moral support." In May 1890, the carpenters, the Deutsch-amerikanische Typographia, and the Granite Cutters won the eight-hour day; the bakers and tailors won ten hours in some cities. A year later the AFL tried again, but "generally depressed business conditions," and "the last minute defection of the United Mine Workers" aborted the campaign. After 1891, Gompers rejected mass, even citywide strikes and decided that the issue "became the responsibility . . . of individual unions . . . rather than the Federation" itself.[5]

THE SLP AND ELECTORAL SOCIALISM

Less than three weeks after the United Labor Party's defeat in April 1887, its more conservative elements seceded and formed the Union Labor Party, "in many respects a revival of the old Greenback-Labor Party of the early Eighties." Its offer of fusion was immediately rejected, and William Gleason continued to try to recapture the original party. Known to the commercial press as "the Free Lunch Party," Gleason's Union Labor Party was in fact a Democratic front and sat out the fall 1887 elections. Although

Morgan's ULP ran a slate, none of its candidates polled more than a fifth of the victorious Republican's total. In January 1888 Morgan's ULP became the Radical Labor Party (RLP); expecting 12,000 votes, it polled all of 3,600 in the spring elections. The RLP survived for one more election, the next fall, when it polled all of 2,183 votes and then folded.[6]

The SLP reappeared in its place. Two hundred of the faithful attended the 1889 nominating convention, which declared

> our present action has been hastened by the demoralization of the local political labor movement, and the desertion of honest, progressive principles by unscrupulous leaders and their infatuated followers, some going to the Democratic party, and the ostracism of the Socialists by scheming politicians, who have used the name of labor to deceive the workers and subserve their own private interests.

The *Arbeiter-Zeitung* judged the whole effort "imprudent" because the party lacked both time and money for an effective campaign. Against a field that included a Joint Labor Party, sponsored by the *Knights of Labor*, as well as the two major parties, the SLP polled all of 167 votes. The SLP ran another full slate for the 1891 municipal elections when the irrepressible Morgan headed the ticket and polled 2,376 votes, not even 2 percent of the total. While the SLP contested all thirty-four aldermanic seats, eight of its candidates failed to draw double-digit tallies and in the worst case J. B. Beel apparently forgot to vote for himself. "Mr. Morgan did not poll a surprisingly heavy vote," noted the renamed *Rights of Labor*, "but he made a surprisingly good canvas . . . and propagated his ideas on social and labor problems to an extent that could not have been accomplished in any other way." Two years later Henry Ehrenpreis polled 830 votes in the 1893 mayoral campaign, less than one percent of the total. The Peoples' Party, not discretion, kept the SLP out of both the 1895 and 1897 campaigns. In the century's last mayoral election, the SLP and the new Social Democracy of America competed against each other and the regular parties. With 541 votes the SLP's mayoral candidate beat both the Prohibition candidate (389) and the Social Democrat (141); yet combined, the two socialists accounted for all of 692 votes.[7]

In the 1890s Chicago's SLP lost votes in each successive election. The same fights between trade union socialists and political socialists erupted again and again. There were two national party conventions in Chicago in the fall of 1889: one of the Rosenberg political faction, the other of De Leonite unionists. Between 1892 and 1896, at both the local and national levels, the party was torn between running its own candidates and fusing with the People's Party. At the national level De Leon dictated an independent course, while in Chicago Morgan tried, quite valiantly in fact, to broaden the party's base, to win new converts, and to maintain the party's precarious existence. De Leon succeeded, Morgan failed. Yet another round of purges ensued, just as they had in 1880. And if the SLP tended to repeat itself, the first experiment with fusion was tragic, the second almost farcical. After McKinley's election, Chicago's SLP was in a shambles, with the turn of the century many of its members joined the new Socialist Party of America. But until then political socialists and electoral socialism in Chicago lapsed into isolation if not impotence.[8]

SOCIALISTS AND THE UNIONS IN THE NINETIES

In July 1889, three full years after Haymarket, the *New Yorker Volks-Zeitung* suggested that "the trade union movement, which in Chicago had been stronger than in any other city in the country, . . . was now at a completely low tide. The Central Labor Union had more than 40,000 members in the spring of 1886. Now a mere 5,000 are left on paper, and of these, not even 1,000 will show up at demonstrations."[9] After Haymarket, the anarchists abandoned dual unionism and returned to their national and international unions. The Progressive Cigarmakers, who had issued the call for the CLU, returned to the International in 1885, but stayed in the CLU. "Remembering its well-established tradition of agitation for the eight hour day," Die Möbel-Arbeiter Union "decided to leave the German-dominated radical Central Labor Union . . . in order to set an example of cross-ethnic agitation." The city's carpenters reorganized in 1888 and a painters' district council re-united unions affiliated with the CLU, the Trades Assembly, and the brotherhood in 1894, on a model provided by the carpenters. Even Typographia Union No. 9, the bulwark of the socialist press, returned to its International. By 1890, and with the first issue of *Der Organisator*, the German and English printers' unions organized in unison. Despite their long rivalry, the CLU and the Trades Assembly reached some kind of detente in 1888. The carpenters and painters, for example, maintained dual membership in both the central and assembly and the two cooperated, not without friction, throughout the 1890s. As the rivalry faded, with time the CLU maintained an independent existence for twenty more years until it quietly expired in 1909.[10]

Despite the double distraction of political action and internal conflict, Chicago's socialists remained active, even prominent, in the organized labor movement in the nineties. Elizabeth Morgan served as an officer in the Women's Federal Labor Union in Chicago and led the citywide fight against sweatshops in the garment industry. George Schilling became District Master workman in DA 24 and, though he had left the socialist movement in 1883, continued to voice workingmen's demands, first as an aide to Governor John Peter Altgeld and later as a functionary of the Chicago Civic Federation. Gustav Hoerich served as Die Möbel-Arbeiter Union's delegate to the national conventions of the Furniture Workers' and Amalgamated Wood Workers' through 1900; Paul Grottkau worked as a traveling organizer for the AFL in California. Thomas J. Morgan stayed with the Chicago Metal Workers Union, serving as a delegate to its national conventions and to those of the AFL, and carried Plank 10—the nationalization of both railroads and telegraphs—to the federation's 1896 convention.[11]

Despite repression, Chicago's ex-anarchists were almost as prominent in the labor movement. After the police closed down *Budoucnost*, Josef Pondelicek continued as the president of the first Bohemian painters' union; two of its next three presidents in the nineties had been anarchists only a decade before. Ex-anarchists continued to serve as the officers of the Furniture Workers', Typographia No. 9, and Metal Workers' unions. Although Mathias Schmeidinger, a master baker and anarchist, was forced out of the Bäcker Unterstüztungsverein in 1887, Oskar Neebe became active in both the brewers' and bakers' locals after his pardon. The more obscure anarchists show up only occasionally: in January 1898, Henry Uhlhorn, a member of Carpenters' Local 521, successfully "introduced a motion to have the union order the *Social Democrat* sent to each member for a period of three months."[12] If only for symmetry, we should return first to the carpenters' union, then to the cigarmakers, finally to the Central Labor Union.

After 1885, when we left them in chapter 2, the carpenters' unions grew dramatically. Three strategic changes were responsible. First, a new set of leaders, "more attuned to the radicalism of the mid-1880s . . . and more willing to enter into alliances with the German-Bohemian Socialists," came to the front in 1885. If they disdained anarchism, their union strongly supported both the defense and amnesty campaigns, and actively participated in the United Labor Party. The second strategy reorganized the brotherhood's locals into a United Carpenters' Council and accommodated hitherto dissident elements; those who had left for the Knights in 1882 and those who had joined the Central Labor Union in 1884 returned. Finally, a new, multiple charter system provided more autonomy and tolerated, even encouraged, ethnic branches. As a result, the Germans rejoined as Locals 240 through 244, the Bohemians as Locals 54 and 256, and "large numbers of the Knights" became Local 73." By 1890, the United Brotherhood had twenty-four locals in Chicago and was the unquestioned leader of the city's carpenters.[13]

The long strike in 1886–1887 had failed, due as much to low levels of unionization as to fractured organization and mutual hostility. All that changed and the union returned to the eight-hour day as the organizing issue. Local 1, "the radical union" led by Anton Johannson, who described himself as both a socialist and anarchist, now belonged to both the CLU and the Trades Assembly, and contained almost half of the brotherhood's membership in the city. The brotherhood finally approached the pieceworkers, who had undermined all previous organizing drives by lowering fees and dues and organizing around the eight-hour day. An eleven-month strike, which started in April 1890, finally won a two-year agreement, which included the eight-hour day, higher wages, and a permanent arbitration committee. By 1891, with between 6,000 and 8,000 men, the carpenters had built the largest union in the city.[14]

The Knights went into a tailspin after the Great Upheaval: at the national level membership dropped from a high of 730,000 in the summer of 1886 to 260,000 two years later. The Knights' *General Assembly Proceedings* recorded a Chicago membership of 22,592 in July 1886; six months later it had slipped almost 20 percent; in the next six months it dropped to 9,819. In 1888, Chicago still boasted four District Assemblies, but membership had sunk to 5,461.[15] That kind of "mushroom growth" had long haunted both local and national leaders, and Powderly insisted he "would rather have ten good men and true than a thousand lukewarm ones." As he explained in 1882, "I am not in favor of too rapid organization. I have observed that those organized hastily are the first to disband." Fully 116 of the 218 (53 percent) local assemblies ever founded in Chicago had been born in 1886. Of 116 new assemblies, 61 percent had lapsed by 1887, and fully 80 percent were gone a year later. Powderly's role in the Crane Brothers boycott in the spring of 1886 and his interference in the packinghouse strike that fall were in part to blame for the order's disintegration. Not even a dramatic change of local leadership could stay those defections.[16]

The Knights lost both unskilled and skilled members, and again the groundwork had been laid before the Upheaval. The Knights had originally organized mixed assemblies that included both skilled and unskilled and mingled different trades. In 1882, the Grand Master approved the decision to organize homogeneous trade assemblies, and they quickly rivalled the older mixed ones. Of the 116 assemblies established in 1886, only twenty-eight were mixed; more than three-quarters of the new assemblies organized along trade lines. In June 1887, Chicago's assemblies wholeheartedly approved a new constitution that mandated national trade assemblies.[17] Many interpreted that decision as a declaration of war. If, in its own words, the Noble Order in Chicago had been "fostered, maintained, and kept alive solely and entirely by trade unionists," their cooperation ended in the summer of 1886. "The storm center was the cigarmaking trade," according to Eugene Staley, "and the bone of contention, the blue label." In 1884, the Knights had stood with the Cigarmaker's International Union (CMIU) in their battle against the Progressive union; in 1886, the socialists stayed with the International against the Knights.[18]

The fight came at the Illinois State Federation of Labor's fourth convention in 1887. The CMIU had adopted a blue union label, the Knights' cigarmakers used white: there was more to the battle than label color. According to the state federation's historian, "The International charged that the Knights were receiving 'scab' cigarmakers rejected by the trade union locals; it refused to recognize the white label as marking 'fair' goods; and a feud developed which rapidly grew in bitterness." The convention was asked to endorse the blue label, both, and the white; by a margin of three votes it chose the blue. The conflict pitted two former allies, two different systems of labor organization, against each other and escalated far beyond the convention. Within Chicago's Trades Assembly, the Knights denounced the convention's decision and DA 24 ordered its local assemblies to withdraw from the Trades Assembly. In turn, the assembly declared war and tried to bring the local assemblies into the AFL. At the national level, the fight betrayed the promise of the trade assemblies and any hope for reconciliation between the CMIU and the Noble Order and between the AFL and the order. At both levels the Knights lost the war and more members.[19]

The SLP's base within the labor movement faded as the nineties progressed. By 1895 and with Daniel De Leon firmly in control, the SLP dropped all pretense of "boring from within" and returned to the praxis of dual unionism. The Socialist Trade and Labor Alliance (STLA) was born in New York in 1895 and came to Chicago six months later. For Morgan, the alliance was a product of the times, "as natural as the advent of the old trade unions, and the more recent K of L., AFL and the ARU." Local Alliance No. 72, a mixed branch, was chartered in June 1896. It opposed the "never ceasing antagonism" of the trades unions and the "nondescript leadership" of the AFL. A year and a half later the movement boasted a District Alliance, No. 11.[20]

The alliance tried to reincarnate the dual unionism of the 1880s: it copied the mixed assembly from the Knights, echoed the insurgency of the Progressive Cigarmakers, and sought the loyalty of the old Central Labor Union. If both the alliance and CLU started small, the former never grew. A year after its charter, it claimed all of four affiliates: the original Local Alliance No. 72, the Progressive Machinists (a caucus surrounding Morgan), Carriage and Wagon Workers Union No. 4, and STLA District Assembly No. 11. By November 1897, a second directory recorded just nine affiliates: the four charter members plus Carriage and Wagon Makers' Union No. 3, Children's Jacket Makers, the Capmakers' Alliance and two branches of the Cloakmakers' Union.[21]

The STLA claimed a national membership of 30,000 but the Chicago branch never published its membership. In June 1897, it announced that it had issued 130,000 copies of *The Socialist Alliance* in the past year, but did not announce its subscriptions. The paper died a year later and by October 1898 the Chicago Alliance was "practically dead." Dual unionism ricocheted within the SLP: at the national level it revived a strategic debate that De Leon had not anticipated; the same debate surfaced in Chicago and split the fragile section. And yet the STLA drew surprisingly little attention from the city's organized labor movement or its press; it captured few defecting unions, even fewer members, and was apparently so pathetic that it did not warrant denunciation.[22]

THE LIMITS OF SOCIALISM AND
THE EXPENDABILITY OF THE SOCIALISTS

The Pullman strike in the summer of 1894 may illuminate the movement's decline. Pullman's model city had attracted anarchist reporters, CLU organizers, and SLP-IWPA speakers before and especially during the Great Upheaval when both the metal and furniture workers' had strong branches in the company town. When the Pullman strike broke out in May 1894, *Die Arbeiter-Zeitung* offered extensive coverage and voiced its outrage with the state militia's bloody action. But as the strike dragged on through the summer—it did not end until October—the paper reduced its coverage. Beyond an almost perfunctory solidarity with the strikers, Chicago's ex-anarchists were distant and uninvolved, and their initial sympathy gave way to a cynical defeatism and then disgust. In part Pullman's work force had few Germans, and "only a minority of the workers had been with the company during the strike of 1886." Those who struck and lost in 1894 knew little of the anarchists, who in turn saw only lessons unlearned or ignored.[23]

If we jump ahead to 1910 we might better see what happened in the nineties. Two German-born historians of German-American radicalism in Chicago have drawn our attention to three demonstrations in the first decade of the twentieth century. *Die Arbeiter-Zeitung* judged the first, on Labor Day 1902, to be the largest workers' parade ever witnessed in Chicago. It featured 47,000 marchers and took almost five hours to wind through the downtown streets. Four years later, the second drew 80,000 of Chicago's foreign-born, who marched with their ethnic organizations to protest another wave of prohibitionism. The third demonstration was arranged in May 1907 when 15,000 people—"the revolutionary core" of Chicago's working class, its radical unions, and the Socialist Party— demonstrated in support of Big Bill Haywood of the IWW.[24]

"It is difficult," write Klaus Ensslen and Heinz Ickstadt, "to assess the proportion and role of the German element on these different occasions. Germans clearly dominated the anti-prohibitionist demonstration but . . . were much less visible amidst the multi-ethnic labor parades." Their declining visibility concerned *Die Fackel*'s editor:

> Where are they gone, the many who only a few years ago helped to build and to extend the organization of the new working-class movement? Many have turned completely bourgeois, and only a small number at least keep in touch with the organized workers by reading a radical paper. . . . Looking back, it seems that this withdrawal is steadily growing in general favor. While it used to be that those active in the movement held on for at least ten years, some years later, one could count oneself fortunate if he saw the same faces for five years. But nowadays, they participate no longer than two years.

"Although the forms and organization of ethnic working-class culture still continued," write Ensslen and Ickstadt, "we can definitely see the decline of a specifically German radical working class movement and the concomitant rise of the Socialist [P]arty as a new radical political force." Despite "the sweet nostalgia" which had "corrupted . . . the pain and fury about the misdeed of those ruling in 1887," *Die Arbeiter-Zeitung* still wanted "to change the world and to take possession of everything that makes life more magnificent and beautiful."[25]

At the turn of the century, the Socialist Party became the linear descendant of the SLP and the IWPA. In 1901, Morgan wrote to his friend Henry

Demarest Lloyd: "The local Socialist movement has changed personnel. The foreign element is submerged by the American inflow. Nearly all the actives are young American enthusiasts." Morgan had devoted twenty-five years to that movement, both he and the SLP had survived the Haymarket Affair, and in 1901 he was still active. In that quarter century the party had become "Americanized" and was now led by a new breed of professionals. Morgan's own career paralleled that trend. His wife had parlayed a $500 loan into a four-room cottage, later a fifteen-room house, and then a forty-eight room hotel. After eighteen years as a machinist and brass polisher in the Illinois Central Railroad shops, he became a lawyer in 1893. His shingle was not alone. The souvenir program of the First Annual International Labor Day Celebration, in May 1897, carried ads for the legal services of Jens Christensen, Jesse Cox, Christian Meier, and Paul Ehmann, as well as Frank Stauber and John Knefel's real estate, loans, and insurance businesses.[26]

What had happened to the movement in the 1890s? Born in 1878, the SLP was essentially a shell after 1900; the IWPA had survived less than three years, from October 1883 to May 1886. Although Chicago's social-revolutionary movement claimed the legacies of 1848 and the First International, its experience was contained by a single generation. The Socialist Party could claim a similar ancestry, but it belonged to another generation, the second; between them the city, its radicals, and their movement had changed. The fury of the riot, arrests, and trial—and the decade-long program of public repression—had thinned the movement's ranks. Beneath that fury lay forces that undercut the movement's ability to survive or reconstitute itself in the nineties. Underlying changes in mobility, urban geography, the patterns of immigration and immigrant acculturation, the conduct of municipal politics, and in the structure of the labor movement militated against a socialist resurgence.

The occupational structures of the movement had changed while the city's had not. That of the IWPA had dramatically changed for, as we saw in the last chapter, the movement was still overwhelmingly blue collar. The city's population had changed as the percentages engaged in skilled and unskilled work declined while the semiskilled had expanded, reversing the pattern within the movement's ranks. This phenomenon is more complex than embourgeoisement. If some moved into low-white-collar positions, others (especially blacksmiths, fringe, tassel, and harness makers) found themselves in dying trades. Within the German community, for example, this stood in marked contrast to the second generation, which "moved into highly specialized and well-paid skilled jobs, especially in the metal industry and other new and expanding industries." [27]

Ongoing changes in urban geography further undercut a socialist resurgence. The IWPA's organizational center was its club life; that center was in turn located in ethnic and working-class neighborhoods. Both moved. The Scandinavian section, as we have seen, dissolved into the party's English sections in 1900, because its members "were living too far apart" to attend the regular meetings. "By 1912 the Aurora Turnverein . . . had moved . . . west as the whole German population in the part of the city was 'inevitably moving westward.' The *Arbeiter-Zeitung* pointed out in 1907 that some of its financial difficulties were caused by subscribers who had resettled in the outlying districts . . . causing delivery costs to rise considerably. . . . [Two years earlier] the area between Randolph, Lake, and Washington Streets . . . the center of German radical activities throughout the turbulent 1880s and 1890s . . . had given way to a railroad station." [28]

Socialist and anarchist club life had centered on a collection of immigrant neighborhood saloons that were supplanted as local unions began to build their own halls. So many of them bought liquor licenses, that, as the historian of Chicago's saloons has noted, "by the turn of the century a great portion, if not a majority of Chicago's labor unions had left the saloon." Heterogeneity had characterized IWPA club life, the mingling of different trades, of skilled and unskilled, of men, women, and children. Union halls were male, skilled, and craft-based. By the turn of the century, that kind of inclusive mingling had been largely replaced by homogeneous and exclusive union halls. [29]

Just as significantly the city's population changed. Between 1890 and 1900, it grew from almost 1.1 million to almost 1.7 million. Not only were there more people and workers, but they were new to America and Chicago. Again, newspapers serve to date their arrival. The Polish community, which numbered about 5,500 in 1880 and 24,000 in 1890, got its first commercial paper (*Zgoda*) in 1881, its second (*Dziennik Chicagoski*) in 1890, and its first socialist paper (*Nowe Zycie*); (New life) appeared in 1889. *L'Italia*, the city's first Italian paper was issued in 1886 when the Italian population was about 4,000; its first socialist paper, *La Parola de Socialisti*, in 1906. The new immigrants took over old neighborhoods, worked unskilled and semiskilled jobs, and pushed the older immigrants up the ladder. [30]

Labor politics changed after Haymarket. At the same level, John Peter Altgeld emerged in the nineties as the Democratic standard bearer. His courageous pardon of Fielden, Neebe, and Schwab in 1893 won him the labor vote; his integrity during the Pullman strike the next year solidified it. Altgeldism, a program of antimonopoly, labor reform, the appointment of labor leaders to state offices, won Anglo-American and German labor voters as it held on to the Irish. Labor politics changed too at the municipal level. John Roche's mayoralty proved less vicious than his election campaign. He had a reputation for being conciliatory toward labor and fired Lieutenant Bonfield before the 1889 mayoral elections. But the defeats of the ULP in 1887 and of the Labor-Populists in the early nineties also marked the rise of the "Grey Wolves" in the city council, the boodle gang. In a sense, the demise of labor politics opened the door for machine politics. Thus, the anarchism of the eighties was outflanked by the corrosive combination of state-level reform and local corruption in the nineties.[31]

Chicago's labor movement shrank from the promise of 1886 as membership dropped and craft sectionalism returned. Under the impact of the Merritt Conspiracy Act and a series of court cases in 1887, the boycott declined. The anarchists had been brutally repressed, but did not disappear; the Knights did. Those who left the Noble Order did not necessarily join the trade unions (many dropped out); without the Knights the unskilled were left without organizers or organization. Skilled workers and their unions reasserted control of a smaller, tighter movement. Haymarket set off a reassessment of labor's local and national prospects, and the movement, not yet wholly committed to "pure and simple unionism," was forced to reassess both tactics and strategy. Ex-anarchists had returned to the conservative unions, to the Trades Assembly, and the AFL after 1890. Their organizational skills, their experience, and their militancy were welcomed—their socialism was not. The class solidarity of the Great Upheaval, a solidarity echoed in the United Labor Party, collapsed into recriminations, then dissolved into memory.

"The times of radical fervor seem to be over," argued Fred Bergmann at the 1909 Communefeier. "The great movement is now stuck in a union mire, and the only questions asked seem to be those of higher wages and shorter hours." In the nineties the anarchists were outflanked on both the political (electoral) and economic (trade union) fronts. Between Haymarket and, say, 1900, the craft culture of both the local and national labor movements matured as skilled workers and their leaders chose to concentrate on the economic ground that held some hope for success. A good number of German and Bohemian socialists who had spent the eighties assailing both Gompers and the AFL, began to fall into line behind him. Socialists could be and were still useful as long as they were disciplined and practical.

Ex-anarchists, like Oskar Neebe (bakers), Gustav Hoerich (furniture workers), Anton Johannson (carpenters), and Lizzie Holmes (Women's Federal Labor Union) could serve unions and their members in official capacities. But active anarchists, like Lucy Parsons or Abraham Issacs, became expendable because they were liabilities.[32]

The first generation of socialists had a unique opportunity. They had made the city's labor movement, they had made the first socialist movement, and in the 1890s they watched the reconstitution of the working class and the remaking of the labor and socialist movements. In Chicago, as in Detroit, "the rhetoric of solidarity endured—most unionists still referred to one another as brother and sister, and the doctrinaires talked as though nothing had changed—but such language was form without substance." It is tempting to steal Richard Cobb's argument and dismiss the question of the social revolutionary movement's failure as "largely irrelevant" since the movement never had any chance of success." Instead we should ask how a vital socialist movement managed ever to emerge at all?[33] The answer to that question takes us back to chapter 9 and the story of the United Labor Party, then to chapter 1, and requires a summary and concluding argument.

The ULP stands as the climax to the Great Upheaval. It reflected the uneasy alliance of Knights, anarchists, and the Trades Assembly; and it pitted that coalition against the two major parties, at the county level in the 1886 campaign, at the city level the following spring. A week before the mayoral election the incumbent Democrat abruptly withdrew, his party fused with the Republicans, and the ULP was defeated. The socialists understood class conflict, especially at the polls; the Knights chose to make ultra-radicals and red-flaggism the scapegoats. The ULP dissolved into recriminations, and the election of a Republican mayor marked the end of the Great Upheaval.

If Haymarket serves now as a window onto the process of radicalization, then the 1879 and 1887 elections serve to illuminate the Great Upheaval and the process of class formation. We need that window and its illumination. Those eight years marked an era spanned by Carter Harrison's four mayoral terms. The SLP's 1879 campaign gave Harrison his first term; the ULP's 1887 campaign compelled him to decline his party's nomination. Both elections featured a labor party, the first Socialistic, the second United. Their platforms were remarkably similar, indeed, some men appeared on both platform committees. And if both parties expected a working class constituency, each hoped to draw both native- and foreign-born voters. Both parties failed. The native-born voted against both the

SLP and the ULP, the foreign-born voted for both. Germans and Irish voters would not or could not support the same candidates, and in 1887, the Irish supported the ULP's candidate for mayor, but not its aldermanic candidates.[34]

The explanation for those differences seems to be ethnic, pitting native-born Republicans against Irish Democrats against German socialists. If the Anglo-Americans were Protestant, and Chicago's Irish were more than 90 percent Catholic, its German community split amongst Protestants, Catholics, Jews, and the irreligious. We might add those two observations and find an "ethno-cultural" explanation of their voting behavior and the sources of their hostility.

> [I]n the political universe of the late nineteenth century, fundamental and irreconcilable belief system differences between distinguishable clusters of ethno-religious groups *primarily* structured partisan cleavage among the mass electorate. The operative word, of course, is *primarily*. And that word should not be construed to imply either *exclusively* or *invariably*, for other social attributes also played roles. Contexts and historical experiences mattered politically.[35]

The context and historical experiences of Chicago's immigrants mattered a great deal. The Irish spoke English, which meant that they could communicate with a political system that consisted at the very least of voter registrars, tavern owners, ward bosses, and election judges. The Irish could read the *Tribune*, the *Times*, or the *Inter Ocean*. They could talk with the native-born, those from Britain, and with the leaderships of the Knights and the Trades Assembly. Scandinavians, who seemed to have learned English faster than any other immigrant group, were almost as fortunate. The Germans and Bohemians did not enjoy such luxuries. The *Adelphon Kruptos*, the Knights' secret work, lay untranslated until 1882; English remained the language of the Trades Assembly, and of the political system. Germans were skilled with preemigration traditions of unionism; the Bohemians were semiskilled and drew on the traditions of 1848; the Irish were unskilled and without such traditions. The Germans had a workingman's paper in the 1850s, Germans, Bohemians, and Scandinavians had socialist papers after 1870. Chicago's Irish may well have read the *Workingman's Advocate* in the seventies, but the New York-based *Irish World and American Industrial Liberator* was not *Der Vorbote* in the eighties. Although the foreign-born comprised the majority of the city's population, they were not just different but antagonistic.

Their conflicts overshadowed the common experiences of industrialization and alienation; and cannot be reduced to either ethnic or religious differences. Beyond both lay the clash of two different republicanisms: one home-grown or Anglo-American, the other imported, almost alien. Despite a common vocabulary those two republicanisms were unintelligible one to the other. Both spoke of liberty, but not the same kind. Both spoke of property, but one cherished it, the other sought to abolish or socialize it. And fraternity got lost in translation. Beyond the common vocabulary and intellectual cognates, lay two different political cultures. One came from a producerite analysis, the other on an eclectic but essentially socialist analysis. Those two cultures had different origins in both time and place, different heroes, symbols, values, and ethics. German socialists in Chicago looked to the SPD for encouragement and inspiration. Scandinavians looked home and within the SLP small branch. So did the French. The Czechs seem to have taken their socialism back to Bohemia from America. And irreligion, in the case of the Scandinavian *fritaenkere,* the German and Bohemian *freidenkers,* and the small native-born contingent of "liberals," further set them apart.[36] Chicago's socialists considered themselves part of an international socialist movement; the native-born, the Irish, and the English-speaking would have none of it. Chicago's socialists looked to the Paris Commune as the model for social revolution; the English-speaking recoiled from the thought of revolution and the horror of the Commune. The conflict between those two political cultures was fundamental and irreconcilable: there was no way, in Andrew Cameron's words, to join "the democratic-republicanism of America" to the red flag of European socialism. We are left then with two notions: of class, and what might have been, and of fragmentation, of competing cultural systems.[37]

THE RECORD OF RADICALISM

A brief recapitulation may serve to highlight the anarchist achievement. The traditional story of Chicago's anarchists has concentrated on the tragedy of Haymarket and on the martyrdom of the executed leadership. However dramatic, the story has remained trapped in a juridical interpretation and a biographical mode. Beyond the trial and executions, outside the courtroom, and behind the Martyrs was a movement that played an important role in the labor movement, in the development of class relations, and in the history of Chicago. That movement should not remain in the shadows of either courtroom or gallows, for it achieved more than martyrdom.

In Chicago, between 1870 and 1900, radicalism emerged out of the reform currents of Reconstruction. It crystallized in a movement composed of immigrant workers alienated and radicalized by the twin processes of industrialization and proletarianization. Under the tutelage of the First International those radicals broke with a producerite identification as "workingmen" and became "socialists." Their movement—never more than a minority in the city's working class—exerted an influence far beyond its numbers. It grew, sporadically in the seventies, explosively in the eighties, as the most militant expression of a working-class presence and consciousness within the city. The socialists were eminently visible in the city's trade unions and its strikes. After the Great Upheaval of 1877 they became an ominous force in municipal politics.

That force dissipated as the socialist and labor movements split internally and confronted economic recovery, vote fraud, and a Democratic regime, headed by Carter Harrison, which served in Richard Schneirov's words, as a "surrogate and safety-valve for worker's power." During the second of Harrison's four terms, one ex-socialist proclaimed that Chicago would become a "working class democracy, the like of which never existed before."[38] The SLP resignedly supported Harrison, still hoping to use elections to educate and agitate the working class. When they rejected parliamentary socialism and embraced revolutionary action to replace the system of private property, Chicago's anarchists split with their erstwhile comrades. As the SLP dwindled to a corporal's guard, the IWPA continued to grow.

The anarchists withdrew from electoral agitation and built their clubs, newspapers, unions, and fearsom reputation. By 1886, there were twenty-six IWPA groups in and around Chicago, and anarchist speakers toured the surrounding states on agitational tours. The groups met weekly, and the clubs served as a library, schoolhouse, benefit society, and social center. By 1886, the movement boasted seven newspapers, issued seven days a week, published in four languages, with a combined circulation of more than 30,000. The movement's membership owned those papers, ran the business, and supervised their editors. Anarchists organized in their neighborhoods, not at the point of production; yet by 1886, they had a strong and growing base within the organized labor movement, including the eleven largest unions in the city. Led by a group of organic intellectuals, the movement's active membership drew upon ethnic culture and traditions to create and maintain a self-consciously visible, vital, and militant movement culture expressed by those clubs, papers, and unions.

Without its club life, press, unions, and culture the ideology of that movement is unintelligible. That ideology might be understood as the last and most radical expression of artisan republicanism. Yet it broke with Anglo-American traditions when it rejected traditional political economy and embraced socialist economics. Such rejection made the anarchists outcast to many of their cohorts; their affinity to revolution made them outlaws, their atheism and free thought made them morally reprehensible. Their "anarchism" was a developing and eclectic ideology, mixing Lassalle and Marx, Gronlund and Kropotkin, St. Simon and Hyndman, Bebel and Kautsky. If "the Chicago Idea" seems to anticipate anarcho-syndicalism or anarcho-communism, it can be better understood on and in its own terms, which were socialist, not anarchist. That ideology rejected the system of private property and the strategy of cooperation. It recognized, even glorified, class struggle.

For all their revolutionary romanticism, and their obsession with armed struggle, Chicago's anarchists retained an intimate relationship with the labor movement. In the Great Upheaval of 1885–86 the anarchists became the cutting edge of the eight-hour campaign and the city's labor organizations. They had already broken with the craft sectionalism of the Anglo-American trade unions in the Trades and Labor Assembly; now they broke with the respectability of the Irish-American Knights of Labor. The IWPA and the CLU organized by disregarding the craft, skill, gender, language, and ethnic lines that fragmented the city's working class. If the IWPA had initially disdained the issue of shorter hours, by October 1885 they had endorsed it; by December, and with the demand for reduced hours at no loss of pay, they gave organizers, organization, and a confrontational edge to that movement.

Confrontation came on the night of May 4 in the form of a police riot and a massacre that was unprovoked but not unprecedented. The repression that followed the Haymarket riot remains unintelligible without that movement. The gang of nine—Engel, Fielden, Fischer, Lingg, Neebe, Parsons, Schnaubelt, Schwab and Spies—were singled out because they were the most prominent leaders of a vital, dangerous, and class movement. Funded by the city's leading businessmen, and carried out by an eager police force, supplemented by a new military garrison, Pinkerton detectives, and agents of the German and Austrian governments, that repression was so brutal and lasted so long because the movement threatened the forces of order.

On the one hand, Selig Perlman once held that "trade unionism . . . in this country originated and grew up in perfect independence of any socialist influence." Herman Schlüter, on the other hand, argued that the positive influence of the IWA, SLP, and the Socialist Party on the American trade union movement had not been acknowledged. By 1903, there were 243,000 trade union members in Chicago and the city could challenge London for the title of trade union capital of the world.[39] Therein lay the legacies of Haymarket and anarchism. For it is the growth, vitality, and militancy of that movement, *not* the prominence, eloquence, or martyrdom of its leaders that ought to be remembered.

Notes

Schilling Papers   George A. Schilling Papers, University of Chicago Library, Chicago.

SLP Records   Socialist[ic] Labor Party of America Records, Wisconsin State Historical Society, Madison.

WSHS   Wisconsin State Historical Society, Madison

Introduction

1. Henry David, *History of the Haymarket Affair: A Study in the American Social-Revolutionary and Labor Movements* (1936; rev. ed., New York: Russell and Russell, 1958); Paul Avrich, *The Haymarket Tragedy* (Princeton: Princeton University Press, 1984), xiii–xiv.

2. Herbert Gutman, "Workers Search for Power: Labor in the Gilded Age," in *The Gilded Age: A Reappraisal*, ed. H. Wayne Morgan (Syracuse: Syracuse University Press, 1963), 38–68, here 37.

3. Clyde Griffen, "Community Studies and the Investigation of Nineteenth-Century Social Relations," *Social Science History*, 10:3 (Fall 1986), 315–338; Kathleen Conzen, "Quantification and the New Urban History," *Journal of Interdisciplinary History* 13 (Spring 1983), 653–677.

4. See, e.g., Theodore Draper, *The Roots of American Communism* (New York: Viking Press, 1957), in which the author argues that the central problems confronting the CPUSA were those posed by the "foreign-language federations," which comprised at least 75 percent of the membership. Despite that thesis Draper cites but a single non-English primary source.

5. E. P. Thompson, *The Making of the English Working Class* (New York: Vintage Books, 1963), esp. p. 13 with its "apology to Scottish and Welsh readers"; William Sewell, *Work and Revolution in France: The Language of Labor from the Old Regime to 1848* (Cambridge: Cambridge University Press, 1980); Wolfgang Renzsch, *Handwerker und Lohnarbeiter in der frühen Arbeiterbewegung: Zur sozialen Basis von Gewerkschaften und Sozialdemokratie im Reichsgrundungsjahrzehnt* (Göttingen: Vandenhoeck und Ruprecht, 1980).

6. See Dirk Hoerder, "The International Labor Market in the Atlantic Economies," and Leon Fink, "Looking Backward: Reflections on Workers' Culture and the Conceptual Dilemmas of the New Labor History" (papers presented to The Future of American Labor History conference, Northern Illinois University, DeKalb, 10–12 October 1984).

Chapter One: A Context for Working-Class Radicalism

1. See Harold Mayer and Richard Wade, *Chicago: Growth of a Metropolis* (Chicago: University of Chicago Press, 1969); Glen Holt and Dominic Pacyga, *Chicago: A Historical Guide to the Neighborhoods, The Loop and The South Side* (Chicago: Chicago Historical Society, 1979).

2. A. T. Andreas, *History of Chicago From the Earliest Period to the Present Time*, 3 vols. (Chicago: A. T. Andreas, 1884–1886); Wyatt Belcher, *The Economic Rivalry Between St. Louis and Chicago, 1850–1880* (New York: Columbia University Press, 1947).

3. See S. S. Schoff, *The Glory of Chicago—Her Manufactures* (Chicago: Knight and Leonard, 1873); Bessie Pierce, *A History of Chicago*, vol. 2: *From Town to City, 1848–1871* (New York: Alfred Knopf, 1940), 77–149; vol. 3: *The Rise of a Modern City, 1871–1893* (New York: Alfred Knopf, 1957), 533.

4. See the encyclopedic chapters on "Chicago's Economic Empire" in Pierce, *A History of Chicago* 3: 64–233; on specific industries see John Jentz, "Bread and Labor: Chicago's German Bakers Organize," *Chicago History*, 12 (Summer 1983), 24–35; Hanns-Theodor Fuss, "Massenproduktion und Arbeiterbewusstsein: Deutsche Arbeiter in den McCormick Reaper Works, 1873–1886," *Amerikastudien*, 29:2 (Summer 1984), 149–168; Sharon Darling, *Chicago Furniture: Art, Craft, and Industry, 1833–1983* (New York: W. W. Norton, 1984), 17–154; Mabel Magee, "The Women's Clothing Industry of Chicago with Special Reference to Relations Between the Manufacturers and the Union" (Ph.D. diss., University of Chicago, 1927); Robert Meyers "The Economic Aspects of the Production of Men's Clothing (With Particular Reference to the Industry in Chicago)" (Ph.D. diss., University of Chicago, 1937); John Jentz, "Skilled Workers and Industrialization: Chicago's German Cabinetmakers and Machinists, 1880–1900," in *German Workers in Industrial Chicago, 1850–1910: A Comparative Perspective*, ed. Hartmut Keil and John Jentz (DeKalb: Northern Illinois University, 1983), 73–85.

5. Samuel Rezneck, "Distress, Relief, and Discontent in the United States during the Depression of 1873–1878," *Journal of Political Economy* 58 (December 1950): 494–512; Herbert Gutman, "Social and Economic Structure and Depression: American Labor in 1873 and 1874" (Ph.D. diss., University of Wisconsin, 1959), 1–30.

6. *Chicago Tribune*, 19 January 1885, 8; *Chicago Herald*, 14 February 1885, 3; *Tribune*, 25 March 1885, 8; Samuel Rezneck, "Patterns of Thought and Action in an American Depression, 1882–1886," *American Historical Review* 61:2 (January 1956), 284–307.

7. *ChAZ*, 10 October 1880, p. 2; *Svenska Tribunen*, 2 March 1888, trans. in CFLPS, reel 63.

8. Hartmut Keil and John Jentz, "German Working-Class Culture in Chicago: A Problem of Definition, Method, and Analysis," *Gulliver* 9 (1981), 128–147, 135; *idem.*, "German Workers in Industrial Chicago: The Transformation of Industries and Neighborhoods in the late 19th Century" (paper presented at the OAH convention, Detroit, 2 April 1981); David Gordon, Richard Edwards, and Michael Reich, *Segmented Work, Divided Workers: The Historical Transformation of Labor in the United States* (Cambridge: Cambridge University Press, 1982), 100–164.

9. Edward Bubnys, "Nativity and the Distribution of Wealth: Chicago, 1870," *Explorations in Economic History* 19:2 (April 1982), 101–109.

10. *Idem.*, "Chicago, 1870 and 1900: Wealth, Occupation and Education" (Ph.D. diss., University of Illinois, Champaign-Urbana, 1978), 153–155.

11. See Pierce, *History of Chicago* 3, 145–191; "American Aristocracy—An Analytical Review of Chicago's Social Directory," *Tribune*, 2 January 1885, 8; and Herma Clark, *The Elegant Eighties: When Chicago was Young* (Chicago: A. C. McClurg, 1941).

12. IBLS, *Third Biennial Report, 1884* (Springfield: H. W. Rokker, 1884), 257–259, 265, 269–270; John Drury, *Old Chicago Houses* (Chicago: University of Chicago Press, 1941), 129. According to the IBLS, *Fourth Biennial Report, 1886* (Springfield: H. W. Rokker, 1886), 249, about 13 percent of Cook County's trade union members owned their own homes.

13. *Northwestern Christian Advocate*, 19 November 1893, 3; cf. *ChAZ*, 30 August 1884, 2.

14. Herbert Gutman with Ira Berlin, "Class Composition and the Development of the American Working Class, 1840–1890," in Gutman, *Power and Culture*, ed. Ira Berlin (New York: Pantheon, 1987), 380–394; Ray Ginger, *Altgeld's America: The Lincoln Ideal versus Changing Realities* (New York: Funk and Wagnalls, 1958), 96.

15. Gruenhut, *Progressive Age*, 15 October 1881, 4; *Herald*, 6 April 1882, 3.

16. On the computation and interpretation of the gini coefficient in Table 1.4, see Charles Dollar and Richard Jensen, *Historian's Guide to Statistics: Quantitative Analysis and Historical Research* (New York: Holt, Rinehart, 1974), 121–126.

17. See a series of articles in the *Tribune*, including: "The Bohemians," 7 March 1886, 3; "Our Polish Citizens," 14 March 1886, 3; "The Scandinavians," 21 March 1886, 14; and the sources cited in note 20, below.

18. Ward-level data obscures concentration, but is accessible; the analysis of smaller units would certainly reveal higher measures. See, e.g., one census enumeration district, about twenty square blocks, on the Northwest side, in which 86 percent of the households were German; or eight square blocks on the North side which were 79 percent German. Keil and Jentz, "Transformation of Industries and Neighborhoods," 20; Christiane Harzig, "Chicago's German Northside, 1880–1900: The Structure of a Gilded Age Ethnic Neighborhood," in Keil and Jentz, eds., *Chicago's German Workers*, 127–144, here 132.

19. See C. J. Calhoun, "Community: Toward a Variable Conceptualization for Comparative Research," *Social History* 5:1 (January 1980); 105–129; Kathleen Conzen, "Immigrants, Immigrant Neighborhoods, and Ethnic Identity: Historical Issues," *Journal of American History* 66:3 (December 1979): 603–615; Howard Chudacoff, "A New Look at Ethnic Neighborhoods: Residential Dispersion and the Concept of Visibility in a Medium Sized City," *Journal of American History* 60 (1973–1974): 76–93; and Gerald Suttles, *The Social Construction of Communities* (Chicago: University of Chicago Press, 1972), 3–18.

20. John Jentz and Hartmut Keil, "From Immigrants to Urban Workers: Chicago's German Poor in the Gilded Age and Progressive Era, 1883–1908," *Vierteljährschrift für Sozial- und Wirtschaftgeschichte* 68:1 (1981): 53–97, 64; Joseph Chada, *The Czechs in the United States* (Washington, D.C.: SVU Press, 1981) 4, 5; Philip

Friedman, "The Danish Community of Chicago, 1860–1920" (Master's thesis, Northwestern University, 1976), 85–91.

On those neighborhoods see Hartmut Keil, "Einwandererviertel und amerikanische Gesellschaft," *Archiv für Sozialgeschichte* 24 (1984); 47–89; Michael Funchion, "Irish Chicago: Church, Homeland, Politics, and Class—The Shaping of an Ethnic Group, 1870–1900," in *Ethnic Chicago,* ed. Melvin Holli and Peter d'A. Jones (rev. ed.; Grand Rapids, MI.: Eerdmans Publishing Co., 1984), 14–45; Ulf Beijbom, *Swedes in Chicago: A Social and Demographic Study of the 1840–1880 Immigration* (Växjö: Scandinavian University Books, 1971); Josefina Humpal-Zeman, "The Bohemian People in Chicago," in *Hull House Maps and Papers* (New York: Thomas Crowell, 1895) 115–128; Joseph Parot, *Polish Catholics in Chicago, 1850–1920* (DeKalb: Northern Illinois University Press, 1981); and Humbert Nelli, *The Italians in Chicago, 1880–1930: A Study in Ethnic Mobility* (New York: Oxford University Press, 1970).

21. Gutman, "Workers Search for Power," 31–53; Richard Schneirov, "Class Conflict, Municipal Politics, and Governmental Reform in Gilded Age Chicago, 1871–1875," in Keil and Jentz, eds., *German Workers in Industrial Chicago,* 183–205.

22. David Montgomery, *Beyond Equality: Labor and the Radical Republicans, 1862–1872* (New York: Vintage Books, 1967), 35–44. Cf. Richard Schneirov and John Jentz, "Social Republicanism and Socialism: A Multi-Ethnic History of Labor Reform in Chicago, 1848–1877" (paper presented at the Social Science History Association convention, Chicago, 21–24 November 1985); *ISZ,* 8 March 1871, 2.

23. On German-Irish tension, see *ISZ,* 6 July 1871, 2; *ChAZ,* 22 July 1882, 4; 2 January 1884, 4; on German-Bohemian relations see *Svornost,* 19 March 1883 (CFLPS, reel 2), 19 March 1896 (CFLPS, reel 1); on Jewish-Irish tension see Abraham Bisno, *Abraham Bisno, Union Pioneer* (Madison: University of Wisconsin Press, 1967), 54–56.

24. Thomas Suhrbur, "Ethnicity in the Formation of the Chicago Carpenters Union: 1855–1890," in Keil and Jentz, eds., *German Workers in Industrial Chicago,* 86–103, here 91, 95; IBLS, *Third Biennial Report, 1884,* 183; Bisno, *Union Pioneer,* 71, 81–83.

25. Montgomery, *Beyond Equality,* 42; Darrel Robertson, "The Chicago Revival, 1876: A Case Study in the Social Function of a Nineteenth-Century Revival," (Ph.D. diss., University of Iowa, 1982); Pierce, *History of Chicago,* 3: 423–454.

26. The "new political history" has focused on the national level. See e.g., Paul Kleppner, *The Cross of Culture: A Social Analysis of Midwestern Politics, 1850–1900* (New York: Free Press, 1970), or Richard Jensen, *The Winning of the Midwest: Social and Political Conflict, 1888–1896* (Chicago: University of Chicago Press, 1971).

27. Paul Green, "Irish Chicago: The Multi-Ethnic Road to Machine Success," in Holli and Jones, eds., *Ethnic Chicago,* 412–459; *Skandinaven,* 10 October 1890, CFLPS, reel 9; *Tribune,* 7 April 1886, 2; *Workingman's Advocate,* 15 February 1868, 1; cf. Michael Ahern, *The Political History of Chicago* (Chicago: Donahue, Henneberry, 1886).

28. The quotations are from Montgomery, *Beyond Equality,* x, 446–447; but the arguments are borne out by more recent research on Chicago. See esp. Kenneth

Kann, "Working Class Culture and the Labor Movement in Nineteenth Century Chicago" (Ph.D. diss., University of California at Berkeley, 1977), ch. 5; Eric Hirsch, "Revolution or Reform: An Analytical History of an Urban Labor Movement" (Ph.D., diss., University of Chicago, 1981); and Richard Schneirov, "The Knights of Labor in the Chicago Labor Movement and in Municipal Politics, 1877–1887" (Ph.D. diss., Northern Illinois University, 1984), ch. 1.

29. David Montgomery, "Strikes in Nineteenth-Century America," *Social Science History* 4:1 (Winter 1980), 81–104; quotations from Eric Hobsbawm, *Labouring Men: Studies in the History of Labour* (1964, reprint, London: Weidenfeld and Nicolson, 1979), 144.

30. David Montgomery, *The Fall of the House of Labor* (New York: Cambridge University Press, 1987), 2.

31. Quoted in Sean Wilentz, *Chants Democratic: New York City and the Rise of the American Working Class, 1788–1850* (New York: Oxford University Press, 1984), 389.

Chapter Two: Socialists, Anarchists, and the Unions

1. *Vorbote*, 4 and 25 May 1887, both p. 5.

2. *Workmen's Advocate* (New Haven, Conn.), 4 October 1885, 2; *Alarm*, 3 April 1886, 4; IBLS, *Fourth Biennial Report, 1886*, 221, 224–225, 226.

3. Hartmut Keil, "The Knights of Labor, the Trade Unions, and German Socialists in Chicago, 1870–1890," in *Impressions of a Gilded Age: The American Fin-de-Siècle*, ed. Marc Chenetier and Rob Kroes (Amsterdam: Universiteit van Amsterdam, 1983), 301–323, here 302.

4. Pierce, *A History of Chicago*, vol. 2: *From Town to City, 1848–1871* (New York: Alfred Knopf, 1940), 160, 166 n. 71; Friedrich Sorge, *Labor Movement in the United States* [1891–1895], ed. Philip Foner and trans. Brewster Chamberlin (Westport, Conn.: Greenwood Press, 1977), 198–204; Keil, "Knights, Trade Unions, and German Socialists," 303.

5. Schneirov and Jentz, "Social Republicanism and Socialism," 19–22.

6. *Workingman's Advocate*, 17 April 1869, 3; 8 October 1870, 3; Keil, "Knights, Trade Unions, and German Socialists," 303.

7. *Inter Ocean*, 17 June 1878, 3.

8. John Jentz, "Chicago's Furniture Industry and its Work Force from 1850 to 1910: A Social and Economic Framework for Interpreting the German-American Furniture Workers and Their Unions," in Chenetier and Kroes, eds., *Impressions of a Gilded Age*, 287–300.

9. Paul Le Blanc, "Pioneer Socialists in America: Beyond the Myth of 'Marxists versus Lassalleans'" (Master's seminar paper, University of Pittsburgh, 1978); cf. Philip Foner, *The Workingmen's Party of the United States: A History of the First Marxist Party in the Americas* (Minneapolis: MEP Publications, 1984), 134, n. 21.

10. *Vorbote*, 6 June 1874; 20 and 27 June 1874, quoted in Philip Foner, ed., *The Formation of the Workingmen's Party of the United States: Proceedings of Union Congress*

Held at Philadelphia, July 19–22, 1876 (New York: American Institute for Marxist Studies, 1976), 2–3; *Vorbote,* 1 January 1876, 4.

11. *Labor Standard* (Paterson, NJ), 11 November 1876, 2, emphasis mine; cf. *ibid.,* 25 November 1876, 2: "Hasty political action . . . will turn us from the economical question, upon which we agree, and lead us into a political labyrinth, in which we shall be lost. Already there are hosts of locusts, called politicians, awaiting the opportunity to jump into and utilize our movement."

12. *The Socialist,* 15 March 1879, 4; *Labor Standard,* 6 January 1877, 3; continued 27 January 1877, 3; *Vorbote,* 2 and 9 March 1878, both p. 3; Selig Perlman, "Upheaval and Reorganization," in John R. Commons et al., *History of Labour in the United States* 4 vols. (New York: MacMillan, 1918–35), vol. 2: 279 n. 34 citing *Vorbote,* 22 June 1878.

13. Paul Grottkau, "Die SAP und die Gewerkschaften," *Vorbote,* 11 October 1879, 3, trans. by Perlman in Commons et al., *History of Labour,* 2: 283.

14. David Roediger, "Albert R. Parsons: The Anarchist as Trade Unionist," in *A Haymarket Scrapbook,* ed. Roediger and Franklin Rosemont (Chicago: Charles Kerr, 1986), 31–35. John Laslett, *Labor and the Left: A Study of Socialist and Radical Influences in the American Labor Movement, 1881–1924* (New York: Basic Books, 1970), 287, called for "further detailed study of rank-and-file opinion." It remains difficult to get below the local leadership: despite rich sources I can identify socialists within the labor movement only when they got elected to office, wrote to labor or socialist papers, or got expelled from their international unions. See Table 4.8.

15. See Walter Galenson, *Rival Unionism in the United States* (New York: Russell and Russell, 1966), esp. 30–40.

16. Fuss, "Massenproduktion und Arbeiterbewusstsein," 149–168; Jentz, "Bread and Labor," 24–35.

17. Henderson quoted in Suhrbur, "Ethnicity in the Chicago Carpenters Union," 95.

18. See Table 4.4 and Chapter Four.

19. I have relied on Thomas Suhrbur, "Unionism among Chicago Carpenters, 1855–1901" (C.A.S. thesis, Northern Illinois University, 1986); *Workingman's Advocate,* 14 February 1873, 3; 22 August 1874, 3.

20. Suhrbur, "Ethnicity in the Chicago Carpenters Union," 93; for an explanation of the branch system, by a Chicagoan, see *The Carpenter* (St. Louis and New York), June 1883, 2.

21. *Carpenter,* September 1882, 8; November 1883, 6; *Carpenter,* 5 February 1896, quoted in Suhrbur, "Ethnicity in the Chicago Carpenters Union," 95, and 93–94; *Carpenter:* March 1885, 2; November 1883, 5.

22. McGuire in *Carpenter,* September 1884, 4, and in German a month later, October 1884, 6; cf. Mark Erlich, "Peter J. McGuire's Trade Unionism: Socialism of a Trades Union Kind?" *Labor History* 24:2 (Spring 1983), 165–197.

23. *Carpenter,* October 1884, 2 and 7; February 1885, 7 and 8; on the Bohemian carpenters, see "History of Local #54," trans. from the Czech by H. Vydra

(typescript, circa 1920), Archives of Local No. 54, Chicago District Council, United Brotherhood of Carpenters and Joiners of America.

24. *Carpenter*, July 1885, 1; *Alarm*, 2 May 1885, 4; Michael Schaack, *Anarchy and Anarchists* (Chicago: F. J. Schulte, 1889), *passim*, identifies thirty-one of his suspects as members of an armed group of the International Carpenters and Joiners' Union. *Carpenter*, October 1885, 5; *Tribune*, 8 September 1885, 3; *Herald*, 7 September 1885, 1.

25. I have relied on Leslee Snyder, "Mobility and Class Consciousness: The Cigarmakers of Chicago, 1864–1886" (paper presented to the Chicago Area Labor History Group, Newberry Library, 6 May 1983); and Hirsch, "Revolution or Reform," 378–435.

26. *CMOJ* (New York City), 15 October 1877, 3; 10 March 1878, 3; H. M. Gitelman, "Adolph Strasser and the Origins of Pure and Simple Unionism," *Labor History* 6:1 (Winter 1965), 71–83.

27. *Inter Ocean*, 14 October 1878, 8; Keil and Jentz, "Transformation of Industries and Neighborhoods," 20–25. Of twelve officers elected in January 1879, for example, ten can be identified as SLP members, see *Socialist*, 11 January 1879, 8.

28. *CMOJ*, 10 April 1879, 5; Snyder, "Cigarmakers of Chicago," 26; *ISZ*, 15 October 1879, 2; *CMOJ*, 10 November 1879, 3; 10 April 1880, 1; October 1883, 5–6; Hirsch, "Revolution or Reform," 409–427.

29. *CMOJ*, May 1880, 3; 10 June 1881, 4; 10 July 1881, 3; April 1884, 4.

30. *Ibid.*, 15 July 1882, 4; *Progress* (New York), 26 October 1883, 1; cf. *CMOJ*, November 1883, 4–5; *Herald*, 24 September 1883, 4.

31. Progressive Local 15's side reported in *Progress*, 26 October 1883, 3; International Local 14's side in *CMOJ*, April 1884, 4; *Herald*, 26 November 1883, 4; 10 December 1883, 4.

32. *Herald*, 5 May 1884, 2; *Progress*, 24 June 1884, 4; 25 July 1884, 6; *CMOJ*, June 1884, 4; August 1884, 4; *Inter Ocean*, 4 August 1884, 8.

33. *ChAZ*, 31 October 1879, 4; *Inter Ocean*, 3 November 1879, 3; *Tribune*, 28 November 1879, 8; *ChAZ*, 3 November 1879, 4.

34. *ChAZ*, 14 November 1879, 8; *Times*, 12 November 1879, 6. On the socialists, see *ChAZ*, 16, 23 and 30 January 1880, all p. 4; on the anti-socialists, see *Tribune*, 23 January 1880, 8; *Times*, 30 January 1880, 8.

35. *ChAZ*, 27 February 1880, 4; 26 March 1880, 4; quotation from *Times*, 2 April 1880, 6; *ChAZ*, 7 May 1880, 4.

36. *Progress*, 26 October 1883, 3; in German, 6; *ibid.*, 24 June 1884, 2. On the CLU, see Perlman in Commons et al., *History of Labour*, 2: 387–389, 391–392, and Jacob Winnen, "Die Geschichte der Arbeiterbewegung von Chicago," *Fackel*, 1 April 1917, 1.

37. *Progress*, 25 July 1884, 6; *Vorbote*, 18 June 1884, 8; 2 July 1884, 8; *ChAZ*, 10 September 1884, 4; *Fackel*, 16 November 1884, 8. Perlman in Commons et al., *History of Labour*, 2: 388, asserts that the SLP "remained with" the Trades Assembly; yet the evidence clearly indicates the SLP joined the IWPA in the CLU. See, for

example, "Notes on the Meetings of the Socialist Labor Party, 1882–1886," in Morgan Collection, reel 6; and the Chicago's SLP's reports in *Der Sozialist* (New York), 9 January 1886, 6; 27 February 1886, 5.

38. See the sources listed in Table 2.1. *Tribune*, 7 January 1884, 7; *Alarm*, 5 September 1885, 1; 24 January 1885, 2; 7 February 1885, 3.

39. Schneirov, "Knights of Labor in Chicago," 311–357: quotations from 343, 350, 356, 351; Chicago Groups of the IWPA, "The Ballot. A Review of the Work of the Illinois State Labor Convention" (circa March 1884), in Parsons Papers; *Progress*, 18 November 1885, 3.

40. *Plan of Organization, Method of Propaganda and Resolutions, Adopted by the Pittsburgh Congress of the International Working Peoples' Association in Session from October 14th to October 16th, 1883* [hereafter *Pittsburgh Manifesto*] (Chicago: IWPA, [1883]), in Parsons Papers; *Progress*, 18 September 1885, 3; *ChAZ*, 16 June 1884, 4.

41. The data comes from the Knights of Labor *Proceedings of the General Assembly*, 1879–1886, and is tabulated in Keil, "Knights, Trade Unions and German Socialists," 309.

42. Philip Van Patten to Terence V. Powderly [hereafter TVP], 28 February 1880, emphasis in original; Van Patten to TVP, 20 May 1880, both reel 2; cf. William Halley to TVP, 28 July 1882, and David McGann to TVP, 20 November 1882, both reel 4, Powderly Papers.

43. Myles McPadden to TVP, 1 February 1882, reel 3; McPadden to TVP, 23 February 1882, reel 2; Richard Griffiths to TVP, 28 October 1881, reel 3; TVP to Griffiths, 31 October 1881, reel 45; John Page to TVP, 11 January 1882 reel 3, all Powderly Papers.

44. Griffiths to TVP, 13 August 1882, reel 4; Halley to TVP, 25 May 1882, reel 3; TVP to Halley, 12 May 1882, reel 45; all Powderly Papers; *Lake Vindicator*, 10 February 1883, 1; 20 April 1883, 2.

45. McGann to TVP, 20 November 1882, reel 4; Thomas Randall to TVP, 8 December 1882, reel 5; Joseph O'Kelley to TVP, 18 March 1883, reel 5; TVP to Griffiths, 26 December 1882, reel 45, all Powderly Papers; *Lake Vindicator*, 3 October 1885, 1; 21 November 1885, 1.

46. David McGann to TVP, 20 November 1882, reel 4, Powderly Papers; Knights of Labor, "District Assembly 24 Minutes, 1882–1886" [hereafter "DA 24 Minutes"], 15 October 1882, in the Schilling Collection, bound vol. 3; IBLS, *Fourth Biennial Report, 1886*, 169.

47. Norman Ware, *The Labor Movement in the United States 1860–1895*, (1929, reprint Gloucester: Peter Smith, 1959), 316; unidentified newspaper clipping, 16 February 1887, Morgan Collection, reel 1; *Vorbote*, 23 February 1887, 8.

48. See Table 4.8 and Chapter Four; delegates names from "DA 24 Minute Book, 1882–1886," Schilling Collection; the composition and identification of LA's from *Progressive Age*, 20 July 1882, 8; and Jonathan Garlock, comp., *Guide to the Local Assemblies of the Knights of Labor* (Westport, Conn.: Greenwood Press, 1982), 65–75.

49. Richard Oestreicher, "Socialism and the Knights of Labor in Detroit, 1887–

1886," *Labor History* 22:1 (Winter 1981), 5–30; Schneirov, "Knights of Labor in Chicago," 98, 112; cf. Keil, "Knights, Trade Unions, and German Socialists," 301–323.

50. *Alarm*, 3 April 1886, 4; Spies in *Autobiographies*, 71; Neebe, *ibid.*, 167; Parsons to TVP, quoted in David, *Haymarket Affair*, 124–125; *Alarm*, 24 April 1886, 3.

51. See two articles in the *Journal of United Labor:* Parsons, "Labor vs. Capital," July 1883, 331–332, and Powderly, "From the Grand Master Workman," 10 March 1885, 931–932.

52. IBLS, *Fourth Biennial Report*, 226; see the sources listed in Table 2.1. Identifying ethnicity by surname is not without problems; see Chapter Four.

53. Keil, "Knights, Trade Unions, and German Socialists," 322, cites *ChAZ*, 30 October 1882, yet the subject had been broached earlier: see John Campbell to TVP, 15 November 1880, reel 2; William Halley to TVP, 28 June 1882, reel 4, both Powderly Papers.

54. Joseph O'Kelley to TVP, 9 January 1886, reel 12; O'Kelley to TVP, 18 January 1886, reel 12; Powderly Papers; *Journal of United Labor*, April 1883, 446. Cf. Schneirov, "Knights of Labor in Chicago," 242–243, 267, n. 82; and Kann, "Working Class Culture and the Labor Movement," 409–410.

55. David, *Haymarket Affair*, 424, n. 96; Richard Oestreicher, *Solidarity and Fragmentation: Working People and Class Consciousness in Detroit, 1875–1900* (Urbana: University of Illinois Press, 1985), 92, 100 n. 53.

56. TVP to J. M. Cannon, 19 November 1882, cited in Vincent Falzone, *Terence V. Powderly: Middle-Class Reformer* (Washington, D.C.: University Press of America, 1978), 140, original emphasis.

57. Griffiths to TVP, 10 July 1882, reel 4; Griffiths to TVP, 28 November 1884, reel 8; Griffiths to TVP, 16 June 1885, reel 10; J. H. Randall to TVP, 5 April 1886, reel 15; all Powderly Papers.

58. TVP to Daniel Cronin, 6 April 1886; TVP to Cronin, 7 May 1886, both Powderly Papers, reel 16.

59. Cf. Kann, Hirsch, and Schneirov, each of whom sees a bipolar rivalry. Kann, "Working-Class Culture and the Labor Movement," 83, 400, 428; Hirsch, "Revolution or Reform," 555–580; and Schneirov, "Knights of Labor in Chicago," 8, 565.

Chapter Three: Socialists, Anarchists, and the Polls

1. *Tribune*, 23 December 1873, 1.

2. The two monographic histories of the SLP inexplicably ignore its first thirteen years. See Charles White, "The Socialist Labor Party, 1890–1903" (Ph.D. diss., University of Southern California, 1959); and Henry Kuhn and Olive Johnson, *The Socialist Labor Party During Four Decades, 1890–1930* (New York: Labor News, 1931). But see the introductory chapters of national studies, e.g., Morris Hillquit, *History of Socialism in the United States* (New York: Funk and Wagnalls, 1910); Howard Quint, *The Forging of American Socialism* (New York: Columbia University Press, 1953); and

Oakley Johnson, *Marxism in the United States Before the Russian Revolution, 1876–1917* (New York: Humanities Press, 1974).

3. Karl Obermann, "La participation à la Première Internationale, avant 1872, des ouvrieres allemands immigrés aux États-Unis," *La Premiére internationale, l'institution, l'implantation, le rayonnement* (Paris: Colloques internationaux du C.N.R.S., 1964), 387–402; *Papers of the General Council of the International Working-men's Association, New York, 1872–1876*, ed. Samuel Bernstein (Milano: Institute Giangiacomo Feltrinelli, 1962), *passim*; Samuel Bernstein, *The First International in America* (New York: Augustus Kelley, 1962); Herman Schlüter, *Die Internationale in Amerika* (Chicago: Deutsche Sprachgruppe der Sozialist Partei der Ver. Staaten, 1918).

4. *ISZ*, 23 December 1873, 4; *Tribune*, 24 December 1873, 1; Arthur Weil, "The Formation of the Workingmen's Party of Illinois, 1873–1874" (Master's thesis, DePaul University, 1952); Kann, "Working Class Culture and the Labor Movement," 226–235.

Historians of the First International in America, including those cited in note 3 above, have focused on German immigrants. For useful correctives see Zdenek Solle, "Die tschechischen Sektionen der Internationale in den Vereinigten Staaten von Amerika," *Historica* (Prague), 8 (1964), 101–134; and on the Scandinavians, *Dagslyset*, January 1872, 4.

5. *ISZ*, 29 December 1873, 4; 13 January 1874, 1; *Times*, 9 February 1874, 1; *Vorbote*, 2 May 1874, 4; Weil, "Workingmen's Party of Illinois"; Josef Polišenský and Jan Staněk, "Počátky české dělnicke emigrace a české sekce I. internacionály ve Spojených státech amerických," in *Začiatky českej a slovenskej emigrácie do USA*, ed. Milos Gosiorovsky (Bratislava: Slovenskj akadémie vied, 1970), 97–124.

6. See "an S[ektion] 3 zu Chicago," in Bernstein, ed., *Papers of the General Council IWA*, 140–144; *Tribune*, 9 April 1874, 5; 16 June 1874, 7; 21 June 1874, 13.

7. *Tribune*, 26 October 1874, 1; *Vorbote*, 7 November 1874, 4.

8. *Morning Courier*, 25 February 1875, 4; *Tribune*, 5 and 20 March 1875, 8.

9. *Dagslyset*, Marts 1875, 6–8; April 1875, 4–5. *Vorbote*, 2 June 1877, 5; Renate Keisewetter, "Die Institution der deutsch-amerikanische Arbeiterpresse in Chicago: zur Geschichte des Vorboten und der Chicagoer Arbeiterzeitung, 1874–1886" (Master's thesis, Ludwig-Maximilians-Universität, München, 1982).

10. *Vorbote*, 29 April 1876, 2; *Hejmdal*, 27 February 1875, CFLPS, reel 9; Sorge, *Labor Movement in the United States*, 199.

11. Foner, ed., *Formation of the WPUS*, 13, 15, 19 and passim. Cf. Le Blanc, "Pioneer Socialists in America," and Foner, *Workingmen's Party of the United States*.

12. Broadside, "The Great Uprising of Labor—The Fifteenth Ward to Send a Workingman to the City Council!" (circa March 1877), Parsons Papers; *CVZ*, 5 March 1877, 4; *Vorbote*, 17 March 1877, 8; election returns in *CVZ*, 4 April 1877, 2; *Vorbote*, 21 April 1877, 8; 16 June 1877, 8.

13. Philip Foner, *The Great Labor Uprising of 1877* (New York: Monad Press, 1977); Richard Schneirov, "Chicago's Great Upheaval of 1877," *Chicago History*, 9:1 (Spring

1980), 3–17; Marianne Debouzy, "Grève et violence de classe aux Etats-Unis en 1877," *Le Mouvement Sociale*, 102 (1978), 44.

14. *Tribune*, 22 August 1877, 4; *Vorbote*, 25 August 1877, 4; *Times*, 20 September 1877, 5; *Progressive Age*, 19 March 1881, 1–2. Cf. Edward Mittelman, "Chicago Labor in Politics, 1877–1896," *Journal of Political Economy*, 28 (1920), 407–418; and Ralph Scharnau, "Thomas J. Morgan and the Chicago Socialist Movement, 1876–1901" (Ph.D. diss., Northern Illinois University, 1969).

15. *Skandinaven*, 9, 16 and 22 October 1877, all 4; *Times*, 29 October 1877, 3; Schneirov, "Knights of Labor in Chicago," 100–103; *Times*, 3 November 77, 3.

16. Elections returns, *Times*, 8 November 1877, 2. See *Vorbote*, 17 November 1877, 7: "In der 5., 6., 7., 14., 15., und 16. Ward lief unser Wahlzettel ausgezeichnet." On the Bohemians and the SLP see *Vorbote*, 30 March 1878, 3; 13 April 1878, 4; and Francis Hlavacek, "Zlomky českého počátečního hnutí dělnické v Americe," *Ročenka Americkych Delnickych Listu* (Cleveland: Delnicky Listy, 1924), 74–91.

17. George Schilling, "History of the Labor Movement in Chicago" ["Brief History"], in *The Life of Albert R. Parsons*, ed. Lucy Parsons (Chicago: By the editor, 1903), xxv; Schneirov, "Knights of Labor in Chicago," 99, 104.

18. *Times*, 8 November 1877, 2; 26 November 1877, 3; *Vorbote*, 17 November 1877, 5.

19. *Platform . . . of the Workingmen's Party of the United States, 1877*, SLP Records, reel 35; *Vorbote*, 5 January 1878, 8.

20. *Times*, 25 February 1878, 2; election returns in *Tribune*, 3 April 1878, 2; *Inter Ocean*, 4 April 1878, 5; *Vorbote*, 13 April 1878, 8.

21. *Hejmdal*, 21 July 1876 (CFLPS reel 9); *Tribune*, 24 April 1878, 4; *Inter Ocean*, 26 April 1878, 8.

22. *Inter Ocean*, 29 April 1878, 8; *ISZ*, 28 April 1878, 2; *Vorbote*, 11 May 1878, 1; *Inter Ocean*, 15 June 1878, 4.

23. *Tribune*, 3 September 1877, 8; *Vorbote*, 6 October 1877, 5; 27 October 1877, 8; *Inter Ocean*, 8 April 1878, 5; *Vorbote*, 4 May 1878, 8.

24. Louis Pio, *Til de Skandinaviske Arbejdere i Amerika* (Chicago: n.p., 1877); Peter Pedersen to editor, *Tribune*, 5 May 1878, 8; and William Scott, comp., *Newspapers and Periodicals of Illinois, 1814–1879* (rev. ed., Springfield: Illinois State Historical Library, 1910), 124.

25. *Times*, 22 July 1878, 3; *Inter Ocean*, 29 July 1878, 8; *Times*, 2 September 1878, 3; *Vorbote*, 7 September 1878, 8; *Inter Ocean*, 19 August 1878, 8; *Times*, 2 December 1878, 5.

26. *Inter Ocean*, 7 November 1878, 2; *The Socialist*, 9 November 1878, 8; 7 and 21 December 1878, both 8.

27. *Times*, 16 September 1878, 5; 4 December 1878, 6; *Tribune*, 13 December 1878, 8; 16 January 1879, 8; *Socialist*, 18 January 1879, 8.

28. *Socialist*, 1 February 1879, 8; 8 March 1879, 8; *Inter Ocean*, 4 November 1878, 8; *Times*, 27 January 1879, 10.

29. National Board of Supervision [NBS] Minutes, 8 August 1878; NBS to editor

Socialist and to editor *Vorbote,* 24 July 1879; 13 October 1879, all SLP Records, reel 34; *Inter Ocean,* 25 January 1879, 8; 21 March 1879, 8.

30. *Socialist,* 22 March 1879, 8; *Vorbote,* 22 March 1879, 6; *ISZ,* 17 March 1879, 4; *Inter Ocean,* 17 March 1879, 3.

31. *Der Westen,* 23 March 1879, 4; *Inter Ocean,* 29 March 1879, 4; *ISZ,* 10 March, 17 March, 27 March–1 April 1879, cited in Kann, "Working Class Culture and the Labor Movement," 315–317.

32. Election returns in *Tribune,* 2 April 1879, 1–2; *Times,* 2 April 1879, 4; cf. the editorials in *ISZ,* 7 April 1879, 4; and *Inter Ocean,* 4 April 1879, 3.

33. Although the city's population grew by at least 50 percent between 1879 and 1886, the time gap between the election and this data may not necessarily compromise its utility.

34. On the computation and interpretation of the Pearsonian correlation coefficient in Table 3.1, see Hubert Blalock, Jr., *Social Statistics* 2d ed. (New York: McGraw Hill, 1972), 385–393. For a non-statistical analysis that corroborates the one here see Hirsch, "Reform or Revolution," 125–129.

Precinct-level data would be preferred, had it been available; nor is data readily available at either level for classification by religious affiliation. The argument here is not intended as a test of the "ethno-cultural" interpretation of voting behavior.

35. See *Svornost,* 27 March 1879, CFLPS, reel 1 and 31 March 1879, CFLPS, reel 2: the editor promised to "publish the names . . . of all who were against us;" *Times,* 21 April 1878, 5.

36. *Platform . . . of the Socialistic Labor Party, 1880,* 38, SLP Records, reel 35. I found no corroboration of Schmidt's association with Marx.

37. Ernst Schmidt, *He Chose: The Other was a Treadmill Thing,* ed. and trans. Frederick Schmidt (Santa Fe: Vegara Printing, 1968), 122–123; *Tribune,* 7 October 1879, 7; 1 and 3 November 1879, 7.

38. Schmidt, *He Chose,* 123; Willis Abbott, *Carter Henry Harrison: A Memoir* (New York: Dodd, Mead, 1895), 140; and Claudius Johnson, *Carter Henry Harrison I, Political Leader* (Chicago: University of Chicago Press, 1928), 179, 190–191.

39. *Vorbote,* 8 February 1879, 8; McLogan quoted in Schneirov, "Knights of Labor in Chicago," 112.

40. *ISZ,* 7 March 1879, 3; *Skandinaven,* 10 June 1879, 4; Carter H. Harrison, Jr., "Ordinances . . . introduced in the Chicago city council by socialist aldermen . . . 1878–1882," (5pp., typescript, n.d.), Carter Henry Harrison Papers, box 1860–1889, Newberry Library.

41. Winnen, "Die Geschichte der Arbeiterbewegung von Chicago," *Fackel,* 1 April 1917, 1; Schilling, "Brief History," xxvii–xxviii; *Svornost,* 2 April 1879, CFLPS reel 1; *Tribune,* 6 November 1879, p. 4; *Skandinaven,* 11 November 1879, 4;

42. *Socialist,* 19 April 1879, 1; *ChAZ,* 19 July 1879, 4; *Tribune,* 4 August 1879, 8; *ChAZ,* 7 October 1879, 4.

43. *Der Westen,* 5 October 1879, 2; *Inter Ocean,* 7 October 1879, 2; *Tribune,* 1 November 1879, 7; 3 November 1879, 8; Schilling to Philip Van Patten [PVP], 20

December 1879; Ed Rose Tangen to PVP, 21 and 22 December 1879, all SLP Records, reel 5.

44. *ChAZ*, 19 January 1880, 4; *Tribune*, 19 January 1880, 8; *Times*, 16 February 1880, 2.

45. *ChAZ*, 20 February 1880, 4; election returns in *Tribune*, 7 April 1880, 1–2.

46. Schilling, "Brief History," xxviii. The Stauber-MacGrath case can be followed in either the *Tribune* or *ChAZ*, May 1880–March 1881.

47. *ChAZ*, 12 June 1880, 2; *Vorbote*, 17 July 1880, 8; Spies to NEC, 20 July 1880; Paul Ehmann to PVP, 30 November 1880, both SLP Records, reel 5. This last item, a ten-page "true synopsis of the disturbance within the party," is especially valuable.

48. Unsigned letter to PVP, 26 February 1880, SLP Records, reel 5: both handwriting and syntax identify the writer as Schilling; T. J. Morgan to NEC, 19 July 1880, *ibid*.

49. John Fossell to PVP, 19 July 1880; M. Schalk to NEC, 4 August 1880; Morgan to PVP, 20 July 1880, George Gaide to PVP, 25 October 1880, all SLP Records, reel 5. Cf. PVP to Schilling, 2 August 1880 and 23 September 1880, both Schilling Collection.

50. Schilling, "Brief History," xxix; cf. PVP to TVP, 15 July 1880, Powderly Papers, reel 2; *Vorbote*, 1 May 1880, 4; 3 July 1880, 1; *ChAZ*, 10 July 1880, 2; 26 June 1880, 2.

51. Mrs. Morgan to PVP, 29 October 1880; Ehmann to PVP, 30 November 1880 both SLP Records, reel 5; Schilling, "Brief History," xxvii.

52. George Gaide to PVP, 15 October 1880; Gaide to PVP, 19 October 1880; Ehmann to PVP, 30 November 1880, all SLP Records, reel 5.

53. *Svornost*, 25 October 1880, CFLPS, reel 2; *Tribune*, 22 November 1880, 8; John Fossell to PVP, 19 December 1880; Ehmann to PVP, 30 November 1880, both SLP Records, reel 5.

54. *Times*, 27 December 1880, 6; 3 January 1881, 3; *Inter Ocean*, 10 January 1881, 5; Scharnau, "Thomas J. Morgan," 92.

55. *ChAZ*, 14 March 1881, 4; *ISZ*, 22 March 1881, 4; Schilling, "Brief History," xxix; election returns in *Times*, 6 April 1881, 2–3.

56. Broadside, "Platform, Plan of Organization [of the] Revolutionary Socialistic Party" (circa October 1881), Parsons Papers; *Times*, 17 October 1881, 6; the standard account is Henry David, *Haymarket Affair*, 69–74.

57. *Herald*, 16 January 1882, 4; *Inter Ocean*, 30 January 1882, 6; *Vorbote*, 18 February 1882, 7; *Tribune*, 27 February 1882, 3.

58. *ChAZ*, 16 February 1882, 4; 25 February 1882, 4; 28–31 March 1882, 4; election returns, 5 April 1882, 4.

59. "Notes on the Meetings of the Socialist Labor Party, 1882–1886," Morgan Collection, reel 6. These are in fact "minutes" not "notes," and will be cited hereafter as "SLP Minutes."

60. *Tribune*, 16 January 1882, 3; 6 March 1882, 8; 10 July 1882, 8; 16 July 1882, 8; 11 December 1882, 8; *Herald*, 8 January 1883, 3; *Tribune*, 5 February 1883, 8.

61. Schilling, "Brief History," xxix–xxx; T. J. Morgan, MS autobiographical

fragment, Morgan Collection, reel 1; Scharnau, "Thomas J. Morgan," 92; James White to PVP, 19 January 1881, SLP Records, reel 5.

62. *Pittsburgh Manifesto*, Parsons Papers. Again, the standard account is David, *Haymarket Affair*, 81–107; cf. Avrich, *Haymarket Tragedy*, 68–78.

63. *Herald*, 22 October 1883, 4; *ChAZ:* 22 December 1883, 3; 21 and 24 January 1884, 4. There was only one block defection from the new IWPA back to the SLP when, in January 1884, the German "Independent Club of Southwestside Socialists," with about 120 members, voted to rejoin the SLP "on condition that the autonomy of the club would be preserved." By the middle of 1885, however, at least twenty-three had rejoined the IWPA.

64. *Herald*, 11 February 1884, 4; 21 January 1884, 4; *Times*, 3 March 1884, 2.

65. *Times*, 7 May 1884, 8; Alexander Jonas, "Socialism and Anarchism," [1885] in *Socialism in America: A Documentary History*, ed. Albert Fried (New York: Anchor Books, 1970), 230–233; Winnen, "Geschichte der Arbeiterbewegung von Chicago," *Fackel*, 8 April 1917, 1.

66. On Langner see Ignaz Auer, *Nach Zehn Jahren: Materiel und Glossen zur Geschichte der Sozialistgesetz* (Nürnberg: Frankischen Verlaganstalt, 1913), 309; on Vahlteich see Franz Osterroth, *Biographisches Lexikon des Sozialismus, Band I: Verstorbene Persönlichkeiten* (Hannover: Deitz Verlag, 1960), 315–316.

67. Hugo Vogt to Julius Krueger, 24 January 1884; W. L. Rosenberg to W. L. Morris, 20 April 1884, both SLP Records, reel 1; "SLP Minutes," 30 June 1884, Morgan Collection, reel 6; *Inter Ocean*, 11 February 1884, 8; *Herald*, 14 July 1884, 4.

68. *Herald*, 2 April 1883, 4; *Inter Ocean*, 21 January 1884, 8. Cf. the *Times*, 17 August 1884, 3: "There are about 10,000 socialistic votes in Chicago, and they have always played a considerable part in political events." *Inter Ocean*, 23 March 1885; 8; *Sozialist*, 18 April 1885, 4.

69. *Vorbote*, 12 March 1884, 8; *Tribune*, 26 May 1884, 8; *Sozialist*, 30 May 1885, 4; 6 June 1885, 4; 9 January 1886, 8; 13 February 1886, 7; cf. the "SLP Membership List," Morgan Collection, reel 7, which covers the period from 1880 to 1886, but includes only 106 names.

70. *Herald*, 12 January 1885, 1; *Vorbote*, 6 January 1886, 8; *Alarm*, 6 February 1886, 1; *Vorbote*, 30 December 1885, 4; *Sozialist*, 25 December 1885, 6; 9 January 1886, 6; 13 February 1886, 6.

71. *Tribune*, 29 March 1886, 8; 5 April 1886, 8; after July 1884 the "SLP Minutes" were kept in German, and do not mention the English section; Scharnau, "Thomas J. Morgan," 105.

Chapter Four: The Forest, Not the Trees

1. *Tribune*, 23 March 1879, 4.

2. The autobiographies were serialized in the *Knights of Labor* in 1887, and reprinted in *The Autobiographies of the Haymarket Martyrs*, ed. Philip Foner (New York: Humanities Press, 1969).

3. See, e.g., Bruce Dancis, "Social Mobility and Class Consciousness: San Francisco's International Workingmen's Association in the 1880's," *Journal of Social History*, 11:1 (Fall 1977), 75–98; and Charles Leinenweber, "The Class and Ethnic Bases of New York City Socialism, 1904–1915," *Labor History*, 22:1 (Winter 1981), 31–56.

4. (SLP) Foner, ed., *Formation of the WPUS*, 13; *Vorbote*, 17 March 1877, 4; *Vorbote*, 8 February 1879, 8; (IWPA) *ChAZ*, 11 August 1884, 4; *Alarm*, 18 April 1885, 1; William Holmes, "A Crime and Its Result," *The Rebel* (Boston), 20 November 1895, 21.

5. "SLP Membership List, 1880–1886," Morgan Collection, reel 6; "List of Anarchists and Socialists" in Schaack, *Anarchy and Anarchists* (Chicago, 1889), 691–693.

6. On the publishing and circulation history of Chicago's socialist press, see chapter 5; also Schaack, *Anarchy and Anarchists*, passim.

7. *Vorbote*, 8 February 1879, 8; *Alarm*, 18 April 1885, 1; see Bruce Nelson, "Culture and Conspiracy: a Social History of Chicago Anarchism, 1872–1900" (Ph.D. diss., Northern Illinois University, 1986), chapter 4.

These samples are neither random nor discrete. The names were conspicuous enough to have been caught, first by a police dragnet, and then a hundred years later in an historian's net. Moreover, 179 of the 724 IWPA members (25 percent) had been SLP members.

8. See Beijbom, *Swedes in Chicago*, 20–38, for an able discussion of these sources.

9. Thomas Mayer, "Some Characteristics of Union Members in the 1880's and 1890's," *Labor History*, 5:1 (Winter 1964), 57–66.

10. Marcus Thrane, "Autobiographical Reminiscences," trans. Vasilia Thrane Struck (typescript, 1917), Marcus Thrane and Family Papers, MSHS; Waldemar Westergaard, "Marcus Thrane in America: Some Unpublished Letters from 1880–1884," *Norwegian-American Studies and Records*, 9 (1936), 67–76; and Aksel Zachariassen, "Marcus Thrane og andre norske socialister i U.S.A." (typescript, 1917) Arbeiderbevegelsens Arkiv og Bibliothek, Oslo.

11. S. J. Loria, *Louis Pio; en biografisk skitse* (København: Loria, 1873); Edvard Wiinblad og Alsing Andersen, *Det Danske Socialdemokratis histoire fra 1871 til 1921* (København: social Demokratiets Fremad, 1921), 19–41; Kenneth Miller, "Danish Socialism and the Kansas Prairie," *Kansas Historical Quarterly*, 38:2 (Summer 1972), 156–168; and Jens Engberg, *Til Arbejdet! Liv eller dod! Louis Pio og Arbejderbevaegelse* København: Gyldendahl, 1979), 322–339.

12. Lev Palda, "Pameti českých osadniku v Americe napsal L.J. Palda," *Amerikan narodní Kalendar na roku 1911* (Chicago: A. Geringer, 1911), 265–288; Baumrucker's obituary, *Svornost*, 21 March 1896, CFLPS, reel 8; Mielbeck's obituary, *Vorbote*, 30 December 1882, 4; and Milan Dostalik, "České dělnické hnutí ve Spojencých státech za hospodářské krize let 1873–1878," in Gosoriovsky, ed., *Začiatky českej a slovenskej emigrácie do USA*, 125–162.

13. Frantisek Cajthmal, "Zivot a smrt Norberta Zouly v Americe," *Americke Dělnicke Listy* (Cleveland), 30 May 1930, 3; "Jakub Mikolanda zemrel," *Dennice Novoveku* (Cleveland), 30 May 1907, 9; Frantisek Soukup, *Pametní List Československe Socialne Demokratie Strany Dělnicke, 1872–1922* (Praha: n.p., 1922), 13–19; Thomas Capek, *The Czechs (Bohemians) in America* (Boston: Houghton Mifflin, 1928), 140–154.

14. Renate Keisewetter, "Die Institution der deutsch-amerikanischen Arbeiterpresse in Chicago: Zur Geschichte des *Vorboten* und der *Chicagoer Arbeiterzeitung, 1874–1886*" (Master's thesis, Ludwig-Maximilans-Universität München, 1982), 50–63.

15. *Tribune*, 26 April 1886, 3; John Flinn, *History of the Chicago Police Force* (Chicago: Police Book Fund, 1887), 232; *Times*, 23 March 1879, 3.

16. Jonathan Mayer, "The Journey-to-Work, Ethnicity and Occupation in Milwaukee, 1860–1890" (Ph.D. diss., University of Michigan, 1977), 54; Elsdon Smith, *The New Dictionary of American Family Names* (New York: Harper and Row, 1973) served as the basic source for the identifications.

17. The data for correcting the SLP's ethnic composition comes from Schaack, *Anarchy and Anarchists*, 62, and *Socialist*, 8 and 22 February 1879, 1. Schaack reported membership figures in early 1878, *Socialist* reported the dues paid by each section in early 1879.

18. Sibley's testimony in *Investigation by a Select Committee of the House of Representatives Relative to the Causes of the General Depression in Labor and Business; and As to Chinese Immigration* (Washington, D.C.: USGPO, 1879), 46th Congress, 2d Session, 112–113; Meilbeck in *Inter Ocean*, 18 May 1886, 12. Cf. T. J. Morgan, three undated mss.: "The Irish in the Socialist Movement: Tommy Ryan"; "Billy Creach [sic];" and "John McAuliffe," all Morgan Collection, reel 2.

19. *ChAZ*, 28 November 1884, 2; Friedrich Engels, "The Labor Movement in the United States," [1887] in Marx and Engels, *Letters to Americans, 1848–1895*, ed. Alexander Trachtenburg (New York: International Publishers, 1953), 289.

20. The category "laborers" is problematic: when asked by a directory agent or census enumerator a socialist machinist or printer may well have given his occupation as "laborer." The presence of two Pinkerton detectives (plainclothes to be sure) is not unexpected, nor is the clairvoyant.

21. The categories are from Stephan Thernstrom, *The Other Bostonians: Poverty and Progress in the American Metropolis, 1880–1970* (Cambridge: Harvard University Press, 1973), appendix B, 289–302; George Engel in *Autobiographies*, 96. Each of the editors listed in Table 4.4 had been a skilled worker: Parsons was a printer, Spies an upholsterer, Schwab a bookbinder, Zoula a silversmith, Pondelicek a painter, and so on.

22. On the computation and interpretation of the occupational index, see Bubnys, "Chicago, 1870 and 1900," 72.

23. *Tribune*, 23 March 1879, 4; and 1 September 1886, 8.

24. Quoted in Schaack, *Anarchy and Anarchists*, 289, 270. The index of segrega-

tion measures SLP segregation at .25 and IWPA segregation at .35, higher than for Germans (.20), those from Britain (.23), and the Irish (.28) but lower than those for the native-born (.39), Swedes (.42) and Bohemians (.64).

On the computation and interpretation of the index of segregation, see Karl and Alma Taeuber, *Negroes in Cities: Residential Segregation and Neighborhood Change* (Chicago: University of Chicago Press, 1965), 28–31, 195–245.

25. Schaack, *Anarchy and Anarchists*, 208–209; *Times*, 7 September 1885, 8; *Vorbote*, 6 January 1877, 5; 25 August 1877, 5; *ChAZ*, 19 February 1883, 4. On their activities see Mary Jo Buhle, *Women and American Socialism, 1870–1920* (Urbana: University of Illinois Press, 1983), 1–48.

26. *ChAZ*, 15 October 1883, 4; *Pittsburgh Manifesto*, in the Parsons Papers; Fielden trial testimony quoted in George McLean, *The Rise and Fall of Anarchy in America* (Chicago: R. G. Badoux, 1889), 105.

27. *Alarm*, 26 December 1885, 4; 6 February 1886, 4; 6 March 1886, 4; *ChAZ*, 7 July 1883, 4; Lizzie Holmes, "The Days of Our Infancy: A Reminiscence," *Progressive Woman*, 5 (August 1911), 7; Meredith Tax, *The Rising of the Women: Feminist Solidarity and Class Conflict, 1880–1917* (New York: Monthly Review Press, 1980), 38–54.

28. IBLS, *Fourth Biennial Report, 1886*, 169.

29. *ChAZ*, 26 December 1883, 4; *Alarm*, 3 October 1885, 3; *ChAZ*, 5 November 1883, 4; *Fackel*, 4 November 1883, 4. See chapter 6 for a discussion of those christenings. Sidney Eastman, *An Open Letter to the Members of the Union League Club* (Chicago: n.p., [1886]), 9.

30. Bubnys, "Chicago, 1870 and 1900," Tables 2.3 and 2.6, pp. 27 and 30; IBLS, *Third Biennial Report, 1884*, 140–141.

31. It remains difficult to get beyond even the local leadership to the membership. Despite rich sources, I can identify socialists within the trade union movement, or the members of anarchist singing societies, for examples, only when they got elected to office, or expelled, or otherwise got their names published. This is why 109 officers can be identified within the total of 146 IWPA members.

32. See Alvin Schmidt, *Fraternal Organizations: Encyclopedia of American Institutions* (Westport, Conn.: Greenwood Press, 1980); Hartmut Keil, "Einwandererviertel und amerikanische Gesellschaft: Zur Integration deutscher Einwanderer in die amerikanische stadtisch-industrielle Umwelt des ausgehenden 19. Jahrhunderts am Beispiel Chicagos," *Archiv für Sozialgeschichte*, 24 (1984), 47–89, esp. 74–85; Eugene McCarthy, "The Bohemian People in Chicago and their Benevolent Societies, 1875–1946" (Master's thesis, University of Chicago, 1950); and Anton Kvist, *Fra Lincoln til Hoover: Amerikas Danske Pioneer Forening Dania, Chicago: 1862–1930* (København: Trykt af Politiken, 1930).

33. Schilling to Lucy Parsons, 1 December 1893, Schilling Collection.

Chapter Five: The Movement's Internal Organization

1. *ChAZ*, 28 January 1884, 4; *Alarm*, 4 October 1884, 4; 14 February 1886, 4; *Vorbote*, 2 September 1885, 8. Cf. Avrich, *Haymarket Tragedy*, 82–84, 471 n. 17, counts between fifteen and nineteen active groups.

2. *ChAZ*, 1 May 1886, quoted in Schaack, *Anarchy and Anarchists*, 110; Schwab in *Autobiographies*, 125; *Die Freiheit* (New York), 14 February 1885, 3. There are five red IWPA membership cards in the Grinnell Collection.

3. *Alarm*, 16 May 1885, 4; Fielden quoted in Schaack, *Anarchy and Anarchists*, 503; *Alarm*, 6 March 1886, 1; cf. Holmes, in *The Rebel*, 20 November 1895, 21.

4. *ChAZ*, 19 February 1883, 4; *Vorbote*, 30 January 1884, 8; *ChAZ*, 11 August, 4; *Vorbote*, 2 September 1885, 8; "A True Bohemian" to editor, *Mail*, 10 May 1886, 1.

5. *ChAZ*, 13 February 1883, 4; 6 March 1883, 4; *Vorbote*, 31 March 1883, 8; *ChAZ*, 5 June 1883, 4; 8 April 1884, 6 August 1884, 4; Seliger quoted in *Concise History of the Great Trial of the Chicago Anarchists in 1886, Condensed from the Official Record*, ed. Dyer Lum (1888, reprint New York: Arno Press, 1969), 79.

6. Engel in *Autobiographies*, 97; Schwab in *ibid.*, 123–125.

7. *Alarm*, 6 February 1886, 4.

8. Thomas Morgan, "Why I am a Socialist," typescript, Morgan Collection, reel 1; *CVZ*, 19 February 1877, 1; Schaack, *Anarchy and Anarchists*, 215, 132, 295, 218–219.

9. Schaack, *Anarchy and Anarchists*, 111, 136, 203; Klaus Ensslen, "Die deutsch-amerikansiche Arbeiterkneipe in Chicago: Ihre soziale Funktion im Spannungsfeld ethnischer und klassenspezifischer Kultur," *Amerikastudien*, 29:2 (Summer 1984), 183–198.

10. Schaack, *Anarchy and Anarchists*, 215, 216, 341; *CVZ*, 26 February 1877, 1. See Table 4.4.

11. Perry Duis, *The Saloon: Public Drinking in Chicago and Boston, 1880–1920* (Urbana: University of Illinois Press, 1983); Harzig, "Chicago's German Northside," 138–140.

On the conjuncture of saloons and socialism, see Peter DeLottinville, "Joe Beef of Montreal: Working-Class Culture and the Tavern, 1869–1889," *Labour/Le Travail*, 8/9 (Autumn/Spring 1981–82), 9–40, and James Roberts, "Wirtshaus und Politik in der deutschen Arbeiterbewegung," in *Sozialgeschichte der Freizeit: Untersuchungen zum Wandel der Alltagskultur in Deutschland*, ed. Gerhard Huck (Wuppertal: Peter Hammer Verlag, 1980), 123–139.

12. *ISZ*, 10 April 1877: "Through nothing else can the German cause be helped as much as through mental stimulation, meetings, and debates. . . . [N]o one has done more in this direction than the socialist organizations. May they continue, grow and thrive, then the German things worthy of preservation will not be in danger." Quoted in Hirsch, "Revolution and Reform," 481.

13. *Alarm*, 31 October 1885, 3; 15 November 1884, 2. Cf. Schwab's description of the groups as "debating societies"; *Autobiographies*, 125.

Notes to Pages 110–114

14. *Socialist*, 31 May 1879, 3; 5 October 1878, 4.

15. *Ibid.*, 30 November 1878, 8; *ChAZ*, 1 June 1882, 4; see the "Regeln für die Leihbibliothek," *ChAZ*, 4 September 1884, 4; 12 April 1884, 4; 12 January 1882, 4; 23 August 1884, 4; *Alarm*, 31 October 1885, 4.

16. *Alarm*, 28 November 1885, 1; *CVZ*, 3 March 1877, 2; Cf. Hans-Josef Steinberg, "Workers' Libraries in Germany before 1914," *History Workshop Journal*, 1 (Spring 1976), 166–180; Stan Shipley, "The Library of the Alliance Cabinet Makers' Association," *ibid.*, 181–184; and Vernon Lidtke, *The Alternative Culture: Socialist Labor in Imperial Germany* (New York: Oxford University Press, 1985), 178–191.

17. Based on a sample of lectures advertised or reported in *ChAZ* and *Alarm*. Cf. Dieter Langeweische und Klaus Schonhoven, "Arbeiterbibliotheken und Arbei-terlekture im Wilhelmischen Deutschland," *Archiv für Sozialgeschichte*, 16 (1976): 135–204.

18. Cf. Richard Ely's argument that "the laboring classes, through their unions, are learning discipline, self-restraint, and the methods of united action, and are also discovering whom they can trust, finding out the necessity of uniting great con-fidence in leaders with strict control of them." Richard Ely, *The Labor Movement in America* (1886, rev. ed.: New York: Thomas Crowell, 1890), 136. The difference between an anarchist group and Ely's unions was the shortage of "discipline" and the lack of "control" by the leadership. Cf. Lidtke, *Alternative Culture*, 17–20.

19. *Times*, 4 April 1881, 1; *ChAZ*, 6 May 1879, 4; *Socialist*, 17 May 1879, 5; *Fackel*, 8 October 1882, 8.

20. *ChAZ*, 1 September 1888, 4; 16 February 1889, 2; 16 March 1889, 4; Schaack, *Anarchy and Anarchists*, 670.

21. Schaack, *Anarchy and Anarchists*, 670, 674, quoting Chicago *Herald*, n.d. Cf. Jane Addams, *Twenty Years at Hull House* (New York: MacMillan, 1919), 91–92.

22. Chapter 6, sketches the cultural dimensions of club life, arguing at some length that the movement's singing societies, theatre groups, dances, festivals, and parades comprised a "movement culture."

23. John Jentz, "Craft Traditions and the Traditions of Craftsmen: Their Role in the Organization of Chicago's Workers in the Gilded Age" (paper presented to the Chicago Area Labor History Group, Newberry Library, 28 June 1983), 4–5. On club life in Europe, see Peter Amann, *Revolution and Mass Democracy: The Paris Club Movement in 1848* (Princeton: Princeton University Press, 1975), P. H. Noyes, *Organization and Revolution: Working-Class Associations in the German Revolutions of 1848–1849* (Princeton: Princeton University Press, 1966); and, especially, Stan Shipley, *Club-Life and Socialism in Mid-Victorian London*, (1971, reprint London: Journeymen Press, 1983).

24. Kenneth Schlichter, " 'By Hammer and Hand All Arts Do Stand': Mechanic's Institutes in America, 1820–1860" (Master's seminar paper, Northern Illinois University, 1974).

25. *Ibid.*, 16–17; Andreas, *History of Chicago*, 1:518–520. Cf. *Inter Ocean*, 3 April 1878, 8. Not a single "mechanic" served on the institute's board of directors in 1880;

of eleven officers, three were manufacturers, two lawyers, one builder, one engineer, one in real estate, and the remaining three were unlisted in the city directory.

26. Jentz, "Craft Traditions," 5; I am indebted to Fred Scheid, who shared his unfinished research on "Die Arbeiter Verein von Chicago" (Ph.D. seminar paper, Northern Illinois University, forthcoming). *ISZ*, 31 August 1861, 2; 26 May 1862, 4; 10 June 1963, 2.

27. See *ISZ*, 30 September 1861, 2; 19 October 1861, 4; Jentz, "Craft Traditions," 6; *ISZ*, 30 March 1866, 2; 13 August 1867, cited in Hirsch, "Revolution or Reform," 483.

28. *ISZ*, 22 February 1876, 3; Montgomery, *Beyond Equality*, x, 446; *ISZ*, 4 September 1861, 2; *Deutsche Arbeiter*, 28 August 1869, 4. The evidence comes from Schlichter, "Mechanic's Institutes," 16–17, 26–27; Scheid, "Die Arbeiter Verein von Chicago"; and Jentz, "Craft Traditions," 6–7.

29. Schneirov and Jentz, "Social Republicanism and Socialism."

30. On the German Turners, see G. A. Hoehn, *Der Nord-amerikanische Turnerbund und seine Stellung zur Arbeiterbewegung* (St. Louis: Union Press, 1897); on the Skandinaviske Turnerbroderna, see Beijbom, *Swedes in Chicago*, 270–271, 279; and on the Bohemian sokols, see "What is Sokol?" [1865] trans. in Jarka Jelinek and Jaroslav Zmrhal, *Sokol Educational and Physical Culture Association* (Chicago: American Sokol Union, 1944).

31. *Vorbote*, 3 April 1880, 1.

32. Foner, ed., *Formation of the WPUS; Constitution . . . of the WPUS, 1877*, 16, SLP Records, reel 35; and Keisewetter, "deutsch-amerikanische Arbeiterpresse in Chicago," 12–25.

33. *Dagslyset*, February 1878, 8; *Vorbote*, 2 June 1877, 5; Winnen, "Geschichte der Arbeiterbewegung von Chicago," *Fackel*, 4 March 1917, 1.

34. Hartmut Keil, "The German Immigrant Working Class of Chicago, 1875–1890: Workers, Labor Leaders, and the Labor Movement," in *American Labor and Immigration History, 1877–1920s: Recent European Research*, ed. Dirk Hoerder (Urbana: University of Illinois Press, 1983), 167; Karl Arndt and May Olson, comps., *Deutsch-Amerikanische Zeitungen und Zeitschriften, 1732–1955: Geschichte und Bibliographie*, (2d rev. ed.; Heidelberg: Verlages Quelle and Meyer, 1965), 58, 69, 86.

35. Louis Pio, *Den Lille Amerikaner, En Forer og Tolk for Skandinaverne i Amerika* (Chicago: Den Christelige Talsmand, 1879–1880); Johannes Wist, "Den Norsk-Amerikanernes Presse, 2: Pressen efter Borgerkrigen," in Wist, ed., *Norsk-Amerikanernes Festskrift, 1914* (Decorah, IA.: Symra Co., 1914), 82–83, 87–88, 92–93; Jens-Bjerre Danielsen, "The Early Danish Immigrant Socialist Press," in *Essays on the Scandinavian-North American Radical Press*, ed. Dirk Hoerder (Bremen: Universität Bremen, 1984), 56–77.

36. *Vorbote*, 4 May 1878, 8; 6 October 1877, 5; *Socialist*, 14 September 1878, 1; *Inter Ocean*, 20 May 1879, 2; *Proceedings of the SLP 1879–1880*, 7, SLP Records, reel 35.

37. *Budoucnost*, 16 June 1883, 1; "A True Bohemian" to editor, *Mail*, 10 May 1886, 1; Frantisek Stedronsky, *Zahraniční krajanské noviny, časopisy a kalendáře* (Praze:

Narodní knihovna, 1958), 388; Josef Polišenský, "Český podíl na předhistorii máje," in Gosiorovsky, ed., *Začiatky českej a slovenskej emigrácie do USA*, 163–185.

38. *Alarm*, 27 December 1884, 2; 22 November 1884, 2; Albert Parsons, *Anarchism: Its Philosophy and Scientific Basis as Defined by Some of Its Apostles* (Chicago: Mrs. Lucy Parsons, 1889), 173; Herbert Gutman, "Alarm: Chicago and New York, 1884–1889," in *The American Radical Press, 1880–1960*, ed. Joseph Conlin, 2 vols. (Westport, Conn.: Greenwood Press, 1974), 2: 380–386.

39. New York *Times*, 7 May 1886, 1: *Tribune*, 7 May 1886, 2; *Svornost*, 7 and 11 May 1886, both 4. Jan Habenicht, *Dějiny Čechů v Amerických* (St. Louis: Hlas, 1910), 607, identifies *Lampcka* as an "anarchistic" paper, although Tomas Čapek, *Padesát Let Českého Tisku v Americe* (New York: Language Press, 1911), 131, identifies it as a "humoristicko-satiricky" weekly. The contradiction cannot be resolved: there are no extant copies.

40. *Vorbote*, 23 December 1885, 8; the entry in Arndt und Olson, comps., *Deutsch-Amerikanische Zeitungen*, 57 is wrong. The Grinnell Collection has two issues of *Die Anarchist*.

41. Pio, *Den Lille Amerikaner*, 12, trans. in Danielsen, "Early Danish Immigrant Socialist Press," 62–63; *Budoucnost*, 16 June 1883, 8; Elisabeth Pitzer, "Burgerliche Presse und Arbeiterpresse in Wandel: Deutsch-amerikanische Tageszeitungen am Ende des 19. Jahrhunderts, dargestellt am Beispiel von 'Illinois Staatszeitung' und 'Chicagoer Arbeiterzeitung'" (Master's thesis, Ludwig-Maximilians-Universität München, 1980).

42. Pio, *Den Lille Amerikaner*, 12, trans. in Danielsen, "Early Danish Immigrant Socialist Press," 62–63; Paul Le Blanc, "Revolutionary Socialism in America, 1877–1887" (Master's research paper, University of Pittsburgh, 1979), 199; Paul Buhle, "German Socialists and the Roots of American Working-Class Radicalism," in Keil and Jentz, eds., *German Workers in Industrial Chicago*, 224–235, here 230.

43. Cf. "By-Laws of 'The Chicago Socialist Press Association,'" *Socialist*, 1 February 1879, 8; "Protokoll-Buch von der Illinoiser Volkszeitung Publishing Association, 1884–1885," Morgan Collection, reel 7; *Alarm*, 30 May 1885, 1; Foner, ed., *Formation of the WPUS*, 31.

44. *Vorbote*, 1 April 1876, quoted in Keisewetter, "Deutsch-amerikanische Arbeiterpresse in Chicago," 37; on the structure of the SPS, see *ibid.*, 28–49; *Vorbote*, 22 December 1883, 6; *Alarm*, 28 November 1885, 1; Foner, ed., *Formation of the WPUS*, 18.

45. See the wonderful account by a Danish printer who worked with Pio in *Ugebladet*, 22 and 29 June 1922, trans. in Marion Marzolf, *The Danish-Language Press in America* (New York: Arno Press, 1979), 42–43.

46. Keisewetter, "Deutsch-amerikanische Arbeiterpresse in Chicago," 74–82. *Vorbote*, 14 July 1877, 2, identified the Board of Directors and Board of Review; of eight elected officers, four were printers, including both presidents. See *Fackel*, 8 June 1879, 8; *ChAZ*, 27 June 1882, 4; and *Alarm*, 30 May 1885, 1.

47. *ChAZ*, 4 December 1883, 4; 3 December 1884, 4; *Vorbote*, 10 August 1882, 7;

24 December 1884, 8. Herman Pudewa inserted the word "Revenge" into the famous Haymarket broadside, see Lum, ed., *Concise History of the Great Trial*, 86.

48. *ChAZ*, 15 April 1882, 4; "Law and Order" to editor, *Tribune*, 7 May 1886, 2; *Inter Ocean*, 5 October 1885, 8; 16 November 1885, 8; on the conflict, see Thomas Robinson, "Chicago Typographical Union No. 16: Fifty Years of Development," (Ph.D. diss., University of Chicago, 1925).

49. Ely, *The Labor Movement in America*, 278.

50. From 1880 to 1886 the city's population increased only 64 percent; see Wesley Skogan, *Chicago Since 1840: A Time Series Data Book* (Urbana: Institute of Government and Public Affairs, 1976), Table 1, p. 18.

51. Habenicht, *Dějiny Čechů v Amerických*, 604–609; Ayer and Sons (firm), *American Newspaper Annuals*, 1880–1886; Rowell, *American Newspaper Directories*, 1880–1886; Pitzer, "Burgerliche Presse und Arbeiterpresse"; Frederick Buchstein, "The Anarchist Press in American Journalism," *Journalism History*, 1 (Summer 1974), 43–46ff.

52. An incomplete run of the *Workingman's Advocate* can be found at the WSHS, but neither the *Telegraph* nor the *Standard of Labor* has survived.

53. *Progressive Age*, 5 March 1881, 1; 24 June 1882, 1; Knights of Labor, "District 24 Minutes, 1882–1886," 3 September 1882, Schilling Collection, vol. 3. Some Chicago Knights opposed the paper, and Powderly disapproved of DA 24's endorsement; see Richard Griffiths to TVP, 26 June 1882, reel 4; and TVP to Griffiths, 17 May 1882, reel 45, both Powderly Papers.

54. *Herald*, 25 June 1883, 4. For the history of the *Progressive Age* and a brilliant exegesis of its leading columnist, see Schneirov, "Knights of Labor in Chicago," 328–336, 318–327.

55. "SLP Minutes," March–June 1884, reel 6; and the ms. "Protokoll-Buch von Illinoiser Volkszeitung Publishing Association, 1884–1885," reel 7, both Morgan Collection; *Herald*, 17 December 1883, 4; 10 March 1884, 4; 24 March 1884, 2; *Inter Ocean*, 12 May 1884, 8.

56. *Inter Ocean*, 22 July 1884, 8; *Sozialist*, 9 and 30 May 1885, both 4; H. Walther to NEC, 9 January 1885, reel 5, L. Bonstein to NEC, 19 January 1885, reel 6, SLP Records; broadside, "An die Abonnenten der Ill. V. Ztg und an der Leser des 'Sozialist,'" 13 April 1885, Morgan Collection, reel 7.

57. Quoted in Schaack, *Anarchy and Anarchists:* 360, 238, 303, and 277.

Chapter Six: Dancing Socialists, Picnicking Anarchists?

1. Sorge, *Labor Movement in the United States*, 71.

2. Hartmut Keil and Heinz Ickstadt, "Elemente einer deutschen Arbeiterkultur in Chicago zwischen 1880 und 1890," *Geschichte und Gesellschaft*, 5:1 (1979), 103–124; Hartmut Keil and John Jentz, "German Working-Class Culture in Chicago: A Problem of Definition, Method and Analysis," *Gulliver*, 9 (1981), 128–147; Buhle, "German Socialists and American Working-Class Radicalism," 224–235. These

studies focus on German-language sources. In contrast, see Avrich, *Haymarket Tragedy*, 131–149, which relies on English-language sources.

3. Klaus Ensslen, Heinz Ickstadt, and Ruth Seifurt, "German Working-Class Culture in Chicago: Problems of Definition and Research" (paper presented at the Chicago Projekt conference, Chicago, 9–12 October 1981), 11: "movement culture . . . does not represent the whole spectrum of the working class." Cf. James Wickham, "Working-class movement and working-class life: Frankfurt am Main during the Weimar Republic," *Social History* 8:3 (October 1983), 315–343, esp. 316–318.

4. Oestreicher, *Solidarity and Fragmentation*, 60–75; Leon Fink, *Workingmen's Democracy: The Knights of Labor and American Politics* (Urbana: University of Illinois Press, 1983).

5. Clifford Geertz, *The Interpretation of Cultures* (New York: Basic Books, 1973), esp. 3–30. See Peter Burke, *Popular Culture in Early Modern Europe* (New York: Harper Torchbooks, 1978), esp. 1–87; Vernon Lidtke, "Die kulturelle Bedeutung der Arbeitervereine," in *Kultureller Wandel im 19. Jahrhundert*, ed. Günter Wiegelman (Göttingen: Vandenhoeck und Ruprecht, 1973), 146–159; Gerhard Ritter, "Workers' Culture in Imperial Germany: Problems and Points of Departure for Research," *Journal of Contemporary History*, 13:2 (April 1978), 165–189; and a special issue of *Geschichte und Gesellschaft*, ed. Jürgen Kocka, "Arbeiterkultur in 19. Jahrhundert," 5:1 (1979).

6. *Tribune*, 14 February 1881, 3; 31 January 1881, 8; *Vorbote*, 15 June 1878, 8; *Socialist*, 12 October 1878, 6; Sandy Mazzola, "When Music is Labor: Chicago Bands and Orchestras and the Origins of the Chicago Federation of Musicians, 1880–1902" (Ph.D. diss., Northern Illinois University, 1984), 29–31.

7. *Vorbote*, 30 March 1878, 8; *Hejmdal*, 11 August 1876, CFLPS, reel 9; *Dagslyset*, Juni 1876, 2; *Socialist*, 29 March 1879, 8; *Inter Ocean*, 24 March 1879, 4.

8. *Abendpost*, 6 July 1935, included the following Gesangvereine in a listing of "German Clubs and Societies in Chicago": Arbeiter Sängerbund des Nordwestens, Stadte-Vereinigung Chicago des Arbeiter-Sängerbunds der Vereinigten Staaten, Ferdinand Lassalle Frauenchor, and Die Arbeiter Liederkranz.

9. Carol Poore, *German-American Socialist Literature, 1865–1900* (Frankfurt, a. M.: Peter Lang, 1982), 111; Mary Corry, "The Role of German Singing Societies in Nineteenth Century America," in *Germans in America: Aspects of German-American Relations in the Nineteenth Century*, ed. E. Allen McCormick (Brooklyn: Brooklyn College Press, 1983), 155–168.

10. Ritter, "Workers' Culture in Imperial Germany," 174; Dieter Dowe, "The Workingmen's Choral Movement in Germany before the First World War," *Journal of Contemporary History*, 13:2 (April 1978), 269–296.

11. *ChAZ*, 17 March 1882, 4; *Tribune*, 7 September 1885, 2; Poore, *German-American Socialist Literature*, 109; Dowe, "Workingmen's Choral Movement," 286, 290; Vernon Lidtke, "Lieder der deutschen Arbeiterbewegung, 1864–1914," *Geschichte und Gesellschaft*, 5:1 (1979), 54–82.

12. J. B. Pecky, N. Zoula, F. Hlavacka, Leo Kochmann, F. Pecha, *Zpevnik dělnicky: sbirka na napevý narodních a jiných znamých pisni s novým textum delnickým*

(Chicago: Spravedlnost, 1901); Čapek, *Čechs (Bohemians) in America*, 146, 148; J. B. Pecky, *Sebrane Básne* (Chicago: Spravedlnost, 1899).

13. *Tribune*, 20 January 1879, 8; broadside, "Socialistic Labor Songs by William Creech (Moulder)," Morgan Collection, reel 6; Schaack, *Anarchy and Anarchists*, 67. One volume of poetry has survived: George Sloan, *The Telephone of Labor* (Chicago: n.p., 1880).

14. *Tribune*, 29 April 1885, 6; Hermann Duncker, "Kunstlicher Kultur" (1904), quoted in Dowe, "Workingmen's Choral Movement," 270.

15. *Fackel*, 5, 12, 19 March 1882; *ChAZ*, 17 and 20 March 1882, 4; Keil and Jentz, "German Working-Class Culture in Chicago," 128.

16. August Spies [W.L. Rosenberg and Paul Grottkau], *Die Nihilisten: Ein Volkstuck in Vier Akten* (Chicago: Social-Democratic Printing Association, 1882).

17. Poore, *German-American Socialist Literature*, 104–105; *Daily News*, 17 and 18 March 1882, 5; *ChAZ*, 15 March 1884, 3.

18. Heinz Ickstadt and Hartmut Keil, "A Forgotten Piece of Working-Class Literature: Gustav Lyser's Satire of the Hewitt Hearing of 1878," *Labor History*, 20:1 (Winter 1979), 127–140, 130, 134; *Vorbote*, 17 and 24 August 1878, 8.

19. *Fackel*, 21 December 1879, 4; 11 March 1883, 4; *ChAZ*, 24 April 1884, 4; *Daily News*, 20 March 1885, 3; *Alarm*, 4 April 1885, 1.

20. *Vorbote*, 13 January 1886, 2; Christine Heiss, "Kommerzielle deutsche Volksbühnen und deutsches Arbeitertheater in Chicago, 1870–1910," *Amerikastudien*, 29:2 (Summer 1984), 169–182.

21. *ChAZ*, 6 and 20 December 1879, 4; *Times*, 28 November 1879, 8. The "Sozial Dramatische Verein" was separate and distinct from the "Working Peoples' Dramatic Association"; see *Times*, 1 April 1880, 6.

22. *Fackel*, 30 March 1884, 8; *ChAZ*, 1 September 1888, 4; Heiss, "Kommerzielle deutsche Volksbühnen," 169–182.

23. Leola Bergman, *Americans from Norway* (Philadelphia: J. B. Lippincott, 1950), 189; Henriette Naeseth and Napier Witt, "Two Norwegian Dramatic Societies in Chicago," *Norwegian-American Studies and Records*, 10 (1938), 44–75.

24. *Denni Hlasatel*, 23 February 1913 (CFLPS reel 3); Rudolf Bubeníček, *Dějiny Čechů v Chicagu* (Chicago: Szabo Westside Press, 1939), 419–423; *Svornost*, 22 June 1878, CFLPS, reel 4; *Budoucnost*, 16 June 1883, 8.

25. *Skandinaven*, 28 July 1882, CFLPS reel 10; *Svenska Tribunen*, 16 January 1878, CFLPS reel 64; 19 December 1883, CFLPS, reel 65; Anne-Charlotte Harvey, "Swedish-American Theatre," in *Ethnic Theatre in the United States*, ed. Maxine Seller (Westport, Conn.: Greenwood Press, 1983), 491–524; Clinton Hyde, "Danish-American Theatre," in *ibid.*, 101–118.

26. Timo Riipa and Michael Karni, "Finnish-American Theatre," in Seller, ed., *Ethnic Theatre*, 119–138; cf. Peter von Ruden, *Sozialdemokratisches Arbeitertheater, 1848–1914* (Frankfurt: Athenaum Verlag, 1973), 55–76.

27. *Alarm*, 1, 8, 15, 22, 29 November 1884.

28. Ritter, "Workers' Culture in Imperial Germany," 173–174; *Times*, 7 September 1885, 8.

29. Klaus Tenfelde, *Sozialgeschichte der Bergarbeiterschaft an der Ruhr im 19. Jahrhundert* (Bonn-Bad Godesborg: Verlag Neue Gesellschaft, 1977), 365, 388–395; *ChAZ*, 26 April 1884, 4; 8 April 1884, 4.

30. *ChAZ*, 4 January 1884, 4; *Alarm*, 22 November 1884, 3; *ChAZ*, 13 April 1884, 4.

31. *Fackel*, 30 March 1884, 8; Dowe, "Workingmen's Choral Movement," 289; cf. the elaborate programs in Lidtke, *Alternative Culture*, 208–222; *Fackel*, 27 January 1884, 8.

32. *ChAZ*, 24 March 1884, 4.

33. *Fackel*, 4 November 1883, 4; *ChAZ*, 26 December 1883; 4; 26 August 1884, 4; *Alarm*, 3 October 1885, 4.

34. Eric Hobsbawm, *Primitive Rebels* (1959, reprint New York: W. W. Norton, 1965), esp. 150–174; *idem.*, "Religion and the Rise of Socialism," in Hobsbawm, *Workers: Worlds of Labor* (New York: Pantheon, 1984), 66–88.

35. *Socialist*, 31 May 1879, 8; 14 June 1879, 8; Schaack, *Anarchy and Anarchists*, 6; *ISZ*, 28 July 1879, 4; 8 September 1879, 4.

36. *ChAZ*, 23, 24, 28 June 1879; *Times*, 23, 27, 28 June 1879; letter to editor, *Skandinaven*, 24 June 1879, 4; Adolf Kraus, *Reminiscences and Comments* (Chicago: Tony Rubovits, 1925), 34–38.

37. *Svenska Amerikanaren*, 3 and 10 July 1879, cited in Beijbom, *Swedes in Chicago*, 332; *Svornost*, 10 July 1879, CFLPS, reel 1; cf. the account of an Irish ("notorious rascals") invasion of a German picnic, *ISZ*, 6 July 1871, 4.

38. *Skandinaven*, 24 June 1879, 4; *ChAZ*, 11 May 1880, 4; 22 June 1880, 4; *Fackel*, 5 September 1880, 12 June 1881, both 8; *ChAZ*, 29 July 1880, 2 August 1880, both 4.

39. *Alarm*, 16 May 1885, 1 and 4; 27 June 1885, 4; *Vorbote*, 1 July 1885, 8; 9 September 1885, 8; *Herald*, 27 June 1885, 4; 7 September 1885, 1; Flinn, *Chicago Police Force*, 249, 250–251; Keil and Ickstadt, "Deutschen Arbeiterkultur in Chicago," 117–118.

40. Schaack, *Anarchy and Anarchists*, 281, 453; "confession" of Herman Muntzenberg, in *ibid.*, 282, 314, 338.

41. *Alarm*, 25 July 1885, 4; *Vorbote*, 29 July 1885, 8; *Inter Ocean*, 17 June 1878, 1; *Times*, 17 June 1878, 3.

42. *Tribune*, 7 September 1885, 2.

43. *Tribune*, 21 April 1879, 7; *Inter Ocean*, 21 April 1879, 7; Illinois Militia Act of May 1879, cited in *Presser versus the State of Illinois*, 116 U.S. 252 (1886), *Supreme Court Reporter* (St. Paul, Minn.: West Publishing, 1886), 6: 580–586.

44. *ISZ*, 3 July 1879, 2; 29 July 1879, 2; *Tribune*, 2 September 1879, 5; *ISZ*, 8 September 1879, 1; Christine Heiss, "Der Lehr- und Wehr-Verein von Chicago: Ein sozialgeschichtliche Beitrag zur Radikalisierung der deutschen Arbeiter in den USA" (Master's thesis, Ludwig-Maximilians Universität München, 1981).

45. *Presser v. Illinois*, 116 U.S. 252; *Times*, 6 January 1886, 1; *Alarm*, 9 January 1886, 2; Robert Shoemaker, "A Fight to Bear Arms," *The Reader* (Chicago), 24 August 1984, 8ff.

46. *Tribune*, 2 July 1880, 5; *ChAZ*, 6 July 1880, 4.

47. *ChAZ*, 28 November 1884, 2; *Alarm*, 29 November 1884, 1; *Tribune*, 28 November 1884, 8; *Inter Ocean*, 29 April 1885, 8; Flinn, *History of the Chicago Police*, 224–228; *Alarm*, 2 May 1885, 1.

48. *Tribune*, 17 June 1878, 2; *ISZ*, 5 July 1879, 1; *ChAZ*, 10 August 1884, 4; *Times*, 26 April 1886, 4; *Alarm*, 24 April 1886, 1; *Vorbote*, 28 April 1886, 5.

49. *Tribune*, 2 June 1878, 4; Flinn, *Chicago Police Force*, 249; *Tribune*, 18 April 1879, 4, 7, 8; Holdridge Collins, *History of the Illinois National Guard* (Chicago: Black and Beach, 1884), 86–96.

50. Samuel Bernstein, "The Paris Commune and American Labor," *Science and Society*, 15:2 (Spring 1951), 144–162.

51. *Deutsche Arbeiter*, 16 July 1870, 1; 1 August 1870, 1 and 3; *ISZ*, 6 August 1870, 1; 8 September 1870, 1; 30 January 1871, 4; 3 April 1871, 4; 30 May 1871, 2; 6 August 1870, 4.

52. *ISZ*, 18 March 1872, 4; *Dagslyset*, Marts 1872, 5–6; *Tribune*, 18 March 1872, 6.

53. *Tribune*, 19 March 1875, 8; *Dagslyset*, Marts 1876, 3; *CVZ*, 20 March 1877, 4; *Socialist*, 29 March 1879, 5; *Fackel*, 21 March 1880, 8; *ChAZ*, 15 March 1884, 4; "History of Local 54," 7, 11, Chicago District Council, United Brotherhood of Carpenters and Joiners of America; *Delnicke Listy* (New York), 17 March 1894, cited by Joseph Chada, in "A Survey of Radicalism in the Bohemian-American Community" (typescript, 1954), CHS; *Alarm*, 20 March 1886, 1; *Daily News*, 20 March 1886, 2.

54. *Vorbote*, 30 March 1878, 4; Ensslen, Ickstadt, and Seifurt, "German Working-Class Culture in Chicago," 12–13.

55. *Vorbote*, 27 March 1875, 2; *CVZ*, 20 March 1877, 4; *Tribune*, 23 March 1879, 8; *Times*, 23 March 1879, 8; *Der Westen*, 23 March 1879, 3; *Skandinaven*, 25 March 1879, 4; *Socialist*, 29 March 1879, 5.

56. *Daily News*, 28 March 1881, 4; *ChAZ*, 19 March 1880, 4; *Daily News*, 20 March 1885, 5; *ChAZ*, 16 March 1885, 4.

57. *Alarm*, 20 March 1886, 1; *Daily News*, 20 March 1886, 2.

58. (NYC) Bernstein, ed., *Papers of the General Council IWA*, 132; Henry James, *Communism in America* (New York: Henry Holt, 1879), 24; (London) Shipley, *Club Life and Socialism in Mid-Victorian London*, 19, 48–49, 68; Hermia Oliver, *The International Anarchist Movement in Late Victorian London* (London: Croom Helm, 1983), 7, 11, 48, 57, 59; (France) Eric Hobsbawn, "Mass Producing Tradition: Europe, 1870–1914," in *The Invention of Tradition*, ed. Eric Hobsbawn and Terence Ranger (London: Cambridge University Press, 1983), 270; (Germany) Heinze Beike und Hans-Jurgen Bochinski, "Die Pariser Kommune und der deutsche Arbeiterbewegung," *Einheit*, 16 (1961), 446–454; Hans-Jurgen Frederici und Jutta Seidel, "Der Widerhall der Pariser Kommune in der deutschen Arbeiterbewegung," *Beitrag zur Geschichte der (deutschen) Arbeiterbewegung*, 3 (1961), 280–298.

59. *Times*, 23 March 1879, 8; *Tribune*, 23 March 1879, 8.

60. *Inter Ocean*, 17 June 1878, 1; *Herald*, 27 July 1885, 4.

61. *Inter Ocean*, 30 June 1878, 8; *Svenska Amerikanaren*, 26 October 1878, cited in Beijbom, *Swedes in Chicago*, 332; *Alarm*, 12 December 1885, 2; *ChAZ*, 17 October 1880, 4; *Vorbote*, 30 September 1882, 4; *Fackel*, 13 April 1884, 8.

62. My use of the term "movement culture" owes much to Lawrence Goodwyn, *Democratic Promise: The Populist Movement in America* (New York: Oxford University Press, 1976), esp. 311; Buhle, "German Socialists and American Working-Class Radicalism," 224–235; Lidtke, *Alternative Culture*, 3–22.

63. Sydney Mintz quoted in Herbert Gutman, *Work, Culture and Society in Industrializing America* (New York: Vintage Books, 1977), 16–17. Cf. Ian McKay, "Historians, Anthropology and the Concept of Culture," *Labour/Le Travailleur*, 8/9 (Autumn-Spring 1981/82): 185–241.

64. Antonio Gramsci, *Selections from the Prison Notebooks*, ed. Quintin Hoare and Geoffrey Smith, (New York: International Publishers, 1971), 5.

65. Walter Jerrold, "The Bohemian Sokol," *Fortnightly Review* 100 (August 1913): 347–358; on the German Turners, see Hermann Schlüter, *Die Anfange der deutschen Arbeiterbewegung in Amerika* (Stuttgart: Dietz Verlag, 1907), 199–214; and Ely, *Labor Movement in America*, 221–225.

66. In 1882, for example, the Sokols were invited, "as usual," to attend a masquerade ball given by the German Turners. They "decided to enact a Bohemian wedding at the ball, with about thirty members in the party, among them ten women, and a bagpiper in costume." The German hosts were reported to have been "charmed." *Svornost*, 1 February 1882, CFLPS, reel 8. When Turnverein Vorwaerts celebrated its fifteenth anniversary it invited the other Turnvereins as well as the Sokols, the Swiss Male Chorus, and Leiderkranz Eintracht. *ChAZ*, 23 September 1882, 4.

67. Samuel Gompers, *Seventy Years of Life and Labour: An Autobiography* (1929, reprint New York: Augustus Kelley, 1967), 66–67, 69–70, 80–81; Bisno, *Union Pioneer*, 86–89; Hutchins Hapgood, *The Spirit of Labor* (New York: Duffield, 1907), 85–91.

68. *Autobiographies*, (Parsons) 32, (Fischer) 83, (Engel) 95, (Schwab) 105; *Times*, 11 August 1884, 8.

69. I am indebted to John Jentz for this insight and phrase. Cf. Riipa and Karni, "Finnish-American Theatre," 119: "Although people were also attracted to the ideologies of the[se] organizations, it was the social activities, like drama, athletics, and dances, that brought and held organizational life together."

70. *Tribune*, 17 June 1878, 5; *Inter Ocean*, 17 June 1878, 1; on the politicization of an earlier set of rituals, see Alfred Young, "English Plebeian Culture and Eighteenth Century American Radicalism," in *The Origins of Anglo-American Radicalism*, ed. Margaret and James Jacob (London: Allen and Unwin, 1983), 185–212, esp. 200–204.

71. *Inter Ocean*, 17 June 1878, 1; *Socialist*, 31 May 1878, 4; 14 June 1878, 3; *ChAZ*, 20 July 1880; Carolyn Ashbaugh, *Lucy Parsons: American Revolutionary* (Chicago: Charles Kerr, 1976), 137.

72. Keil and Jentz, "German Working-Class Culture in Chicago," 140.

73. *Vorbote*, 26 June 1875, 2; *Svornost*, 18 May 1878, 2 July 1878, both CFLPS, reel 4; and Heiss, "Lehr- und Wehr-Verein von Chicago," 56–63.

74. Hobsbawm, "Inventing Traditions," in Hobsbawm and Ranger, eds., *Inven-

tion of Tradition, 1–14; Burke, *Popular Culture in Early Modern Europe,* 116–124. Cf. Hobsbawm, "Labour Traditions," in his *Labouring Men,* 371–385.

75. See, e.g., *Dagslyset,* Marts 1876, 8; *CVZ,* 19 March 1877, 2; and L. J. Palda, *Komuna Pařížska na zaklade ruznych pramenu, zvláště dle dila Lissagarayova* (New York: n.p., 1885).

76. Ickstadt and Keil, "Forgotten Piece of Working-Class Literature," 127; cf. Hirsch, "Revolution or Reform," 478.

77. Gramsci, *Prison Notebooks,* 349; Sorge, *Labor Movement in the United States,* 210.

Chapter Seven: Bakunin Never Slept in Chicago

1. Le Blanc, "Revolutionary Socialism in America," 6; David, *Haymarket Affair,* 142. I am indebted to Paul Le Blanc for many of the ideas in this chapter.

2. Albert Parsons et cl., *Anarchism;* broadside, "A. R. Parsons' Appeal to the People of America," 21 September 1887, Grinnell Collection.

3. David, *Haymarket Affair,* 82–156; David Behen, "The Chicago Labor Movement, 1874–1896: Its Philosophical Bases" (Ph.D. diss., University of Chicago, 1954); Michael Johnson, "Albert R. Parsons: An American Architect of Syndicalism," *Midwest Quarterly* 9 (1968): 195–206; Billie Stevenson, "The Ideology of American Anarchism, 1880–1910" (Ph.D. diss., University of Iowa, 1972); Rodney Estvan, "The Political Thought of Albert R. Parsons" (typescript, 1978), CHS; and Avrich, *Haymarket Tragedy.*

4. Parsons in *Autobiographies,* 42–43; *Alarm,* 7 March 1885, 1. Schilling first used the label "anarchist" to describe the Grottkau-Morgan fight, see [Schilling] to PVP, 26 February 1880, SLP Records, reel 5.

5. Cf. Avrich, *Haymarket Tragedy,* 133–134.

6. Broadside, "Platform, Plan of Organization [of the] Revolutionary Socialistic Party," circa October 1881, Parsons Papers; *Fackel,* 30 October 1881, 2, 4–5; *ChAZ,* 24 April 1884, 4; *Times,* 7 May 1884, 8; cf. Jonas, "Socialism and Anarchism" [1885] in Fried, ed., *Socialism in America,* 230–233. *ChAZ,* 25 May 1884, 4; *Diskussion über des Thema 'Anarchismus oder Kommunismus' gefuhrt von P. Grottkau und J. Most am 24 Mai 1884 in Chicago* (Chicago: Das Central-Comite der Chicagoer Gruppen der I.A.A., 1884).

7. Fischer in *Autobiographies,* 81: Most in *Tribune,* 25 December 1882, 8; Griffen in *Alarm,* 11 July 1885, 3; Schwab in Sorge, *Labor Movement in the United States,* 211.

8. Chester Destler, *American Radicalism, 1860–1901* (New London, Conn.: Connecticut State College, 1946), 79; William Trautmann, *The Voice of Terror: A Biography of Johann Most* (Westport, Conn.: Greenwood Press, 1980); Le Blanc, "Revolutionary Socialism in America," 166–186.

9. See Priscilla Robertson, *The Revolutions of 1848: A Social History* (1952, reprint, Princeton: Princeton University Press, 1971); Stanley Pech, *The Czech Revolution of 1848* (Chapel Hill: University of North Carolina Press, 1969); Halvdan Koht, "Die 48er Arbeiterbewegung in Norwegen," *Archiv für die Geschichte des Sozialismus und der Arbeiterbewegung,* 2 (1912): 237–274; Carl Wittke, *Refugees of Revolution: The*

German Forty-Eighters in America (1952, reprint Westport, Conn.: Greenwood Press, 1970); and esp. Bruce Levine, "In the Heat of Two Revolutions: The Forging of German-American Radicalism," in *"Struggle a Hard Battle": Essays on Working-Class Immigrants,* ed. Dirk Hoerder (DeKalb: Northern Illinois University Press, 1986), 19–45.

10. *ISZ,* 11 September 1878, 2; 25 July 1879, 3.

11. Eric Foner, "Abolitionism and the Labor Movement in Ante-bellum America," in Foner, *Politics and Ideology in the Age of the Civil War* (New York: Oxford University Press, 1980), 58–59; cf. Schneirov and Jentz, "Social Republicanism and Socialism;" David Montgomery, "Labor and the Republic in Industrial America, 1860–1920," *Le mouvement social,* 111 (Avril–Juin 1980), 201–215; and Nick Salvatore, *Eugene V. Debs: Citizen and Socialist* (Urbana: University of Illinois Press, 1982).

12. Kann, "Working-Class Culture and the Labor Movement," 304–306, 337, 343, 351, 382; *Socialist,* 9 November 1878, 2; *ChAZ,* 2 July 1879, 2; Lehr- und Wehr-Verein von Chicago, *Constitution und Nebengesetze* (Chicago: Social-Democratic Printing Association, 1878).

13. *Vorbote,* 1 May 1875, 4; *Inter Ocean,* 21 April 1879, 7; on the LWV's German roots see Heiss, "Lehr- und Wehr-Verein von Chicago," 56–64.

14. *Inter Ocean,* 17 June 1878, 5; *ChAZ,* 1 April 1880, 2; *Alarm,* 14 November 1885, 2.

15. Chicago Groups of the IWPA, "The Ballot," Parsons Papers; *Inter Ocean,* 21 April 1879, 7; *Herald,* 29 August 1881, 4; *Alarm,* 11 October 1884, 1.

16. *ChAZ,* 23 September 1882, quoted in Hirsch, "Revolution or Reform," 477; *Socialist,* 23 November 1878, 2; *Vorbote,* 10 June 1881, 5; *Alarm,* 1885.

17. Frantisek Zdrûbek, "Kco je socialismus?" *Kalendar amerikan* (Chicago: A. Geringer, 1880), trans. in Chada, "Radicalism in the Bohemian-American Community," 5.

18. *Inter Ocean,* 4 March 1878, 8; *Alarm,* 22 November 1884, 2; 4 October 1884, 2.

19. See chapter 5. Also *Socialist,* 19 July 1879, 2.

20. Spies in *Autobiographies,* 66, 68; Engel in *ibid.,* 95; Neebe in *ibid.,* 166.

21. *Budoucnost,* 16 June 1883, 7; Broadside, "To the Socialists of North America," 15 August 1883, Parsons Papers; Johann Most to August Spies, 11 July 1883, Grinnell Collection.

22. Parsons, *Anarchism,* 22–40; David, *Haymarket Affair,* 82–107; Le Blanc, "Revolutionary Socialism in America," 221–238.

23. *Vorbote,* 20 February 1884, 4; David, *Haymarket Affair,* 128; Parsons, *Life of Albert Parsons,* 101; Le Blanc, "Revolutionary Socialism in America," 217–221.

24. *Alarm,* 6 December 1884, 1; 18 April 1885, 2; 2 May 1885, 3; 30 May 1885, 4; 25 July 1885, 3; 14 November 1885, 4; Avrich, *Haymarket Tragedy,* 160–177.

25. Neebe quoted in David *Haymarket Affair,* x; Johann Most, *Revolutionäre Kriegswissenschaft* (3rd ed.; New York: Die Freiheit, 1885).

26. Avrich, *Haymarket Tragedy,* 150–159; Bruce Nelson, "Das Attentat: The Propaganda of the Deed in the American Anarchist Movement" (Bachelor's seminar paper, Northern Illinois University, 1972), 41–47, 70–73.

27. Floyd Dell, "Socialism and Anarchism in Chicago," in *Chicago: Its History and Its Builders*, ed. J. Seymour Currey, 5 vols. (Chicago: S. J. Clarke, 1912) 2: 361–405, 391; George Schilling to Lucy Parsons, 1 December 1893, Schilling Collection.

28. David, *Haymarket Affair*, 124–125; see "Die Baboeufisten," *Vorbote*, 30 December 1885, 2; "Theorie und Praxis," *Vorbote*, 27 March 1880, 1.

29. This discussion draws on a sample of eighty-five slogans and banners carried in WPI, WPUS, SLP, and IWPA parades between 1873 and 1886. Chicago's press proved the best source, but see also Schaack, *Anarchy and Anarchists*, 69, 85, 91 and 109; and Flinn, *Chicago Police Force*, 249–251.

30. Georges Haupt, "La Commune comme symbol et comme exemple," *Le Mouvement social* 79 (Avril–Juin 1972): 205–226; *Fackel*, 21 March 1880, 1; (Holmes) *Alarm*, 4 April 1885, 4.

31. Parsons in *Tribune*, 26 April 1878, 3; Holmes in Avrich, *Haymarket Tragedy*, 34; Schneirov, "Chicago's Great Upheaval of 1877," 17. See Jeremy Brecher, *Strike! The True History of Mass Insurgency in America* (San Francisco: Straight Arrow Books, 1972), 1–25.

32. Simmens quoted in Pierce, *History of Chicago*, 2: 243, 244; *ChAZ*, 23 February 1885, 2; *The Accused and the Accusers* (1887, reprint New York: Arno Press, 1969); *Pittsburgh Manifesto* in Parsons Papers.

33. Letter to E. A. Stevens, cited in David, *Haymarket Affair*, 226. David dismissed that evidence commenting, "This point is made nowhere else. Perhaps this element may explain some of the police brutality. It is at best a remote possibility." *ibid.*, 233, n. 16.

34. Gutman, "Protestantism and the American Labor Movement," in Gutman, *Work, Culture and Society*, 90; Montgomery, *Beyond Equality*, 42.

35. See Albert Post, *Popular Freethought in America, 1825–1850* (1943, reprint New York: Octagon Books, 1974); and Sidney Warren, *American Freethought, 1860–1914* (New York: Columbia University Press, 1943). There is some fascinating material on Chicago's fritaenkere in the Marcus Thrane Papers, MSHS. Wittke, *Refugees of Revolution*, 122–146 is useful, but see also Bettina Goldberg, "Deutsch-amerikanische Freidenker in Milwaukee, 1877–1890: Organisation und gesellschafts-politische Orientierung," (Master's thesis, Ruhr-Universitat Bochum, 1982).

36. *Times*, 20 May 1884, 6; *Svornost*, 27 May 1884, CFLPS, reel 6; *Tribune*, 10 December 1885, 7; C. F. Gates, *First Annual Report of the Chicago City Missionary Society* (Chicago, 1884), 10, quoted in *Svornost*, 16 September 1884, CFLPS, reel 1.

Svornost claimed that half of Chicago's 35,000 Bohemians were "liberal thinkers," *Svornost*, 19 August 1883, CFLPS, reel 4. Rev. Adams believed "that half and maybe two-thirds of the local Bohemians are not active members of those [Catholic] churches." *Svornost*, 27 May 1884, CFLPS, reel 6. A Czech-American historian has estimated the ratio between the "progressive" and "religious" movements at six-to-one over the period from 1861 to 1911 (Chada, *Czechs in the United States*, 92). Even after the massive "new immigration," Chicago's Czechs were still "about evenly divided between Catholics and free-thinkers." (Karel Bicha, "Settling Accounts with an Old Adversary: The Decatholicization of Czech Immigrants in America," *Social History-Histoire sociale*, 8 [November 1972], 45–60).

37. [Joseph Martinek?], "One Hundred Years of the Bohemian Freethinkers in Chicago," in *Panorama: A Historical Review of the Czechs and Slovaks in the U.S.A.*, ed. Vlasta Vraz (Cicero, Ill.: Czechoslovak National Council of America, 1970), 82–83; *The Semi-Centennial Jubilee of the Bohemian National Cemetery Association in Chicago, Illinois* (Chicago: Bohemian National Cemetery Association, 1927), 4; Karel Bicha, "Community or Cooperation? The Case of the Czech-Americans," in *Studies in Ethnicity: The Eastern European Experience in America*, ed. Charles Ward et al. (New York: Columbia University Press, 1980), 100, 93–102.

38. Frantisek Zdrûbek, "The Creed of the Freethinkers," *Hlas jednoty svobodo-myslných*, (Iowa City) 3 June 1872, trans. in *The Czechs in America, 1633–1977*, ed. Vera Laska (Dobbs Ferry, NY: Oceana Publications, 1978), 97; Chada, "Radicalism in the Bohemian-American Community," 3–9.

39. Solle, "Tschechischen Sektionen der Internationale, 101–134; Dostalik, "České dělnické hnutí ve Spojencých státech za hospodářské krize let 1873–1878," in Gosiorovsky, ed., *Začiatky českej a slovenskej emigrácie do USA*, 125–162.

40. *Svornost*, 24 March 1879, CFLPS, reel 1, 27 March 1879, CFLPS, reel 2, 31 March 1879, CFLPS, reel 2, 2 April 1879, CFLPS, reel 1; Richard Schneirov, "Free Thought and Socialism in the Czech Community in Chicago, 1875–1887," in Hoerder, ed., *"Struggle a Hard Battle"*, 121–142.

41. *Inter Ocean*, 20 May 1879, 2; cf. *Times*, 2 September 1878, 8; 30 April 1879, 6.

42. *Tribune*, 5 September 1881, 3; *Inter Ocean*, 20 March 1882, 8; *Socialist*, 19 April 1879, 1; cf. Gutman, "Protestantism and the American Labor Movement," 106–107, n. 90; Hobsbawm, *Primitive Rebels*, 126–149.

43. *Tribune*, 24 June 1878, 8; cf. *Times*, 21 May 1878, 3; *Skandinaven*, 31 July 1882, CFLPS, reel 11; *Alarm*, 25 July 1885, 1; 17 October 1885, 4; *Tribune*, 10 August 1885, 8.

44. Schilling, "Brief History," xxx–xxxi; *Inter Ocean*, 24 August 1885, 8; *Tribune*, 10 August 1885, 6; *Mail*, 29 December 1885, 8; *Herald*, 26 October 1885, 1.

45. Parsons in *Tribune*, 4 November 1887, 2; George MacDonald, *Fifty Years of Freethought*, 2 vols. (1929–1931, reprint New York: Arno Press, 1972), 1: 265, 315, 381–382, 396–397; Fielden in *Autobiographies*, 155; on socialists in the Liberal League, see *Express*, 17 September 1879, 4; and *Herald*, 10 October 1881, 1; Robert Roberts, "The Freethought Movement of Chicago," (Master's thesis, University of Chicago, 1947).

46. TVP to Charles Keegan, 12 July 1882, reel 45; O. H. Barthel to TVP, 22 May 1886, reel 16; Dan [no last name] to TVP, 8 December 1884, reel 8; all Powderly Papers.

47. Parsons to editor, *Knights of Labor*, 11 December 1886, 11. The United Labor Party expelled William Gorsuch, a member of the IWPA's American Group, for atheism. *Knights of Labor*, 8 January 1887, 4.

48. Schilling, "Brief History," xxx; *Herald*, 5 April 1886, 1. Eric Hirsch first noted the ministers' prominence, "Revolution or Reform: Chicago's Eight Hour Move-

ment in the Mid-1880's" (paper presented to the Chicago Area Labor History Group, Newberry Library, 24 April 1981), 14.

49. Post, *Popular Freethought in America*, 155–158; Warren, *Freethought in America*, 135–136. Both Post and Warren's bibliographies are monolingual; see instead "Notes on Ethnic Freethought," in *Freethought in the United States: A Descriptive Bibliography*, ed. Marshall Brown and Gordon Stein (Westport, Conn.: Greenwood Press, 1978), 95–105.

50. Schneirov, "Freethought and Socialism," 142; Adams in *Svornost*, 27 May 1884, CFLPS, reel 6; cf. *ISZ*, 7 September 1887, 2.

51. Marx, "Contribution to the Critique of Hegel's Philosophy of Law: Introduction," [1843] in *Marx-Engels Collected Works* (Moscow: International Publishers, 1975–), 50 vols. 3: 175. Cf. Eric Hobsbawm, "Religion and the Rise of Socialism," in Hobsbawm, *Workers*, 33–48.

52. State's Attorney Grinnell's closing argument in the Haymarket Trial, quoted in Schaack, *Anarchy and Anarchists*, 560, and in Parsons, "Notes Taken During the 1886 Trial," Parsons Papers.

53. *Alarm*, 28 November 1885, 2; Le Blanc, "Revolutionary Socialism in America," 255–273, 259; *Alarm*, 5 September 1885, 4.

54. Schmidt, *He Chose*, 107; E. H. Carr, "Bakunin's Escape from Siberia," *Slavonic Review*, 15 (January 1937): 377–388.

55. Chicago Groups of the IWPA, "The Ballot," 3.

56. *Ibid.*, original emphasis.

57. *Pittsburgh Manifesto*, Parsons Papers.

58. Geertz, *Interpretation of Cultures*, 193–233.

Chapter Eight: Eight Hours, Riot, and Repression

1. Bisno, *Union Pioneer*, 66–71.

2. *Tribune*, 15 October 1885, 8; 7 December 1885, 8; *Express*, 10 October 1885, 8; 19 December 1885, 8; *Herald*, 2 February 1885, 4. The printers, for example, did not endorse the movement until spring; see Typographical Union No. 16 Minutes, 28 February 1886, 18 April 1886; Chicago Typographical Union Records, CHS.

3. *Alarm*, 23 January 1886, 2; 6 February 1886, 2; *Vorbote*, 31 March 1886, 5; the circular appeared in the *Express*, 10 April 1886, 6, almost a month after it had been issued.

4. *Vorbote*, 10 March 1886, 3; 14 April 1886, 3; both trans. in Keil, "Knights, Trade Unions, and German Socialists," 317.

5. *Alarm*, 3 April 1886, 4; *Vorbote*, 10 March 1886, 4; Neebe in *Autobiographies*, 167.

6. Unidentified newspaper clipping, 12 October 1885, Parsons Papers; *Alarm*, 5 September 1885, 1; 12 December 1885, 2; *Tribune*, 26 October 1885, 8; *ChAZ*, 12 November 1885, 4. The same arguments appeared within the remnants of Chicago's SLP, see *Der Sozialist*, 26 December 1885, 6.

7. *Mail*, 27 February 1886, 3; Robert Ozanne, *A Century of Labor-Management*

Relations at McCormick and International Harvester (Madison: University of Wisconsin Press, 1967), 3–21.

8. See the report of a "Polnischer Achtstunden Verein," with seventy members, *Vorbote*, 30 December 1885, 8; and the ad for a meeting of the "Polnischer Arbeiter Club," *ibid.*, 3 February 1886, 8; *Tribune*, 28 December 1885, 8; *Times*, 12 January 1886, 6.

9. *Alarm*, 3 April 1886, 4; 24 April 1886, 4; *ISZ*, 19 April 1886, 4.

10. On Die Möbel-Arbeiter Union see *Vorbote*, 14 April 1886, 7; on the bakers, *ibid.*, 17 March 1886, 3; on the butchers, *ibid.*, 24 March 1886, 3; and Hermann Schlüter, *The Brewing Industry and the Brewery Workers' Movement in America* (Cincinnati: United Brewery Workmen of America, 1910), 122–123.

11. *Vorbote*, 7 April 1886, 8; *Alarm*, 3 April 1886, 3 and *Tribune*, 1 May 1886, 2. On the lumber shovers, see Schneirov, "Free Thought and Socialism," 132–134.

12. *Vorbote*, 21 April 1886, 8; the *Tribune*, 19 April 1886, 2, confirms all of the numbers claimed by *Vorbote*; *Der Sozialist*, 10 April 1886, 6. On Die Metall-Arbeiter Union, see Fuss, "Massenproduktion und Arbeiterbewusstsein," 162–168.

13. On the Trade Assembly see *Express*, 19 December 1885, 2; *Tribune*, 22 March 1886, 3; on the CLU see *Vorbote*, 21 April 1886, 8; 28 April 1886, 8; Perlman in Commons et al., *History of Labour*, 2: 387.

14. *Tribune*, 20 March 1886, 1; IBLS, *Fourth Biennial Report, 1886*, 221, 224–226; Keil, "Knights, Trade Unions, and German Socialists," Table 2, p. 309.

15. Compare, e.g., *Svornost*, 12 and 27 April 1886; *ISZ*, 12 and 27 April 1886; and *Vorbote*, 14 and 28 April 1886.

16. IBLS, *Fourth Biennial Report, 1886*, 479–480, 491.

17. *Tribune*, 1 May 1886, 2; cf. *ChAZ*, 3 May 1886, 2: "The capitalist press has good grounds for busing the 'Reds'—without them no agitation!"

18. Parsons in *Autobiographies*, 34; Schneirov, "Chicago's Great Upheaval of 1877," 3–17; Philip Foner, *The Great Labor Uprising of 1877* (New York: Monad Press, 1977), 139–156.

19. Spies *Herald*, 21 and 22 July 1884, 4; Joseph Kaufman to August Spies, 23 July 1884, Grinnell Collection: on the Pinkertons, see *Tribune*, 20 July 1885, 8.

20. Kann, "Working Class Culture and the Labor Movement," 417–421; Schneirov, "Knights of Labor in Chicago," 372–384.

21. Wesley Skogan, comp., *Chicago Since 1840: A Time-Series Data Handbook* (Urbana: University of Illinois, 1976), Table 8, p. 89; Richard Marohn, "The Arming of the Chicago Police in the Nineteenth Century," *Chicago History*, 11:1 (Spring 1982), 40–49; *Svornost*, 8 February 1882, CFLPS, reel 2.

22. Citizens Association, *Annual Reports, 1874–1901* (Chicago: Citizens Association of Chicago, 1901); Bruce Grant, *Fight for a City: The Story of the Union League Club of Chicago and Its Times, 1880–1955* (Chicago: Rand McNally, 1955), 96–103; Emmett Dedmon, *A History of the Chicago Club* (Chicago: The Chicago Club, 1960); John Glessner, *The Commercial Club of Chicago* (Chicago: privately printed, 1910); Wayne Andrews, *Battle for Chicago* (New York: Harcourt, Brace, 1946), 127–141.

23. *Daily News*, 6 January 1885, 4; *New York Times*, 3 January 1885, 2; 7 January

1885, 2; 12 January 1885, 5; *Inter Ocean,* 10 January 1885, 6; *Daily News,* 12 and 13 January 1885, 4.

24. *Tribune,* 27 November 1885, 8; 28 December 1885, 8; *Times,* 18 January 1886, 8; 20 March 1886, 6; and Richard Sennett, "Middle-Class Families and Urban Violence: The Experience of a Chicago Community in the Nineteenth Century," in *Nineteenth-Century Cities: Essays in the New Urban History,* ed. Stephan Thernstrom and Richard Sennett (New Haven: Yale University Press, 1969), 386–418, here 391–394.

25. *Tribune,* 27 April 1886, 8; 30 April 1886, 8.

26. *ChAZ,* 1 May 1886, quoted in Lum, ed., *Concise History of the Great Trial,* 20–21.

27. *Tribune,* 1 May 1886, 2, 8; 2 May 1886, 9, 10.

28. *Ibid.,* 3 May 1886, 2.

29. The sample was compiled from every available account of the riot: the commercial and radical, English- and foreign-language press, trial testimony, and the police account. It remains far from complete.

30. Lieutenant Ward's 130 officers were identified in Flinn, *Chicago Police Force,* 304–323; and Schaack, *Anarchy and Anarchists,* 150–155.

31. Parsons in *Autobiographies,* 57; *ChAZ,* 19 July 1888, 2; David, *Haymarket Affair,* Preface to the Second Printing, and 508–527; Avrich, *Haymarket Tragedy,* 437–445; *idem.,* "The Bombthrower: A New Candidate," in Roediger and Rosemont, eds., *A Haymarket Scrapbook,* 71–74.

32. John Altgeld, "Reasons for Pardoning Fielden, Neebe and Schwab, The So-Called Anarchists" [1893], in *The Mind and Spirit of John Peter Altgeld,* ed. Henry Christman (Urbana: University of Illinois Press, 1960), 97–98; David, *Haymarket Affair,* 224; Schaack, *Anarchy and Anarchists,* 120, 122.

33. Bonfield quoted in *Evening Journal,* 5 May 1886, 1; on the tailors, see Bisno, *Union Pioneer,* 79, 80–81; Schilling to editor, *Knights of Labor,* 11 September 1886, 2.

34. Of 723 IWPA members identified in chapter 4, 342 were listed in the 1886 city directory; but of them only 198 (58 percent) also appeared in the 1887 directory.

35. Quoted in McLean, *Rise and Fall of Anarchy,* 133–135.

36. The *Official Record of the Haymarket Trial* can be found at the CHS. The trial has been extensively reviewed; see e.g., Matthew Trumbull, *Trial of the Judgement: A Review of the Anarchist Case* (Chicago: Heath and Home, 1888); Lum, ed., *Concise History of the Great Trial;* Joseph Gary, "The Chicago Anarchists of 1886," *Century Magazine,* 45:6 (April 1893), 803–837; Altgeld, "Reasons for Pardoning Fielden, Neebe and Schwab," [1893]; and Sigmund Zeisler, *Reminiscences of the Anarchist Case* (Chicago: Chicago Literary Club, 1927).

37. Salomon had been corresponding secretary of Cigarmakers' No. 15, an active member of the IWPA's Gruppe Sudwestseite III, advertised as a "deutsche advocat" in *Die Arbeiter-Zeitung,* and served as Die Möbel-Arbeiter Union's lawyer.

38. Grinnell quoted in Parsons, "Notes Taken During the 1886 Trial," typescript, Parsons Papers.

39. On the trial and appeals, I have relied on Altgeld, "Reasons for Pardoning

Fielden, Neebe, and Schwab"; David, *Haymarket Affair*, 236–392; and Avrich, *Haymarket Tragedy*, 260–296.

40. Charles Russell, *These Shifting Scenes* (New York: Hodder and Stoughton, 1914), 89.

41. *Daily News*, 10 May 1889, 9; see Mayor Harrison's comments in *Herald*, 14 and 15 November 1891; *Times*, 15 November 1891; cited in David, *Haymarket Affair*, 504, n. 24.

42. McLean, *Rise and Fall of Anarchy*, 28; Holmes in *The Rebel*, 20 November 1895, 21; Schaack, *Anarchy and Anarchists*, 445–446; and M. E. Walter's notarized statement on the Pinkertons, *Knights of Labor*, 20 November 1886, 4. One spy's report, 8 May 1886, on Chicago police department stationery, is in the Grinnell Collection.

43. Schaack, *Anarchy and Anarchists*, 206, 210–212, 219, 207–208, 213–214, 202–204.

44. *Tribune*, 23 September 1886, 8; *Alarm*, 3 December 1887, 1; see David, *Haymarket Affair*, 461 and 476, n. 34.

45. Joseph Pasteris, "The Haymarket Riot of 1886; An Analysis of the Popular Press" (Master's thesis, Northern Illinois University, 1966); *ISZ*, 4 September 1886, 2; 28 January 1887, 2; *Svornost*, 17 May 1886, CFLPS, reel 1; *Times*, 19 May 1886, 8.

46. See one of the treasurer's reports, *Vorbote*, 24 November 1886, 5; Schmidt, *He Chose*, 147.

47. *Vorbote*, 15 February 1887, 8; *Alarm*, 17 December 1887, 4; *ISZ*, 28 January 1889, 4; *ChAZ*, 28 January 1889, 4; The Pioneer Aid and Support Association Papers at CHS; and "Minute Book, 1892, of the Committee of 21 [of the Amnesty Association]," Schilling Collection.

48. *ChAZ*, 6 July 1886, 4; *Daily News*, 9 December 1886, 6; *ISZ*, 29 November 1888, 2; *Der Sozialist*, 18 June 1887, 4; *ISZ*, 12 November 1891, 2; *Tribune*, 2 May 1892, 8; *ChAZ*, 2 May 1892, 4.

49. (Hronek) *Tribune*, 18 July 1888, 1–2; Schaack, *Anarchy and Anarchists*, 676–681; *Alarm*, 28 July 1888, 3; 8 December 1888, 3; (Bodendeick) *Alarm*, 29 September 1888, 3.

50. For the constitution, see *Vorbote*, 28 November 1888, 7; *ChAZ*, 28 December 1888, 4; the trial can be followed in *Tribune* or *ChAZ*, 4–8 January 1889; the judge quoted in David, *Haymarket Affair*, 482; *ChAZ*, 16 January 1889, 4; *Tribune*, 27 January 1889, 10.

51. *Fackel*, 2 September 1888, 8; *Times*, 5 January 1889, 1; *Tribune*, 6 January 1889, 9; *Alarm*, 12 January 1889, 3.

52. *ChAZ*, 12 November 1888, 4; *ISZ*, 12 November 1891, 3; Perry Duis, "The Saloon and the Public City: Chicago and Boston, 1880–1920" (Ph.D. diss., University of Chicago, 1975), 641–642; *Tribune*, 18 May 1886, 8; 16 April 1891, 3; 7 December 1891, 8.

53. *Herald*, 4 and 5 January 1892; cited in David, *Haymarket Affair*, 482–484.

54. *Die Abendpost*, 23 September 1895, CFLPS, reel 14.

55. *Berliner Tageblatt*, 31 January 1890, *Berliner Börsen-Zeitung*, 1 February 1890, *Berliner Volksblatt*, 18 February 1890, cited in *Plutokraten und Sozialisten: Berichte*

deutscher Diplomaten und agenten über die amerikanische Arbeiterbewegung, 1878–1917, ed. Dirk Hoerder (München: K. G. Saur Verlag, 1981), 371, 386.

56. Hoerder, ed., *Plutokraten und Sozialisten,* 367–372; *Inter Ocean,* 14 May 1886, 4; Polizeipräsidium, Pr. Br. Rep: 30, Berlin C. Tit. 94, Lit. A, No. 204: "Nachrichten über die anarchistischen Bewegung in Amerika," 8585, 95–98, Brandenburgisches Landeshauptarchiv, Potsdam, DDR. I am indebted to Dirk Hoerder and Hartmut Keil for making typescripts available to me.

57. *Times,* 9 May 1886, 1; *Möbel-Arbeiter Journal* (New York), 18 June 1886, 7 July 1886, 18 June 1887, quoted in Helmut Keil, "The Impact of Haymarket on German-American Radicalism," *International Labor and Working Class History,* 29 (Spring 1986), 16–27, 22.

58. Quoted in Grant, *Fight for a City,* 102; on the activities of other businessmen, including Armour and McCormick, see Andrews, *Battle for Chicago,* 127–137.

59. *ChAZ,* 23 August 1888, 4; 1 October 1888, 4; 15 January 1889, 2; *Socialist Alliance,* June 1897, 5.

60. David, *Haymarket Affair,* 480.

Chapter Nine: Martyrs and Survivors

1. Avrich, *Haymarket Tragedy,* 446–448; *IVZ,* 20 May 1893, 4; *Chicago Labor,* 9 December 1893, 7; by fall 1894 Neebe's Hall was the meeting place of the SLP's Central Committee.

2. Čapek, *The Čechs (Bohemians) in America,* 148–149; (Zoula) Frantisek Cajthaml, "Zivot a smrt Norberta Zouly v Americe," *Americke Delnicke Listy* (Cleveland), 30 May 1930, 12; (Mikolanda) *Dennice Novoveku* (Cleveland), 30 May 1907.

3. (Goldwater) Robert Rockaway, "The Laboring Man's Champion: Samuel Goldwater of Detroit," Detroit Historical Society *Bulletin,* November 1970, 4–9; (Schnaubelt) Avrich, *Haymarket Tragedy,* 238–239, 439–441; (Waller) *Vorbote,* 30 November 1887, 8; *Alarm,* 3 December 1887, 1; (Petersen) *Vorbote,* 1 May 1889, 8.

4. (Rau) city directories: 1890, 1895, 1900; (Kalbitz) *Tribune,* 3 July 1893, 3; *Chicago Labor,* 17 February 1894, 4; (Grottkau) *Vorbote,* 16 January 1889, 8; *Tribune,* 16 July 1894, 8; and his obituary, *Fackel,* 5 June 1898, 4.

5. Morgan, in "Proceedings of the Socialist Unity Convention . . . 1901," quoted in Aileen Kraditor, *The Radical Persuasion, 1890–1917* (Baton Rouge: Louisiana State University Press, 1981), 210. (Rollinger) *Vorbote,* 10 July 1880, 1; (Neudeck) *Vorbote,* 25 February 1885, 1.

6. Thernstrom, *Other Bostonians,* 222–223.

7. The data is drawn from the 1890 and 1900 city directories, and the occupational categories are again those of Thernstrom, *Other Bostonians,* appendix B, pp. 289–302.

8. Theodore Polling, for example, had different partners in 1890 and 1900 in a painting company; August Heun quit the *Arbeiter-Zeitung* and became a partner in a printshop. A painter in 1870, O. A. Bishop became a patternmaker and machinist in the early eighties, a patent solicitor in 1884, and a notary in 1890 and 1900.

William Jeffers had been a post office carrier in 1880, and molder in the mid-eighties, a machinist in 1890, and opened his own picture-frame shop in 1900.

9. Bisno, *Union Pioneer*, 181–182: "A neighbor of mine who was not a socialist, . . . tried to persuade me to go into the real estate business. 'Because of your intelligence and the people you mix with, and the kinds of friends you're acquainted with even if you were an efficient cloakmaker and were able to hold a job as well as anyone else, the money earned in the trade won't be enough for you or for your wife. Better take my advice—go into the real estate business with me. . . . You can make money.'"

10. (Reuter) Obituary, *IVZ*, 6 Mai 1893, 4; Montgomery, *Beyond Equality*, 208; (Bonnefoi) city directories for 1890 and 1900; Rowell, *American Newspaper Directory*, *1888*, 179; Ayer and Sons, *American Newspaper Annual, 1890*, 126. Moses Salomon became a Democratic State Senator in the 1890s.

11. See Mittleman, "Chicago Labor in Politics," esp. 417–418. I have relied on Scharnau, "Thomas J. Morgan and the Chicago Socialist Movement," 104–141; and Schneirov, "Knights of Labor in Chicago," 485–547.

12. *Express*, 16 August 1886, 8; MS "Minutes of Meeting at Greenebaum's Hall, 21 August 1886," in the Morgan Collection, reel 6; *Sozialist*, 4 September 1886, 5; (Powers and Rowan) *Tribune*, 22 August 1886, 8; (Owens) *Express*, 18 September 1886, 8; (CLU) *Vorbote*, 24 September 1886, 8.

13. Scharnau, "Thomas J. Morgan," 107; *Skandinaven*, 6 October 1886, 12; *ChAZ*, 5 October 1886, 4; 6 October 1886, 2 and 4.

14. *Tribune*, 24 October 1886, 4; election returns in *ChAZ*, 4 November 1886, 4.

15. *Knights of Labor*, 6 November 1886, 1. *Tribune*, 5 November 1886, 2; *ChAZ*, 30 January 1887, 1; *Sozialist*, 12 March 1887, 5.

16. "Minutes of Feb. 26 [1887] Convention," Morgan Collection, reel 6, 70–97; the ULP platform appeared in *Vorbote*, 28 February 1887, 8; *Labor Enquirer*, 2 March 1887, 4; *Skandinaven*, 2 March 1887, 12.

17. *Times*, 3 April 1887, 4; broadside, dated 5 April 1887, Parsons Papers, *Tribune*, 22 March 1887, 4.

18. Election returns in *Tribune*, 6 April 1887, 1–2; 28 February 1887, 8; *Knights of Labor*, 9 April 1887, 6; *Times*, 5 April 1887, 5.

19. *Tribune*, 23 August 1886, 1; *ChAZ*, 6 October 1886, 2; 18 October 1886, 4; MS Minutes of Executive Committee ULP, Morgan Collection, reel 6; for the Committee of 21, 7–8; for speakers and ward captains, 50; on the cigarmakers tax, 11 October 1886; on the CLU tax see *Knights of Labor*, 24 September 1887, 3.

20. LA 522 assessed its members for the ULP, see *Knights of Labor*, 16 October 1886, 3; LA 6037 appropriated $50, only to withhold payment when Powderly protested; see MS Minutes of Executive Committee, ULP, 11 October 1886, Morgan Collection, reel 6; Schneirov, "Knights of Labor in Chicago," 499.

21. Schneirov, "Knights of Labor in Chicago," 532. I am indebted to Richard Schneirov, who generously shared his data and computer runs for the statistical analysis of the ULP.

22. *Tribune*, 7 April 1887, 1; Schneirov, "Knights of Labor in Chicago," 533. In

testing the relationship between ethnicity and turnout, Schneirov (p. 546, n. 93) found "the only significant coefficient was a negative one of .32 for the Irish, [i.e.] a one percent increase in the number of Irish registered voters yielded a .32 percent decrease in turnout."

23. Rank order correlation measures the ward-level association between the 1879 SLP vote and the 1887 ULP vote, $r_s = + .85$, $r_s^2 = .72$. For the computation and interpretation of the statistic, see Blalock, Jr., *Social Statistics*, 416–418.

24. *Tribune*, 11 September 1886, 7; unidentified newspaper clipping, 25 March 1887, Morgan Collection, reel 1; on Ryan, see MS "The Irish in the Socialist Movement: Tommy Ryan," Morgan Collection, reel 2.

25. Spies to Lum, in *Alarm*, 23 June 1888, 4; Keil, "German Immigrant Working Class of Chicago," 175.

26. Eugene Dietzgen, "Joseph Dietzgen: A Sketch of His Life," in Joseph Dietzgen, *Philosophical Essays on Socialism and Science, Religion, Ethics, Critique-of-Reason and the World-at-Large*, (Chicago: Charles Kerr, 1914); on Belz, see *Vorbote*, 5 September 1888, 7; and his obituary, *ChAZ*, 10 October 1888, 1.

27. *ChAZ*, 1 November 1886, 4; *Vorbote*, 10 November 1886, 8. Arguing that the *ChAZ* was "not radical enough" the Jewish Workingmen's Educational Club bought one page of *Die Freiheit* and subscribed for 1,500 issues per week. The CLU rejected their petition for financial aid, judging it "a competitive matter" between the two papers, see *ChAZ*, 16 July 1888, 4.

28. Stedronsky, *Zahraniční krajanský noviny, časopisy a kalendáře*, 104; Habenicht, *Dějiny Čechů v Americkych*, 608.

29. "History of Local No. 54," Chicago District Council, United Brotherhood of Carpenters and Joiners of America; *Times*, 28 February 1887, 3 and *Vorbote*, 18 May 1887, 8.

30. Joseph Buchanan, *The Story of a Labor Agitator* (New York: Outlook Co., 1903), 343ff. The *Enquirer's* rival was the *Daily Star Telegram* "published by the Knights of Labor Publishing Co.," a single clipping (25 April 1887) has survived in the Parsons Papers.

31. *Alarm*, 1 September 1888, 3; 8 September 1888, 3 (signed G. A. S.); Buchanan, *Labor Agitator*, 456–457.

32. On Lum, see William Reichert, *Partisans of Freedom: A Study of American Anarchism* (Bowling Green: Bowling Green State University Press, 1976), 237–244; and Paul Avrich, *An American Anarchist: The Life of Voltairine de Cleyre* (Princeton: Princeton University Press, 1978), 54–69.

33. *Vorbote*, 14 May 1888, 4; 30 May 1888, 1; e.g., *Alarm*, 16 June 1888, 2; the third page carried "Our Chicago Letter," signed "H.", probably William Holmes.

34. *Alarm*, 25 February 1888, 1; *Vorbote*, 14 March 1888, 8. *Die Arbeiter Stimme* is listed in Arndt and Olson, comps., *Deutsch-Amerikanische Zeitungen*, 58. On *The Record*, see *Vorbote*, 20 June 1888, 8; 11 July 1888, 8; *Alarm*, 14 July 1888, 3.

35. The earliest extant issue of *Der Illinoiser Volks-Zeitung* (1:7) is dated 22 April 1893. There are but five extant copies (April–May 1893) at WSHS; see Arndt and Olson, comps., *Deutsch-amerikanische Zeitungen*, 78.

36. The Labor News Co. of St. Louis, "a socialist newspaper union," offered "an eight page paper, [with] local matter . . . confined to the last page." By 1895 it was published under different names in thirty-three cities, *Chicago Labor*, 12 August 1893, 8. On De Witt, see *ibid.*, 13 October 1894, 8.

37. *Denni Hlasatel*, 1 May 1901, CFLPS, reel 4; Habenicht, *Dějiny Čechů v Americkych*, 608–609; Danielsen, "Early Danish Immigrant Socialist Press," 56–76 and Odd-Stein Granhus, "Scandinavian-American Socialist Newspapers," 79–99, both in Hoerder, ed., *Essays on the Scandinavian-North American Radical Press*; Henryk Nagiel, *Dziennikarstwo Polskie w Ameryce* (Chicago: n.p., 1894), 86–90.

38. *Tribune*, 25 July 1886, 9.

39. *Tribune*, 18 September 1886, 3; *Vorbote*, 30 March 1887, 8; 12 November 1890, 7.

40. *ChAZ*, 11 November 1886, 4; Christine Heiss, "German Radicals in Industrial America: The Lehr- und Wehr-Verein in Gilded Age Chicago," in Keil and Jentz, eds., *German Workers in Industrial Chicago*, 221, 223 n. 53.

41. *Vorbote*, 4 May–15 June 1887; 21 December 1887, 3; *Alarm*, 14 July 1888, 2, emphasis mine.

42. *ChAZ*, 31 December 1886, 4; 10 January 1887, 4; 22 April 1887, 2; 19 May 1887, 1; (Vahlteich) *ChAZ*, 28 November 1890, 1; Schwab to Hermann Schlüter, 4 June 1897, quoted in Keil, "Impact of Haymarket on German-American Radicalism," 24.

43. *Sozialist*, 11 June 1887, 8; 7 February 1891, 4; see *IVZ*, 6 May 1893, 4, for a directory of Chicago's section. *ChAZ*, 29 March 1894, 4; *Chicago Labor*, 7 April 1894, 8; 29 September 1894, 8. Krzysztof Groniowski, "Socjalistyczna Emigracja Polska w Stanach Zjednoczonych, 1883–1914," *Z Pola Walki* 1 (1977): 1–31. I am indebted to Mary Cygan for this last source.

44. *Sozialist*, 31 October 1891, 3; *IVZ*, 20 May 1893, 4; *ChAZ*, 10 May 1894, 4; *Chicago Labor*, 16 June 1894, 4; *IVZ*, 22 April 1893, 4; *Chicago Labor*, 14 April 1894, 8; *Vorbote*, 13 February 1889, 8.

45. *Chicago Labor*, 28 July 1894, 8; 12 May 1894, 8; *Socialist Alliance*, September 1896, 7; *Arbejderen*, 3 December 1896, 3.

46. McLean, *Rise and Fall of Anarchy*, 44.

47. *Revyen*, 4 February 1899, CFLPS, reel 10; *Arbejderen:* 11 March 1897, 1; 6 July 1899, 1; *Revyen*, 13 October 1900, CFLPS, reel 9, 13 August 1904, CFLPS, reel 9, 13 January 1906, CFLPS, reel 10; Danielsen, "Early Danish Immigrant Socialist Press."

48. Philip Bregstone, *Chicago and Its Jews: A Cultural History* (Chicago: By the author, 1933), 10, 13–14, 60; Bisno, *Union Pioneer*, 66, 75–77; *Vorbote*, 12 November 1890, 7. Jews like Moses Salomon and Abraham Hermann had been prominent in the IWPA, but without exception they were German Jews who had little or no contact with the *Ostjuden*. See Edward Mazur, "Jewish Chicago: From Diversity to Community," in Holli and Jones, eds., *Ethnic Chicago*, 46–68.

49. Bregstone, *Chicago and Its Jews*, 14, 60–61; Bisno, *Union Pioneer*, 84–91; Elias Tcherikower, ed., *The Early Jewish Labor Movement in the United States*, trans. and rev.

by Aaron Antonovsky (New York: Yivo Institute for Jewish Research, 1961), 294–298. Cf. *Vorbote*, 13 February 1889, 8; *ChAZ*, 2 January 1895, 4.

50. *Revyen*, 15 April 1911, 4, CFLPS, reel 9. That same optimism, "the socialistic atmosphere," and the "chummy comradeship," might have been reported in *Vorbote, Budoucnost*, or *Alarm* three decades earlier.

51. *Chicago Labor*, 7 April 1894, 8; 20 October 1894, 8; *Socialist Alliance*, September 1896, 7; *Arbejderen*, 17 June 1897, 4.

52. Voltairine de Cleyre, *The First May Day: The Haymarket Speeches, 1895–1910*, ed. Paul Avrich (Minneapolis: Cienfuegos Press, 1980); *Vorbote*, 6 February 1889, 1; 29 May 1889, 8; 31 July 1889, 8; and the "Souvenir Program of the First Annual International Labor Day Celebration," *Socialist Alliance*, May 1897.

53. *Vorbote*, 23 March 1887, 5; 27 March 1889, 5; (Bohemians) 8 October 1890, 8; *ChAZ*, 14–16 March 1894, 4; *Chicago Labor*, 17 March 1894, 8.

54. Klaus Ensslen and Heinz Ickstadt, "German Working-Class Culture in Chicago: Continuity and Change in the Decade from 1900–1910," in Keil and Jentz, eds., *German Workers in Industrial Chicago*, 236–252, here 252, 244.

55. *ChAZ*, 12 November 1909, trans. in Ensslen and Ickstadt, "German Working-Class Culture in Chicago," 249; Buhle, "German Socialists and the Roots of American Working-Class Radicalism," 225.

56. David, *Haymarket Affair*, 531.

Chapter Ten: Ex-Anarchists in the Gay Nineties

1. Perlman in Commons et al., *History of Labour*, 2:392; *Knights of Labor*, 22 May 1886, 2; 5 June 1886, 2; Schilling to editor, *John Swinton's Paper* (New York) 30 May 1886, 2. On the Great Upheaval in five other cities, see Fink, *Workingmen's Democracy*.

2. David, *Haymarket Affair*, 534–539; Schneirov, "Knights of Labor in Chicago," 445–453; Perlman in Commons et al., *History of Labour*, 2:385.

3. *Knights of Labor*, 8 May 1886, 1; Typographical Union No. 16 Minutes, 7 May 1886, Chicago Typographical Union Records; *Inter Ocean*, 7 May 1886, 1.

4. AFL, *Proceedings of the Third Annual Convention*, 1888; *Workmen's Advocate*, 19 and 26 October 1889; both quoted in Sidney Fine, "The Eight-Hour Day Movement in the United States, 1888–1891," *Mississippi Valley Historical Review*, 40:1 (1953), 441–462, here 443, 454.

5. Knights of Labor, *Proceedings of the General Assembly*, 1889, 7–8, 51–52; Samuel Gompers, *Seventy Years of Life and Labour: An Autobiography*, 2 vols. (London: Macmillan, 1925), I:295, both quoted by Fine, "Eight-Hour Day Movement," 451, 462.

6. Scharnau, "Thomas J. Morgan," 125–141, 125; on the "Free Lunch Party," see *Inter Ocean*, 8 January 1888, 3; on the Union Labor Party, see *Tribune*, 23 April 1887, 6, and *Knights of Labor*, 23 April 1887, 6 and 11.

7. *Inter Ocean*, 23 March 1889, 8; *ChAZ*, 23 March 1889, 4; 4 April 1889, 4;

Scharnau, "Thomas J. Morgan," 142–160; *Sozialist*, 18 April 1891, 1; *Rights of Labor*, 11 April 1891, 1; *Socialist Alliance*, November 1892, 2; *Tribune*, 5 April 1893, 2; *ChAZ*, 26 March 1894, 4; *Socialist Alliance*, April 1897, 3; *Tribune*, 5 April 1899, 1.

8. *Fackel*, 6 January 1894, 4; Winnen, "Geschichte der Arbeiterbewegung von Chicago," *Fackel*, 3 June 1917, 1; Destler, *American Radicalism*, 175–211.

9. *New Yorker Volks-Zeitung*, 21 July 1889, trans. in Hartmut Keil, "Impact of Haymarket on German-American Radicalism," 23.

10. Keil, "Knights, Trade Unions, and German Socialists," 307; *Der Organisator*, September 1890; *Pamětní list vydaný k jubileu 30-lété činnosti česke natěracske unie cis 273, Bratstva Natěraču, Dekoratoru a Papirovacu v Americe, 1895–1925* (Chicago: n.p., 1925?); I am indebted to Steven Sapolsky for this last source. *ChAZ*, 11 April 1894, 1 and 4; *Fackel*, 19 June 1910, 1.

11. The Morgans' activities after 1900 are documented in the Thomas J. Morgan Papers, University of Chicago, and Scharnau, "Elizabeth Morgan, Crusader for Labor Reform," *Labor History*, 14:3 (Summer 1973), 340–351. Schilling's activities after 1900 are documented in the George A. Schilling Papers, University of Chicago, but see also August Gans to Franklin MacVeagh, 18 November 1900, National Civic Federation Papers, New York Public Library.

12. *Jubileu 30-lété činnosti česke natěracske unie cis 273*; John Jentz, "Artisan Culture and the Organization of Chicago's German Workers in the Gilded Age, 1860–1890," *Amerikastudien* 29:2 (1984), 133–148, here 138–143; *Social Democrat*, 13 January 1898, 4.

13. Suhrbur, "Ethnicity in the Chicago Carpenters Union," 97–99; Suhrbur and Schneirov, *Union Brotherhood, Union Town: The History of the Carpenters of Chicago, 1863–1987* (forthcoming, Carbondale: Southern Illinois University Press, 1988).

14. Hapgood, *The Spirit of Labor*; Schneirov, "Knights of Labor in Chicago," 448–451, 557–558, 562–563; "Rollbook of Delegates to the United Carpenters' Council, 1892–1896," Chicago District Council, United Brotherhood of Carpenters and Joiners of America.

15. Knights of Labor *General Assembly Proceedings*, 1879–1888, tabulated in Keil, "Knights of Labor, Trade Unions, and German Socialists," Table 2, p. 309.

16. TVP to William Halley, 12 May 1882, TVP to Halley, 29 May 1882, Powderly Papers, reel 45; Schneirov, "Knights of Labor in Chicago," 453, 466; Garlock, *Guide to the Knights of Labor*, 63–92.

17. DA 24 Minutes, 3 September 1883, Schilling Collection, bound volume 3; *Tribune*, 29 June 1887, 1; *Alarm*, 31 December 1887, 3; for complaints against mixed assemblies, see *Labor Enquirer*, 9 March 1887, 2.

18. DA 24 Minutes, 15 October 1882, Schilling Collection; Eugene Staley, *History of the Illinois State Federation of Labor* (Chicago: University of Chicago Press, 1930), 60; Dennis East, "Union Labels and Boycotts: Cooperation of the Knights of Labor and the CigarMakers International Union, 1885–6," *Labor History*, 16:2 (Spring 1975), 266–271.

19. Staley, *Illinois State Federation of Labor*, 60. Again, the cigarmakers' story has

usually been written as a New York phenomenon; see, e.g., Ware, *Labor Movement in the United States*, 271–279.

20. Philip Foner, *History of the Labor Movement in the United States* (New York: International, 1955), 2: 296–298, 389–390, 398–401; Morgan to Henry Demarest Lloyd, 9 June 1896, Henry Demarest Lloyd Papers, WSHS, cited in Scharnau, "Thomas J. Morgan," 271–272.

21. *Socialist Alliance*, June 1897, 6; January 1898, 6; Winnen, "Geschichte der Arbeiterbewegung von Chicago," *Fackel*, 3 June 1917, 1.

22. *Socialist Alliance*, June 1897, 1; Peter Damm to Henry Kuhn, 7 October 1898, SLP Records, reel 21.

23. *ChAZ*, May–October 1894; *Vorbote*, May–October 1894; Stanley Buder, *Pullman: An Experiment in Industrial Order and Community Planning* (New York: Oxford University Press, 1967), 168.

24. *ChAZ*, 2 September 1902; 26 March 1906; and 20 May 1907; *Fackel*, 24 May 1908; cited and trans. in Ensslen and Ickstadt, "German Working Class Culture in Chicago," 236–252.

25. The first quotation is of Ensslen and Ickstadt; the second from *ChAZ*, 12 November 1909; the third from *ChAZ*, 12 November 1907; both second and third trans. in Ensslen and Ickstadt, "German Working Class Culture in Chicago," 250, 249, 241–2.

26. Morgan to Lloyd, 18 July 1901, Lloyd papers, quoted in Scharnau, "Thomas J. Morgan," 327; *Socialist Alliance*, May 1897.

27. See Tables 9.1 and 1.3; Hartmut Keil, "Chicago's German Working Class in 1900," in Keil and Jentz, eds., *German Workers in Industrial Chicago*, 19–36, here 34.

28. *Revyen*, 13 October 1900, CFLPS, reel 9; *ChAZ*, 13 April 1912; *ChAZ*, 14 October 1907; *Fackel*, 19 June 1910, all cited and trans. in Ensslen and Ickstadt, "German Working Class Culture in Chicago," 248.

29. Duis, *Saloon and the Public City: Chicago and Boston*, 641–643; Ensslen, "Deutsch-Amerikanische Arbeiterkneipe in Chicago"; Cf. the report that the SLP's Danish section sought a "suitable meeting place not connected with a saloon," *Chicago Labor*, 12 May 1894, 8.

30. Paul Cressy, "Population Succession in Chicago, 1898–1930," *American Journal of Sociology*, 44 (July 1938): 59–69; *Dziennik Chicagoski*, 10 March 1894; 21 April 1894; *Narod Polski*, 22 August 1897, all CFLPS, reel 50.

31. Harry Barnard, *Eagle Forgotten: The Life of John Peter Altgeld* (Indianapolis: Bobbs-Merrill, 1938); Ginger, *Altgeld's America*; Lloyd Wendt and Herman Kogan, *Lords of the Levee* (Indianapolis: Bobbs-Merrill, 1943).

32. *ChAZ*, 18 March 1909, 2. On her activities after 1890, see Ashbaugh, *Lucy Parsons*, 188–266; on Isaacs, see "Nachrichten über die anarchistischen Bewegung in Amerika," Brandenburgisches Landeshauptarchiv.

33. Richard Oestreicher, "Solidarity and Fragmentation: Working People and Class Consciousness in Detroit, 1877–1895" (Ph.D. diss., Michigan State University, 1979), 466; Richard Cobb, *The Police and the People: French Popular Protest, 1789–1820* (London: Oxford University Press, 1972), xiv.

34. See Table 9.3

35. Paul Kleppner, *The Third Electoral System: Parties, Voters, and Political Cultures* (Chapel Hill: University of North Carolina Press, 1979), 364, original emphasis.

36. See Professor Masaryk's lecture "The Development of Czech Socialism since 1848," *Denni Hlasatel*, 15 May 1902, CFLPS, reel 4; and Josef Polišenský, "America and the Beginnings of Modern Czech Political Thought," in *The Czech Renascence of the Nineteenth Century*, ed. Peter Brock and H. Gordon Skilling (Toronto: University of Toronto Press, 1970), 215–223.

37. Cameron, *Tribune*, 3 May 1886, 2. Working with different sources, and a different research strategy, Richard Schneirov has come to similar conclusions. Cf. Oestreicher, *Solidarity and Fragmentation;* and, for a later period, James Barrett, "Unity and Fragmentation: Class, Race and Ethnicity on Chicago's South Side, 1900–1922," *Journal of Social History*, 18:1 (Fall 1984), 37–55.

38. The first phase (and argument) is Schneirov's, see "Knights of Labor in Chicago," 271–305; the second quotation is of Joe Gruenhut, in *Progressive Age*, 10 September 1881, 4.

39. Selig Perlman, "History of Socialism in Milwaukee, 1893–1910" (Bachelor's thesis, University of Wisconsin, 1910), 19; Schlüter, *Die Internationale in Amerika*, 399, 511; Montgomery, *Fall of the House of Labor*, 269.

Selected Bibliography

There are useful bibliographies on the Haymarket Affair in both David and Avrich; this one is focused instead on the movement.

Primary Sources

MANUSCRIPT COLLECTIONS

Chicago Trade and Labor Assembly Collection. Chicago Historical Society, Chicago.

"History of Local 54" and "Rollbook of Delegates to the United Carpenters' Council, 1892–1896." Archives of Local No. 54, Chicago District Council United Brotherhood of Carpenters and Joiners of America.

Thomas and Elizabeth Morgan Collection. Illinois Historical Survey, University of Illinois, Champaign-Urbana.

Thomas J. Morgan Papers. University of Chicago Library, Chicago.

"Nachrichten über die anarchistische Bewegung in Amerika." Polizei Präsidium, Brandenburgisches Landeshauptarchiv, Potsdam, DDR.

Albert R. Parsons Collection. State Historical Society of Wisconsin, Madison.

Pioneer Aid and Support Association Papers. Chicago Historical Society, Chicago.

Terence V. Powderly Papers. Catholic University of America. Microfilm edition: Microfilming Corporation of America, Glen Rock, New Jersey, 1970.

George A. Schilling Collection. Illinois State Historical Library, Springfield.

George A. Schilling Papers. University of Chicago Library, Chicago.

Socialist[ic] Labor Party of America Collection. Microfilm edition: State Historical Society of Wisconsin, Madison, 1970.

Marcus Møller Thrane and Family Papers. Minnesota Historical Society, St. Paul.

Workingmen's Party of the United States Collection. Microfilm edition: State Historical Society of Wisconsin, Madison.

NEWSPAPERS (Chicago, unless otherwise noted.)

The Alarm, 1884–1886, 1886–1889.

Arbejderen. 1896–1900. (Danish).

Budoucnost. 16 June 1883. (Czech).

The Carpenter. St. Louis and New York. 1881–1901.

Chicago Labor. 1893–1894.

Chicagoer Arbeiter-Zeitung. 1879–1900. (German).

Chicagoer Volks-zeitung. 1877. (German).

Cigarmakers' Official Journal. New York and Chicago. 1875–1895.

Dagslyset. 1869–1878. (Norwegian).

Daily News. 1872–1886.

Denní Hlasatel. 1891–1901. (Czech).

Der Deutsche Arbeiter. 1869–1870. (German).

Dziennik Chicagoski. 1894–1898. (Polish).

Express. 1879–1893.

Die Fackel. 1879–1900. (German).

Hejmdal. 1874–1878. (Danish).

Hemlandet. 1859–1900. (Norwegian).

Herald. 1880–1887.

Illinois Staats-Zeitung. 1871–1900. (German).

Illinoiser Volks-zeitung. 14 February 1885. (German).

Illinoiser Volkszeitung. April–May 1893. (German).

Inter Ocean. 1872–1889.

Journal of United Labor. Marblehead, Mass.: Washington, D.C. 1880–1885.

Knights of Labor, 1886–1887.

Labor Enquirer. 1887–1888.

Mail. 1880–1887.

Morning Courier. 1875.

Právo Lidu. 1893–1894. (Czech).

Progress. New York. 1882–1885.

Progressive Age. 1880–1882.

Revyen. 1895–1900. (Danish).

Rights of Labor. 1890–1893.

Skandinaven. 1877–1886. (Norwegian).

The Socialist. 1878–1879.

Socialist Alliance. 1896–1898.

Der Sozialist. New York. 1885–1890. (German).

Svenska Amerikanaren. 1877–1880. (Swedish).

Svenska Tribunen. 1876–1882. (Swedish).

Svornost. 1875–1885. (Czech).

Times. 1872–1889.

Tribune. 1870–1900.

The Vindicator. Town of Lake, Illinois. 1883–1885.

Der Vorbote. 1874–1900. (German).

Der Westen. 1878–1890. (German).

Workingman's Advocate. 1866–1877.

Workman's Advocate. New Haven, Connecticut. 1885–1893.

ARTICLES, PAMPHLETS, SPEECHES

A.D. [Adolph Douai?]. "Bericht über den Fortgang der sozialistischen Bewegung: Amerika." *Jahrbuch für Sozialwissenschaft un Sozialpolitik.* 1:1 (1879): 186–191.

Grottkau, Paul. *Diskussion über das Thema Anarchismus und Kommunismus geführt von P. Grottkau und J. Most.* Chicago: Central Committee of the Chicago Groups of the IWPA, 1884.

Hansen, Alfred William. "Louis Pios Forsog paa at oprette en socialistisk Stat i Kansas" [Louis Pio's plan for a socialist community in Kansas]. *Dannevirke* (Cedar Rapids, IA): 14 February 1906.

Hudek, Prokop. "Osudy prvotních českych osadniku chicagskych" [Memoirs of the early Czech settlement in Chicago]. *Amerikan narodní Kalendar na roku 1884.* Chicago: A. Geringer, 1884, pp. 185–204.

Palda, Lev J. "Pameti ceskych osadniku v Americe" [Memories of Czech settlers in America by L. J. Palda]. *Amerikan narodni Kalendar na roku 1911.* Chicago: A. Geringer, 1911, pp. 265–288.

Westergaard, Waldemar (trans. and ed.). "Marcus Thrane in America: Some Unpublished Letters from 1880–1884." *Norwegian-American Studies and Records* 9 (1936): 67–76.

Winnen, Jacob. "Geschichte der Arbeiterbewegung von Chicago." *Die Fackel.* 25 February–17 June 1917.

Zdrubek, Frantisek. "Kco je socialismus?" [What is Socialism?]. *Kalendar Amerikan.* Chicago: A. Geringer, 1880, pp. 114–118.

BOOKS

The Accused and the Accusers. Chicago: Socialist Publishing Society. 1887. Reprint: New York: Arno Press, 1970.

Bernstein, Samuel, ed. *Papers of the General Council of the International Workingmen's Association, New York, 1872–1876.* Milano: Institute Giangiacomo Feltrinelli, 1962.

Bisno, Abraham. *Abraham Bisno: Union Pioneer.* Madison: University of Wisconsin Press, 1967.

[Bohemian National Cemetery Association.] *Padesátílété Jubileum českeho národního hřbitova v Chicagu Illinois* [The fifty year jubilee of the Bohemian National Cemetery Association in Chicago]. Ed. John Jelinek. Chicago: R. Mejdrich, 1927.

Buchanan, Joseph. *The Story of a Labor Agitator.* New York: The Outlook Co., 1903.

Chicago Directory of Lodges and Benevolent Societies, 1883. Chicago: C. F. Lichtner and Bro., 1883.

Edwards, Richard. comp. *Edward's Thirteenth Annual Directory . . . of the City of Chicago.* Chicago: Richard Edwards, 1870.

Flinn, John. *History of the Chicago Police Force from the Settlement of the Community to the Present Time.* Chicago: Police Book Fund, 1887.

Hoehn, G. A. *Der Nordamerikanische Turnerbund und seine Stellung zur Arbeiterbewegung.* St. Louis: Union Press, 1892.

Hoerder, Dirk, ed. *Plutokraten und Sozialisten: Berichte deutscher Diplomaten und*

Agenten über die amerikanische Arbeiterbewegung, 1878–1917. Munich: K. G. Saur Verlag, 1981.

Hutchinson, Thomas, comp. *The Lakeside Annual Directory of the City of Chicago.* Chicago: Chicago Directory Co., 1875–1886, 1890, 1900.

Kebabian, John, ed. *The Haymarket Affair and Trial of the Chicago Anarchists, 1886. A Rare Book Monograph on the Contents of the Julius Grinnell Manuscripts.* New York: H. P. Kraus, 1970.

Keil, Hartmut, and John Jentz, eds. *Deutsche Arbeiterkultur in Chicago von 1850 dis zum Ersten Weltkrieg: Eine Anthologie.* Ostfildern: Scripta Mercaturae Verlag, 1984.

Kvist, Anton. *Fra Lincoln til Hoover: Amerikas Danske Pioneer Forening Dania, Chicago: 1862–1930* [From Lincoln to Hoover: America's first Danish society, Dania]. Copenhagen: Trykt af Politiken, 1930.

Lum, Dyer, ed. *The Concise History of the Great Trial of the Chicago Anarchists in 1886. Condensed from the Official Record.* 1888. Reprint. New York: Arno Press, 1969.

McLean, George. *The Rise and Fall of Anarchy in America.* . . . Chicago: R. G. Badoux, 1888.

Most, Johann. *Revolutionäre Kriegswissenschaft: Ein Handbüchlein zur Anleitung betreffend Gebrauches und Herstellung von Nitroglyzerin, Dynamit, . . . usw.* 3rd ed. New York: Die Freiheit, 1885.

Pamětní list vydáný k jubileu 30-lété činnosti česke natěracske unie cis 273, Bratrstva Natěraču, Dekoratoru a Papirovacu v Americe, 1895–1925. [Memorial of the 30th anniversary of the Czech painters' union local 273, Brotherhood of Painters, Decorators and Paperhangers of America, 1895–1925] N.p. n.d. [1925?]

Parsons, Albert, et al. *Anarchism: Its Philosophy and Scientific Basis as Defined by Some of Its Apostles.* Chicago: Mrs. A. R. Parsons, 1887.

Parsons, Lucy, ed. *Life of Albert R. Parsons with a Brief History of the Labor Movement in Chicago.* Chicago: Mrs. Lucy Parsons, 1889.

[Pio, Louis.] *80 Louis Pio breve og en bibliografi* [80 letters from Louis Pio and a bibliography]. Ed. Borge Schmidt. Copenhagen: Forlaget Fremad, 1950.

Presser versus The State of Illinois, 116 U.S. 252. *Supreme Court Reporter.* St. Paul: West Publishing Co., 1886, 6: 580–586.

Salmonsen, Morris. *Brogede minder. fra fyrretyve aars ophold i Chicago* [Mixed memories from a forty-year sojourn in Chicago]. Copenhagen: Gyldendal Nordisk forlag, 1913.

Schaack, Michael. *Anarchy and Anarchists: A History of the Red Terror and the Social Revolution in America and Europe.* . . . Chicago: F. J. Schulte and Co., 1889.

Schmidt, Ernst. *He Chose: The Other was a Treadmill Thing.* Ed. and trans. by Frederick Schmidt. Santa Fe: Vegara Printing Co., 1968.

Schoff, S. S. *The Glory of Chicago—Her Manufactories.* Chicago: Knight and Leonard, 1873.

Sloan, George. *The Telephone of Labor.* Chicago: n.p., 1880.

Spies, August. *Reminiscenzen von August Spies: Seine Rede vor Richter Gary, sozial-*

politische Abhandlungen, Briefe, Notizen, usw. Ed. Albert Currlin. Chicago: Mrs. Christine Spies, 1888.

Spies, August. [Wilhelm Rosenberg and Paul Grottkau] *Die Nihilisten: Ein Volkstück in Vier Akten.* [1882] St. Louis: n.p., 1886.

Secondary Sources

UNPUBLISHED PAPERS, THESES, AND DISSERTATIONS

Bizjack, Jack. "The Trade and Labor Assembly of Chicago, Illinois." Master's thesis, University of Chicago, 1969.

Bubnys, Edward. "Chicago, 1870 and 1900: Wealth, Occupation and Education." Ph.D. diss., University of Illinois, 1978.

Chada, Joseph. "A Survey of Radicalism in the Bohemian-American Community." Typescript. Chicago Historical Society, 1954.

Friedman, Philip. "The Danish Community of Chicago, 1860–1920." Master's thesis, Northwestern University, 1976.

Heiss, Christine. "Der Lehr- und Wehr-Verein von Chicago, 1875–1887: Ein sozialgeschichtlicher Beitrag zur Radikalisierung deutscher Arbeiter in den U.S.A." Master's thesis, Ludwig-Maximilians-Universität, München, 1981.

Hirsch, Eric. "Revolution or Reform: An Analytical History of an Urban Labor Movement." Ph.D. diss., University of Chicago, 1981.

Kann, Kenneth. "Working Class Culture and the Labor Movement in Nineteenth Century Chicago." Ph.D. diss., University of California at Berkeley, 1977.

Keil, Hartmut, and John Jentz. "German Workers in Industrial Chicago: The Transformation of Industries and Neighborhoods in the Late 19th Century." Paper presented at the OAH convention, Detroit, 3 April 1981.

Kiesewetter, Renate. "Die Institution der deutsch-amerikanischen Arbeiterpresse in Chicago. Zur Geschichte des Vorboten und der Chicagoer Arbeiterzeitung, 1874–1886." Master's thesis. Ludwig-Maximilians-Universität, München, 1982.

LeBlanc, Paul. "Revolutionary Socialism in America, 1877–1887." Master's seminar paper, University of Pittsburgh, 1979

Nelson, Bruce. "Culture and Conspiracy: A Social History of Chicago Anarchism, 1872–1900." Ph.D. diss., Northern Illinois University, 1986.

Pitzer, Elizabeth. "Burgerliche Presse und Arbeiterpresse im Wandel: Deutsch-amerikanische Tageszeitungen am Ende des 19. Jahrhunderts, dargestellt am Beispiel von 'Illinois Staats-zeitung' und 'Chicagoer Arbeiterzeitung.'" Master's thesis, Ludwig-Maximilians-Universität, München, 1980.

Scharnau, Ralph. "Thomas J. Morgan and the Chicago Socialist Movement, 1876–1901." Ph.D. diss., Northern Illinois University, 1969.

Schneirov, Richard. "The Knights of Labor in the Chicago Labor Movement and in Municipal Politics, 1877–1887." Ph.D. diss., Northern Illinois University, 1984.

Selected Bibliography

Stevenson, Billie. "The Ideology of American Anarchism." Ph.D. diss., University of Iowa, 1972.
Suhrbur, Thomas. "Unionism among Chicago Carpenters, 1855–1901." C.A.S. thesis, Nortern Illinois University, 1986.
Zachariassen, Aksel. "Marcus Thrane og andere norske socialister i U.S.A." [Marcus Thrane and other Norwegian socialists in the USA]. Typescript, Arbeiderbevegelsens Arkiv og Bibliotek, Oslo.

ARTICLES IN JOURNALS, ESSAYS IN BOOKS

Bicha, Karel. "Settling Accounts with an Old Adversary: The De-Catholicization of Czech Immigrants in America." *Social History-Histoire sociale* 8 (November 1972): 45–60.
Danielsen, Jens-Bjerre. "The Early Danish Immigrant Socialist Press." In *Essays on the Scandinavian-American Radical Press*. Ed. Dirk Hoerder. Bremen: Universität Bremen, 1984. pp. 56–77.
Georg, Adolph. "Aus der Geschichte der Chicago Turngemeinde." *Deutsch-Amerikanische Geschichtsblatter* 5:3 (July 1905): 42–51.
Groniowski, Krzysztof. "Socjalistyczna Emigracja Polska w Stanach Zjednoczonych, 1883–1914." [Polish Socialist Emigration to the United States]. *Z Pola Walki* 1 (1977): 1–31.
Hlavacek, Francis. "Zlomky Českého Počátečního Hnutí Dělnického v Americe" [Elements of the first Czech labor movement in America]. *Ročenka Americkych Delnickych Listu*. Cleveland: Delnicky Listy, 1924. pp. 74–91.
Ickstadt, Heinz, and Hartmut Keil. "A Forgotten Piece of Working-Class Literature: Gustav Lyser's Satire of the Hewitt Hearings of 1878." *Labor History* 20:1 (Winter 1979): 127–140.
Jentz, John. "Bread and Labor: Chicago's German Bakers Organize." *Chicago History* 12 (Summer 1983): 24–35.
Jentz, John, and Hartmut Keil. "From Immigrants to Urban Workers: Chicago's German Poor in the Gilded Age and Progressive Era, 1883–1908." *Viertaljährschrift für Sozial- und Wirtschaftsgeschichte* 68:1 (1981): 52–97.
Johnson, Michael. "Albert R. Parsons: An American Architect of Syndicalism." *Midwest Quarterly* 9 (1968): 195–206.
Keil, Hartmut, ed. "Chicago-Projekt: Untersuchungen zur Arbeitswelt und Lebensweise deutscher Arbeiter in Chicago, 1850–1915." Special issue of *Amerikastudien* 29:2 (1984).
Keil, Hartmut. "The German Immigrant Working Class of Chicago, 1875–90: Workers, Labor Leaders, and the Labor Movement." In *American Labor and Immigration History, 1877–1920s: Recent European Research*. Ed. Dirk Hoerder. Urbana: University of Illinois Press, 1983, pp. 156–176.
Keil, Hartmut, and Heinz Ickstadt. "Elemente einer deutschen Arbeiterkultur in Chicago zwischen 1880 und 1890." *Geschichte und Gesellschaft*. 5:1 (1979): 103–124.

Keil, Hartmut, and John Jentz. "German Working-Class Culture in Chicago." *Gulliver: Deutsch-Englische Jahrbucher.* Band 9. (1979): 128–147.

Klima, Arnost. "Die Entstehung der Arbeiterklasse und die Anfange der Arbei-terbewegung in Böhmen." In *Wirtschafts- und sozialgeschichtlicher Probleme der Frühen Industrialisierung.* Ed. Wolfram Fischer. Berlin: Colloquium Verlag, 1968, 434–448.

Kocka, Jurgen, ed. "Arbeiterkultur in 19. Jahrhundert" Special issue of *Geschichte und Gesellschaft.* 5:1 (1979).

Kořalka, Jiří. "Über die Anfange der Zusammenarbeit zwischen der Arbeiterbe-wegung in Deutschland und in dem böhmischen Landern." In *Aus 500 Jahren deutsch-tschechoslowakischer Geschichte.* Ed. Karl Obermann und Josef Polišen-ský. East Berlin: Rütten und Loening, 1958, 299–330.

Lahme, Hans-Norbert. "Der deutsche sozialdemokratisches Arbeiterverein in Kopenhagen und die danische Arbeiterbewegung." *International Review of Social History* 21 (1976): 240–255.

Mai, Joachim. "Der gemeinsame Kampf der deutschen und polnischen Arbeiter-bewegung in der Zeit des Sozialistengesetzes, 1878–1890." *Jahrbuch zur Geschichte von Stadt und Landkreis Kaiserlautern* 7 (1963): 103–144.

Martinek, Josef. "Padesat let ceskeho casopisy delnickeho v Americe" [Fifty years of the Czech labor press in America]. *Rocenka Americkych Delnickych Listu* Cleveland: Delnicky Listy, 1924, pp. 15ff.

Mittleman, Edward. "Chicago Labor in Politics, 1877–1896." *Journal of Political Economy.* 28:5 (May 1920): 407–418.

Obermann, Karl. "La participation a la Première internationale, avant 1872, des ouvriers allemands immigrés aux États-Unis." In *La Première internationale, l'institution, l'implantation, le rayonnement.* Paris: Colloques internationaux du C.N.R.S., 1964, 387–402.

Schneirov, Richard. "Free Thought and Socialism in the Czech Community in Chicago, 1875–1887." In *"Struggle a Hard Battle": Essays on Working-Class Immigrants.* Ed. Dirk Hoerder. DeKalb: Northern Illinois University Press, 1986, pp. 121–142.

Solle, Zdenek. "Die tschechischen Sektionen der Internationale in den Vereini-gung Staaten von Amerika" [The Czech sections of the First International in America]. *Historica* (Prague) 8 (1964): 101–134.

BOOKS

Andreas, A. T. *History of Chicago from the Earliest Period to the Present Time.* Vol. 3: *From the Fire of 1871 to the Present Time.* Chicago: A. T. Andreas Co., 1886.

Arndt, Karl, und May Olson, comps. *Deutsch-amerikanische Zeitungen und Zeit-schriften, 1732–1955: Geschichte und Bibliographie.* Heidelberg: Quelle und Meyer, 1955.

Ashbaugh, Carolyn. *Lucy Parsons: American Revolutionary.* Chicago: Charles Kerr, 1976.

Selected Bibliography

Avrich, Paul. *The Haymarket Tragedy*. Princeton: Princeton University Press, 1984.

Beijbom, Ulf. *Swedes in Chicago: A Demographic and Social Study of the 1846–1880 Immigration*. Växjö, Sweden: Scandinavian University Books, 1971.

Bubenicek, Rudolf. *Dějiny Čechů v Chicagu* [History of Czechs in Chicago]. Chicago: Szabo Westside Press, 1939.

Čapek, Tomas. *Padesát let Českého Tisku v Americe*. New York: The Language Press, 1911.

Chenetier, Marc, and Rob Kroes, eds. *Impressions of a Gilded Age: The American Fin De Siècle*. Amsterdam: Amerika Instituut, Universiteit van Amsterdam, 1983.

David, Henry. *The History of the Haymarket Affair: A Study in the American Social-Revolutionary and Labor Movements*. 1936. Rev. ed. New York: Russell and Russell, 1958

Ely, Richard. *The Labor Movement in America*. 1886. Rev. ed. New York: Thomas Crowell, 1890.

Engberg, Jens. *Til Arbejdet! Liv eller dod! Louis Pio og Arbejderbeveagelse* [To labor! Life or death! Louis Pio and the labor movement]. Copenhagen: Gyldendahl, 1979.

Gosiorovsky, Milos (ed.). *Začiatky českej a slovenskej emigrácie do USA: Česká a slovenská robotnícka emigrácia v USA v období I, internacionály* [The beginnings of Czech and Slovak immigration to the USA: the emigration of Czech and Slovak workers in the era of the First International]. Bratislava: Slovenskej akadémie vied, 1970.

Habenicht, Jan. *Dějiny Čechů v Amerických*. [History of Czechs in America]. St. Louis: Hlas, 1910.

Keil, Hartmut, and John Jentz, eds. *German Workers in Industrial Chicago, 1850–1910: A Comparative Perspective*. DeKalb: Northern Illinois University Press, 1983.

Metzner, Heinrich. *A Brief History of the American Turnerbund*. Trans. Theodore Stempfel, Jr. Rev. ed. Pittsburgh: National Executive Committee of the American Turnerbund, 1924.

Moses, John, and Joseph Kirkland, eds. *The History of Chicago, Illinois*. Chicago: Munsell and Co., 1895.

Pierce, Bessie. *A History of Chicago*. 3 vols. Vol. 2: *From Town to City, 1848–1871*. New York: Alfred Knopf, 1949. Vol. 3: *The Rise of the Modern City, 1871–1893*. New York: Alfred Knopf, 1957.

Poore, Carol. *German-American Socialist Literature, 1865–1900*. Frankfurt: Peter Lang, 1982.

Roediger, Dave, and Franklin Rosemont, eds. *A Haymarket Scrapbook*. Chicago: Charles Kerr, 1986.

Schlüter, Hermann. *Die Anfange der deutschen Arbeiterbewegung in Amerika*. Stuttgart: Dietz Verlag, 1907.

Schlüter, Hermann. *Die Internationale in Amerika: Ein Beitrag zur Geschichte der Arbeiter-Bewegung in Vereinigten Staaten*. Chicago: German-speaking Groups of the Socialist Party, 1918.

Sorge, Friedrich. *Friedrich Sorge's Labor Movement in the United States* [1891–1895]

Trans. Brewster Chamberlin and ed. Philip Foner. Westport, Conn.: Greenwood Press, 1977.

Soukup, Frantisek. *Pametní List Československe Socialne Demokraticke Strany Dělnicke, 1872–1922.* [Memorial of the Czechoslovak social-democratic labor party]. N.p., 1922.

Stedronsky, Frantisek. *Zahraniční krajanské noviny, časopisy a kalendáře do roku 1938.* [Newspapers and journals from abroad.] Praze: Narodni knihovna, 1958.

Vraz, Vlasta, ed. *Panorama: A Historical Review of Czechs and Slovaks in the U.S.A.* Cicero, Ill.: Czechoslovak National Council of America, 1970.

Index

297